Building Quality Software

Robert L. Glass

Computing Trends

PRENTICE HALL

Englewood Cliffs, New Jersey 07632

Editorial/production supervision: *Brendan M. Stewart*
Prepress buyer: *Mary McCartney*
Manufacturing buyer: *Susan Brunke*
Acquisition editor: *Paul Becker*
Editorial Assistant: *Noreen Regina*

The publisher offers discounts on this book when ordered in bulk quantities. For more
information, write: Special Sales/Professional Marketing, Prentice Hall, Professional &
Technical Reference Division, Englewood Cliffs, NJ 07632.

Printed in the United States of America
10 9 8 7 6 5 4 3 2 1

ISBN 0-13-086695-4

Prentice-Hall International (UK) Limited, *London*
Prentice-Hall of Australia Pty. Limited, *Sydney*
Prentice-Hall Canada Inc., *Toronto*
Prentice-Hall Hispanoamericana, S.A., *Mexico*
Prentice-Hall of India Private Limited, *New Delhi*
Prentice-Hall of Japan, Inc., *Tokyo*
Simon & Schuster Asia Pte. Ltd., *Singapore*
Editora Prentice-Hall do Brasil, Ltda., *Rio de Janeiro*

Contents

2   The Technology of Quality

Preface

This is a book on software quality.

Wait, now! Don't quit reading yet!

I know that many books on software quality are about as inspiring as a hex dump. But this one is different.

Why is it different? For one thing, this book is primarily about the technology of quality. There is a section, toward the back, about the management of quality, where quality assurance is discussed. But the underlying philosophy here is that quality is at heart a technical problem. That's why the book is called *Building Quality Software,* and not the more traditional *Software Quality* or even *Software Quality Assurance.*

Now this technology-first approach requires an explanation. In most other books on software quality, the assumption is that quality equals quality assurance, and that indeed is a management topic.

That is not the assumption here. Let me explain why.

No matter how carefully management plans for and provides for quality processes in software development, I believe that it is no more possible to *manage* quality into a software product than it is to *test* it in. It is well accepted that quality cannot be tested into software (because testing only looks at reliability, one facet of quality, and because testing comes too late in the life cycle to have a preventive effect on poor quality), but it is not at all commonly accepted that quality cannot be managed in. In fact, that is a radical viewpoint.

The reason I believe that you can't *manage* in quality is that quality is a deeply intimate software trait. As we explore what quality *really* is in this book, we see that the injection of quality, and the detection of quality, occur far below the surface of software's facade. How can you put modifiability, one of the quality attributes, into a software product? How can you find out if it was put there? There are no easy answers to these questions, but the fact is that only a technical person can do the putting and the finding. Modifiability is so deeply technical that it is simply not assessable by the casual viewer. Management, for better or worse, is in this sense only a casual viewer of the software product. Management in general is not and should not be comfortable with the technical tasks necessary for either instilling or detecting modifiability.

That is not to say, however, that management has no role in building quality software. To the contrary, there is an essential role for management to play. Management must construct and maintain a climate in which quality is fostered and nurtured.

What do I mean by a quality climate? One where processes that facilitate quality are enabled and followed. One in which tools to assist in providing quality are procured and used. One in which people who think quality are hired and helped. One in which advocacy of product quality occurs right up there with advocacy of schedule and cost constraint conformance.

It is easier to say these things than to do them. We are passing through an era in which schedule and cost have been the dominant factors in evaluating software management and software products. There are some good reasons for that. Software's schedule and cost performance have often been abysmal. With rampant problems in that area, management has rightfully concentrated on trying to solve those problems.

But there is a danger here. As the pressure of meeting schedule and reducing cost intensifies, it is quality that inevitably suffers. How can we accelerate a late product? Cut back on whatever is happening when the problem is discovered, usually verification and testing. What is the result? Reduced product quality.

The software manager of the twenty-first century must find a new equation for software. It must not simply be

software product = on schedule + within budget

It must instead be

software product = quality + on schedule + within budget

And achieving good results in that more complicated equation requires management commitment to quality as an end goal right up there with schedule and cost.

Fortunately, it is not hard for management to facilitate the construction of quality software. Most technical people fundamentally want to do a good, quality job. In fact, sometimes in the trade-offs between quality and cost and schedule, technical people lean too heavily on the side of quality! But what that means is that management usually will find very willing partners in the task of facilitating quality software.

There, then, is the basic philosophy of this book. Quality is at heart a technical problem. Management's job is to create a facilitating environment.

The rest of the book is an elaboration on these themes. After an introductory section that defines quality and its importance, the next and longest section of the book talks about the quality techniques available to the dedicated technologist. Following that, there is a smaller but equally important section on ways that management can facilitate quality. Then there is a case study section, showing how some companies and governments have gone about meeting the challenge of building quality software. In the final section, the whole book is distilled into a set of project-dependent quality approach recommendations.

If what you expect here is yet another book on software quality assurance, I am going to disappoint you. But if you are the reader whose attention was arrested with that *"Wait"* plea several paragraphs back, I hope you will be pleased.

It is my intention to write a book that gets at the *essence* of software quality. That essence is much more than quality assurance. I hope, after you have finished reading this book, that you will agree with me.

—*Robert L. Glass*

P.S. Some readers may recognize portions of this book, especially some of the whimsy (I strongly believe that technical material goes down better when it is leavened with humor). This book evolved from many things I have done in the past, especially the now out-of-print *Software Reliability Guidebook.*

1

Introduction

1.1 OVERVIEW

Software and *quality* are both intangibles. Those of us in the software business, or the quality business, have a pretty good idea of what they are. But it would be hard to point to something and say to someone not in our business "that's software" or "that's quality" and have that person know what we are talking about.

And yet in the last few decades, software has come to play a key role in the lives of individuals, in our society, and in fact in our whole culture. And because of that key role, it is essential that software have quality.

It is the purpose of this book to make a tangible contribution to the achievement of that intangible called *quality* in that intangible called *software*. In order to do that, we tackle several problems:

1. We must first define quality in such a way that we will know how to go about achieving it, and know whether we have achieved it when we are finished.

2. We must define software in such a way that we will know clearly what it is we are trying to give quality to.

1

3. Finally, we must define the intersection of those two terms in such a way that we can clearly identify technical and managerial ways of achieving quality, and meaningful ways of evaluating the quality that we have achieved.

In this look at software quality, we try to confront the elusive problem of achieving quality head on. Technical people and their technology are the keys to software quality, we believe, and we devote a lot of space to dealing with those topics. (Chapter 2 is a large— some would say huge!—treatment of the technology of quality.)

Management is the facilitator of the quality technologist and technology, and we devote additional space to that topic in Chapter 3 about the management of quality.

Because the *product* of the software process is the entity that must have quality, we look at evaluation of the product even though we know a lot less about that subject than we wish we did (rather than looking at the more convenient focus of evaluation of the *process*).

The result of this approach is that software quality is seen as a complex topic, one with many ramifications, one with no magic solutions, and one with a lot of different approaches to its achievement. The result, in short, is an honest view of software quality and how to achieve it, but *not* one that gives comfort to people seeking easy answers to difficult questions.

Because these two entities, software and quality, are so intangible, let us try to make them come alive through a little story about software quality in the society of the 1990s. After the story, we begin taking a serious look at how to achieve software quality.

The tiny computer under the hood of the car ran on, executing instructions far faster than the driver of the rapidly moving car could imagine. Data flowed toward the computer from various automotive devices; once it arrived at the computer, it was chewed, digested, and spat out to the control systems that played a key role in whether the car kept going or not.

There were no moving parts inside the computer, nothing much there in fact except circuitry, and yet there *was* something else there. Unseen and unseeable, the software at the heart of the computer was the life pulse that made the hardware box worthwhile.

The driver behind the wheel of the car never thought about the software, and rarely thought about the computer. That was good. If the software and the computer were doing their job, if they were of high *quality*, then this user need not think about them.

But there is a problem here. The software is unseen and unseeable. How does anyone know if it has quality? What does quality even mean under these circumstances?

Suddenly the software controlling the computer entered a previously unentered logic path. There, it found instructions that had never been tested. There, it executed a part of those instructions that were in error. There it foundered; the software failed, the computer stopped running, and the car itself could go no further. Somewhere in that complicated system, the driver knew, something had gone wrong. The driver would find out what it was later. The software was lacking in the quality of *reliability*, and the system had temporarily failed.

Suddenly, in an alternate scenario, the software entered a previously unentered path. There, it found complicated and lengthy sets of instructions, and the execution of the software, and of the computer, and of the car, slowed dramatically. As data continued to flow to the computer, the computer became unable to keep up with the flow. Signals were missed, and logic paths were not taken, and only a fraction of the control data that should have been produced was actually produced. The car began performing erratically. The driver, concerned, slowed and pulled to the side of the road. The software was lacking in the quality of *efficiency*, and the system had temporarily failed.

How do we know if software has quality? Often, by the symptoms of the system in which it resides. If the system is unreliable, it may be because the software is unreliable. If the system is slow or erratic, it may be because the software is inefficient.

Suddenly, in yet another alternate scenario, the software left the unused path, directed away from the faulty logic by self-test facilities in the software that detected a problem and overcame it by bypassing the bad path. The performance of the car smoothed. The driver, at first untrusting, slowly relaxed. The car continued, swiftly, down the highway. The tiny computer under the hood was doing its job well again. The unseen software and its unseeable attributes of quality were doing their job again, through use of a technique called *software fault-tolerance*. (Software fault tolerance is just one of the five dozen or more approaches to software quality that we examine in this book.)

A smile crept slowly across the driver's face, and he began to whistle.

1.2 THE BASIC PREMISE OF THIS MATERIAL _____

You have already seen that this is an unusual book about software quality. Let's talk about how unusual it is.

First, implicit in this material is the thought that software is exceedingly complex. There may be some applications that are fairly trivial in nature, but most software is complicated. It is complicated because software solves complicated problems—any problem from any discipline is potentially within the software application domain set—and because software solutions tend to escalate in complexity faster than the problems they solve, often exponentially.

Some say software is the most difficult mental task humanity has ever undertaken. Others, such as well-known computer scientists David Parnas and Donald Knuth, say it more simply: "Software is hard" (to create).

Because software itself is complex, the achievement of software quality is complex. There are, in this fifth decade after the advent of software as a problem-solving tool, still no "best" approaches to achieving software quality. You will not find any magic best solutions in this book. (In a milestone paper on software engineering, noted author Fred Brooks referred to the lack of "silver bullets" to slay the software werewolf.)

In the absence of best approaches to achieving software quality, quality approaches must depend on several factors:

1. The application problem being solved. (Some applications are extremely data dependent, for example, and require data-oriented quality approaches. Others are algorithm dependent and require more functional quality approaches.) Unfortunately, there is not yet sufficient research on quality-oriented, application-focused techniques to be definitive about even the best approaches for specific applications.

2. The organization solving the problem. Some organizations use extremely formal, disciplined approaches to software and quality. Others use informal, creative approaches. Although computer science tends to favor the former approach, many software organizations tend to continue to use the latter successfully.

3. The people within the organization solving the problem. Data show that some people are up to 35 times better at software's tasks than others. Certainly the best route to software quality in the 1990s is using the best quality people to do the job.

But using good people is not enough. People need support. Tools and techniques can help good people—or even mediocre people—do a better job. So can good organizational strategies.

In this book you will find a menu of quality tools and techniques and organizational strategies. Some of them may be appropriate for your application, your organization, and your people. Others may not. Some of them are frequently mentioned in the computer science literature but are of dubious value. Others are quietly used by top practitioners but never mentioned in the literature. Both are covered here (with appropriate warnings when a technique sounds better than it really is).

The philosophy of the book is to present that menu of ideas in breadth rather than in depth. A brief explanation of a good, new idea is certainly more valuable than an in-depth explanation of a bad one. References are presented for those wishing to pursue a particular idea from the menu in more depth. In addition, in the back of the book there is a set of recommendations for the use of particular tools and techniques on particular kinds of projects.

The underlying presumption here is that you, the reader, do not need a primer showing a few application-independent, organization-independent, person-independent techniques, but rather an understanding of the set of choices that faces you in building quality software, and enough information to help you make informed judgments about those choices, no matter what problem you are solving.

1.3 THE IMPORTANCE OF SOFTWARE QUALITY IN THE 1990S _____

Computers and software have permeated every part of people's lives. It is not just that they control our cars. They direct our appliances, they facilitate and control our travel, they handle our finances, they make more convenient all the necessities and nonnecessities of life. Without computers and software, our society, like the car in the previous section, would probably come slowly to a halt.

With that as a given, the ante for software quality has been upped immeasurably. Poor quality software could inconvenience us; it could entangle society; it could kill people.

Is that an exaggeration? Not at all.

Picture some very large software. TWA's computerized reservation system, when it was first developed, was flawed. A high-priority quality program, undertaken at considerable cost, saved the company $1.75 million once it was completed. They bet the corporate coffers on software quality.

Picture some very widely-used software. Microsoft had to recall a product a few years ago because of serious bugs it contained. We are talking here about thousands, even hundreds of thousands, of customers who were inconvenienced because of software quality. But more to the point, Microsoft had alienated a large part of its customer base. Quickly, they formed a quality organization to monitor product quality. They couldn't afford to make that mistake again; they bet their company on every software product.

Picture software produced by a careless person. Some day soon a software-producing company—and its programmer—are going to get sued for malpractice. It happens to doctors and other professionals now. It could happen to you. You may bet your financial future on every line of software you write.

Picture software produced by a normally careful person. In early 1990, AT&T's telephone system suffered what *Business Week* called "nine hours of chaos" because special software to help the system be fail-safe was itself flawed and took the system down with it.

Picture life-critical software. Computers and software control the newer aircraft and are capable of taking off and landing an airplane without a pilot on board. You literally bet your life on software when you

ride on one of those airplanes. When an Airbus A320 crashed at the Paris
air show in 1988, the press initially assumed the flight control computer
hardware and software were at fault. (The real reason was discovered later
to be "pilot error.")

For the most part, software quality was a much less visible thing until
a few years ago. Software applications were smaller then, and they were
less critical and less pervasive. All that, in this rapidly growing field, has
changed. Most of us, excited by the promise of the future, are glad for that
growth and change. But the dimension of the change is almost overwhelm-
ing.

Now, when we consider software quality:

- Huge amounts of money are at stake.
- Corporate success or failure is at stake.
- Your personal future is at stake.
- Lives are at stake.

Software quality is no longer an option, an add-on whose cost we may
debate and consider doing without. Software quality, to some degree that
we will talk about later, is a requirement.

REFERENCES

CSN87—"NCR Loses 'Malpractice' Judgment," *Computer Systems News,* May 25,
    1987. *A popular press news article on an arbitrator award of half a million dollars
    to an NCR customer for faulty software on a reservations application. Files were
    corrupted and data lost for no apparent reason.*
DUNHAM89—"V&V in the Next Decade," *IEEE Software,* May 1989; Janet R.
    Dunham. *Predicts specific improvements in verification and validation practices
    in the 1990s.*
JOYCE87—"Software Bugs: A Matter of Life and Liability," *Datamation,* May 15,
    1987; Joyce. *Describes the legal and human consequences of "Malfunction 54" on a
    linear accelerator radiation machine. More than one person is alleged to have died
    because of faulty treatment caused by hardware or software problems in the
    machine.*

1.4 DEFINITIONS

Defining the title material of this book is no small task. What is software?
We've already decided that it is unseen and unseeable.

What is quality? The pursuit of that elusive issue is complex.

Zen and the Art of Motorcycle Maintenance, by Pirsig, is a fascinating book that can be read on many levels . . . a philosophy of maintaining motorcycles, a philosophy of sustaining life, a travel odyssey, a relationship of a man and his son, a quest for meaning. . . .

But one thing it is especially about is quality. The chief character of the book, as we learn in a series of flashbacks, is a former college professor who specialized in pursuing the meaning of quality. As he got closer and closer to a valid definition, his personal life fell more and more into chaos.

Finally, just as he apparently had reached the meaning he had sought, he became mentally unbalanced, a trauma from which he is just recovering as the book begins.

Pursuing the notion of quality had cost him his sanity.

Here are our definitions:

- *Software*—a set of instructions that can be loaded into a computer to direct the computer to perform tasks.
- *Quality*—the degree of excellence of something. We measure the excellence of software via a set of attributes.

The remainder of this book focuses on these attributes and how to achieve them.

Before we use these definitions, it is important to discuss certain definitions of quality that have *not* been used here.

Sometimes quality is equated to "satisfying requirements." This is a tempting definition, since

1. The prime task of the software developer is to create a solution that solves the user's problem as stated in the requirements.
2. The quality targets for that solution can be explicitly included in the requirements.

However, there is a trap here. Let us discover that trap through an analogy.

Suppose we define requirements for an automobile. In fact, let us define two sets of requirements. The first set of requirements, let us say, heavily emphasizes quality and treats cost as a less important consideration. The second set of requirements, let us also say, places a much heavier emphasis on cost.

Now suppose we build an automobile to each of these sets of requirements. When we complete the first automobile, we call it a "Rolls Royce." When we complete the second automobile, we call it a "Hyundai." Now both automobiles, by definition, satisfy all of their requirements. But are they of equal quality?

The answer, of course, is "No." Simply stated, there are certain elements of quality that are absolute, or at least independent of the requirements underlying the product. That is why, in this book, we define quality not as satisfying requirements (even though that is a vitally important goal), but as achieving a set of attributes.

There is another reason why quality cannot be equated to satisfying requirements. Part of the software developer's task is to define those requirements, and part of the quality task is to make sure those requirements are right. (Some people say there are two tasks here, "getting the right requirements" and "getting the requirements right.") If quality is merely satisfying requirements, then although that covers "getting the requirements right" it does not cover "getting the right requirements." We see later in the chapter on the technology of requirements, for example, that some of the quality focus techniques and tools, such as modeling and simulation, are for "getting the right requirements" more than they are for "getting the requirements right." Thus, the focus of quality as satisfaction of requirements leaves out a vitally important consideration.

Another popular definition of quality closely related to the one just discussed is "user satisfaction." But again, that entity is something rather different from quality. Customers of McDonald's restaurants are generally satisfied with the meals they buy there, but hardly anyone would call McDonald's "quality dining." In this book we discuss how to satisfy requirements, and techniques for satisfying users, but in no way do we pretend that in doing so we are discussing quality. Many people would make the point that users want satisfaction more than they want quality (see, for example, Redenbaugh [90]), and that may well be true; but in this book we focus primarily on quality. The reason we do so is that we software people are still struggling with quality as a goal in itself, as we saw in the previous section.

REFERENCES

REDENBAUGH90—"Beware the God of Quality," *Business Month,* June 1990; Russell G. Redenbaugh. *"Customers do not buy quality. They buy satisfaction. The two are dramatically different." Goes on to say that companies that pursue quality to the exclusion of satisfaction will probably fail.*

It is not unusual, we have already seen, to have radically different definitions for commonly used terms in the software field. Probably the most dramatic such term is *quality* itself.

The vocabulary list that follows is from the July 1990 special issue of *System Development*; the topic for that issue was a report on the 1990 International Conference on Information Systems Quality Assurance, and the definitions emerged from that conference.

We do not necessarily agree with all of these definitions, but it is important that the quality-concerned software person of the 1990s at least be aware of the latest words and the meanings sometimes attributed to them.

MODERN QUALITY VOCABULARY

- *Customer*—As in customer satisfaction, customer focus, customer driven. Without doubt, the customer has become the absolute determinant for quality improvement. And while the traditional definition implicitly leans to someone outside an organization who receives a product or service, the modern definition explicitly includes internal and external customers. Everyone at some point in any basic process is a customer and a supplier: we generally all receive input in our jobs, act on it, and deliver it as output to somebody else. All customers have an obligation to demand a certain level of quality from their suppliers.
- *Employee empowerment*—This is certainly not a new idea. Thomas Jefferson, third president of the United States, admitted this: "I have never been able to conceive how any rational being could propose happiness to himself from the exercise of power over others." An essential characteristic of quality improvement programs, empowerment encourages employees to take ownership of the quality of their work. Empowerment also means that anyone can stop a flawed process without negative consequences. It goes hand in hand with a nonthreatening work atmosphere and a corporate culture based on respect for the individual. William Perry, Executive Director of the Quality Assurance Institute, says: "Empowering employees scares managers to death." Nevertheless, it is something they will have to learn to do.
- *Kaizen*—A Japanese word meaning "continuous improvement." Kaizen in the context of quality assurance means that quality improvement is a journey without end. Because it is continuous, orders of improvement may only be incremental, but this has become the preferred approach. "Revolutions" of quality improvement are certainly possible, but they are harder work.
- *Mistake-proofing*—Is a step in process evaluation and management. It involves eliminating, or at least minimizing, the opportunity for error within any process.
- *Process*—As in process improvement, process simplification, and so on. Processes provide the greatest opportunities for quality improvement via automation, elimination of redundancy, shortened cycle times, and so on. Process improvement also affords every employee the opportunity to get involved in a corporate quality effort.

- **Quality in fact, quality in perception**—"Quality in fact" is synonymous with "compliance to standards." It is the producer's or supplier's view of quality, whereby a product must meet all appropriate internal standards. "Quality in perception," on the other hand, is synonymous with "fit for use." It is the customer's or user's view of quality, whereby the product performs according to the customer's or user's expectations. It follows that for a quality product to exist, it must pass all tests for quality in fact, and quality in perception.
- **Six Sigma**—Though coined and used in Motorola Inc., this metric, borrowed from statistics, has the chance of becoming a standard to which all companies will aspire. Sigma is a figure of merit based on defects in parts per million. Average companies operate at Four Sigma, whereas Six Sigma companies achieve a defect rate of three or four parts per million or better.
- **Total Quality Management** (TQM)—The draft DoD standard says it best: "TQM consists of continuous process improvement activities involving everyone in an organization—managers and workers—in a totally integrated effort toward improving performance at every level.

  This improved performance is directed toward satisfying such cross-functional goals as quality, cost, scheduling, mission need, and suitability. TQM integrates fundamental management techniques, existing improvement efforts, and technical tools under a disciplined approach focused on continuous process improvement. The activities are ultimately focused on increased customer/user satisfaction."
- **"Walk the talk"**—This is an improved extension to simply "talking the talk," whereby quality improvement efforts only receive lip service. Every employee who has subordinates must walk the talk; that is, demonstrate, on a daily basis and in every activity, a sincere preoccupation with quality improvement.
- **Waste elimination**—Even prior to automation or restructuring, many processes can be improved simply by eliminating waste. Not confined to removing redundancy and emphasizing reuse in a process, waste elimination also means excluding a feature from a product that a customer does not want, or for which the cost cannot be recovered.

1.5 THEORY AND PRACTICE

Often when we discuss the forefront of the field, we speak of the "state of the art." Unfortunately, that expression is ambiguous. Theorists, when they say it, mean "the most advanced concepts and ideas available." Practitioners, when they say it, mean "the most advanced concepts and ideas commonly in use." Between those two interpretations, there is quite a gulf.

From the very origins of computing as a field—not so very long ago, only about 40 years if we count the beginnings of common applications—

there has been a discontinuity between those who do research into computer science, and those who practice it. The outlooks are different, the judgments on values are different, even the terminology is different.

Researchers and theorists are interested in things that are "interesting," ideas that are an intellectual challenge to pursue.

Practitioners are interested in things that are "useful," ideas that will prove helpful in achieving a goal or performing a task.

The difference between "interesting" and "useful" is more profound than most researchers and practitioners realize. It has been said (about other fields, but it applies to computing as well) that scientists do in order to learn, and engineers learn in order to do. That is the difference we are discussing here.

There is even a difference of opinion about which comes first, theory or practice. At first thought, most of us would say "theory, of course." But it is not that obvious. Compiler writing was done in practice, for example, before there was any theory defined for it. The practice of computing, as another example, preceded the offering of computer science coursework by about ten years [Glass89]. "Thermodynamics owes much more to the steam engine than the steam engine owes to thermodynamics. . . . If we look at the usual course of events in the historical record . . . there are very few examples where 'technology is applied science.' Rather it is much more often the case that 'science is applied technology.'" [Price83]

But all this is a bit of a chicken and egg problem. It doesn't matter very much which came first; what matters a lot more is where we go from here.

In the next two sections of the book we examine this issue of "state of the art" as it applies to software quality. But because of the dichotomy that we have been discussing, we divide the discussion into the "state of the theory" and the "state of the practice." In the field of quality software, we will see, the differences are significant.

REFERENCES

GLASS89, GLASS90—"The Temporal Relationship Between Theory and Practice," January 1989, and "Theory vs. Practice— Revisited," May 1990, *Journal of Systems and Software*; Robert L. Glass. *An analysis of which comes first, theory or practice, that shows (surprisingly) a belief among many scientists that practice precedes and helps form theory. Proposes two curves to show how that relationship may progress over time.*

PRICE83—"Sealing Wax and String: A Philosophy of the Experimenter's Craft and its Role in the Genesis of High Technology," *Proceedings of the American Association for the Advancement of Science* annual meeting, 1983; D. D. Price.

1.5.1 State of the Theory

What is the state of the theory? Many theorists are looking at automated, formal approaches to producing quality software.

1. *Formal specifications.* The problem to be solved by the construction of software must be clearly and unambiguously stated. Theorists see the best hope for clarity and removing ambiguity to be formally defined languages. We discuss these languages in more detail in Chapter 2.2.2, but basically we are talking about languages with strong rules for expressing the necessary content of a requirements specification. Since the requirements specification becomes the platform upon which the entire software product eventually rests, the theorists say we must take our best and strongest shot at doing that job right.

2. *Prototyping.* It is not easy to see the best set of requirements for a complicated problem. Sometimes it is necessary to build a model, simple solution in order to expose the results of the solution to the people who have the problem to be solved. Often, when this is done, these "users" realize that the problem they wanted to solve is different from that demonstrated by the prototype. As a result, the requirements are modified, and the real problem solution is undertaken. We discuss prototyping in more depth in Chapter 2.2.2.

3. *Automatic generation of prototype and final solution code.* Given a strong underpinning in the problem statement by means of the preceding techniques, theorists would next move toward the building of tools which could automatically translate requirements statements into code. By means of such tools, all possibility of design and programming errors would be eliminated, and maintenance would be drastically simplified into a process of maintaining a requirements specification.

4. *Proof of correctness.* Mathematical proofs of theorems have always been considered to be rigorous and undeniable. If we could prove software to be correct with the same degree of confidence, say the theorists, we would then be sure of its reliability. Experimentation into proof methodology has been under way for over two decades, and portions of programs have indeed been proven correct.

Remember the previous discussion about "interesting" versus "useful?" There is no doubt in anyone's mind that all of the theory approaches just listed are interesting, but are they useful? As we study each of these concepts in a different context later, we address that issue. For now, let us consider these thoughts:

1. Specifications must be read and understood by users as well as processed into a problem solution, so that the user can determine whether the problem statement does indeed match the problem to be solved. Users may not be very interested in or capable of reading formally expressed requirements.

2. Prototyping solidifies the process of defining requirements, but it makes the software estimation problem complex. How can you estimate how long it will take to build a software product if the requirements won't be firm until after the prototype findings are evaluated?

3. Automatic generation of code is a very hard problem. Except for carefully tailored requirements specifications, it really has not yet been successfully accomplished.

4. Small proofs of correctness for simple problems have been performed. Many of the proofs have been found to be flawed. Large-scale proofs have not been successful.

We have just dissected "interesting" theory from the "useful" point of view. From that viewpoint, theoretical approaches appear unsuccessful. But there is an important further thought here. What is useful can change, as research progresses. Although the usefulness of these theory approaches is in some doubt today, their future usefulness is yet to be determined. Success in any of these theory areas would have a profound effect upon the ability to achieve software quality. Even today's successes—prototyping is the best example—pay off now in certain kinds of applications.

There are other forces at work to move these kinds of theory into practice. For example, the British Ministry of Defense for two years required certain standards of safety-critical software applications:

1. no assembly language
2. limitations on higher-level languages to "safe subsets"
3. static analysis (similar to proof of correctness) of all code
4. accredited formal-method training for all software engineers
5. independent sign-off by an accredited software engineer

(This program was a two-year experiment, and at this writing it is not yet known whether these standards will be continued.)

There are other more specialized or localized theory approaches. IBM has explored profoundly new ideas in its *cleanroom* studies under noted theorist Harlan Mills (now retired from IBM and head of his own company), involving approaches to producing error-free software, and to testing it to substantiate that it is error free.

The Office of Naval Research has worked with noted computer scientist David Parnas to try out the Parnas requirements specification and "information hiding" concepts on a complicated application to see how well they scale up to what is commonly called *programming in the large,* as opposed to *programming in the small.*

In other research labs in other settings, new ideas are being brought forth, tried, and evaluated. The theory community is as interested in software quality as the practitioner community, even though its approaches are dramatically different.

REFERENCES

IEEE90—Special issue on "Formal Methods," *IEEE Software,* September 1990. *Contains seven papers on formal approaches to specification, development, standards, and verification. One paper, for example, presents "Seven Myths of Formal Methods."*

1.5.2 State of the Practice

The practitioner sees software quality as a many-faceted problem. It is an organizational problem (how can we best organize our people to achieve quality?). It is an economic problem (how best do we spread our dollar resources to achieve quality?). Most fundamentally, it is still a technical problem (what techniques can software developers and quality specialists best use to achieve quality software?).

Viewed from that standpoint, what is the state of the practice in achieving software quality?

1.4.2.1 Software developer emphasis.

The software developer has prime responsibility for putting quality into the software product. Approaches to achieving software quality start from that point of view.

1.4.2.2 Software quality assurance organization emergence.

The approach of a software quality assurance (SQA) organization is rapidly gaining strength. We see data later in this chapter that demonstrates that the number and size of such organizations have been increasing rapidly in recent years.

Early SQA attempts were seriously flawed. SQA people tended to be retreads from older QA disciplines with little or no software knowledge. Because of this lack of knowledge, they tended to focus on the superficial and measurable rather than on the true indicators of quality.

The quality assurance team was reviewing the software, primarily for standards conformance.

I don't know why they were doing it in the middle of the formal flight test sequence for the missile which carried the computer which carried the software—that's probably a symptom of a greater problem.

Sure enough, they found a standards violation. "Fix it," the QA team said, with all the fervor that a politically strong team can employ.

"But," said the software developers, "we shouldn't change the software for anything other than a severe error during flight testing."

"Fix it," said the QA team again.

And so the software developers fixed it. They modified the software to eliminate the standards violation, they held a peer code review to evaluate the change, and they tested the change. Then they took a poll about the wisdom of installing it in the flight test software.

Two programmers voted to install. One did not, with the opinion that he wasn't sure the fix was correct. The majority ruled.

The missile moved swiftly through the sky, hugging the spring-green California countryside. As it veered upward in response to a chase plane signal, the missile crossed over 3,000 feet altitude, still climbing.

But not for long. Suddenly, it lost power, dropped, struck the ground, and exploded in flames.

The software fix had been valid, all right. But only up to 3,000 feet.

To some extent, the problem of software-ignorant software quality assurance persists. In a 1984 survey conducted by Laventhol and Horwath, a public accounting firm, the findings were:

- Current QA programs do not usually improve our ability to complete systems that meet their goals within planned budgets and time frames.
- Current QA programs do not usually result in lower costs for enhancing or debugging systems.
- Current QA programs do not usually result in a significant increase in time spent on development relative to maintenance.

Even today, skilled software practitioners tend to avoid working in a QA organization. The undeniable challenge of the software field lies in the *creation* of a product. Watching someone else do it, no matter how responsibly the task is defined, is not the same.

Yet the movement toward SQA approaches is accelerating. In 1983 a survey was conducted on this trend. Its findings were:

- 50 percent growth per year in the number of QA organizations
- between 1:100 and 5:100 ratio of QA people to developers

- average QA organization history—2.7 years
- average experience of QA people in software:
  - analyst—3.5 years
  - manager—11.8 years
- number of projects per QA analyst—> 3
- median number of reviews per project—3.4
- top QA manager average salary—$65,000

Some of these numbers reflect the trend, some of them are simply interesting. The latter figure is especially interesting. That kind of salary (in 1983 dollars) will go a long way toward overcoming the natural reluctance of software development people to move to QA!

1.4.2.3 Risk inhibits change

It is both the best and worst of the practitioner's habits that approaches which add risk to the construction of a product are avoided. It is the best because this approach tends to result in relatively reliable, achievable products. It is the worst because this approach tends to inhibit the use of new and better approaches when they become available.

As an example, the technology of debugging using a source code debugger has been known since the late 1960s, but it did not come into common use in practice until a full decade after that. While the development programmers created programs in high-level language and reaped the productivity and quality benefits of doing so, they checked out their code using archaic assembly-code, machine-intimate debuggers which slowed the checkout process immensely.

As another example, the ability to measure how well a set of test cases covers a software product has been available now for over a decade, but software developers and managers rarely employ tools providing that capability.

In a world where software managers still tend to be rated more on schedule and cost performance than on product quality, there has been little motivation at the management level to take the risks to overcome the problems.

Complicating this tendency to avoid risk has been a generally negative reaction to the advances of theory. Too often theoretical approaches are presented to practitioners without experimental verification. When theorists come to a software organization to promote new methodologies which the practitioners know are simply not ready for use (e.g., automatic generation of code), the negative practitioner reaction to that experience tends to carry over into a rejection of all things new.

The gulf widens. Practice tends to be stuck in place, and theory tends to lack the force and the knowledge to budge it.

1.4.2.4 Framework for quality

The realities of building quality software to cost and schedule constraints have resulted in some very practical trade-offs in emphasis on quality. Consider the chart that follows.

PROJECT CRITICALITY

		High	Medium	Low
PROJECT SIZE	Large	Large emphasis on quality. Resources available.	————decrease———→ quality emphasis	
	Medium	decrease resources		
	Small			Least emphasis on quality. Resources un-available.

As this chart shows, approaches to quality vary with the criticality and the size of a project. Some projects simply do not warrant a complete peer code review of every line of code (a quick and dirty one-execution program [assuming it is truly that!] is one example).

Some projects simply do not have the resources available for full-blown quality approaches even when the criticality is there. For example, a one-person project of a critical nature may not be able to afford a full design review approach, with preliminary and critical peer and management reviews and full design documentation.

Thus, we see that there is no single "best" way of developing software.

That statement is reinforced by the following chart which results from a survey of tools usage made by a research organization and published in the periodical, *System Development* in July 1984. The message of the chart is that there is no well-defined "toolset" in common usage; there is only a scattering of tools used with varying emphasis in various computing installations. Although more recently there is increased usage of fourth-generation languages and CASE tools to match organization-chosen methodologies, including strong moves by such vendors as IBM and Digital Equipment to standardize such approaches (see Chapter 3.2), as of the writing of this book it is still true that there is no universally accepted problem-solving toolset.

SURVEY OF TOOLS USAGE

Report generation	77%
Debugging aids	65%
Screen generators	61%
Data dictionaries	60%
Librarians	58%
Program analyzer/optimizer	48%
Cross-reference analyzer	38%
Documentation aids	34%
Application development system	33%
Precompilers	20%
JCL processors	18%
Comparators	17%
Test data generators	12%

We come back to many of these tools in Chapter 2 and do a proper job of defining and discussing them. But the point here is that considering these commonly known tool concepts, there is great variance in how much they are actually used. Whether that is because they are unavailable in certain environments, or because practitioners are not aware of them, or because different people find they have different value profiles, the fact remains that there is not a consistent picture of tools usage.

1.4.2.5 Out-company supplements

In what we have said so far, the underlying assumption has been that the achievement of software quality at Company X is the task of the people of Company X. Surprisingly enough, that is not always the case.

In an earlier section, we saw increasing need for emphasis on software quality in the 1990s. Because of the factors leading to that need, it is more and more common to find software developers reaching outside their own company walls to obtain help in producing a quality product.

When this trend began, it tended to take these forms:

- Seminars on software quality. An expert would be brought in to provide, or employees would be sent to, a several-day seminar on the specifics of software quality. The seminars would cover the same sorts of material presented in this book.
- Management consulting on software quality. An expert would be brought in by management, perhaps to help solve a critical problem which had just occurred, or perhaps to do longer-range planning, in either case focusing on software product quality.

- Independent verification and validation. In the high-criticality world, a company would be hired to parallel the efforts of the developers in creating and evaluating a quality product. This has been especially common in space and military software.

In recent years, new dimensions have been added:

- Test and tool support. A company which specializes in testing techniques is hired to test the company's software using advanced tools and techniques.
- Code and data analysis. A company which specializes in verification techniques is hired to examine the company's code and data.
- Performance analysis. A company which specializes in evaluating sizing and timing efficiency is hired to examine the company's computing performance, perhaps using automated tools to help fine tune system performance.

An interesting twist to these services is the company that provides one or more of the preceding services, and then gives the software a "seal of approval." Especially in the highly competitive micro software world, this seal has both a marketing and technical meaning.

1.4.2.6 International standards

Most of the preceding approaches have examined the relationship between a software-developing institution, its software developers, and perhaps a small interfacing world outside the company.

There is a broader spectrum at work. Various national and international bodies are beginning to work on defining standards for achieving software quality.

For example, an engineering-oriented organization, the IEEE (Institute of Electrical and Electronics Engineers, Inc.) has been working for a number of years on developing software guidelines and standards.

Although these standards have no power with respect to a particular company and its software developers, the expectation is that the force of the creating people and organization will make their use inherently desirable—the better mousetrap approach—and that eventually these standards will come to be commonly accepted at the corporate level. Currently existing standards relevant to software quality are:

- a standard for the creation of quality assurance plans
- a glossary of terminology
- a standard for software test documentation
- a standard for configuration management plans

Efforts are under way to develop a number of additional standards and guidelines relevant to software engineering. We return to this topic later when we discuss the management of quality.

1.4.2.7 Summary

What we have seen here is that the state of the practice of software quality is diverse and complicated. It is stuck at some traditional levels. It is resistant to theory, some of which it should not resist, and some of which it should. It increasingly often uses a quality assurance organizational additive, and yet over all it still relies heavily on the software developer for product quality.

We can also see ways in which the practice has acknowledged the growing importance of quality in software with new organizational concepts (both in-company and out-company), even international bodies overseeing the problem.

REFERENCES

BROOKS87—"No Silver Bullet—Essence and Accidents of Software Engineering," *IEEE Computer,* April 1987; Fred Brooks. *A pragmatic summary of the state of the art and practice of software engineering. Sees no breakthroughs coming.* Must reading.

PARNAS85—"Software Aspects of Strategic Defense Systems," *American Scientist,* November 1985; David Parnas. *Looks at software research from the point of view of the then-proposed "Star Wars" system. Concludes that no major developments that could help build such a huge system are foreseeable.*

REIFER87—"Final Report: Software Quality Survey," *American Society for Quality Control,* November 1987; Donald J. Reifer, Richard W. Knudson, and Jerry Smith. *One of several recent surveys of quality assurance practice. Finds significant differences between aerospace QA (requirements compliance oriented) and nonaerospace QA (testing, defect removal oriented). Sees major issues of QA as being management awareness, customer/user awareness, finding and training qualified people.*

1.6 QUALITY AS ATTRIBUTES

In an earlier section, we defined quality as a collection of attributes, but failed to say what those attributes were. It is time now to fulfill that task.

Many writers on quality have defined many sets of attributes. Probably the best such definition was given by [Boehm78], and it is Boehm's definition that we use throughout this book.

Many writers on quality have also taken the following attributes, or some like them, and broken them down to a finer grain. For example, simplicity is an important characteristic of software at a different level, in that it contributes to almost all of the following seven attributes; simple software is more understandable and modifiable, and simple user interfaces make for better human engineering.

Here, however, we stay at this level of seven. The notion of attributes is so fundamental to the approach to quality we take in this book that it is important to focus on the top level and not dilute the concept.

- *Portability*: the ability of the software to be transferred easily from one computer to another for the purposes of execution.
- *Reliability*: the ability of the software to satisfy its requirements without error.
- *Efficiency*: the ability of the software to perform with minimum use of computer resources such as internal memory, external memory, and machine cycles.
- *Human engineering*: the ability of the software to be easily understood and used by human users.
- *Testability*: the ability of the software to be easily verified by execution.
- *Understandability*: the ability of the software to be read by a software maintainer.
- *Modifiability*: the ability of the software to be revised by a software maintainer.

These seven attributes make up our true definition of software quality. Software which has these attributes is said to be of high quality.

Note that with this definition, we have neatly sidestepped Pirsig's dilemma from *Zen and the Art of Motorcycle Maintenance*. We have converted the elusive notion of quality into a collection of easily (intuitively) understood attributes.

Note also that this definition meshes well with the experiences of software developers. Building software of high reliability is an everpresent challenge. Building software that is portable is a less common challenge, but one most of us have confronted on a few occasions. At one time or another, all software developers build software that requires special attention to one or more of these attributes.

That brings us to an important point. The construction of a software solution *should always begin with the establishment of a prioritized list of the attributes*. Does this software require special attention to its human engineering? (Microcomputer products frequently have this requirement.) Are changes expected in this software, so that special care should be taken with its understandability and modifiability? (Software in a brand-new application area will nearly always have this requirement.)

It is not enough to establish one key attribute and focus on it. To one degree or another, for any software solution all of the attributes are important. For example, software that has a high requirement for portability still must be reliable, efficient, testable, and all the other attributes. But portability requires special attention if it is to be well achieved. While not ignoring the other attributes, the builder of portable software will give his or her product the necessary special attention.

In a later section of this chapter, we talk about which techniques for achieving quality help most in achieving each of these attributes. For now, however, let us continue with a more philosophical discussion.

One of the difficulties in building software to match a prioritized list of quality attributes is that achieving one of them may degrade one or more of the others.

TRADE-OFFS IN ACHIEVING THE ATTRIBUTES

	P	R	E	H	T	U	M
Portability			X			X	X
Reliability			X	X			
Efficiency	X	X		X	X	X	X
Human Engineering		X	X		X	X	X
Testability			X	X		X	X
Understandability	X		X	X	X		
Modifiability	X		X	X	X		

In the preceding chart, X represents a negative correlation between achieving one attribute and another. For example, in the first row, the chart shows that achieving portability may have a negative effect on achieving E (efficiency), U (understandability), and M (modifiability).

When you are building portable software, for example, one technique is to use a common and standard subset of a high-order language. Because you are not using all the functional power of the language, your program may be less efficient than it could be. Because you are not using all the expressive power of the language, your program may be harder to understand and modify than it could be. Similar examples could be used to show the other negative correlations.

The point of the chart and this discussion is *not* to be precise about which attributes correlate negatively with others, and by how much. This kind of discussion is primarily philosophical since no good data are available to substantiate any particular point of view. (In fact, this chart is purely an intuitive presentation expressing the author's own biases!)

Instead, the point of the chart and this discussion is to show that preparing and using a prioritized list of attributes to define the quality goals of a software product is not an easy task.

Because of this problem, several other problems occur:

1. Achieving quality in a software product naturally tends toward conflict. If there is a quality assurance organization working with a software development organization, the conflict may become an organizational one.
2. People responsible for software quality must understand and agree on overall system goals.
3. People responsible for software quality must understand software and how to achieve the attributes. If they do not, when these conflicts arise, naive solutions will be proposed.
4. Even with a clearly prioritized set of quality goals, it is necessary to pay attention to all of the attributes, not just the key ones. Otherwise a perfectly beautiful software product fulfilling all of its quality goals will founder on poor quality from an unexpected source.

The Intel 432 was to be the computer of the future. It had an advanced architecture that was the subject of enthusiasm at every computing conference where its creators spoke.

They called it an "object-oriented machine" (a data object and its manipulation mechanisms were emphasized and facilitated by special hardware). They called it an "Ada machine" (the architecture of the machine paralleled the Department of Defense programming language Ada). They called it a "system programmer's machine" (the instruction set was enormous and contained a number of operating system functions, such as scheduling and dispatching, normally done in software).

But when the smoke cleared away in the marketplace, they had to call the Intel 432 a dud. It met all those design goals mentioned in the previous paragraph. But it failed in another.

The 432 was slow as molasses. It was 10 to 20 times slower than its competition. It was, in fact, unacceptably slow.

Somewhere, in the quest to build a high-quality product, one of the quality attributes had slipped through the crack. It was a fatal mistake.

Achieving software quality through its attributes may be a complex process, but it is also a manageable one. The individual quality attributes are well understood in practice, and there are commonly accepted ways of accomplishing them.

REFERENCES

BOEHM78—*Characteristics of Software Quality,* North-Holland, 1978. Barry W. Boehm et al. *A book whose goal is to explore the notion of quality through its characteristics. Much of the philosophy of this section is taken from that material.*

1.7 QUALITY IN THE LIFE CYCLE

If you asked the average software developer when quality considerations enter into the software development process, the "shoot from the lip" answer might be "during testing." But upon further thought, he or she might reconsider and say, "from the very beginning."

It is the latter approach that we examine and advocate in this book.

In childrearing, if the parents fail to steer a child in desirable directions in the first four years of life, it may be too late to do it after that. The analogous situation is true of software. If the software developer waits until testing to put the quality in, it is too late. Quality evolves from correct requirements, creative design, careful coding, and then comprehensive testing.

We call this full-project philosophy the *life-cycle approach* to building quality software. In this book, we talk a great deal about the techniques that a software person concerned with quality can use in all the phases of the life cycle. Only after we have taken this chronological approach to obtaining quality do we return once again to the attribute approach, and single out those life-cycle concepts which best help to achieve a prioritized list of attributes.

What is this life cycle? It is the series of steps that make up the software development and maintenance process. In this book, we call those steps *requirements, design, implementation, checkout,* and *maintenance.* In a few moments we will define those terms. But first, let's acknowledge some controversy about life cycles in general, and this definition in particular.

There is some opposition to the whole idea of the life cycle—an article entitled "Life Cycle Concept Considered Harmful" [McCracken82] has appeared in the literature—on the grounds that a rigid approach to the life cycle tends to preclude the use of new concepts such as prototyping. Others have found [Zelkowitz88] that a rigid approach to the life cycle is simply unrealistic, as it does not match what practitioners really do.

There is also disagreement on what the steps are within the life cycle. Different software engineering experts advocate different sets of phases and phase names. For example, in this book we use the term *implementation* for what others call *programming* or *coding.* (The term implies that a design is being implemented into code.)

For the purpose of this book, however, we sidestep these arguments. The life cycle we use here is only a framework for discussion. If you do not agree with this life cycle, simply substitute your own. The most important thing is not which life-cycle definition you use, but that you use the one you have chosen with care. No one should use anyone's life cycle without the willingness to bend that usage to meet project needs. For example, it is often true that design is an iterative task, and may include preliminary coding to verify that a design technique will work. This conflicts with a rigid look at the life-cycle sequence specify-design-code. When such conflict occurs, it is the fault of rigidity, not the life-cycle concept.

Viewed in this way, prototyping is simply an iterative approach to the development of a requirements specification, and thus it fits comfortably within the life-cycle concept.

Now, let us return to defining the life cycle we have been talking about. It is the sequence of steps we usually go through to develop software.

Requirements. This is the first phase of software development, usually consuming roughly 10 percent of total software costs (see Figure 1.1, and recall that total costs include maintenance). It is here that the user's problem is stated, analyzed, understood, and translated into a problem definition. Some call this phase *systems analysis.*

The result of the requirements phase is a requirements specification, a document describing what the finished product must do and be.

The greatest hazard in the requirements phase is the temptation to

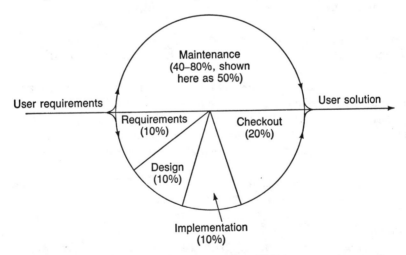

Figure 1.1 Software life cycle: costs per phase. Maintenance costs range from 40–80% of total system costs. Recent emphasis on "front end" (requirements and design) process tends to raise these percentages (to perhaps 15-15) and lower checkout (to perhaps 10). Small projects have higher implementation percentages.

define a solution to the problem, rather than simply stating the problem. If a solution or partial solution is specified, then it will have the force of a requirement and alternative solutions will be prematurely precluded.

Design. This is the second phase of software development, usually consuming another 10 percent of software costs. Here the "what" of requirements is translated into the "how" of a solution. Computing-specific decisions are made: What computer? What language? What modules? What sequence of functions? What data structures? What else?

The greatest hazard in design is quitting too soon (leading to an inadequate solution) or quitting too late (leading to an implementation phase which severely overlaps with design, wasting time and money).

Implementation. This is the third phase of software development, usually consuming yet another 10 percent of costs. The design is coded into a computer-readable, computer-processable solution.

Here the computer software takes actual shape and becomes an executable, problem-solving entity. The intricacies of the computer are met head on and dealt with. There is the illusion—or perhaps the reality—of crafting a hold-it-in-your-hands product, a Stradivarius capable of making the computer play fine music.

The greatest hazard in implementation is carelessness. Computer programs are a mass of fine details, many of them interrelated and many of them brain-busters in their own right. There is the ever-present danger that carelessness can turn a Stradivarius into a kazoo.

Checkout. This is the fourth phase of software development, usually consuming 20 percent of costs. Here, the Stradivarius is played to see if it meets its requirements.

Another analogy applies here. Checkout is playing Sherlock Holmes to a frustrating series of "crimes" caused by program flaws, sifting through clues to identify (and rehabilitate) the criminal code. Checkout is seeking programming errors, seeking design errors, questioning questionable requirements, and putting the final polish on the soon-to-be-usable computer program.

The greatest hazard in checkout is impatience. Program checkout must be a painstaking process of trying out all the requirements, all the structural elements, and as many of the combinations of logic paths as common sense and cost/schedule considerations permit. The temptation is to stop short, declare the program fit, and ship it off to its users. A disgruntled user, one who loses trust in a computer program, may never regain that trust. And a computer program can die from lack of trust.

Maintenance. Here is the final and continuing phase of software evolution. While the user begins to use the production software system which has passed the checkout process, the maintainer removes residual errors and installs the inevitable changes. To the surprise of many, maintenance has been found to consume 50 percent or more (sometimes much more) of software costs.

The greatest hazard of maintenance is ineptitude. A finely tuned Stradivarius can be reduced to high-quality firewood by an inept maintainer. All the good of the previous phases can be undone in the glamorless, unheralded world of maintenance.

Several studies have been conducted on actual costs of the different phases of the software life cycle. Although there are variations between them, Figure 1.1 presents a roughly accurate breakdown. Note the dominance of the maintenance phase.

Studies have also been conducted on when errors are generated during the software life cycle (Figure 1.2). These studies typically start after the requirements phase, assuming that the specification is a baseline against which the errors are measured. They also typically measure only errors detected after integration or acceptance or delivery. Design errors dominate the picture.

Studies also show that recorded errors are often not detected until very late in the software life cycle (Figure 1.3). The predominant number are found during or after the acceptance test.

The cost of fixing an error rises dramatically as the software progresses through the life cycle (Figure 1.4). Maintenance costs (per error) are enormous.

The preceding figures paint a depressing picture. They show software errors occurring early in the software life cycle (predominantly in design), and being detected late (predominantly in maintenance). They show dramatically increasing costs for removing errors as time passes by. How much better it would be to find the errors as they are created.

The beginnings of an approach for doing so are shown in Figure 1.5. Here, as the software development transitions from one phase to the next,

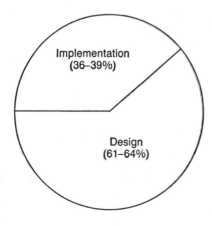

Figure 1.2 Software life cycle: error sources per phase. Design errors dominate; most errors are introduced early in the life cycle.

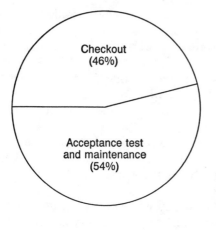

Figure 1.3 Software life cycle: error discovery per phase. Error discovery occurs very late in the life cycle.

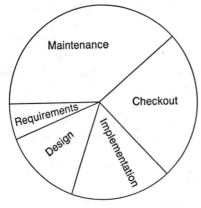

Figure 1.4 Software life cycle: per error fix cost per phase. Cost of error removal rises dramatically through the life cycle.

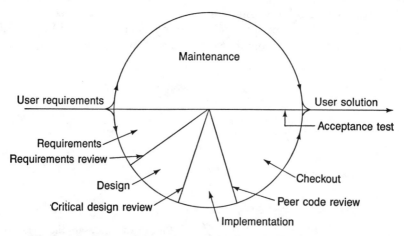

Figure 1.5 Software life cycle: interphase reliability techniques. Many reliability activities are scheduled at phase transitions.

quality checking practices are employed. In this figure, we show the requirements review, the critical design review, the peer code review, and the acceptance test. These interphase quality processes and many more are discussed in the material which follows.

In the next two major sections, we first look at a set of techniques organized by life-cycle phase. Then we look at the same set of techniques organized by attributes.

With these two views of the same topic, we can then define a set of techniques to be used on a project to satisfy its attribute goals, and organize their use chronologically.

REFERENCES

BOEHM88—"A Spiral Model of Software Development and Enhancement," *IEEE Computer,* May 1988; Barry W. Boehm. *Summarizes life-cycle concepts; presents what is arguably the most rational definition for a software life cycle.*

COLLOFELLO87—"Introduction to Software Verification and Validation," Software Engineering Institute Curriculum Module SEI-CM-13, October 1987; James S. Collofello. *Defines a framework for a discussion of life-cycle quality approaches, for use by an educator wanting to teach the topic.*

GLASS91—"My Trivial/Brilliant Concept Called 'Problem-Solving,'" *Software Conflict,* Yourdon Press, 1991; Robert L. Glass. *Points out that the "software life cycle" is not unique to software, but rather is used in all problem-solving processes.*

McCRACKEN 82—"Life-Cycle Concept Considered Harmful," *ACM Software Engineering Notes,* April 1982; D. D. McCracken and M. A. Jackson. *Finds the use of the software life cycle has been counterproductive.*

SCACCHI87—"Models of Software Evolution: Life Cycle and Process," Software Engineering Institute Curriculum Module SEI-CM-10, October 1987; Walt Scacchi. *Presents an introduction to most of the models of software development (including the traditional "waterfall" life cycle); for use by an educator wishing to teach the topic.*

ZELKOWITZ88—"Resource Utilization During Software Development," *Journal of Systems and Software,* September 1988; Marvin R. Zelkowitz. *Finds via practitioner project data analysis that the traditional software serial waterfall life cycle is not realistic; software developers frequently do some work in one phase of the cycle while nominally working in another. Advocates changing the life cycle, not the practice.*

1.8 THE ZEROTH OPTION (REUSE)

It is easy to fall into the trap of discussing software quality from the point of view of *creating* quality software, starting from scratch.

But in fact the most effective route to quality software is not to create it at all! In this book we use the term *zeroth option* to discuss the choice that should be examined *before* the choice of software development approach: "Do I need to write any software at all to solve this problem?"

Increasingly often, the answer to that question is "No." *Off-the-shelf products* such as spreadsheets and report generators allow us to solve some problems without writing software. *Reuse* allows us to borrow packages from past software to use like software parts in our current work. *Application generators* allow us to write programs for narrowly defined, well-understood applications by responding to questions posed by an intelligent, application-focused tool. *Fourth-generation languages* (often called 4GLs to distinguish them from more general, third-generation languages like COBOL or Ada or Modula) allow us to write complex programs in terms appropriate to a particular class of application, frequently report generation from a database. *Natural language interfaces* allow us to specify a problem to a particular software product in English-like, rather than computer-programming-like, phrases. Each of these approaches is in general preferable to creating new software from scratch, so long as the quality goal of efficiency is met, and the technique to be used is powerful enough to solve the application in question.

However, the promise of the zeroth option is often not borne out in practice. Packages, special-purpose languages, and natural language interfaces frequently apply only to part of a more complicated problem to be solved. Reusable parts are available, but sometimes for the wrong application or hardware or language or operating system.

The zeroth option, interestingly enough, has had a strong presence throughout the history of software. In the 1950s, math libraries and sort/merge routines were commonly available. Problem-oriented languages were the focus of research in the 1960s and into the 1970s.

Then progress slowed. The easy problems of the zeroth option had all been solved. Further progress required application-specific approaches, and for a particular class of applications it was not so clear what functions could be reused, and how such reusable parts could be built.

Renewed interest in reuse in the 1980s led to increased research into the problem, but not much progress. It became clear that further progress in reuse depended on

- reuse of design, not just code
- motivation of both creators (reusable software must be "generalized" and users (the "not invented here" syndrome must be overcome) of reusable parts
- taxonomies to make it easy to find appropriate parts
- broadening the notion of reuse to data and objects as well as functions.

As a result, although the zeroth option remains the option of choice before beginning the creation of new software, all too often it has not been a practical option. The remainder of this book is about the creation of new software (or the maintenance of software that was at one time "newly created"). But before proceeding, let us take a look at how reuse might be employed (see box).

You work for one of the leading timber companies. You have been assigned a second specialized report program to extract data from the tree growth measurement database.

When you received the first assignment, you looked through the collection of fourth-generation languages and application generators available to you, and found that although they might solve 85 percent of the problem you had to solve, it was the easy 85 percent and the hard 15 percent was going to be very hard in any 4GLs you could find. Because of that, you had decided to write your own report generator from scratch, trying to reuse all or parts of it in later similar applications.

With this second assignment, you find the payoff of this approach is beginning. The overall design framework of the first program is appropriate to the second. Many parts of the code need only tailoring to this second application to be used. The tailoring is somewhat clumsy, but as you do it you begin to look at ways to simplify the tailoring for the next time you need to write a similar program. You identify logic and data that are different from the prior solution, and you begin to isolate those elements into modules that will be easier to modify next time. The rest you package in such a way that the changeable elements are parameters to the unchanging elements.

By the time you get a third similar assignment, your solution has been parameterized and generalized. This time, you can move quickly from a rudimentary design solution to the simple changes to parameterized code that you planned during the second implementation. The process works, and works well. You begin to think of documenting what you have done in order to submit it to your corporate reuse library. It feels good to know that your work will be useful to others, and that you will be recognized in your profession and company as a capable contributor.

REFERENCES _____

TRACZ89—IEEE Tutorial on Reuse, IEEE, 1989; Will Tracz. *A good collection of papers defining the state of the art and practice of software reuse.*

TRACZ91—"Software Reuse Rules of Thumb," *The Software Practitioner,* March 1991; Will Tracz. *A "how-to" paper on building reusable software.*

2

The Technology of Quality

The viewpoint of this book, as we have already seen, is that product quality is at heart a technical issue. The creator of the software must strive for product quality, using the best technical tools and methods at his or her disposal, or quality will not happen. That is the subject of this chapter. Later we see what approaches management can use to help assure that quality has been an important part of the development process.

2.1 A LIFE-CYCLE APPROACH TO QUALITY

In the previous chapter, we discussed what the software life cycle is and why a life-cycle approach to quality is important. In the sections that follow, for each life-cycle phase we present a set of techniques and tools that can be useful in helping to improve the quality of the eventual software product.

As you will see, the set of technologies and tools is rich. Approximately five dozen are presented here. It is important to point out, however, that some of these technologies and tools are more useful than others. Judgment is passed on particular techniques and tools in the section where each is discussed; in addition, at the end of the book there is a summation where the author's pick of the "best" techniques and tools is presented.

These judgments and choices are, of course, subject to controversy. Techniques and tools appear in the literature of software quality because someone is advocating them. It is important for you the reader, as you work your way through this material, to begin forming your own framework for judgment as to the value of the techniques of quality. You may prefer to accept the positive opinion of the original advocate for a technique which, for example, the author of this book sees as having little value.

It is a fair assessment of the state of quality technology that diverse opinions are healthy. In the short history of software engineering as a profession, we have found no best route to software development. That fact is even more true in the pursuit of software quality. It is the intent of the author of this book to provide the reader with the judgment to resolve those controversies at a personal level, rather than to define and advocate any "best" approach.

2.2 REQUIREMENTS

The quest for quality must begin early in the software development cycle.

The statement of requirements defines what problem will be solved, and therefore what product will be built. If it is not right—and all too often, getting it right is very difficult—then the software product itself, no matter how flawlessly designed, implemented, and tested, cannot be right.

This high leverage of requirements in the quality of the final software product has led to a great deal of research in recent years into ways of doing requirements better. Much of that research has been focused on representational issues, that is, how to state the requirements in the form of a specification once they are obtained. That topic is dealt with in a later section. A burgeoning tools industry has, in fact, formed to support requirements representation.

But requirements for a software system are a representation problem and a lot more. Most fundamentally, in fact, requirements are a communication problem.

First, let us introduce the players in the requirements gathering process. There is the person with the problem to be solved, commonly called either the *customer* because he or she is providing the resources for the solution, or the *user* because he or she will eventually use the solution to solve the problem. (The customer and the user may be different people, different institutional organizations, the same person, or from the same organization.)

Then there is the computing specialist who is gathering the requirements in order to provide the computing solution. This person is called by different names depending on the application domain: *systems analyst* for commercial data processing applications, *math analyst* for scientific/engineering applications, and systems engineer for real-time applications.

The communication problem comes about because these problem-solving specialists must clearly and unambiguously agree on what characteristics they see in the problem and what characteristics they demand in the problem solution. For a problem of any magnitude, that is a massive communication task. Typically, the customer/user is a specialist in some problem discipline, usually not computing, and is used to talking to other specialists with a similar background. The requirements gatherer, on the other hand, is usually a software specialist more skilled in employing a computer than in the problem discipline. There is a built-in communication gap at the beginning of the problem solution, therefore, and it is primarily the task of the requirements gatherer to overcome it.

Often, in addition to the fundamental communication problem, there is also a technology problem. That is, the customer/user may still be exploring the solution methodology from the point of view of his or her own discipline. The requirements gatherer, steeped in the knowledge of the computing discipline, suddenly is thrust into the forefront of an unfamiliar technology and is expected to produce a solution in an application domain space that even the customer/user is still struggling to understand. Thus, the ability of the requirements gatherer to grow in the direction of one or more application domain specialties is vital to the success of the requirements-gathering exercise.

The existence of this larger customer/user world, the world of the application discipline, is reflected in several important ways in the requirements process. One way is that the software solution is often part of a larger system solution. The immediate software problem may be a carburetor control mechanism or an on-line teller user interface, for example, but the encompassing problem—the "system"—is an automobile or a bank.

The other way the customer/user world is reflected in the requirements-gathering exercise is that the nature of the application plays a heavy role in the techniques used by the requirements gatherer to define and specify the requirements. For that automotive application, for example, real-time control representation methods will be vital for understanding and specifying the eventual requirements specification. For the banking application, on the other hand, the problem may be heavily flavored by database and human interface implications. The requirements techniques and tools to be used (and, as we see later, the design techniques and the testing techniques) are heavily influenced by the kind of application problem being solved.

In fact, the system aspects of the requirements problem are often complex enough that a separate discipline known as *systems engineering* has been established to help bridge the communication and technology problems that would otherwise separate the problem solvers. Let us look a little more at the nature of systems before we move further into the subject of software requirements.

2.2.1 System Requirements

Basically, there are two kinds of software-related problems: those that have only a software flavor, and those where the software is part of a larger system. This section is about the latter.

If the software is part of a larger system (see Figure 2.1 for a pictorial view), then a great deal of systems-related work must precede the definition of the software requirements. First, the requirements for the total system must be obtained and stated. This is a requirements-gathering exercise similar to the one we discussed earlier, except that the requirements-gathering specialist is a systems engineer rather than a software engineer.

Once the total system requirements are understood—and that, of course, is a sizable task in its own right, usually much larger than the problem of understanding the software requirements—then it is time to allocate those requirements to the disciplines that will provide the solutions. For example, somehow a decision must be made as to which of the system requirements will be solved by nonsoftware components, and which by software. This allocation process is usually accomplished by a preliminary design of the total system. The design, to be sure, is only conducted to the level of allocating functions to disciplines such as software, but nevertheless this is a design process since the decision is being made as to how

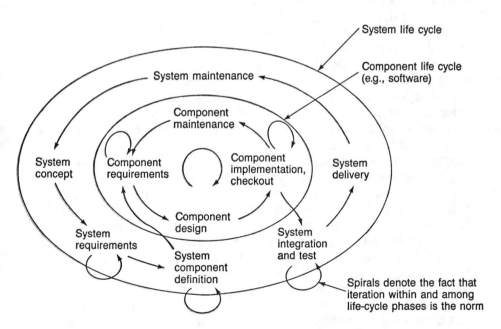

Figure 2.1 A system view (spiral life cycles within spiral life cycles).

the problem solution is to occur. It is only after this preliminary system design that the software problem is understood well enough to begin to pursue the software requirements.

Under these circumstances, the determination of software requirements may often be a process of referring to the preliminary system design while combing through the total system specification, looking for those requirements that may apply to the software subproblem. This may be a more impersonal process than that described earlier because the system specification serves as a surrogate for the customer/user, but the communication and technology problem are just as pernicious as if the communication were firsthand.

Modeling and simulation. That preliminary system design task essential to the establishment of software requirements is as complex as the application system to be built. That is often, as mentioned before, complex indeed.

In fact, it is often complex enough that the skilled systems engineer may need help in getting a firm grip on the system requirements. Modeling and simulation are important techniques for doing that.

Modeling is the construction of something that represents an object or process; simulation is causing a model to interact with a real or simulated external environment. For example, building a scaled-down replica of a space vehicle is modeling; exercising that model in a wind tunnel to determine its flight characteristics is simulation.

One of the powerful capabilities of the computer is the fact that it can be made to behave like other objects or systems. For example, via the computer it is possible to test fly a space mission defined as a computerized scenario in order to see if the real space flight will encounter problems that could not have been anticipated with a simple paper and pencil analysis. Most complicated, high-cost systems are now exercised via simulation before the real thing is built. Simulations explore such issues as completeness of the understanding of a system, or adequacy of its performance characteristics. In other words, simulation is an excellent support for exploratory systems requirements definition. Are the current structural requirements sufficient for the system in question? We'll build a simulation and subject it to simulated stress testing to find out. Are the performance requirements sufficient to allow a successful mission? Let's simulate the timing characteristics and see whether things happen on time.

Thus, one of the principal benefits of building a model and simulating its execution is the opportunity for requirements analysis. Not only can the proposed requirements be analyzed, but feasibility tests can be run to see if the proposed requirements are sufficient, or if they need augmentation, or if they are simply so far off that the proposed system cannot be built. The cost of building a computerized simulation is often high, but not nearly as high as the cost of building the corresponding real system, especially if that is done and the system fails!

Modeling and simulation may be accomplished in a variety of ways in the software world. Basically, any simulation can be coded using any software language or methodology. But there are some language systems designed specifically for building simulation applications. For example, GPSS (General Purpose System Simulator) is a language designed for simulation development; and Simscript and Simula add simulation capabilities to standard programming languages (Fortran and Algol). (Simscript has evolved from its Fortran base into a language in its own right.) Thus, the technology for simulation construction is well advanced and has been for over two decades.

Modeling and simulation language systems provide a wide variety of facilities for modeling continuous, periodic, or stochastic (statistically distributed, random) discrete functions. Some functions commonly provided that are particularly useful to simulating computer-related systems include:

- Computer hardware. The hardware features of a single processor, multiprocessor, or distributed system may be simulated.
- Control flow. The execution sequences of various activities may be simulated.
- Data flow. The movement of data through activity nodes may be simulated.
- Interface. Inputs, outputs, and data rates may be simulated.
- Performance. Timing and sizing may be simulated.

Simulation generally involves a fairly complex system of software tools: a compiler, capable of translating the simulation language into machine-executable code; a scenario processor, capable of understanding a statement of the problem to be executed by a particular simulation run; and a postprocessor, capable of performing data reduction on the often voluminous outputs of the simulation run.

EXAMPLE OF SYSTEM MODELING AND SIMULATION

You have been asked to construct a fault-tolerant computer system for the control of carburetion in a Formula One racing car. Your job places heavy emphasis on a fully reliable fuel system, and less emphasis on costs. To assure fault tolerance (the owner and driver would both feel badly and be irritated if your carburetor failed one lap before the checkered flag dropped on a world championship race with $50,000 prize money), you decide to use a triply redundant system of processors—that is, the same software runs continuously in three computers, and if their results differ, they vote to determine which computer has failed, dropping it from further use.

Because of the reliability requirements and the complexity of the application, you convince your customer to spend the extra money needed to simulate the system. You elect to use GPSS as the modeling language, and you begin gathering data on automobile and engine performance to serve as the basis for the model. The engineer who designed the car and the engineer who designed the engine have most of the information you need, and the skilled mechanics in the owner's shop can estimate the rest. You model the engine at the level of each piston stroke and corresponding electrical system and carburetor actions, and stress the functioning of the software-hardware system controlling the carburetor.

You choose to define *transactions*, the units upon which GPSS operates, as pulses through the engine's electrical system and elements of the fuel flow. The transactions move through blocks you have specified for them—the gas tank, the fuel lines, the fuel pump, the carburetor, the battery, the electrical connections, the distributor, and the ignition chamber. In each of these blocks, a series of actions you specify impacts the transactions. Such functions as throttle pressure, heat and humidity, and car attitude are applied to define the actions. When the model is executed, the transactions flow through the blocks of the system, and a record is made of the resulting modeled actions. Interactions between the transactions and the computer hardware/software system are also tracked.

The model, when run, verifies that your software as specified will do the job. However, you discover a fuel slosh problem which will only occur on hard braking and report that result to the owner. The fault is corrected, both in the system and in the model, and the subsequent runs of the model make the upcoming championship season look promising.

REFERENCES

MERRIMAN87—"Automated Interactive Simulation Modeling System: AISIM," *Journal of Systems and Software*, March 1987; Michael F. Merriman. *Describes an Air Force general-purpose simulation tool with application in the areas of communication nets, computer systems architectures, and data processing functions during the conceptual stages of system development.*

VARHOL89—"Modeling Business Systems," *MIPS*, April and June 1989; Peter D. Varhol. *Description of a case study of the use of a GPSS simulation for studying a business application, the provision of telephone hotline service support for customer service in a large company.*

2.2.2 Software Requirements

Once the system requirements are refined enough to allow an understanding of what problems the software is to solve, the software requirements analysis may proceed. Here we determine the "what" of the problem to be solved by software. This includes the functionality of the problem solution, the interfaces to the remainder of the system, and the degree of quality to be achieved in building the software solution.

What we must not determine at this point is the "how" of the problem. This is a problem to be deferred until the design phase.

2.2.2.1 Kinds of requirements

We have already seen that software requirements may either emerge from a system specification and design, or from communication with a customer/ user.

Given that background, common sense would tell us that there is no more taxonomizing of requirements; requirements from here on in are requirements. But common sense would be wrong.

The word *requirements* has blurred in meaning over the years in defining the "what" of problem solution. It has been used, by various authors, to mean the following [Davis88]:

- the needs of the software user
- the solution space as the set of all legitimate solutions
- the external behavior of the as-built product
- the set of architectural components that make up the as-built product
- the set of specifications for the individual modules of the to-be-built product
- the algorithms which define the function of the individual modules of the to-be-built product

In each of these cases, the definition of requirements defines the "what" of something related to software, and the next step of problem decomposition would result in a "how." Therefore, each author using one of these meanings feels fully justified in choosing that definition.

But clearly this blurring of definition can lead to trouble. Some of these definitions of *requirement* are problem specific, for example, and others are program specific. The problem lies to some extent in the word which defines the representation of the requirements, the *specification*. Whereas *requirement* at least has some intrinsic meaning, *specification* does not. *Specification* has been used to mean the following [Rombach87]:

- the statement of the problem requirements
- the output of any life-cycle phase (e.g., the requirements specification is the product of the requirements analysis phase)
- the input to the next life-cycle phase (e.g., the requirements specification is the input to the design phase)
- the statement of the program requirements

- any software document (e.g., the maintenance manual is referred to in some circles as the "computer program development specification")

For the purposes of this book, the two words are used as follows:

- Requirements define the "what" of the problem, not the program.
- Specification is the written output of the requirements analysis phase.

The mischief of all this blurring of definitions is that while computing and software people seem to be talking about the same thing when they use the terms, they in fact are not. For example, there is much discussion and study in the computer science research world of the possibility of automatic generation of code from specifications. As the definition of requirements and specification becomes more program specific, it becomes much more possible to actually automate the generation of code. But to someone who thinks that requirements are at a considerably higher level—the problem level—the notion of automatic code generation verges on either the miraculous or the laughable, depending on the naivete of the listener.

There are other taxonomies into which the topic of requirements may be divided. For example, the requirements for a system may take two forms: problem requirements and project requirements. The latter might include the milestones to be used to measure project progress and the schedule by which they are to be achieved, for example. Usually this dilemma is resolved by leaving the project requirements out of the requirements specification and putting them into another document, sometimes called the *statement of work,* so that the problem requirements are purely about the problem, and not the management aspects of its solution.

Another possible division of terms is in the categories of requirements that might be considered. These are often divided into behavioral requirements as the things software will do for the user, and nonbehavioral requirements as the quality with which it will do those things.

The quality attributes that form the focus of much of this book are the nonbehavioral requirements. To the extent that the software is portable or modifiable, for example, the requirement to achieve those quality attributes is nonbehavioral. Some requirements representation techniques are very good at allowing the formal specification of behavioral requirements, for example, but specifying nonbehavioral requirements formally is much harder and is usually done with informal specification techniques.

In spite of all of these differences about what requirements might be, there is one thing that everyone agrees on: Requirements are the "what" of the software life cycle, design is the "how," and it is vital to make sure that design does not creep into the requirements. It is vital because to the extent that design becomes a requirement, it constrains the eventual designer to solutions that may not be optimal, and it is vital because the task of defining requirements is difficult enough without contaminating it by sliding into a design solution unknowingly.

REFERENCES

BRACKETT89—"Software Requirements," Software Engineering Institute Curriculum Module SEI-CM-19, 1989; John W. Brackett. *Presents an overview of software requirements identification, analysis, representation, communication, and acceptance. Written for someone who wants to teach the topic.*

DAVIS88—"A Taxonomy for the Early Stages of the Software Development Life Cycle," *Journal of Systems and Software,* September 1988; Alan M. Davis. *Identifies a multiplicity of definitions of the word* requirements *in software engineering. Points out that many tools and techniques are good at some definitions but not at others, and that it is easy in this situation to be comparing apples with oranges.*

ROMBACH87—"Software Specification: A Framework," Software Engineering Institute Curriculum Module SEI-CM-11, October 1987; H. Dieter Rombach. *Defines the word* specification *and gives examples of its use. Points out the many definitions that have evolved for the word. Contains information for someone wanting to teach the topic.*

2.2.2.2 Problem analysis

The essence of software engineering is application problem solving.

What is the process of problem solving? If we think in terms of a general problem, not just a software one, we very quickly run into our old friend, the life cycle. To solve any problem, we must study the requirements, design a solution, build the solution, test the solution to see if it works, and then if the solution stays around long enough, provide operational support for the maintenance of the solution.

Now, with the insight that this problem-solving process is universal, are there any universal truths to accompany that insight? Unfortunately, after that initial general insight, the problem-solving process gets application specific fairly quickly. (Computer scientists are just beginning to appreciate the role of application dependency in the computing process.)

We *can* say, however, that problem analysis is the first step in the problem-solving process; if we don't understand what the problem is, we are unlikely to be able to solve it. There are some general, high-level statements that can be made about approaches to problem analysis.

First of all, for a technique to be both general and useful, it should meet these criteria as suggested by Davis [Davis89]:

- facilitate communication between the person with the problem and the problem solver

- provide a means of defining system boundaries
- support the notions of partitioning, abstraction, and projection
- steer the problem solver toward the problem rather than its solution
- allow for an examination of alternatives
- identify conflicting alternatives where possible

There are several possible starting points for problem analysis. These starting points are defined by the nature of the problem to be solved:

- Inputs and outputs. Examine all inputs to and outputs required from the problem. For particularly simple problems, this may be the most appropriate starting point.
- Major functions. Identify all the functions to be performed in solving the problem. Extract from those functions the definition of the inputs needed to perform the functions, and the outputs needed to demonstrate satisfactory performance of the functions.
- Objects. Identify all the objects to be manipulated by the system, the operations to be performed on them, and their interrelationships. (This is known as object-oriented analysis.)
- Users. Interview all the potential users of the system. Extract from the list of users those whose usage is in some or all ways unique. Identify the outputs expected by each unique user. Working backward, identify the inputs required to produce those outputs.
- Environment. Study the environment in which the solution will function. Identify the effects the solution is to have on the environment. Identify what outputs must be produced to create those effects. Working backward, identify the inputs required to produce those outputs.

Once the inputs and outputs, basic functions, and objects are identified, analysis shifts from problem identification to problem decomposition. Techniques useful in the decomposition process are partitioning, abstraction, and projection [Yeh80].

Partitioning is a bottom-up process in which the whole problem is so difficult to grasp that it is partitioned into a set of smaller problems, each of which is then broken down into *its* constituent requirements. The totality of the software requirements is the sum of the requirements of the subproblems. Abstraction is a top-down process in which the essence of the problem at a high level is identified. Then that high-level essence is decomposed into a set of more specific and concrete constituents. The totality of the software requirements is the sum of the requirements of the most concrete constituents of the abstract problem.

Projection is a multiviewed approach to the aspects of the total problem. The problem is examined from the point of view of the key players in the eventual problem solution, for example, the users. The totality of the software requirements is the sum of the requirements from each key player projection.

In each of these problem decomposition approaches, the point is not so much to identify all the requirements per se, but to see the system at a sufficient level of detail that all aspects of the system become visible. With this visibility, the system requirements are easily extracted.

There are many specific methodologies created to support this problem analysis process. A discussion of such methodologies is beyond the intended scope of this book; here, we want only to cover the essence of the tasks involved in doing problem analysis. The reader interested in further study of particular methodologies might look at *IEEE Computer* [85] which contains an excellent summary of some of the leading candidate methodologies in a special issue entitled "Requirements Engineering Environments: Software Tools for Modeling User Needs." That publication also contains further references for the specific techniques it covers.

If the reader is particularly interested in methodologies for real-time software, then Ward [86] may be interesting; for commercial data processing, Orr [81] or Marca [88] may be of special value. There are, in fact, a large number of techniques and methodologies available; what is missing is a good analysis leading to a basis for associating the techniques and their most appropriate application domain. That analysis will inevitably come, and probably soon, as researchers become increasingly aware of the special needs of the various application domains.

The end result of this problem analysis process should be the set of requirements defining the problem to be solved. It is easy to say that, but as we have already seen, doing it is a complicated process. Often the problem is that not all the pertinent requirements get identified. Systematic approaches such as partitioning, abstraction, and projection should help make sure that sufficient depth is encountered so that the analyst sees all aspects of the problem.

A common problem is to omit key requirements. For example, in one particularly naive specification for complex software, in this case a compiler, the procurement specification defined the outputs of the compiler in total as "the compiler shall output symbolic assembler language statements as specified in the computer programming manual for the target computer." Superficially, this may sound adequate. But think of the possible outputs of a compiler:

- the listing of the source program
- diagnostics for source errors
- interface requirements, such as for a loader or a source debugger

- cross-reference listings, load maps, object code listings
- object code optimizations

Clearly, the person who performed this particular problem analysis had not employed either partitioning or projection, and if abstraction were used, no decomposition had followed it!

Sometimes, for particularly difficult or new problems, this process is still not enough to allow identification of the full set of requirements. Under those circumstances, a useful approach is prototyping, which is discussed in a following section.

REFERENCES

DAVIS89—*Software Requirements: Analysis and Specification,* Prentice Hall, 1989; Alan M. Davis. *A particularly practical view of the requirements definition process, with lots of insight into how requirements analysis should be performed.*

IEEECOMPUTER85—*IEEE Computer,* April 1985. *Special issue on "Requirements Engineering Environments," with information on such methodologies as SADT, SREM, TAGS, and others.*

MARCA88—*Structured Analysis and Design,* McGraw Hill, 1988; David Marca and C. McGowan. *Describes one of the better-known "structured" approaches to requirements and design.*

ORR81—*Structured Requirements Definition,* Ken Orr and Associates, 1981. *Describes one of the better-known "structured" approaches to requirements.*

RINALDI89—"The CASE Way of Life; to Each His Own Method," *Software Magazine,* April 1989; Damian Rinaldi. *Popular-press summary of commercially available systems analysis and design CASE tools.*

WARD86—"The Transformation Schema: An Extension of the Data Flow Diagram to Represent Control and Timing," *IEEE Transactions on Software Engineering,* February 1986; P. Ward. *Presents the result of extending data flow techniques toward the real-time application domain.*

YEH80—"Specifying Software Requirements," *Proceedings of the IEEE,* 68, 9, September 1980; Raymond Yeh and Pamela Zave. *First reference to the use of partitioning, abstraction, and projection as systematic approaches to requirements identification.*

2.2.2.3 Prototyping

Sometimes a problem is not clearly understood, even after an exhaustive requirements study. Perhaps the customer doesn't quite see all the ramifications of the problem to be solved, or perhaps the systems analyst can't quite wrap his or her arms around the problem even after it is fully laid out by the customer. Under these circumstances, it is useful to build a preliminary working model of the system. Such a model of a software system is called a *prototype*.

How does this idea differ from modeling, discussed in a preceding section? A model is a scaled-down version of, or a pattern for, a larger entity, whereas a prototype is a preliminary version of a future entity, an *original* model. Prototyping is covered separately here because a great deal of special study has occurred in the use of prototypes in the construction of software, and because whereas modeling generally applies to the greater system, prototyping more often applies to portions of systems, such as a software portion.

There are essentially two kinds of prototypes. One is the construction of a processor for just the inputs and outputs of a system, to give the customer the ability to visualize the working interface of the product. (One commercial software builder, Dan Bricklin, has built a general-purpose product called "Demo" which does just that.) The other is a scaled-down version of the whole product, to give the customer and the analyst a feel for the workability of the algorithms to be used in the eventual solution.

Each kind of prototype may be appropriate to use under the right circumstances. In either case, what we are doing is giving visibility to the requirements, as they are understood, to see if they are the requirements to be used as the basis for the final product. Prototyping can also be used to experiment with a design approach, but that is not the context in which we are discussing it here.

What happens in the prototype approach is that the prototype's usage and interface form the basis for an experiment in the workability of the proposed requirements. Perhaps the prototype demonstrates the viability of those requirements; then no further work is needed before a full-scale implementation of those requirements. Or perhaps the prototype demonstrates some inconsistencies or inadequacies; in that case, the requirements are adjusted, the prototype is similarly adjusted to try out the revised requirements, and this process continues iteratively until the requirements are perceived to be the ones desired.

Building a prototype means extracting the essence from the software requirements and building just that narrowly focused portion of the software. For example, if the user interface is all that is in question, the prototype developer will not implement the internal processing model of the system. Or if the processing of a particular area is in doubt, then the prototyper will not build an elaborate user interface, or construct the other processing modules unless they are needed to support implementation of the area of doubt. Thus, a prototype is a skeletal version of the final software product.

There are two problems with the prototyping approach. The first is related to a fundamental problem in the field of software quality. It is generally acknowledged that we software developers are very bad at estimating how long it will take us to build a software product, and yet the state of the profession is that we are expected to come up with an estimate before the fact anyway. Using the prototyping approach, of course, we are dealing with a rather large schedule unknown: How many iterations of the prototype are needed to understand the requirements well enough to begin the full implementation? And how can we say how long it will take to build the software if we do not yet understand the requirements? If an up-front estimate of the full software development schedule is made, then prototyping will almost certainly destroy that schedule. (The correct answer to this dilemma, of course, is to split the estimate into at least two parts: one for the requirements phase, to be made up front; and one for the remainder of development, to be made after the requirements are sufficiently well understood. The requirements estimate may still be uncertain, but the development estimate is much more likely to be accurate once the requirements are well understood).

The second problem with the use of prototyping is that, under typical cost and schedule pressure, there is a great temptation to let the original prototype evolve into the final software product, rather than start over once the requirements are understood. In a small percentage of cases, this may indeed be a valid approach; but much more often, the skeletal nature of the prototype and its "quick and dirty" implementation may simply not lend themselves to use as a structure for a full-scale implementation. And if it is used anyway, the final product may have severe quality problems. For example, a prototype system might be fully functional, but be extremely slow and difficult to maintain.

Nevertheless, the prototype concept is an important one, and for certain types of requirements problems, there is really no substitute for its use. In his pioneering book [Brooks75] of over a decade ago, Fred Brooks said "build one to throw away." That advice is still valid today.

Have any studies been conducted to *measure* the value of the prototyping method? The answer is "Yes." Two experiments have resulted in published papers, both appearing (interestingly) in mid-1984. The first [Alavi84] used 63 MBA and MIS students in an experiment to determine the differences between a prototype approach and a traditional approach. In general, the preferences were split along user/developer lines. The users liked the prototype-generated results better than the traditionally developed ones, seeing the reports produced as more accurate and helpful. The software developers, however, saw the prototype process as harder to manage and control (probably because the idea was somewhat new to the participants, and because the iterative nature of prototyping removed some traditional control mechanisms from management).

The second study [Boehm84] used seven teams of professional software developers in a study similar to the first one mentioned. The users found the prototype results to be easier to use but not as good functionally (?), whereas the software developers found the prototype approach produced smaller final programs, was easier to code, with more coherent designs and an easier integration process.

The findings of the two experiments are not entirely consistent with each other, and yet the overall conclusion of both is that prototyping can be seen to have significant value under the right circumstances.

Some people see the prototyping and life-cycle approaches as being competitors. That is, if the prototype methodology is used, then we are not using a true life-cycle approach. Especially in the artificial intelligence application domain, prototyping is an essential part of the development process, and those application specialists see the life cycle as a bad idea because it inhibits the use of the prototype methodology. The problem here, once more, lies in applying the life-cycle principle too rigidly. If the life cycle is seen as a process which permits digressions and iterations, then prototyping is simply an iterative approach to the requirements analysis phase of the life cycle, and the two concepts are indeed compatible.

EXAMPLE OF PROTOTYPING

You are the team leader for a small software house preparing a product for demonstration at the next Winter Joint Software Conference. From a marketing point of view, it is vitally important that your product be ready. As an experienced software developer, you know that the schedule time left before the conference is inadequate to build a proper product. Furthermore, you still have doubts as to the proper user interface for the product.

Acting according to these constraints, you decide to build a prototype version of your product that implements only the important requirements of the system and uses an experimental user interface. At the conference, you will be up front with the people who visit your exhibit, telling them that this is an experimental version of the product, and in fact inviting them to vote on and critique the user interface. This way, you can use the time before the conference effectively, and get important feedback as part of the conference process.

The product you take to the conference is about one fourth the size of your estimate of the final product. It lacks most exception handling features; there is a generic exception module that simply announces to the user that the feature in question has not yet been implemented. It has not been made efficient, but because of the lack of exception handlers the speed will be fast enough for the conference environment. Maintainability considerations, such as appropriate levels of commentary, have been left out since the program will be rewritten after the conference. Portability requirements have been ignored for the same reason.

The stripped-down version of the product is intended to serve only two purposes: to announce your presence with a viable product in the marketplace, and to gather input to refine the user interface further. Anything else is left out of the prototype.

REFERENCES _____

ALAVI84—"An Assessment of the Prototyping Approach to Information Systems Development," *Communications of the ACM*, June 1984; Alavi. *Describes an experiment in the use of prototyping versus traditional approaches in an academic environment. Finds that users liked the prototyped results better, software developers found the process harder to manage.*

BOEHM84—"Prototyping vs. Specifying: A Multiproject Experiment," *IEEE Transactions on Software Engineering*, May 1984; Boehm, Gray and Seewaldt. *Describes an experiment similar to that in [Alavi84] conducted in an industry setting. Users found the prototype results easier to use but poorer in functionality; developers found the resulting final products easier to develop and better (smaller programs, more coherent designs, easier to integrate).*

BROOKS75—"Build One to Throw Away," *The Mythical Man-Month*, Addison-Wesley, 1975; Brooks. *Advocates considering the first implementation of any complex software product to be a prototype on the grounds that it takes an experiment to see the problem clearly enough to get it right.*

HECKEL80—"Designing Translator Software," *Datamation*, February 1980; Paul Heckel. *Describes the creation of a hand-held language translator to be used by tourists for word-at-a-time translations. Provides analysis of the prototyping approach taken—why it was used, and how. An excellent discussion of a real application of prototyping.*

2.2.2.4 Representation (specification)

Once the requirements are firmly established, they usually must be written down in a document called the requirements specification. The purposes of this document are to:

- allow the key players visibility into a shared and agreed upon vision of what problem is to be solved
- provide a definition for follow-on technical life-cycle activities, such as design, testing, and even maintenance
- provide a baseline which can be used by management to control system development

Actually, as the requirements are gathered, a preliminary version of the requirements specification is usually created. Both the preliminary and final versions of the specification allow the systems analyst to check the consistency and completeness of the requirements as they are derived, and allow the customer/user to see if the requirements definition is proceeding appropriately. All of that is easy to say. But what, exactly, does a requirements specification look like?

There are many potential answers to that question. Some would say a specification should be written in natural language (e.g., English) to facilitate readability for the customer/user. Some would say that a specification should be written in a formal language to facilitate verification of the specification itself and unambiguous communication with the designer who will use it as a starting point for the software design.

Even with those two prime categories of specification languages, there are many alternatives. Davis [84] and *IEEE Software* [85] are particularly good references for more information. Some of the alternatives are:

- natural language—everyday English
- *structured English*—English constrained to a restricted vocabulary of nouns and verbs relevant to the problem and its solution
- *formal specification languages*—one of several formal notations using defined operators and syntactic rules, similar in concept to a programming language, for expressing relations and constraints
- *decision tables, decision trees*—a concise notation for expressing alternatives (one tabular, one graphical)
- *finite state machine*—a concise notation for representing states of a system and the functions that map actions to states
- *data structure model*—graphical notation used to represent relationships between major data entities
- *data flow diagram*—graphical notation used to represent flow of data through a system, and the nodes at which the data are processed
- *data dictionary*—a table of definitions of the data items to be used as the basis for the requirements

Already we can see that there are a number of choices for writing specifications, independent of what the content of the specification should be. But what of the content? What kinds of information should be contained in a requirements specification?

Well, requirements, of course. But what does that really mean? It means the list of things which must come true in the software solution in order for it to be a correct and successful solution. That list, in fact, should be both necessary and sufficient, that is, it must contain only the things that the software must do, and all the things the software must do, in order to be what it should be. A requirement not written down is a requirement which will probably not be achieved.

How can we further identify what ought to be in a requirements specification? Some would suggest checklists of information, where in general the checklists would contain certain fundamental categories of information and then some application-domain-specific considerations. For example, one author [Meyer85] has defined the "seven deadly sins of the specifier," a nonapplication-specific checklist of bugaboos to avoid in gathering and stating requirements:

1. *Noise*—do not include irrelevant information.
2. *Silence*—do not underspecify.
3. *Overspecification*—do not include solution-oriented material.
4. *Contradiction*—do not include incompatible information.
5. *Ambiguity*—do not include material with multiple interpretations.
6. *Forward reference*—do not reference not-yet-defined material.
7. *Wishful thinking*—do not include requirements which cannot be validated.

This checklist, though interesting, is not specific enough to provide the detail level of guidance required by a systems analyst writing a real problem specification. However, at the conceptual level, it is an accurate picture of the worst pitfalls the analyst can fall into, and by implication the strengths that should be present in a specification.

Another useful approach to defining the content of the requirements specification is to use one of the standard outlines provided by various international and governmental standards agencies. Glass [88] provides a discussion of such standards.

2.2.2.4.1 Formal versus informal specification languages: Specifications have traditionally been written in natural language (that is, English). To be sure, the form of that natural language is rather unnatural, heavily flavored as it is with sentences containing words like "shall" or "must." Be that as it may, even with this mild unnatural flavor, natural language has proven useful and is presently the specification methodology of choice among practitioners.

Researchers, however, are focusing on the use of more formal language for specifications, just as they have explored formal languages for writing program code and documenting program design. A rudimentary example of such a formal language is found at the end of this section; more comprehensive examples may be found in the references.

Given the traditional natural language approach and the research formal language approach, the question then arises, which works better in practice?

There are strong advocates on both sides of the issue, and a few advocating a middle ground with the use of formality where it is most helpful, and the use of (informal) natural language elsewhere [Meyer85]. (In this middle ground, the formal language might be used to express the problem rigorously to another computer person, such as a reviewer of a set of requirements, or the designer, while the natural language is used to communicate with the customer.) This issue has been put in better focus by several recent studies (see the references at the end of this section). The first finding of the studies has been a clearer picture of where formal approaches succeed, and where they fail.

Those arguments which support formal specifications are:

- A formal language is rigorous.
- Formal specifications can be computer analyzed (e.g., for consistency).
- Formal specifications may some day allow automated generation of code.
- Prototypes may be generated, perhaps automatically, from formal specifications.

Those arguments which support informal (natural language) specifications are:

- Informal specifications are easier to write.
- Informal specifications are easier to read.
- Specifications must often be evaluated by computer-naive customers, who are unlikely to have the background which allows them to read formal material.
- Automated code generation of code or prototypes is of dubious feasibility.
- People-to-computer communication is at its best when it is formal, but people-to-people communication is at its best when it is informal.

An interesting experiment in the value of formal specifications was reported in Avizienis [84]. Although the paper was an exploration of fault-tolerant software design, during the course of the work the authors analyzed the relative merits of three approaches to problem specification:

- a formal specification language, OBJ
- English
- an informal specification language much like Program Design Language (PDL)

The findings were in many ways surprising. The three languages were evaluated on several criteria: length of the resulting specification in pages (the English specification was the shortest, and the PDL the longest); length of the resulting program (the PDL specification resulted in the shortest program in many cases); the speed of the resulting program (the English language specification produced the fastest programs); and the test results (the English language specification resulted in the fewest errors, and the formal specification the most).

Not only did the experimental findings show no particular benefit derived from formality, they actually showed that traditional approaches were better. Obviously, one experiment should not be taken as conclusive; more studies are needed in this area. However, this experiment showed at least as much of the negative as the positive side of formal language usage.

This is one of the most heated battles in the realm of software quality. The ultimate payoff of formal languages, if all their benefits are achievable, is enormous (but see [Rich88]). However, there are many barriers to achieving that payoff, and traditional techniques appear for the present to be more appropriate in practice. The present-day solution to the problem of choosing a language for stating requirements, then, is natural language; but carefully chosen natural language, to provide the maximum rigor that such an essentially unrigorous approach can allow.

EXAMPLE OF FORMAL REQUIREMENTS LANGUAGE

You have been asked to design and implement a program to simulate the playing of a game of baseball as a management training tool for a school for baseball managers. Because the customer has been relatively unclear in the requirements he presented you, you feel it would be wise to write a clear specification of the problem he wants solved, both as a baseline for further development efforts and as a check on your understanding of his wishes. You elect to use a formal language to do so.

Since your computing installation has no standard language, you decide to use one of your own design. After a survey of the literature on specifications languages, you define the following available language forms:
SPEC
   INPUT (list of inputs)
   OUTPUT (list of outputs)
   ACTIONS (list of verbs and explanations)
   CONSTRAINTS (list of bounds on actions)
END_SPEC
For input, based on your understanding of the customer's wishes, you have a roster of players, each player accompanied by his statistical data (batting and fielding averages, and so on). You also have the ability to name a starting lineup and to change that lineup as the game proceeds. For output, you will print the result of each pitch (ball and strike count, type of pitch, and so on), an end-of-inning summary, and an end-of-game summary. The game will be played interactively by two managers-in-training, or one manager against the computer; each manager may make lineup changes (per baseball's normal rules) after each pitch, if he wishes. The playing of the game will rely heavily on a random-number generator whose results will be weighted by individual player statistics to determine what happens on each pitch (curve, fastball, . . . , hit, walk, error, . . .). You have misgivings about naming the existence of the random-number generator at the specification level—it is more of a "how" statement than a "what" one—but you anticipate that your customer will want to know that particular design detail, and it is a fundamental enough part of your notion of the problem that you decide to include it.

With this background, you represent the specifications as follows, and submit them to both your customer and a few carefully selected peers for review.

```
SPEC
   INPUT (ROSTER OF PLAYERS:
      PLAYER, PLAYER STATISTICS;
   STARTING LINEUP (IN BATTING ORDER):
      PLAYER NAME, PLAYER POSITION;
   LINEUP CHANGE:
      REMOVED PLAYER NAME, REPLACEMENT PLAYER
      NAME, POSITION;)
   OUTPUT (PITCH_BY_PITCH RESULT (LINEUP CHANGE
         ALLOWABLE): TYPE OF PITCH, BATTER ACTION;
      END_OF_INNING SUMMARY:
         SCORE OF GAME, HITS_RUNS_ERRORS_
         LEFT ON BASE;
      END_OF_GAME SUMMARY:
         SCORE OF GAME, HITS_RUNS_ERRORS_
         LEFT ON BASE;
         PLAYER STATISTICS UPDATE;)
   ACTIONS (GENERATE RANDOM NUMBER
         FOR EACH PITCH;
         APPLY PLAYER STATISTICS TO RANDOM NUMBER;
         DETERMINE TYPE OF PITCH AND BATTER ACTION;
         TRACK CONTENT OF ROSTERS, LINEUP, AND BASES;
         TRACK SCORE AND STATISTICS;)
   CONSTRAINTS (NORMAL RULES OF BASEBALL;)
END_SPEC
```

The customer is reasonably satisfied with your spec. However, he reminds you that the user-manager needs to be able to access updated player statistics interactively in order to make lineup changes, and that you have not included "ALLOW LINEUP CHANGE" under "ACTIONS" even though it is provided for under "INPUT." You make that change in your representation and proceed to the design phase. "How to," rather than "what to," now becomes your problem.

REFERENCES

AVIZIENIS84—"Fault Tolerance by Design Diversity: Concepts and Experiments," *IEEE Computer*, August 1984; Avizienis and Kelly. *Explores methods of software fault tolerance; experimentally examines the value of formal specifications, and finds them wanting.*

BERZTISS87—"Formal Specification of Software," Software Engineering Institute Curriculum Module SEI-CM-8, October 1987; Alfs Berztiss. *Presents a view of methods for formal specification of programs and large software systems, for use by an educator wanting to teach the topic.*

DAVIS89—*Software Requirements: Analysis and Specification*, Prentice Hall, 1989;

Alan M. Davis. *Contains a summary and comparative analysis of the alternative forms for stating specifications, such as decision tables and finite state machines.*

GLASS88—*Software Communication Skills,* Prentice Hall, 1988; Robert L. Glass. *Presents outlines proposed by standards organizations for the various documents the software engineer may produce, including the requirements specification.*

IEEE SOFTWARE85—IEEE Software, January 1985. *Special issue "On Formalism in Specifications," including [Meyer85].*

JORGENSON87—"Requirements Specification Overview," Software Engineering Institute Curriculum Module SEI-CM-1, July 1987; Paul C. Jorgenson. *Discusses the content and construction of a requirements specification. Presents several alternatives. For use by an educator wanting to teach the topic.*

MEYER85—"On Formalism in Specifications," *IEEE Software,* January 1985; Bertrand Meyer. *Contains an excellent set of references on formal specifications. The author concludes "we in no way advocate formal specifications as a replacement for natural language specifications; . . . rather . . . as a* complement *to them."*

RICH88—"Automatic Programming: Myths and Prospects," *IEEE Computer,* August 1988; Charles Rich and Richard C. Waters. *Sees automatic programming as defined by many to be a "cocktail party" myth; goes on to summarize the state of the theory, and what* is *possible.*

WASSERMAN77—"The Evolution of Specification Techniques," *Proceedings of the 1977 Annual Conference,* Association for Computing Machinery; T. Wasserman. *Outlines the goals and trends in specification techniques. Identifies reliability and customer communication as the driving factors. Names several languages and discusses when they are most applicable.*

WING88—"A Study of 12 Specifications of the Library Problem," *IEEE Software,* July 1988; Jeanette M. Wing. *Presents the findings of a study in which 12 different specifications were prepared from the same set of requirements. A fascinating look at the variance possible in specification technology.*

2.2.2.5 Traceability

It is one thing to define requirements and write specifications. It is quite another to keep track of them once the deed is done. In a system of any size, tracing requirements as they are interpreted into design and then into code can be a major problem. What design elements or code satisfy requirement "A"? What requirements are this design element or code intended to satisfy? The answers to those questions can be quite illuminating, especially if a requirement changes or the value of a section of design or code is questioned. Perhaps even more important, questions about the existence of code for particular requirements can quickly be resolved.

One way of tracking requirements is to note the driving requirements for each design element or section of code in the design representation or as comments in the code listing. Additionally, a master requirements tracking document, perhaps part of the eventual maintenance manual, can summarize for each requirement where the related design elements or code sections may be found. Even better, the elements related to a particular requirement may be "threaded" from one element to the next (e.g., each element not only identifies its driving requirements, but the "next" and perhaps even "previous" element related to each requirement). Then the master requirements document need only point to the first element on the "thread."

One company—Computer Sciences Corp.[Glass82]—has formalized this requirements threading process, deriving several fringe benefits from doing so. All system requirements are threaded from the relevant system inputs through the processes that manipulate them to the resulting outputs. The technique is especially useful in design verification and in forcing the early definition of interfaces between threaded system elements. In addition, *threads* have proven useful in the organization and management control of large software projects. Threads that are functionally related in a practical way are gathered into what are called *builds,* where a build is an element of the total software system that can be implemented more or less autonomously from the rest. A build is constructed and integrated as an entity, prior to total system integration. A *build leader* is responsible for all technical decisions related to a build. And overseeing the entire threads/builds organization is an automated *threads management system,* which tracks progress of threads and builds as a vehicle for management control and customer status reporting.

Whether this degree of formality is needed or not is a valid question, but in any case the tracing of requirements/specifications through a design and implementation has significant merit, especially in large and complex systems.

Traceability is an idea that sounds promising in theory, but a decade after its birth is seldom used in practice (although contracts for software let by the U.S. Department of Defense are beginning to require it). Why is it so seldom used?

As the requirements for a software solution evolve into a design, there is an explosion of the original requirements into the design requirements needed to implement the design solution into code. That is, the process of design augments the user-specified or "explicit" requirements by solution-necessary "implicit" or "derived" requirements. Preliminary data on this subject, collected at IBM's System Integration Division and presented at a workshop by Mike Dyer, suggest that this explosion of requirements is by a factor of not just tens but actually hundreds. That is, every explicit requirement stated by a user is multiplied by several hundred in the process of deriving the design requirements necessary for a problem solution. Thus, we see that the promise of traceability may be buried in the cost of providing a solution.

Automated tools are beginning to be available in the marketplace to help manage this explosion problem, but as of this writing most of them are too rudimentary to solve the problem in any effective way.

Thus, for the complex software for which traceability is most important, the task of doing it taxes the intellect and tools of the software builder.

EXAMPLE OF REQUIREMENTS/SPECIFICATIONS TRACEABILITY

You elect to employ traceability in a program to simulate the game of baseball, partly because your customer has indicated that he wants close visibility on your implementation efforts.

Each requirement in your requirements language specification is assigned an identifying designation, to simplify the job of recording all implications of the requirements. All input requirements, for example, are assigned the key first letter I, and each requirement is then given a mnemonic name (for a larger system, a number, although less meaningful, might be more practical). I_ROSTER, for instance, defines the roster of players input requirement and I_CHANGE the requirement to allow the input of lineup changes. Similarly, A is used as a key first letter for actions, and A_PITCH defines the requirement to generate a pitch of a defined set of characteristics (fastball, forkball; thrown by lefthander; and so on).

As the design is formulated and emerges in design representation form, the driving requirements are noted as part of the representation, as parenthetic expressions for each element of the design. And as your design is programmed into code, the requirement mnemonics are carried through as comments within the code itself. Successor and predecessor references for each noted requirement are also encoded and noted. The documentation of the program, as well as its coded representatives, also reflects the thread notation. Progress reports to your management, too, are thread specific; thus threads and their references permeate the software at every level of its existence.

The system pays off when your customer decides to modify the way in which the user-manager is allowed to make lineup changes. Each software element which must be changed is attached to the requirement by a threaded list, and the impact of the change is quickly defined, scoped, and implemented. The "nuisance" of recording apparently extraneous information has paid off technically as well as managerially.

REFERENCE

GLASS82—"Requirements Tracing," *Modern Programming Practices*, pages 59–62, Prentice-Hall, 1982; Robert L. Glass. *Excerpts from government reports prepared by TRW and Computer Sciences Corp. describing their practice of tracing requirements through the development of the software product.*

2.2.2.6 Review

The requirements for a system are essentially a contract between the prospective software developers and the software buyers. It is essential that this contract be an accurate and complete representation of the expectations of both. No matter how carefully the requirements specification is prepared, it needs analysis and feedback from the concerned parties. The requirements review is the event where that happens.

The function of a requirements review is to reach agreement on the requirements specification. This agreement, when it is achieved, is signified by the concerned parties signing the requirements specification.

The review may happen remotely or in a meeting. If it happens remotely, the proposed requirements specification is presented to the concerned parties (usually the systems analyst presents it to the customer) and the concerned parties read it, critique it, and either ask for changes or sign it. If changes are requested, after a revision of the specification, another iteration of reading is called for. Once the specification is signed, it has been accepted and, in essence, the requirements phase of the software development process is ended and design may begin.

If the review happens in a meeting, generally the attendees at the meeting will have read the specification beforehand and the purpose of the meeting will be to resolve any differences that the readers have identified. Sometimes new wording will be created at the meeting, and the completed version can be signed as soon as the clerical updates are made to the specification. At other times, agreement in principle on changes will be made, and the authors of the document will revise it and present the revision for one last review process.

Occasionally the attendees at the requirements review meeting will not have read the document beforehand, and the authors will use a lecture mode of presentation to present the document and stimulate agreement or change requests. Obviously this technique may dangerously reduce the thoroughness needed to evaluate the specification, but it is a lower-cost approach to the review.

As we proceed through the rest of this book, we see that review is an important quality process in all of the life-cycle phases, not just at requirements time. However, the personnel makeup of the review changes dramatically as the life cycle proceeds. Figure 2.2 shows this change graphically. At the outset and near the end, managers, customers and users play a vital role in reviews, making sure that requirements are appropriate and that test results are correct, as measured against the problem to be solved in the context of its application domain. The intermediate reviews, which we discuss in subsequent sections, become more and more heavily peer oriented. What is happening here is that software development is a trip from the customer problem into the intricacies of software and back out to a

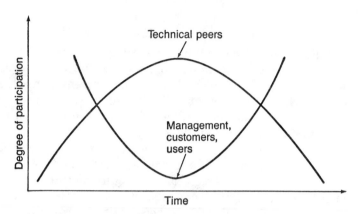

Figure 2.2   Phasing of review participation.

customer solution. Reviewers must be chosen appropriate to how far along we are on this trip.

REFERENCES

COLLOFELLO87—"The Software Technical Review Process," Software Engineering Institute Curriculum Module SEI-CM-3, April 1987; James S. Collofello. *An overview of review processes with a good bibliography of review-relevant material. Written for the educator who wants to teach the topic.*

MARTIN90—"N-Fold Inspection: A Requirements Analysis Technique," *Communications of the ACM,* Feb. 1990; Johnny Martin and W. T. Tsai. *Explores the use of multiple review teams for the requirements of critical software systems.*

YOURDON77—*Structured Walkthroughs,* Yourdon Press, 1977; Edward Yourdon. *A how-to book on conducting review walkthroughs of all kinds.*

2.3 DESIGN

Software design is a complex, thought-intensive process in which the *what* of requirements gets translated into the *how* that leads to a coding solution.

Traditionally, we have seen design as a combination of a methodology and a representation. That is, the designer needed a set of processes to steer the creation of the design, and one or more languages to write the design down in when it emerged from the mind.

But we are now beginning to see that methodology + representation is not enough. It is not enough because it does not account for the cognitive processes, the processes that go on inside the mind. (See Figure 2.3.)

Studies of those cognitive design processes are beginning to yield results. At the highest level, these studies have found that design involves

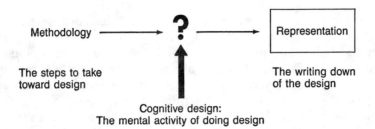

Figure 2.3 Cognitive design as a missing link.

- understanding the problem
- decomposing the problem into goals and objects
- selecting and composing plans to solve the problem
- implementing the plans
- reflecting on the process and the product

But this is not surprising. In fact, this set of steps is analogous to the software life cycle, which in turn is strongly analogous to any problem-solving process.

It is when we examine the step involving selecting and composing plans of the preceding list in more depth that we begin to see what the cognitive portion of design is all about. Protocol studies of designers at work [Adelson84, Curtis87] have shown that there is a well-defined series of steps the designer takes.

First, the designer mentally creates a model of a proposed solution for the problem at hand. This solution, being an initial attempt, is usually woefully inadequate.

Next, the designer mentally executes the model, simulating its working via sample input data to see if it comes close to handling the problem. Normally, the model will fail, but in the act of simulation the designer will spot inadequacies in the model, and mentally enhance it to cover the discovered problem areas.

The new version of the model will then be executed again, more inadequacies will be discovered, and the model will be reenhanced. This process will proceed in iterative fashion until a simulation run fails to show any more inadequacies. At that point, the design will be a candidate for recording in a representation.

Note that although the description of the process took several paragraphs, all of it happened inside the mind at mind-speed. It is probably because of the speed of the mental process, in fact, that this essence of design was so long in being studied experimentally and described.

Because these findings are relatively new, there has not been a family of tools and techniques built up to assist in the process. Those who have conducted the studies of the process suggest that such tools as a model builder and simulator might be useful. An idea archiver and retriever might also help, since during this rapid mental process ideas sometimes sprout but then get forgotten as the mind brushes past them too quickly. And similarly helpful would be a tool that kept track of strategic assumptions so that they were kept freshly in mind during the model simulation and enhancement process to ensure that the design did not veer off in the wrong direction. But these tool/technique ideas are purely speculation as this book is being written; no one has tried building or testing one.

What we are dealing with in design, then, is the raw spark of creativity. The designer acts at mind-speed, and that is of course different for different people. One person's catalyst for creativity may well be another's mental straightjacket.

The design phase is critical to the quality of the product that results. It may be possible to produce a poor implementation from a good design, but it is seldom possible to produce a good implementation from a poor design. Design, then, is a make-or-break phase for software construction.

In the overall picture of the software process, design is preceded by a requirements definition. The designer, therefore, should have a fairly firm problem definition to work with, and be able to concentrate on methods of solution rather than methods of problem definition. But in practice, this may not be the case. The requirements definition may be incomplete or overly constraining, and either way the designer has leftover requirements tasks to complicate the already complex design process.

Given all of this, where does the designer start? Many skilled designers suggest starting with the hard problems, the places where the designer really doesn't see a solution. These same designers (for example, Gary Kildall and John Page, quoted in [Lammers86]) suggest that in solving these hard problems, the designer may even need to write a little code and physically or mentally execute it in order to prove out the design concept before entering the proposed solution into the overall design. This is considerably at odds with a rigid view of the software life cycle, which requires that all design stops before any coding begins. The problem here is that this rigid view is simply wrong. Design is a complex process that should not be constrained by rigid procedures; the designer needs the latitude to try out ideas before being locked into using them. In fact, one study [Zelkowitz88] has shown that when software practitioners are engaged in what we call the design process, they may actually be doing exploratory coding and more in-depth requirements analysis, and when they are doing what we call coding they may be reviewing a design and perhaps doing early testing. In other words, in practice the life-cycle phases are not (and should not be) crisply delineated.

There is another important consideration in the starting point for design. Most designers have available design analogies from past problem solutions; it is almost as if the designer is carrying around a backpack full of past solutions to draw on. When a new problem is encountered, usually the first version of the model that goes through the simulation process described earlier is not a raw, untried, new model, but rather a candidate borrowed from a past problem. Thus, reuse of designs at the mind level, at least, is common practice.

When, then, does the design process end? Historically, design has blurred more or less indistinctly into the implementation process. It is often hard to know exactly when design should cease and coding should begin. Butler Lampson [Lammers86] suggests that

> Design should be carried down to a level . . . where two things are true. First, I already know about the primitives I write the programming in—they have been implemented many times before . . . Second, I understand the primitives well enough to estimate within a factor of two or three how much memory they are going to cost.

This advice, coming from an all-time computing professional, is wise; but notice that it means that the ending of design is person dependent, since the collection of well-understood primitives will differ from one programmer to another. If I am preparing a design to code myself, for example, I will stop the design process much sooner than if I am designing for a novice programmer to code, since the novice will have a much smaller supply of well-understood primitives.

The final result of the design process should be an algorithm-specific, computer-specific solution to the original problem. Of course, the design should allow for modification. If it is anticipated that better algorithms may become available later, then these algorithms should be isolated into modules and become potentially plug replaceable. And if the computer to be used is actually a collection of computers, such that portability is a requirement, then the hardware-specific parts of the design should likewise be isolated into modules. But all in all, the design, when completed, must be a workable blueprint of a problem solution, such that the chosen programmer(s) can begin work at sculpting the final problem solution.

As the cognitive process ends and the design becomes more formal, and before the design process concludes, it is important that ways be found to work with the emerging design. The next section on design approaches discusses some of these ways.

REFERENCES

ADELSON84—"A Model of Software Design," Yale University Department of Computer Science, October 1984; Beth Adelson and Elliot Soloway. *A report on empirical findings about design from the protocol studies conducted by Soloway and his students.*

CURTIS87—"Empirical Studies of the Design Process: Papers for the Second Workshop on Empirical Studies of Programmers," MCC Technical Report Number STP-260-87; Bill Curtis, Raymonde Guindon, Herb Krasner, Diane Walz, Joyce Elam, and Neal Iscoe. *A collection of papers describing the findings of empirical studies of design conducted at the Microelectronics and Computing Consortium. (These papers also appeared in the Proceedings of the subject workshop, published by Ablex.)*

LAMMERS86—*Programmers at Work,* Microsoft Press, 1986; Susan Lammers. *Contains interviews with key people in the computing world, especially software developers in the microcomputer industry. Presents considerable insight.*

PARNAS86—"A Rational Design Process: How and Why to Fake It," *IEEE Transactions on Software Engineering,* February 1986; David Lorge Parnas and Paul C. Clements. *Presents an idealized design process; discusses why it is difficult to achieve; and recommends that the final product of design look like it came from the idealized process even if it did not.*

ZELKOWITZ88—"Resource Utilization During Software Development," *Journal of Systems and Software,* September 1988; Marvin V. Zelkowitz. *Reports data from the study of several NASA projects that show that life-cycle processes, rather than being distinct, actually overlap in practice.*

2.3.1 Design Approaches

In the previous section, we discussed the cognitive model of design while mentioning that traditionally design has been discussed in terms of methodology and representation. This section contains a brief introduction to methodology. It is no more than a brief introduction because much in-depth material on this subject is available elsewhere. For the same reason, there is no discussion of design representation in this book.

From the quality point of view, the most important determiner of design approaches must be the nature of the application problem being solved. With this in mind, either a top-down or bottom-up approach (and either a functional approach, a data approach, or an object-oriented approach) may be chosen. The nature of the specific problem and the specific application will determine which should be used.

The first level of choice should be the function versus data versus object-oriented approach. For problems that are heavily data oriented where the bulk of the work centers around a database or a collection of files, a data-oriented design method is appropriate. Data-oriented design approaches are discussed in a later section.

For problems that are heavily logic oriented where the bulk of the work centers around algorithms and logic, a function-oriented design method is best. Function-oriented design is discussed later in the section on top-down design.

It is not yet clear for which application domains the object-oriented approach is best. Object-oriented design is based on the application's collection of data objects, each with its associated operations, abstracted in such a way that characteristics of one data object can easily be inherited from another. Although there is enormous enthusiasm in the academic world about the value of this approach with some who say it is a much more natural representation of many problem domains, there are few case studies from which we can draw conclusions about the characteristics and success of the application of this technique.

In addition to the function, data, and object-oriented design approaches, there is another emerging design approach: business-rules based design.

This is an approach specific to business data processing applications. It addresses the concern that, during maintenance, most software changes are caused by changes in the business rules implemented in the software. With business-rules based design, those rules are represented in some isolated and easily-changed way. For example, if business rules are represented as a table of data or a file, then a change in the rule may be effected by changing the table or the file, usually a much simpler task than changing program logic.

The second level of choice should consider top-down or bottom-up design. Top-down design has so long been a part of software's list of best practices that it is difficult to imagine anyone advocating anything else. Yet when there is a wealth of reusable modules or objects, a bottom-up approach in which the design is based on using these artifacts can be quite successful.

Top-down design starts with the big picture, and breaks it down through a decomposition process into increasingly smaller hierarchic subprocesses. Bottom-up design starts with existing small solutions and builds a big solution out of them.

It has been popular for some time to advocate data design and top-down design. Certainly, with the advent of database-centered solutions, data design is extremely useful. And with the management emphasis on cutting software costs and adding discipline to the software process, top-down approaches (which keep a strong focus on the eventual top-level problem solution) are appealing.

But many scientific and systems programs, and some real-time programs, are much more functionally oriented than they are data oriented. And the emerging thrust toward more software reuse (building new software from a catalog of existing software parts, such as library routines) argues on behalf of at least a partial bottom-up design approach.

Note that it is possible to mix and match these design approaches. For example, top-down functional approaches might be appropriate for a relatively new scientific application having few reusable parts. Top-down data designs might be appropriate for relatively new business application. The bottom-up functional approach might be appropriate for a systems programming application with a lot of existing parts, such as building a compiler with the LEX and YACC tools. And the bottom-up data approach might be appropriate for business applications with a lot of reusable data objects from a previous object-oriented design. There is not one best way to approach design; there are ways that are more appropriate depending on what the needs of a particular design are.

In the two sections that follow, there is an elaboration of the two currently most popular design approaches: top-down and data structure. Certainly in a world where reuse is still not clearly achievable at the application parts level, bottom-up approaches are probably premature. That is why there is no discussion of bottom-up approaches here. And the discussion of top-down design focuses on a function-oriented top-down approach; that is why data structure design is given additional attention.

REFERENCES

AP89—Special issue on "Object-Oriented Observations," *American Programmer,* Summer 1989. *Contains twelve papers by key players in the object-oriented approach to software.*

BUDGEN87—"Introduction to Software Design," Software Engineering Institute Curriculum Module SEI-CM-2, July 1987; David Budgen and Richard Sincovec. *Provides an overview of software design topics and a bibliography for further information, for educators wanting to teach the topic.*

GOULD85—"Designing for Usability: Key Principles and What Designers Think," *Communications of the ACM,* March 1985; Gould. *Recommends that designers of user-friendly software (1) focus on users and tasks, (2) measure usage empirically, and (3) design iteratively based on early use of (1) and (2).*

IEEE86—"Special Issue on Software Design Methods," *IEEE Transactions on Software Engineering,* February 1986. *Contains several papers on each of these topics: "Systems Decomposition," "Documentation of Designs," "Quantitative Evaluation of Design Methods," "Analysis of Concurrent Designs," and "Prototyping and Program-Generation Environments."*

IEEE88—Special issue on "What is Object-Oriented Programming?" *IEEE Software,* May 1988. *Contains two papers that take a programming language oriented view of object orientation.*

KELLY87—"A Comparison of Four Design Methods for Real-Time Systems," *Proceedings of the Ninth International Conference on Software Engineering,* 1987; John C. Kelly. *Finds that "there is no single methodology which is superior to all others for all problems," and "the search for them may be counterproductive."*

MANNINO87—"A Presentation and Comparison of Four Information Systems Development Methodologies," *ACM Software Engineering Notes,* April 1987; Mannino. *Compares SASD (Yourdon), JSD (Jackson), Application Prototyping (Boar) and Box Structure (Mills) methodologies. Finds no methodology is superior to the others overall.*

MEYER87—"Reusability: The Case for Object-Oriented Design," *IEEE Software,* March 1987; Bertrand Meyer. *Presents a good analysis of the value of object-oriented and bottom-up (reuse) approaches to software design.*

PETERS77—"Comparing Software Design Methodologies," *Datamation,* November 1977; Peters and Tripp. *Presents, analyzes, and evaluates five different design approaches. Concludes that no single approach is valid for all problems, and that "designers produce designs, methods do not."*

SEL86—"Measuring Software Design," NASA Goddard Software Engineering Lab report SEL-86-005, November 1986. *Reports on research into design approaches. Presents surprising findings ("module size is not an effective criteria for software design" . . . "Neither parameter nor common coupling is generally better than the other").*

TRIPP88—"A Survey of Graphical Notations for Program Design—An Update," *ACM Software Engineering Notes,* October 1988; Leonard L. Tripp. *Shows examples of many different design representations.*

WEBSTER88—"Mapping the Design Information Representation Terrain," *IEEE Computer,* December 1988; Dallas E. Webster. *Examines and organizes a view of present design representation alternatives.*

YOURDON89—"OOPSLA '89," *American Programmer,* November 1989; Ed Yourdon. *A practitioner-view report on a 1989 conference on object orientation, saying "it seemed adrift when it came to applying useful software concepts to real-world projects."*

2.3.1.1 Top-down design

Top-down design is a design approach that begins with the most abstract description of a system. From the single highest-level system description, successively more detailed subsystems are designed. This process is repeated until the level of design is sufficient for coding. The result is a hierarchic or tree-structured design. Each level must consist of a complete description of the system before the next level of finer detail is built.

The value of top-down design is that it provides manageable levels of complexity at each stage of the design process. Additionally, at each stage the relation of each constituent to the other is known. Via such an organized approach, there is early visibility into design problem areas, and avoidance of focusing on low-level details until their overall context has been decided. Top-down design is also sometimes referred to as *hierarchic decomposition* because of the cascading nature of the process.[1]

Given that the problem of a design approach is really one of chopping a software specification into manageable and digestible chunks, one ob-

---

[1]For an interesting philosophical (noncomputing-oriented) discussion of hierarchic systems, see *The Ghost in the Machine,* App. I, Macmillan, 1967; Arthur Koestler. Rules, strategies, equilibrium, and disorder are among the aspects of hierarchies discussed. The *open hierarchical system* is discussed and advocated.

vious and successful approach is to identify and separate the functions to be performed. Most software designers tend to work in this way. Top-down design applies an ordering to that approach.

There is, however, a fundamental question raised by top-down design concepts; what *is* the most abstract description of the system? If the specification is written properly, it is clearly identified; if it is not, however, the designer is left with the problem of believing in top-down design but being unable to locate the top.

For example, one design of a real-time operating system clearly labeled by its designer as *top-down* began with the real-time computer's interrupt structure as the top. It is no more apparent that the particular aspect of the real-time system is its "top" than, say, the user services which the operating system is to provide. In this case, the design had the aura of top-down design but not necessarily any of its characteristics. (This is not to say that such a design is wrong, just that it is not clearly top-down.)

There is one other problem with top-down design as first described. If the hierarchic decomposition is to occur one level at a time before passing to the next level, it may well delay the detection of feasibility problems lurking at a low level. It is true in the software world that serious problems occur at all levels of detail, and it is not uncommon to flush them out only when the bottommost detailed implications of a process are dealt with. A hierarchic structure may, of course, crumble if one of its lowest-level elements collapses.

However, this does not change the fundamental fact that top-down is a good approach. The alternative may be to bog down early in the details of a system while neglecting its overall structure. The problem of lurking low-level problems is usually solved by an iterative top-down process, in which the implications of low-level problems are dealt with in a redesign starting down from the top.

Note that top-down design and top-down programming, discussed elsewhere in this material, are different concepts. Top-down programming is one approach to implementing a design; there are others. There *are* those who interrelate the two concepts—design and implementation are to occur in tandem, in top-down order. Few actually follow this philosophy, however. The current emphasis is usually on separating design and implementation further, not intermingling them.

EXAMPLE OF TOP-DOWN DESIGN

You have been asked by an apparently serious manager to build an elephant simulation program. (Actually, the simulator is one of a series commissioned by a local veterinary school to demonstrate the relationship between animal subsystems and behavior.) Your customer hands you a good specification for an elephant, including characteristics of its simulator, and you decide to employ the top-down approach.

First, you do a hierarchic decomposition of the elephant simulation's component parts. At the top, you put the behavioral aspects of the simulation. Subsidiary to that are each of the subsystems whose impact on behavior you wish to analyze. And each of those subsystems, in turn, is broken down into its significant components:

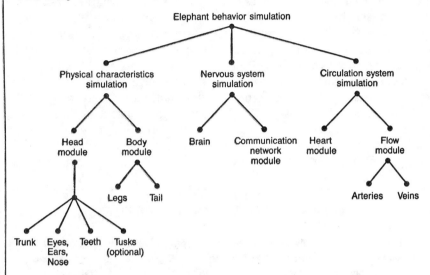

Figure 2.4 Elephant behavior simulation, top-down design.

From the point of view of the total simulation, each design element represents the model representation of that physical component of the elephant. For example, the "brain" element represents a block of the simulation through which neurological pulse flow will be measured, and the "heart" another such block, which processes circulatory transactions.

You have managed to segment the originally elephantine task into a manageable set of individual modules.

1.2.1.2 Data structure design

Contrasted with the functional approach of top-down design, which tends to decompose specifications into functional components, is the *data structure design* approach. This approach focuses on the structure and flow of information rather than on the functions performed.

The value of data structure design (sometimes called the *Jackson method*) is that it attempts to narrow the choices of the designer—as shown in the preceding paragraphs, there is sometimes ambiguity in defining the top of a top-down design. However, the data structure designer has a more clear-cut series of tasks to perform—define the data structures, identify data flow, define the operations that enable data flow.

As with top-down design, this approach focuses on the task of breaking up the design into manageable chunks. The chunks, in this case, are data oriented rather than function oriented.

One problem that can arise with data structure design is the *structure clash,* where the data structures to be processed by a program are in some sense not synchronized (e.g., the input file is in sequence by employee name, the output file is to be sorted on salary rate; or in the input stream is a continuous stream of characters, with logical records asynchronous to physical records, while the output stream is a more traditional logical-records-blocked-into-physical-records structure). Solutions to the clash problem are defined in the references—the creation of an intermediate file, or the conversion of one structure processor into a subroutine for the other, are among the possible solutions. Data structure design is an approach commonly used in data-oriented programs such as business data processing applications (e.g., producing reports from and updating data bases).

EXAMPLE OF DATA STRUCTURE DESIGN

Once again, you have been asked by an apparently serious manager to build an elephant simulation program. In this case, you elect to employ a data structure design approach.

First, you identify the simulation data structures. There are scenario input data, which define the overall actions of the simulation; transaction data, which define the elements to flow and queue in the simulation; event queue definitions themselves; and report output data, which contain the simulation results. For example, the transactions will include (as before) neurological pulses and circulatory elements, and the actions will include brain events and heart pulses. Printed outputs will show the dynamic and final states of the queues, events, and overall behavior. Figure 2.5 shows a summary diagram of the data structures.

Next, you design the form and content of each of the structures shown. In so doing, you are forced into a deeper understanding of the specific data items which will make up your simulation. The layout of the input and output formats may seem fairly mundane, but the makeup of event queues and the impact of elephant elements on them begins to introduce you to the depths of the physical problem.

Then you design the flow of information between the structures. The scenario, for example, is used to initialize the event queue; transaction flow through the simulated events is defined; and event results are reformatted into output reports. Now you are really coming to grips with both the data structure and the functional elements of the simulation.

Finally, you define the operations necessary to cause this flow of information to occur. You have effectively concentrated first on the simulator's data instead of the elephant's structure.

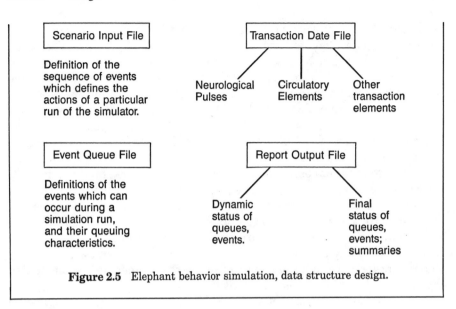

Figure 2.5   Elephant behavior simulation, data structure design.

REFERENCES

DE LAVIGNE77—"Basic Program Design—the Jackson Way: An Example," *Proceedings of the 1977 Annual Conference, Association for Computing Machinery;* de Lavigne. *A contrast is drawn between functional decomposition and data structure as design approaches via a census data problem example. Limitations of the functional approach and methodology of the data structure approach are discussed. A complete bibliography of articles and books authored by Michael Jackson is presented.*

JACKSON75—*Principles of Program Design,* Academic Press, 1975, Jackson. *Takes a problem-oriented approach to design concepts—each concept is followed by a problem solution illustrating the concept. Problems are taken from the data processing realm, and sample code is in COBOL. Data structure design is stressed.*

2.3.2 Fault-Tolerant Software

Some software is so important that it must not fail. Yet everything we know about software says that getting it to be completely error free is virtually impossible. "Good" software is said to have 10 to 50 faults per 1,000 lines of code; rigorous testing is said to reduce that range to .1 to .5.

How do we resolve this dilemma? We build software as error free as we can, and then we add a dimension of reliability to it through a technique called *fault tolerance.* Even though much work has been done in practice, especially in the aerospace and rail industries, with even more work done in the research world, particularly in Europe, both the state of the theory and the state of the practice of fault-tolerant software are still more in the research and development stage than in the demonstrated practice stage.

In the world of hardware fault tolerance, where hardware failures must be worked around, redundancy is the way to achieve it. Multiple copies of key hardware components are put on line, and when one breaks or wears out another replaces it. Note that the transformation from a failed hardware component to a working one is often performed by software; however, such software is not in itself fault tolerant unless it guards against *software* errors as well.

The redundant component approach does not work, however, for software. Since software does not break or wear out, but instead fails only because of a lingering development or maintenance error, all copies of a piece of software will have the same error.

However, there is a software analogy to hardware redundancy. It is called *diversity*. Via diversity, software redundancy may be achieved by having multiple versions of a piece of software designed and implemented by entirely different teams. Or it may be achieved by having more than one implementation of a piece of software logic, not necessarily designed by different teams, but simply written such that one comes into play only when the other fails, and works around the failure. Diversity, then, implies multiple and different copies, but it does not imply identicality.

The essential principles of software fault tolerance are:

1. *Error confinement.* Software must be written in such a way that when an error occurs, it cannot contaminate portions of the software beyond the local domain where it occurred.

2. *Error detection.* Software must be written such that it tests for and reacts to errors when they arise.

3. *Error recovery.* Software must be written such that after detecting an error, it takes sufficient steps to allow the software to continue to function successfully.

4. *Design diversity.* Software and its data must be created in such a way that there are fallback versions available following error detection and recovery.

How might these principles be achieved? As mentioned previously, answers to that question are still more in the research stage than in working practice. However, there *are* some answers.

Error confinement can be achieved by software using the *principle of least privilege*. Procedures and data should have limited and well-defined functions such that no procedure offers more capabilities needed for its intended function and no procedure can access data outside its own limited-access database.

Error detection can be achieved by extra code placed at strategic and frequent intervals throughout the software. Its purpose is to test known conditions to ensure that they have been correctly obtained. The notion of assertions, to be discussed in a later section, is useful here. An assertion is a statement of what should be true if the software is functioning correctly. An assertion violation, then, would constitute error detection.

Error recovery can be achieved by special-case diversity, where extra code and extra data are available to fall back on when the primary logic or data fail. Design diversity is the key to error recovery. There are several known ways of striving for design diversity:

1. the use of recovery blocks, sections of code whose task is to accommodate and recover from whatever problem has occurred
2. N-version programming, the closest thing there is to hardware redundancy, in which multiple teams of software designer/implementors build multiple versions of software which meet the same set of requirements
3. rollback/restart, where the software periodically saves its status and simply rolls back to the most recent status if a problem is detected
4. data diversity, where special provision is made to defend against loss of data.

Recovery blocks are probably the most commonly used of these techniques in practice; they have been used on such software applications as Boeing commercial aircraft avionics software. With recovery blocks, every error detection point is accompanied by a section of code (the recovery block) whose sole purpose is to recover from the detected error if it occurs. Recovery, of course, will be very application specific. It may be as simple as replacing a known erroneous data value with a known "safe" value, or it may be as complex as obtaining the same result just found to be erroneous through an entirely different algorithm or section of code.

With *N-version programming,* critical sections of code are created at design time by different design teams working to the same set of requirements. When the software is implemented, the multiple versions are all available for execution. Perhaps they all execute "simultaneously" (in parallel if there are multiple processors, or serially with wait if there is a single processor) and compare results at error detection points, using a sort of "majority rule" decision if they differ in their results. Or perhaps one version operates until it fails at an error detection point, whereupon it turns control to another. (The first technique, in hardware, is referred to as a *hot spare* approach because all versions are executing; the second technique is a *cold spare* approach, because only the active version is executing.)

There is an assumption that goes with N-version programming, and there is a problem with that assumption. The assumption is that different teams of software developers will design software with different errors; that is, each team may create software with errors in it, but they will not be the same errors. With that assumption, when one version of software fails, the majority will still likely succeed at that detection point. However, that assumption has been tested in recent research [Knight86] and found wanting. Apparently there are some errors that are more likely to be made than others. Boundary value errors are an example (errors where the software fails at a particular point in an algorithm, such as a point of discontinuity or a switchover from one expression to another). Because of that, N-version software is disturbingly likely to have multiple failures at an error detection point, complicating the choice of a "correct" answer. Thus, there is serious question about the usefulness of N-version programming as a fault-tolerance technique.

Rollback/restart is probably the oldest of the fault-tolerance techniques. It involves saving a baseline set of data periodically as the software executes, and when an error is detected restoring the baseline and trying again. This approach was particularly useful in the early days of computing when hardware and data device errors were frequent, and ways of recovering from such problems were essential.

Data diversity is vital to heavily data-oriented software. Here, redundancy is added to the data in whatever application-specific way makes sense. For example, in threaded lists of data, where pointers are used to attach one item of data to the next, and where the loss of a pointer means the loss of all subsequent data, a set of backward pointers as well as a set of forward pointers might be maintained. Or as another example, in sets of data where a sentinel is used to signal the last data item, a count of the data items might also be used.

These design diversity concepts need not, of course, be used in isolation. For example, data diversity could be used with recovery blocks, and in fact N-version programming with a recovery block fallback might be used. Because multiple techniques may be appropriate, the failure of the independency assumption in N-version programming, for example, might be overcome by backing up N-version with other approaches.

Note that an interesting idea arises from the discouraging findings about N-version software. If some kinds of software errors are indeed more frequent, then software reliability techniques which concentrate specifically on those frequent errors are probably needed.

Software fault tolerance, of course, has a cost attached to it. The diversities of design, whether in logic or in data, will cost extra in design time, in coding time, and in testing time. That extra cost may well be recovered, of course, if the software has the benefit of ultra-safe reliability as it executes. Nevertheless, as with any other high-quality approach, fault-tolerant software has a higher up-front cost than its alternatives.

EXAMPLE OF FAULT-TOLERANT SOFTWARE

You have just learned that your baseball-playing simulator will be delivered to the despotic leader of a remote nation and that you personally will be invited to perform the installation. You are warned by your management, in a friendly gesture, that the despot takes unkindly to faulty technology and has been known to remove the coding fingers of programmers whose work is below par.

Because you now perceive your application to be what is called "critical software," you decide to employ all possible quality techniques. As a "safety play," in case all else fails, you use fault-tolerant technology. You perform a new analysis of your baseball simulator, studying the modularization with new criteria in mind. Fortunately, your modules were selected and implemented using the principle of information hiding, and you decide that they effectively confine errors as well. However, you design a new error detection and recovery mechanism: anomalous conditions are to be tested for at every stage of the program's execution. The result, you realize, is a rigorous blanket of assertions and assertion checks manually and permanently inserted in the program. Detected assertion violations are processed by a central recovery module, which mixes specific assertion violation responses with a general recovery mechanism designed to keep the program properly operating. For example, if the value of variable *outs* is ever (inappropriately) less than zero or more than three, the program, having detected the condition, branches to the *next inning* label, meanwhile logging the assertion violation on an audit file for later review.

You also define the areas where backup code is necessary and the mechanisms for control transfer from mainline to backup. Most of these are situation specific. The entire base-path manager for example is backed up so that if a violation occurs on the assertion that each base can be occupied by no more than one player, the program (after logging the violation) can backtrack to the preceding play and repeat its impact with the newly-switched-in backup code.

You then select your most skilled peer to write the backup code and, without explaining all the details to him, you invite him to participate in the delivery and installation.

He accepts. You decide to fill him in on the political details later.

REFERENCES

AVIZIENIS84—"Fault Tolerance by Design Diversity: Concepts and Experiments," *IEEE Computer*, August 1984; Avizienis and Kelly. *Describes experiments in the use of different methodologies for doing requirements analysis and design.*

BLACK81—"A Case Study in Fault-Tolerant Software," *Software Practice and Experience*, 1981; Black, Taylor and Morgan. *Describes the use of data diversity to assist in fault tolerance.*

BREMERHAVEN87—*Proceedings of the Third International Conference on Fault-Tolerant Computing Systems*, Bremerhaven, September 1987, Springer Verlag. *A collection of relatively recent findings on fault tolerance.*

CMU87—*Digest of Papers, the Seventeenth International Symposium on Fault-Tolerant Computing*, Carnegie Mellon University, July 1987, IEEE Computer Society Press. *Another collection of relatively recent findings on fault tolerance.*

ECKHARDT88—"Fundamental Differences in the Reliability of N-Modular Redundancy and N-Version Programming," *Journal of Systems and Software*, September 1988; Dave E. Eckhardt and Larry D. Lee. *Contrasts hardware redundancy with software diversity (N-version programming). Finds the approaches fundamentally different but concludes "both approaches can improve system reliability."*

KNIGHT86—"An Experimental Evaluation of the Assumption of Independence in Multiversion Programming," *IEEE Transactions on Software Engineering*, January 1986; John Knight and Nancy Leveson. *Reports experimental results showing that N-version programming does not eliminate common requirements-driven errors.*

PRADHAN86—*Fault-Tolerant Computing—Theory and Techniques*, Prentice-Hall, 1986; Dhiraj K. Pradhan (editor). *Yet another collection of papers on fault tolerance.*

VOGES88—*Software Diversity in Computerized Control Systems*, Springer-Verlag, 1988; Ugo Voges (editor). *Presents both applications of, and experiments about, software diversity.*

2.3.3 Automated Design Checking

There are many ways of representing a software design: data flow diagrams, program design language, structure charts, decision tables, hierarchic-input-process-output charts, Nassi-Shneiderman charts, box diagrams, flow charts. The length of the list exemplifies the complexity of the design task. Each possible representation technique may be best at a particular kind of application or may be preferred by a particular software designer, but there are few acknowledged best solutions. Perhaps the one most commonly used in practice is data flow diagrams (Figure 2.6) for the transition from requirements specification to design, supplemented by a structure chart (Figure 2.7) of the static organization of the design, with program design language text (Figure 2.8) for elaborating the detail-level components.

Whatever the design representation chosen for the task at hand, one characteristic which the representation should have is that it be checkable by an automated processor. For many years, this considerably narrowed the field. Only textually-based design languages could conveniently be computer checked, and the program design language became popular for that reason.

More recently, a plethora of computer-aided software engineering (CASE) tools have made it possible to automate the drawing and checking of graphic representations. Name a representation, and there are one or more CASE tools available to support its construction and check conformance of the resulting product to the rules for the representation.

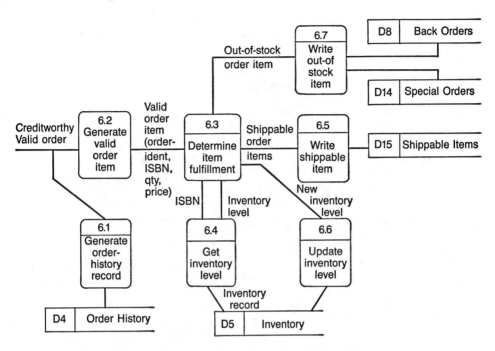

Figure 2.6 Design as representation: dataflow diagram.

Because the program design language (PDL) is still a part of many design methodologies, and because its checking techniques are more oriented toward logic errors in the design than to drawing errors in the representation, we discuss automated design checking from that point of view.

What could a PDL look like? The reading of this book could be represented by a PDL in the following form:

```
Open book;
While page not back cover;
  Read page;
  Turn page if odd-numbered;
End while;
Close book;
```

There are many specific PDLs, each with a different set of somewhat formal syntax rules, but the essence of the PDL is that it is a textual language, source-code like, with a fairly formal control structure but flexible in the definition and use of names to represent functions and data.

What is an automated checker, and what can it do? It is a computer program that accepts as input the design representation, analyzes the representation, and produces a list of flaws detected in the design as well as other analytic information about the design.

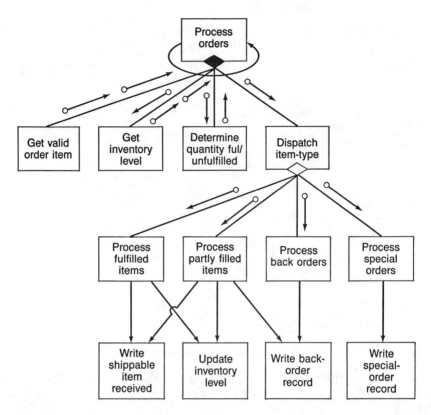

Figure 2.7   Design as representation: structure chart.

```
DO-WHILE  MORE INPUT

      GET VALID ORDER ITEM
      GET INVENTORY-LEVEL
      IF        NO INVENTORY RECORD
       THEN     DO SPECIAL-ORDER-ROUTINE
      ELSE      (STOCK CARRIED)
          SO    IF      INVENTORY-LEVEL IS ZERO
               THEN     DO BACK-ORDER-ROUTINE
              ELSE      (STOCK IS HELD)
                  SO    SUBTRACT ORDER-QTY FROM INVENTORY-LEVEL
                             GIVING NEW-INVENTORY-LEVEL
                        IF        NEW-INVENTORY-LEVEL GE ZERO
                         THEN     DO FULFILLED-ORDER-ROUTINE
                        ELSE      (PART ORDER FULFILLMENT)
                            SO    SUBTRACT INVENTORY-LEVEL FROM
                                     ORDER-QTY GIVING QTY-UNFILLED
                                  DO PARTLY-FULFILLED-ORDER-ROUTINE
END-DO
```

Figure 2.8   Design as representation: program design language.

Such a design checker can easily analyze syntactic information, but semantics are more difficult or impossible to check. For example, such a processor could detect functions defined but not used, functions used but not defined, inconsistent functional interfaces, and functions that are not terminated properly. But it could not detect, for example, inadequate logic.

Design checkers can also produce tables of useful information for further human analysis. Commonly they produce cross-reference lists of the design—where data items or functions are defined, and where they are referenced—much like a compiler does at the code level. They can also produce call structure charts, showing what functions call what other functions. This kind of information is useful for consistency checks by the designer, and for assisting in the functional division of a program that is going to be overlaid in a single processor or divided among distributed processors.

In addition, the automated checker can audit the design for certain kinds of standards conformance. For example, the presence of a GOTO-like direct branch could be flagged if the design standards call for GOTOless code. If the checker were analyzing data flow diagrams, it could ensure that appropriate levels and balancing were present.

EXAMPLE OF AUTOMATED DESIGN CHECKING

You are worried about the design of your elephant simulation program. You have represented the design in a relatively formal program design language. (It has a predefined list of allowable verbs, and each line of PDL must contain one of them.) As a result, since the PDL is computer readable and the formality makes it computer decipherable, you decide to use a fortuitously available automated design checker.

You provide your PDL to the checker as input data, run the checker, and await the results.

The checker output is largely positive. It catches a few improperly nested IF _THEN_ELSEs, notes several PDL statements that failed to use an acceptable verb, and locates a program segment that cannot be logically reached. (The trunk simulation was misplaced.) In addition, an inspection of the data items cross-reference listing shows several items referenced but not defined, and one defined but never referenced.

Correcting these errors does not give you total confidence in the design, of course. You are glad to eliminate those errors, but you are realistic enough to know that semantic errors may remain in your design. However, you do feel confident that the types of errors checked for are now removed from your design.

REFERENCES

BOEHM75—"Some Experience with Automated Aids to the Design of Large Scale Reliable Software," *Proceedings of the International Conference on Reliable Software,* 1975; Boehm, McClean, and Urfig. *Summarizes experience in analyzing and eliminating design error sources. Categorizes design error causes.*

CARD90—*Measuring Software Design Quality,* Prentice Hall, 1990; David N. Card with Robert L. Glass. *Defines and describes what can be usefully measured in the process of design evaluation, and what those metrics tell us about good and bad design.*

2.3.4 Design Reviews

Designers of their first computer program (or elephant) may begin to feel a little insecure around the edges as their design efforts progress. (Designers of their 100th program often feel that way, too.) Unless afflicted with a severe ego problem, they will probably begin to wish that they could share their design with a few skilled and sympathetic peers, especially those who have designed similar computer programs (or animals). They may also wish that their customer would make a pass over their design, to make sure that the customer's real requirements (presumably reflected in the program specifications) are in sync with what has been designed.

It is to satisfy these needs that the design review was created. (It was also created, of course, so that management and the customer could better monitor the designer's progress!) The design review is an analysis of the design of a computer program conducted to determine if the proposed implementation is capable of (1) meeting specified performance, design, and verification requirements; and (2) has a high probability of successful realization within the projected schedule and budget allocated for the task.

Design reviews, especially in the government world, usually come in two flavors—the *preliminary design review* (generally referred to as the PDR), and the *critical design review* (CDR).

The PDR comes early in the design process and is an attempt to make sure that the proper design course has been set.

The CDR comes at the end of the design process and is a last chance to correct design flaws before they are cast in the concrete of code.

Design reviews can be organized in several different ways. Most commonly, one of these two approaches is used: (1) the designer makes a verbal presentation of the design, augmented by graphic aids, and the review becomes a seminar between the designer and the reviewers; (2) the designer issues a written design document prior to the review, and the reviewers submit written comments which are dealt with at the review. The first concept involves a review driven by the design; the second, a review driven by comments on the design. (See also [Parnas87] for some alternative approaches to design reviews.)

The question arises: What information should form the basis for a review? One answer to that question is the following—a PDR presentation should include a computer program development plan, outlining schedule and task chronology, and a function, interface, and data structure breakdown of the problem at a fairly high level; and the CDR should include a proposed user manual, a first-draft maintenance manual (sometimes called a computer program development specification), a proposed test plan, and a complete breakdown of major functions, algorithms, interfaces, and data structures. All of the presentation material should be subjected to design review analysis.

Most important, the success or failure of a design review is dependent on people. The people who attend must be intelligent, skilled, knowledgeable in the specific problem area, cooperative, and have the time available to dedicate themselves to the review. Only the interactions of capable people can make a design review successful. The review should be chaired by someone with both authority and technical skills, and who is also able to motivate and direct the participants into staying on course. This may be the designer, his or her manager, or a technically knowledgeable customer.

The concept of egoless programming, presented in Weinberg's *The Psychology of Computer Programming,* fits nicely with the design review technique. The responsibility for the design, resting primarily on the designer, is at the same time shared among the design review attendees.

EXAMPLE OF DESIGN REVIEW

You have completed your elephant simulation program design, but because you have never seen an elephant, you are extremely dubious about what you have done. You ask your management (or perhaps your management asks you!) to schedule a design review, in this case a CDR. (Even if you were not ignorant about elephants, you would still see the merits of an independent design review in helping to eliminate errors early in the software development process.)

Because you want competent reviewers, you select as participants your colleagues who have just completed a camel simulation and a cocker spaniel simulation. Additionally, you invite the customer who is paying you to build an elephant simulation, and your manager.

In preparation for your review (and as part of your overall documentation task), you document the functional, interface, and data structure characteristics of the design; the simulation algorithms you have developed; draft a user manual and test plan; and ship the CDR package to each of the attendees. Several days before the review, their comments on the CDR package arrive. You scramble to prepare a response to each comment prior to the review.

> Some of the comments are trivial, dealing with typographical errors. Some
> are antagonistic, and your hackles rise at the cavalier way in which "your"
> design is "attacked." But some are extremely valuable. The comment that you
> have inadvertently appended the simulated trunk to the rear of the simulated
> body, for example, will prove very helpful in restoring design credibility once it is
> acted on.
>
> The review itself is very taxing. You have been selected to chair the review,
> with authoritative support provided by your management. Keeping the partici-
> pants moving through the comments and your responses, while at the same
> time allowing digressions that appear productive, requires a great deal of group
> discipline. Since the goal of the review itself is to reach agreement on resolution
> of each comment, you must be constantly mentally alert and aware of the
> consequences of resolutions. This requires intense self-discipline.
>
> At the conclusion of the review, however, you are elated. A few problems have
> been unearthed and corrected, and your design has been stamped feasible and
> acceptable by knowledgeable peers, your management, and your customer.
>
> The implementation of the elephant simulation can now begin.

REFERENCES

MYERS75—*Reliable Software Through Composite Design,* pages 117–119, Pe-
trocelli/Charter, 1975; Glenford Myers. *Defines the design review as an element of
"management of design." Lists questions participants should ask.*

PARNAS85—"Active Design Reviews: Principles and Practices," *Journal of Systems
and Software,* December 1987; David L. Parnas and David M. Weiss. *Proposes a
technique for design reviews in which there are specific expectations of the designers and reviewers: reviews are held in groups of two to four, designers question
the reviewers rather than vice-versa, reviewers are chosen because of the characteristics important to the design, and so on.*

WEINBERG71—"Programming as a Social Activity," *The Psychology of Computer
Programming,* Von Nostrand Reinhold, 1971; Gerald Weinberg. *The classic book
that discusses egoless programming. Advocates, through an anecdotal approach,
a team approach to software development and review.*

2.4 IMPLEMENTATION

The "what" and "how" of software development have, we hope, been effectively completed in the preceding requirements and design phases. Now it
is time to pour the concrete into those foundations, to write the computer
program that turns the "how" into a problem solution. Although some call
this process programming or coding, recall that here we call it *implementation.*

If quality-producing considerations have been ignored in the first two life-cycle phases, no amount of brilliant work can produce a quality product here. ("You can't turn a sow's ear into a silk purse.") But a complete requirements specification and a brilliant design solution can still be ruined if this implementation phase isn't just as carefully done.

In the early days of software, when problems were smaller and everything was newer, this is the phase where programmers tended to start their efforts. True, there was a bit of discussion with the customer, and a back-of-the-envelope design was sketched out, but getting down to the business of the code was what programming was all about.

Nowadays, for some simple software problems, that may still be the best way to produce software, even quality software. But for the vast majority of today's complicated problems and solutions, a more carefully planned approach must precede the writing of code.

That carefully planned approach has been described by some as a more disciplined approach. Discipline, in this sense, is taken to mean following the proper set of steps along the well-marked, rather formal path to a completed software project, that is, the kinds of steps that we are talking about in this chapter of this book.

But discipline is a controversial word in this context. For all the advances we have made in our ability to build software, the construction of software products is still partly a creative endeavor, in this sense something of an art form. Although most would acknowledge that software builders must use both discipline and creativity, no one has really defined how to do that.

What makes all of this relevant to the implementation phase of the life cycle is that those who stress the disciplined approach tend to see the implementation phase as perfunctory, spelled out in elaborate detail by the skills of the systems analysts and designers. In that context, this phase is often referred to as *coding,* where coding is taken to mean something that is almost clerical. This same philosophy leads researchers in the direction of building automated coders, programs which can translate requirements or design into code automatically, without human intervention. After all, if the task is clerical, why not automate it?

Perhaps someday this will be possible. For well-understood applications, such as simple report generation from well-defined databases, it is possible today. But there are indications that automated code generation will not progress beyond these straightforward applications.

Recall from our discussion of design (Chapter 2.3) that the ending of design is person dependent. (We stop our design process when we have reduced the problem to the primitive solutions we understand.) Unless the programmer and the designer are the same person, this creates a problem. Either the designer has a stronger set of primitives than the programmer, in which case the programmer must "complete" the design before coding it, or the designer has fewer primitives than the programmer, in which case the programmer is likely to discard parts of the ("over") design. Either way, for all our assumptions of a disciplined, clerical process, this implementation phase almost always involves additional design (and thus creative) activity.

Therefore, quality considerations in the implementation phase are important. In the sections that follow, we talk about the options open to the developer concerned with quality during the implementation phase.

2.4.1 Top-Down versus Bottom-Up Programming

Top-down programming is the practice of implementing and testing software in hierarchic sequence, starting first with those modules closest to the top-level requirements for the software product.

Bottom-up programming is the practice of implementing and testing software in a reverse hierarchic sequence, starting first with the lowest-level modules, those farthest from the highest requirements.

Advocates of top-down stress that their approach is more natural, gives better management visibility, and eliminates the often painful software integration process where bottom-up developed modules must be glued together.

Advocates of bottom-up stress that their approach leads to more solidly tested software modules, better definition and use of shared, common modules, and is easier to staff with programmers.

To understand top-down and bottom-up programming, a program should be viewed as a tree structure or network of modules, with the top level of the structure containing the control elements as defined by the requirements. Typically, the structure widens downward from the top, as the control module invokes subordinate functions, each of which invokes others.

A top-down implementation is one in which the highest level is coded first; the next level is then coded and integrated via testing into the program; and similarly until the bottom of the structure is reached. Each uncoded module is represented in the integrated whole by a stub code, which satisfies the interface requirements of the missing module but performs few or none of its functions. Stubs are replaced by, or augmented to become, the real thing when appropriate in the implementation plan. At any point in the implementation process, the implemented program should be correctly functioning down to the level of its current completeness.

Bottom-up programming, on the other hand, is implementation beginning at the lowest-level modules. It is typically tested via the concept of test drivers, starting with unit testing of the lowest levels and concluding with integration testing of the fully combined units.

It is the elimination of the separate integration phase of software development that makes top-down attractive from a quality viewpoint.

Since each piece of program is tested as it is screwed into the whole, when the program has been completely implemented, it has also been completely tested. Integration is incrementally accomplished rather than occurring as an indigestible whole. Errors and misunderstandings are identified and corrected early in the implementation.

Bottom-up uses testing techniques of known feasibility. Top-down, being newer, is less well understood. Bottom-up eliminates risk; top-down may reduce cost and increase reliability.

Both require their users to exercise special care—with bottom-up, keeping overall project goals in mind; with top-down, gaining a good understanding of the operating environment before coding. Failure in either case may lead to serious redesign during implementation.

A compromise between the two may actually resolve this problem. Top-down is most attractive for its elimination of integration; bottom-up is most attractive for its use of common, well-checked-out building blocks. It may well be possible to do both. Using the top-down/bottom-up approach (some people call it a *sandwich approach*), initial software development would first implement the overall logic framework, then the lowest-level and most commonly used building blocks, and then proceed via the top-down approach. Levels of implementation and checkout would proceed downward from the top, but building blocks would be added as the need arose. This compromise can result in the best of both technologies.

EXAMPLE OF TOP-DOWN AND BOTTOM-UP PROGRAMMING

You are now at the point of implementing the baseball-playing simulation program which you specified in an earlier section. (It will be used for training baseball managers, you may remember.) You wonder about the relative wisdom of the top-down and bottom-up methodologies. Your design, emerging from the specification, has been performed in top-down fashion.

After some research, you elect to use a sandwich approach. This will track well with the elements of your top-down design, and you like the notion of eliminating the integration phase and of having a demonstrable product early in the implementation process (it will impress your manager and your customer, and may even ward off a project abort if times get tough, you know). Your implementation will proceed in top-down manner, but there are some bottom-level building blocks you will immediately need. For one, you need a random-number generator able to incorporate statistics-based factors specific to individual simulated players; for another, you need a database management scheme for keeping and updating statistics and for such mundane things as base contents management.

However, with these building blocks designed, implemented, and tested, you are able to proceed in a top-down manner. You have already determined in your design that the top level of abstraction—simulation of a game of baseball—is immediately followed by a next lower level, consisting of roster manipulation, basepath management, a play-by-play simulator, and a report generator. You begin work on the play-by-play simulator, stubbing off for the moment the roster manipulation and report generation. You implement the basic framework of play-by-play actions, coding stubs for specific actions (e.g., what to do if a left-handed batter faces a right-handed pitcher). You then go to work on the roster manipulation, replacing the stubs with high-level mechanisms for initiating and updating roster information. However, you stub off the lineup selection process as being too detailed for this level. It is now obvious that in order to see whether your simplistic simulator is functioning properly, you must have at least rudimentary report generation capability. You implement the inning-by-inning summary point but stub off the statistics and final summary modules.

　　Now that your simulator is running and printing results, you can go to work on the deeper details. The routine that distinguishes between hits and outs is coded, but the code for specific kinds of hits (singles, home runs, ...) is deferred. Lineup selection is added to roster management, but use of individual player statistics is deferred. Report generation is expanded to printing opening lineups and names of batters. You are proceeding level by level, implementing and testing new capabilities one at a time, at each level producing a working program version with somewhat more in-depth capability than the previous version.

　　Your customer is especially pleased. Whenever he drops by, he can see that you have a functioning program, one that prints baseball-like results. Progress is discernible and measurable. You have come to like the top-down (albeit bottom-up!) approach.

REFERENCES

MYERS76—Testing Principles, *Software Reliability,* Wiley-Interscience, 1976; Myers. *Contrasts top-down and bottom-up testing techniques; suggests a middle ground called* sandwich testing *which preserves the best of both. Evaluates the various methods.*

MILLS71—"Top Down Programming in Large Systems," *Debugging Techniques in Large Systems,* Prentice-Hall, 1971; Mills. *Describes and advocates top-down programming. Stresses structured programming and its top-down implementation.*

2.4.2 Modular programming

Modular programming is the practice of implementing software in small, functionally oriented pieces. These pieces are called *modules* and are usually implemented as subroutines or functions or clusters of subfunctions. (In some languages, *paragraphs* or *procedures* may be used.) Each module is devoted to one or more tasks related to a function; the module may be accessed from one or several places in a software system.

By isolating functions into separate code units, several advantages are gained—the software is more easily designed, built, comprehended, tested, and modified, since the structure is easily related to the tasks being performed. Additionally, the concept of a library of software procedures is made possible; pluggable modules may be built and used in a large number of different software systems. The latter is an especially powerful quality concept, since a library typically contains oft-tested, highly stable codes (such as a Fortran math and I/O library).

Superimposed over these discussions of structure must be a discussion of data communication. Most commonly data are passed to and from modules by parameter lists. Data are also passed by means of globally-known data, or common blocks (Fortran) or compools (JOVIAL). The term *completely closed* is sometimes used to describe a module whose data are passed only through parameter lists. Such modules can have no "side effects" on common database items and are transportable to other tasks or projects without carrying along a database. Because of this, they are a preferred form of module.

However, the data needs of a module, especially in a complex program, are sometimes sufficiently diverse that a global or common/compool database must be used instead of, or in addition to, a parameter list. These may be called *partially closed* modules. Internal procedures often utilize this form of data communication because the database is readily and inexpensively accessible without the sometimes tedious manipulation of external data blocks.

An emerging concept is that of the *package* which consists of a database associated with one or more procedures or subroutines that access it. Limitations are placed on accessing the data from outside the package. Thus, the need for globally accessible data is effectively merged with the need for database reliability.

A word of warning should be made about the readability of modular code. Because closed modules are usually off-page references—that is, the executable code is not present in the program listing at the point of invocation—it is at first reading difficult to follow a modular program. However, once the module functions are understood, code reading is improved by modular programming.

There is conflict between modular programming and some interpretations of structured programming. Top-down design, an SP concept, often is defined as being the process of defining the structure of a program downward from its requirements, with each "branch" of the program's tree structure being self-contained. The notion of a tree structure, if taken literally (as it has been by some authors), implies no cross-communication among branches. This is at odds with the multiple-use subfunction concept, where one module may be accessed from several branches of the tree. Thus, modular programming and the development of project-independent libraries of common subfunctions are incompatible with this project-driven interpretation of top-down design. Fortunately, few software-knowledgeable people advocate this interpretation.

EXAMPLE OF MODULAR PROGRAMMING

You have already begun a functional, building-block breakdown of your baseball simulation program in the preceding section. Remember that it consists of a couple of bottom-up entities—a random-number generator and a database manager—and then a host of top-down entities. Each of those entities will now become a module of code.

As you proceed further in defining functional modules, the top-down/bottom-up implementation proceeds. The player roster manipulator, the play-by-play simulator, and the report generator become modules each containing many calls to tasks performed by them for other modules. The play-by-play simulator, for example, delegates several of its functions as follows: There is a base-path manager module, which keeps track of the answer to Abbott/Costello questions about "Who's on First"; there is a play-by-play decision-maker module, which mixes the individual player statistics and the random-number results to come up with the result of each batter's action; and there is a statistics update module, which accesses the database to record the results of the play-by-play decision maker. Modules correspond to the elements in the top-down design and to the building blocks of the implementation "tree structure." Each module with elements "below" it in the tree invokes those elements in a modular fashion, usually by a procedure call.

You find your implementation process to be one of "thinking modular"— when a function appears to be needed more than once, or subject to change, or sufficiently complex to clutter up main-line logic, you modularize it. The resulting program, you know from experience, will be relatively easy to revise when the inevitable requirements changes start coming in.

REFERENCES _____

Myers75—*Reliable Software Through Composite Design,* Petrocelli/Charter, 1975; Myers. *Advocates modularity, if done properly, as the key to effective software development. Describes proper modularizing—how to design them and how to interrelate them. Stresses the importance of the design phase.*

Parnas72—"On the Criteria to Be Used in Decomposing Systems into Modules," *Communications of the ACM,* December 1972; Parnas. *Uses an example to discuss two strategies for defining modules. Recommends modularizing to promote infor-*

mation hiding, such that modules contain design decisions that are likely to change.

2.4.3 Structured Coding

Structured coding is the practice of implementing software using a small number of simple logic forms. It is part of a totality called *structured programming,* treated in this book by dealing with its components, since structured programming as a whole has been subject to fuzzy definition and some exaggeration. A program which has structured code uses only these logic constructs:

- a sequence of operations
- a conditional branch to one of two sequences (IF_THEN_ELSE)
- return repetition of a sequence (DO_WHILE and DO_UNTIL)
- multibranch selection between sequences (CASE)

Notice that the GOTO statement is not in the preceding list and, by implication, is not to be used.

The essence of structured code is that the code is straightforward, using that word almost literally. That is, the code is straight (in the sense that sequences are stressed and needless branches are eliminated) and forward (in the sense that only one form of backward branching is allowed).

Enough has been said about the merits of structured programming in general and structured coding in particular that not much more is said here. If you are not familiar with the general principles of these ideas, refer to one of the references at the end of this section for more information. The benefits of structured coding from a quality point of view are:

- The original coding of the problem will be cleaner and easier.
- The resulting code is easier to read and understand.
- The code is easier to modify.
- Errors are less likely to be hiding in a labyrinth of code.

It is important to note, however, that the benefits of structured programming have been oversold by some enthusiasts. It is certainly true that structured code is of better quality than unstructured code. When the question of how much better arises, however, the answer is not at all clear. While there are few experiments whose results shed any light on this issue [Vessey84], one did find a gain in quality of 5 percent to 10 percent due to using the structured methodologies. (This finding was not reported in the literature, but was stated in the question-and-answer session at a conference!)

REFERENCES

BAKER75—"Structured Programming in a Production Programming Environment," *Proceedings of the IEEE International Conference on Reliable Software,*
1975; Baker. *Discusses structured coding and programming standards in the
context of structured programming methodology.*

LINGER77—"On the Development of Large Reliable Programs," *Current Trends in
Programming Methodology,* Prentice-Hall, 1977; Linger and Mills. *Advocates
structured programming as a tool for coding error-free programs; uses illustrative
examples.*

MILLS86—"Structured Programming: Retrospect and Prospect," *IEEE Software,*
November 1986; Harlan Mills. *A glowing review of the history and future of
structured programming by its strongest proponent.*

VESSEY84—"Research in Structured Programming: An Empiricist's Evaluation,"
IEEE Transactions on Software Engineering, April 1984; Iris Vessey and Ron
Weber. *An analysis of the literature which found no experimental research to
substantiate the claimed benefits of structured programming, even though the
authors believe benefits are there.*

2.4.4 High-Order Language

A high-order language is a programming language closer to the application domain than to the machine domain. An assembler language, for
example, is *not* high order because it is nearly the same language that the
computer executes. Pascal, COBOL, and Ada are high-order languages
(sometimes called *third-generation languages*) because the computer cannot execute them without help from an elaborate compiler or interpreter. A
fourth-generation language (4GL) is an even higher-order language because it is focused on a particular application domain or collection of
domains.

Ultimately, an application program which has an input language by
means of which the user communicates his or her goals to the program is
the highest-level language of all. Thus, language is a spectrum ranging
from machine code at the lowest level to application-specific languages at
the highest level.

In general, quality is achieved by using the highest-level language
consistent with the problem to be solved. That is, if an off-the-shelf application solution is already available (and presuming it possesses reasonably
strong quality attributes), then that is the best solution to the problem. If,
stepping down one level, a 4GL is available which addresses the problem,
then it should be used. Exhausting those possibilities, then a good traditional programming language (e.g., Modula 2, Fortran, COBOL, or . . .)
should be chosen. And finally, if all else fails, then a machine-level or
assembly-level solution must be used. .

What are the factors which drive us down the chain of choice from highest to lowest? Capability is one. Highest-level languages are often narrowly focused on a very specific problem and may not be useful for the presumably new problem at hand. Efficiency is another. Generally there is a loss of computer resource efficiency as we move up the language levels, and sometimes that loss may be intolerable at the highest level. Each of the quality attributes, in fact, must be evaluated against the proposed level of solution to ensure that the reduced price of a cheaper programming solution up front is not more than paid for in time by a lower-quality solution.

The quality benefits of the highest possible language level are many:

- High-order languages finesse whole levels of solution effort, eliminating chances for error. For example, assembler-level programmers must manipulate hardware-specific registers, and run the risk of making many register allocation errors. It is not possible for a higher-level language programmer to make register errors, because the programmer cannot and does not need to access registers.
- There are fewer lines of code in a high-level solution, and thus fewer chances for errors.
- Structured code is facilitated by high-level languages. Interestingly, in the highest-level solutions the code may not even need to be structured since it can be presented to the computer in a nonprocedural way. (Order of execution is a function of the language processor, not the programmer.)
- Portability, maintainability, and testability are facilitated by the higher-level languages.

In essence, what we are saying here is that most of the quality attributes are made better by the highest-level language solution possible. As we mentioned before, efficiency is a counterexample, and problems which need an extremely efficient solution will find themselves moving down the language-level chain until the best compromise between the needed quality attributes can be obtained.

REFERENCES

MISRA88—"Third-Generation versus Fourth-Generation Software Development," *IEEE Software*, July 1988; Santosh K. Misra and Paul J. Jalics. *Findings from a case study in comparative language selection. Concludes that 4GLs are not always better than 3GLs.*

See the references for the preceding section, many of which are applicable here as well. See also material on comparative analysis of programming languages, such as:

GHEZZI82—*Programming Language Concepts,* John Wiley and Sons, 1982; Ghezzi and Jazayeri.

LEDGARD81—*The Programming Language Landscape, SRA,* 1981; Ledgard and Marcotty.

MACLENNAN83—*Principles of Programming Languages,* Holt, Rinehart and Winston, 1983; MacLennan.

See also material on specific languages, such as special issue of *IEEE Software* on Modula-2, November 1986.

2.4.5 Standards and Enforcers

Programming standards are the requirements placed on a programmer by organizational control structures such as management, customers, or perhaps peers. Standards supplement the product requirements as stated in the requirements document and have to do with the craft of programming, not so much the shape of the final product. Enforcers are tools which check standards conformance. Standards which are levied but not enforced result in the same thing as not having standards.

The purpose for having standards is to increase product quality and programmer productivity. Standards, for example, may specify ways of naming data variables. Such a naming convention increases productivity and improves quality because it lessens the chance of committing time-wasting errors in naming variables, and increases the readability of the resulting program to the benefit of the checkout specialists and the maintainers.

Typical standards might include:

- language requirements
- limits on code complexity
  - structured programming constraints
  - avoidance of undesirable language forms
- requirements for modularity
- requirements for maintainability
- naming conventions
  - data names must reflect the content of the variable OR
  - data names must reflect the structure of the program and data OR
  - a combination of both of the preceding requirements
- commentary conventions
- code elements traceable to design or requirements
- interface structures

It is the task of a standards enforcer to check for conformance to as many of the standards defined in the standards manual as is possible. That is easier said than done. Enforcers may easily check for limits on code complexity, for example. But checking for the use of meaningful variable names has semantic implications and can only be done by a person. Typically, standards enforcers can detect less than half of standards violations, and the use of a human enforcer is essential.

Recall from an earlier section of this book that there are international bodies proposing standards of general usefulness. The present state of the practice is, however, that most standards are homegrown.

There are two serious problems with the use of standards and enforcers in current practice. The first is that most computing installations have too many standards. The second is that most computing installations do almost no enforcing. The two problems are related.

In most programming shops, if there is a standards manual at all it is probably at least 100 pages long, chock full of wonderful rules for building software. It was probably written by a group of people who either (1) could be spared from writing software because their talents were not in as high demand as their peers, or (2) had developed what they perceived to be a best way of writing software and wanted to make sure that everyone else did it their way.

All of this is the wrong way to establish software standards. First of all, standards should be terse and to the point. The *must* rules for writing software, no matter what the installation, should be distilled into a short manual which can be digested quickly, applied easily, and enforced conveniently. If there are more elaborate, preferred but not required ways of building software, a different document—one which specifies *guidelines, not standards*—should be established. This document may be as long as it needs to be, because it contains helpful hints which most programmers will want to read, and length will be less of a problem since there is no need or even intention of enforcing these rules.

Second, standards should be written and reviewed by the best programming talent in the shop—not whoever happens to be available at the moment, or whoever has an ax to grind. Rules on which a great deal of emphasis and enforcement is to be placed deserve the best knowledge available.

Third, enforcement of standards should be mandatory, not something done if there happens to be time. Once the decision is made to shorten the standards document to only those things which are essential, the pain of enforcement diminishes rapidly. Enforcement processes should include automated enforcers where possible (sometimes called *code auditors*), and the use of reviews as necessary where automation is not possible. Peer code reviews are one important way of enforcing standards, although the main focus of such a review should be on quality as a whole, not just standards enforcement.

There is another problem in the area of enforcement. Often quality assurance organizations will perform standards enforcement activities, and pronounce the software to be of high quality. It is important to distinguish between standards conformance and product quality. Standards are a narrow subset of the total issue of quality, and although it would be nice to establish the definition of quality in terms of conformance with a sufficient set of standards, it is simply not possible. If you go back over the definition of quality in terms of attributes, and think about ways of demanding achievement of those attributes in terms of rules, you will quickly see that software quality cannot simply be legislated, it must be performed. Efforts to measure quality in terms of standards conformance are doomed to letting poor quality software slip through undetected.

The emphasis here may seem negative. That is, quite a point is made earlier about the historic problems in levying standards. This should not be taken as a vote against the use of standards to improve software quality. Properly chosen, carefully enforced standards can definitely improve the quality of the software product. They are one of the tools a quality-concerned software professional must employ.

REFERENCES

GLASS82—*Modern Programming Practices: A Report from Industry,* Prentice-Hall, 1982; Glass. *Discusses standards and guidelines used by several successful large-scale software companies.*

IEEE—*IEEE Standards on Software Engineering,* a series of volumes on different standards topics, available from IEEE Service Center, 445 Hoes Lane, Piscataway, NJ 08854. *Standards and guidelines prepared by a professional society.*

POSTON86—The series, *Software Standards,* published in *IEEE Software.* See, for example, "Instant Productivity Gains," November 1986; Poston. *Interesting and diverse series of discussions on the issues and successes surrounding standards.*

2.4.6 Standardized Elements

The benefits of standardization reach beyond the rules defined for programmers. It is possible to build whole software systems based on off-the-shelf components. When this is done, all kinds of quality benefits accrue, starting with the fact that components which have been used elsewhere are generally relatively bug free and thus reliability will be high. What kind of standard solution elements might be available to programmers?

- libraries of modules
- programming languages

- operating systems
- computer instruction sets

Let us consider each of these possibilities in turn.

Standard libraries of modules: We have already seen the benefits of modular programming and reuse in earlier sections of this book. Libraries are simply an extension of that concept. The wise programmer will choose library modules over homegrown modules whenever an appropriate library module is available, unless there is a serious flaw with the module which makes it unusable in the application in question. (For example, on some real-time systems where timing is critical and the need for accuracy in trigonometric functions can be relaxed, quick-and-dirty trig functions have been used in place of library trig functions. This, however, is an extremely unusual circumstance.)

Standard programming languages: Many computing installations choose to do all of their programming in a particular language. This choice reduces programmer training costs, makes maintenance easier since systems are maintained in a language that all the programmers understand, and assists in making the software more portable should the need arise. The ultimate in language standardization is the Department of Defense (DoD) language Ada, where the DoD defined the language for the express purpose of requiring all embedded, real-time DoD applications to be coded in it.

Standard operating systems: Through the early years of computing, operating systems were hand-tailored to the computer hardware in question, and no one thought to do things differently. Two things have happened that are beginning to change that. First, the Unix operating system was defined and gathered an enthusiastic following, such that the system was rehosted onto a large number of popular computers. Second, as microcomputers and de facto standardized chips became popular, the number of available operating systems was held to a standard few: CP/M for 8-bit computers, MS-DOS for 16-bit, IBM PC compatible computers, and OS/2 or Windows for more recent IBM personal computers. The programmer who chooses to use a standard operating system for application development reaps the same kinds of benefits as the programmer choosing a standard language—reduced training costs, easier maintenance, and especially increased portability.

Standard computer instruction sets: The world of computer hardware has improved dramatically over the years, especially in the area of price and performance. There is one area, however, that has not received the attention it should. Computer hardware still is designed with the marketing department and the hardware engineer, not the software engineer, in mind. Each computer by each hardware vendor tends to have its own instruction set, requiring new compilers for each machine and inhibiting portability of both programs and data. There are two trends currently at work which may change that. The first is within the Department of Defense where, as with the Ada language, a hardware standardization effort is well under way. The DoD has defined two instruction sets, called MIL-STD-1750A (16 bit) and MIL-STD-1862 (32 bit), which hardware vendors must use if they are to sell hardware to the DoD for embedded, real-time applications. Benefits to the DoD include reduced training costs, increased application portability, and reduced support software costs (one compiler for MIL-STD-1750A, for example, will support *all* vendor's 1750 computers).

The second trend is a de facto trend which began with the origins of the microcomputer industry. The number of basic chips, and thus instruction sets, which underlie all the microcomputers in that market is very small. Most hardware vendors buy off-the-shelf chips from a chipmaker such as Intel or Motorola, rather than inventing their own. The reason the hardware vendors chose to do this was that it reduced the cost and risk of bringing out a new computer, but software engineers can reap the benefits which go with standardization, such as (once again) decreased training and increased portability.

2.4.7 Wizards

Thus far we have talked about achieving quality through tools and methods rather than through people. This is a misleading approach. Data from a variety of studies have consistently shown over the years that the road to quality and productivity in the construction of software is through the selection of the best people available, not the best methodologies. This is, of course, sometimes easier said than done. First of all, we do not have good objective criteria in our field which allow us to decide who is truly best. Most of us who have worked with or managed software professionals have intuitive and subjective ways of making that choice, but there is not yet any method which allows us to point to a particular programmer and say "he or she is the best one in the shop" and be certain that we have made the correct choice.

Second, the set of criteria for "best" programmers is diverse. They must program well, of course, but that is only the beginning. They must be thorough and user friendly in performing requirements gathering. They must be imaginative and complete in doing design. They must pay close attention to detail in programming. They must be open to admitting error in checkout. They must be able to invent and sell a concept, and invent and sell a product. They must understand costs and benefits and how and when to compromise. Most programmers who are good at some of those criteria are not good at others. The supply of top-quality people who can do even some of these things extremely well is limited.

Nevertheless, the fact remains that the top-quality person or team will generally build the top-quality software. People who are able to do this are often called gurus, hackers (by those who like the concept of hacking), or wizards. A small set of wizards will do more for the creation of quality software than an army of nonwizards using the best methodologies in the land.

REFERENCES

AP90—Special issue on "Peopleware," *American Programmer,* July/August 1990. *Contains several articles emphasizing "the best way to improve software productivity and quality is to focus on people." One especially important article, "Managing the Real Leverage in Software Productivity and Quality," by Bill Curtis, proposes a five-stage maturity process for the managing of the peopleware of an organization—herded, managed, tailored, institutionalized, and optimized— where increasingly more useful ways of utilizing people are discovered.*

2.5 CHECKOUT

The emphasis of the preceding sections has been on the *front-end loading* of software quality activities. That is, problems that are avoided in requirements and design cannot come back to plague the programmer during testing, and the user during operation.

It is tempting but naive to believe that this will totally rid a program of problems. The fact is that in these earlier phases no program even existed from which to remove problems! *Checkout* is the term that is used in this book for the phase of software development when the now-formed software product is to be cleansed of its flaws.

This section divides checkout activities into two classes: static methods (analysis of a program without executing it), and dynamic methods (execution of a program under test input conditions). Static methods generally involve high people costs and low computer costs; dynamic methods incur some computer costs, and may involve people costs as well. As will be seen, testing has traditionally been, and will continue to be, the largest focus of software error-removal efforts. However, static methods have generated a great deal of enthusiasm in recent years, and may play an increasingly important role in the years to come.

REFERENCES

BASILI87—"Comparing the Effectiveness of Software Testing Strategies," *IEEE Transactions on Software Engineering,* December 1987; Victor Basili and Richard Selby. *Evaluates functional testing versus structural testing versus code review in a controlled experiment; finds code review the most effective and cost effective.*

COLLOFELLO89—"Evaluating the Effectiveness of Reliability Assurance Techniques," *Journal of Systems and Software,* March 1989; James Collofello and Scott Woodfield. *Evaluates testing versus code reviews versus design reviews on an industrial software project; finds reviews more effective and cost effective.*

FAIRLEY78—"Tutorial: Static Analysis and Dynamic Testing of Computer Software," *IEEE Computer,* April 1978; Richard Fairley. *Defines static and dynamic methodologies. Describes techniques, pointing out both advantages and disadvantages/limitations.*

MYERS78—"A Controlled Experiment in Program Testing and Code Walkthroughs/ Inspections," *Communications of the ACM,* September 1978; Glenford Myers. *Describes an experiment in error seeking using testing and code review. Sees these techniques as complementary, with both being necessary.*

2.5.1 Static Methods

During checkout, a piece of software actually exists. It has emerged from the requirements and design and coding efforts in the form of a machine-readable representation but, more important, it exists in human-readable form. The listing of a program, output by its compiling or assembling program, is that human-readable representation.

When most software people think of a computer program, they think of its listing. Fortunately, since the listing and the machine-readable representation are usually produced by the same processor, there is every reason to believe that each faithfully represents the other. The reason this is fortunate is that the listing serves as the basis for almost all understandings about a program and, more specifically from the point of view of this section, it serves as the basis for most static quality methodology. Methodologies that do not involve examination of the listing usually involve an automated analysis of the source program itself. In either case, what distinguishes static methodologies from dynamic ones is that they do not involve execution of the program.

Specific static methodologies are described in the material that follows.

2.5.1.1 Desk Checking

Desk checking is probably computing's "oldest profession." Of all the elements of software development methodology, desk checking has been the most necessary for the longest time. Nothing is likely to change that situation (although, unlike other oldest professions, desk checking lacks stimulation and excitement and is sometimes avoided for those reasons).

It is a little difficult to define the concept. Desk checking covers the totality of checkout efforts performed manually. Most commonly, it refers to (1) reviewing a program listing for faults, (2) doing arithmetic calculations to verify output value correctness, and (3) "playing computer" (i.e., manually simulating program execution) in order to understand and verify program logic and data flow. What these three processes have in common is that they are performed at the desk rather than on the computer.

One or more of the facets of desk checking just described is an essential part of any verification process. The choice among those facets is generally debug driven—that is, desk-checking efforts concentrate on areas of special problems, especially suspected errors or code inefficiencies, and involve techniques appropriate to that problem.

Arithmetic verification of output is especially essential. Although it is sometimes possible to do this by checking against already known correct answers, more often the only way to do it is by manual or calculator performance of the arithmetic chores of the program.

Part of the focus of modern software technology has been to develop computer-assisted desk checking. "Let the computer do it" has become today's programmer cry, with good reason. Computer resources have grown increasingly cheap, and human resources increasingly dear, as the costs of computing evolve. Source language debug, interactive debug, and perhaps even symbolic execution are in some sense automated desk checking—they let the computer itself "play computer" while providing enough visibility for the programmer to monitor program flow.

However, there is really no significant substitute for manual at-the-desk checking, especially listing review and arithmetic calculation. Unfortunately, there is evidence that the latter is becoming a neglected art. Manual arithmetic calculations are drudgery, and programmers would in general be happy to avoid them. Since there is no known effective substitute, this neglect may someday have tragic implications.

A particularly interesting example of desk checking is described in [Shuttle84]. In the early days of the Space Shuttle, as the software was first developed, an especially vicious set of bugs was uncovered and corrected. The nature of the bugs was that a variable was used in one branch of a program, but it was not reset to the proper value needed by another branch of the program.

This kind of error is particularly difficult to detect and remove because its discovery is dependent on executing a particular pair of logic segments in just the right order. Because of the importance of the Space Shuttle missions, a task force was set up to look through all portions of the Shuttle software, checking for just this kind of error. Probably no larger-scale use of desk checking has ever been undertaken.

EXAMPLE OF DESK CHECKING

Suppose that your program for the generation of probabilistic odds for bookmaking on games of chance has gone awry. The blackjack option is producing obviously erroneous results under test.

You suspend testing activities and begin an earnest and detailed review of the program listing. Statement by statement you proceed through the blackjack portion of the program, looking for flaws in the logic and the mathematics. But in spite of your dedicated efforts, no error manages to permeate your consciousness. (You have just employed desk checking of the listing-analysis variety.)

Getting a little more concerned, you perform the probabilistic arithmetic as your mathematical algorithm specifies it, keeping track of all intermediate results in case you need to check them later against program-provided results. As you were fairly sure would be true, the hand-calculated results differ from those obtained by your program. Obviously, in spite of your listing review, there is an error somewhere in your coding of the algorithm. (You have just employed desk checking of the arithmetic-calculation variety.)

You decide to play computer. Statement by statement, algorithmic term by algorithmic term, you read the program listing and perform the act dictated by the program. After each step, you check the results against the saved arithmetic results of the previous paragraph.

After several statements, you obtain a difference between the algorithmic hand-calculated results and your computer simulation hand-calculated results. Your brow indicates that an "ah-ha" reaction has occurred. The coded representation of the algorithm has used the wrong variable in a minor term of the probabilistic equation.

Having invested this much time in hand calculation, you decide to finish the playing-computer approach to the algorithm, using the corrected equation, to see if any other errors remain. Fortunately, algorithmic and coded results track perfectly, and you now feel much more confident that the code is correct. (You have just employed desk checking of the playing-computer variety.)

REFERENCES

LEDGARD75—Proverb 20, *Programming Proverbs for Fortran Programmers,* Hayden, 1975; Henry Ledgard. *Advocates and describes "hand-checking your program before running it." Uses an example containing several hand-check-detectable errors.*

SHUTTLE84—"The Space Shuttle Primary Computer System," *Communications of the ACM;* September 1984. *Case study of the development of Space Shuttle computing through interviews with key people.*

2.5.1.2 *Peer Code Review*

A peer code review is a process by which a team of programming personnel do an in-depth review of a program or a portion of a program, by inspection. Other terms for variations on this activity are *code verification, code/ program reading, walkthrough,* and *code inspection.*

The primary reason for a peer code review is to improve program quality. The peer team examines the subject program intimately, from the various points of view of the participants, seeking flaws that may have eluded the programmer's less diverse frame of reference.

In addition to flaw elimination, peer code reviews have fringe benefits. Programmers are motivated to do a better job, knowing that their work will be scrutinized by their peers. Additionally, programmers collectively improve their techniques and style as they share ideas at a review, and reviewers will gain sufficient knowledge to serve in a backup capacity on the program if necessary.

There is great enthusiasm for the peer review among software professionals, and with good reason. Yourdon [77] says "Walkthroughs are one of the most effective ways known to improve the quality of a computer program," and "programming groups using walkthroughs report . . . reducing the number of errors . . . by as much as a factor of ten."

J. F. Clemens of IBM Federal Systems Division and the Space Shuttle program said "The payoff is tremendous. If I had it to do over, I would insist on independent code inspections as a mandatory part of the verification process for the entire program" [Clemons 84].

Several studies of the relative value of testing and review processes have found reviews to be both more effective at removing errors and less costly than testing. And in addition to these enthusiastic qualitative findings, there is quantitative data as well. Kouchakdjian [89] and Bush [89] independently found that over 90 percent of the errors in significant software could be removed by review processes *before testing even began.* There seems little doubt that careful peer review is an essential part of any software quality program.

However, there are also problems with peer reviews. Code review is often drudgery; the methodical and thorough pace necessary for effective review is taxing. Because of this, motivation of participants is difficult. Motivation is vital, however, because only through intense reviewer concentration can the peer code review have value.

In addition, peer code review is expensive. Experience indicates that about 100 source statements may be reviewed in an hour, and the concentration of the participants wanes after an hour. For a program of any size, the cost and duration of a peer review may seem prohibitive. Because of the value of the review, in such circumstances it is wise to review at least key program portions and to select other portions for review randomly.

Several questions regarding the application of the peer code review need to be dealt with here.

Who attends a peer code review?: Only technologists should attend a peer review. Managers should be excluded, to avoid any emphasis on *programmer* review as opposed to *program* review (which, in turn, would lead to programmers attempting to conceal problems rather than openly searching for them).

Typically, three to four peers should attend, varying in experience level to maximize learning. Preferably, these participants should have a sense of responsibility for the program, such as:

- being members of the same team
- having responsibility for an interfacing program
- having responsibility for the program's product test or quality assurance
- being assigned to maintenance of the program

Or, at the very least, participants should assume backup responsibility as a result of review attendance.

In addition, it is important that someone represent specific interests at the review. Yourdon [77] suggests a

- "maintenance oracle," who looks for maintainability
- "standards bearer," who looks at standards conformance
- "user representative," who cares for the user's needs

Participant attitude is important. Those who cannot be cooperative and tactful in pursuing flaws, and those who are defensive about flaws detected, should be excluded from peer reviews (and, perhaps, from the organization!).

When should a peer code review be held?: There is no clear answer to this question. There are those who suggest that they should occur as early as possible in the development cycle. However, it is probably preferable to rid the program of easily-computer-detected problems before engaging in the taxing mental effort of the review. That would mean reviewing only code that is thought by its developer to be complete, well annotated, and syntactically correct. A "clean compile" and perhaps early, trivia-removing unit tests could precede the review.

What is the sequence of events at a peer code review?: The methodology of a peer code review should be considered in advance. Some suggest very formal review processes, with a trained facilitator conducting the review, well-defined roles played by the participants, and a requirement that participants have conducted an in-depth study of the program prior to the review itself.

Others would suggest that it is the rigor of the review, not its formal processes, that gives value, and that review conditions should facilitate that rigor with a minimum of formality. In these circumstances, the responsible programmer will verbally lead the participants sequentially through the data areas and logic flow of the program. Someone should be assigned in advance to the role of scribe, recording all significant comments and making sure that action items are recorded and assigned.

Each statement of the program should be discussed as it is encountered. All logic branches should be taken at least once. Requirements and design documents must be present for correlation of function to the original problem and its design solution. Participants should focus on flaw identification, not flaw correction. The end product of the review should be the set of action items with responsible person assignments, and a decision to accept the product as is, accept it with specified revisions, or reject it (requiring a future review after revisions are made).

EXAMPLE OF PEER CODE REVIEW

You have completed a bookmaking program for simulating outcomes from certain games of chance, and it has occurred to you that it might prove personally useful. But since any such use would involve your own money rather than a customer's, you are determined to leave no reliability stone unturned in removing all potential errors in advance. As a result, you hand-pick a few skilled friends, explain what you have in mind, and invite them to a peer code review in your recreation room.

In preparation for the review, you obtain a projection device for displaying the computer-resident program listing for all to see, and you flank the projector with ample supplies of cheese, chips, and chip dip. The requirements specifications, detailed design, and user manual are readily available in supplementary windows on your display computer. There is a pitcher of beer and several icy bottles of Pepsi. Arranging empty glasses strategically, you are ready for the arrival of your guests.

After a few convivial remarks, and a top-level program overview, you get down to business. Line by line you explain the function of the program, stopping to field questions from participants and to wipe chip dip off the projector. The participants are positive in their approach, and a feeling of camaraderie permeates the group.

As time progresses, however, the pace at which you move through the code lessens noticeably, and some comments become more testy than constructive. Recognizing the symptoms, you bring the review to a close.

You hold a summary discussion. Everyone agrees that a great deal of progress has been made, and you have detected three programming errors and the need for improved self-documenting code. (You could not remember, under questioning, the function of a couple of flag variables.) The group parts amiably, and you put away the list of action items for further review, and move the dead soldiers to the sink.

Realizing that only 112 statements out of a 1,500 line program have been reviewed, a week later you call your friends and invite them to the second in a proposed series of ten code reviews. No one agrees to come.

(Absurd as it may sound, this scenario actually happened!)

REFERENCES

ACKERMAN89—"Software Inspections: An Effective Verification Practice," *IEEE Software,* May 1989; A. Frank Ackerman, Lynne S. Buchwald, Frank H. Lewski. *Defines a specific kind of review—the "inspection"—that has six well-defined steps, four well-defined participant roles, a formal data collection process, and a supporting infrastructure.*

BUSH89—"The Jet Propulsion Laboratory's Experiences with Formal Inspections," *Proceedings of the Fourteenth Annual Software Engineering Workshop,* Goddard Space Flight Center, Maryland, November 29, 1989; Marilyn Bush and John Kelly. *Describes the use of formal inspections at JPL. Finds that the cost is $84 to $108 per error, and the savings over 300 inspections to be $7.5 million!*

CLEMONS84—"The Space Shuttle Primary Computer System," *Communications of the ACM,* September 1984; J. F. Clemons. *Case study material on approaches used on the Space Shuttle.*

KOUCHAKDJIAN89—"Evaluation of the Cleanroom Methodology in the SEL," *Proceedings of the Fourteenth Annual Software Engineering Workshop,* Goddard Space Flight Center, Maryland, November 29, 1989; Ara Kouchakdjian, Scott Green, and Vic Basili. *Evaluated a modified cleanroom process in which rigorous inspection techniques replaced formal verification. Studied a production software project using professional programmers. Found that 91 percent of the software errors were detected prior to the first test case execution.*

MYERS78—"A Controlled Experiment in Program Testing and Code Walkthroughs/Inspections," *Communications of the ACM,* September 1978; Glenford Myers. *Sees code review as a necessary but somewhat expensive component of the overall checkout process. Suggests the evolution of computer-assisted review techniques.*

SELBY84—"Evaluating Software Testing Strategies," *Proceedings of the Ninth Annual Software Engineering Workshop,* NASA-Goddard, 1984; Richard W. Selby, Jr., Victor R. Basili, Jerry Page, and Frank E. McGarry. *Compares error-testing strategies; finds code reading the most effective.*

YOURDON77—*Structured Walkthroughs,* Yourdon Press, 1977; Edward Yourdon. *A how-to book on conducting walkthroughs of all kinds.*

2.5.1.3 *Structural analysis*

There is a class of software problems which could be unearthed by human-oriented static methodologies such as desk checking and peer code review if human beings were sufficiently patient. This class involves problems emerging from the structures—data structure and especially logic structure—of a program.

However, the elaborate efforts necessary to perform these kinds of analysis has led to the automation of the process. As a result, a variety of automated tools have been developed to explore a program looking for certain classes of structural problems. These tools fall into the static category because, even though they involve the use of a computer, the analysis is performed on the subject program without executing it.

A structural analyzer, then, is an automated tool that seeks and records errors in the structural makeup of a subject program. Examples of problems sought by structural analyzers include:

1. Data variables undeclared or improperly declared
2. Data variables used before they are initialized, or initialized and never used
3. Use of unauthorized language forms (e.g., GOTO in structured programming, ALTER in COBOL, mixed-mode arithmetic)
4. Violation of naming conventions (data variables, procedure names, statement labels)
5. Overly complicated constructs (loops or conditionals too deeply or improperly nested)
6. Procedure argument checking (actual and formal parameter mismatching)
7. Inconsistencies in procedure calling trees (recursion where not allowed)
8. Inconsistent global data layout (*common* blocks)
9. Unreachable logic
10. Missing logic
11. Erroneous logic (potentially infinite loops)

Some of the preceding errors fall into the category of standards violations. That is, the technique may be proper from the point of view of the language and compiler being used, but not from the point of view of the installation or project needing the code. We have already discussed static analysis tools which look for this kind of problem, calling them standards enforcers or code auditors.

Structural analyzers are almost always language specific and perhaps even installation or project specific. Most structural analyzers are built to date accommodate only a particular language; for example, DAVE [Osterweil76] processes Control Data Fortran programs looking for uninitialized variables; Meta COBOL, a COBOL preprocessor and auditor, looks for unauthorized language forms (ALTER), questionable constructs (deeply-nested IFs), and other similar violations; and software sneak circuit analysis uses computer hardware concepts to look for software logic "short circuits" in assembler language code.

EXAMPLE OF STRUCTURAL ANALYSIS

Still determined to rid your bookmaking program of errors before you use it, you decide to subject it to a fortuitously available structural analyzer. You have coded the program in Fortran, and your installation procured a Fortran structural analyzer and standards enforcer several years ago. (In fact, your decision to use Fortran was based partially on the existence of such tools). You invoke the structural analyzer, and it checks for referencing variables before they are initialized, inconsistencies of logic structure, and conformance to your installation's standards.

When the results of the analysis come back, there is good news and bad news. The good news is that the peer code review had discovered all uninitialized variables and violations of naming conventions; no such error message came from the analyzer. The bad news is that a couple of your common blocks are inconsistent, one statement number is never referenced, and your statement numbers are occasionally out of order (that violates an installation standard).

The bad news is not very bad, however. The errors are easy to fix. Straightening out the common blocks is a near-clerical matter. Fixing the statement numbers is a little harder, since you need to detect and correct all references to them as well as correcting the numbers themselves. The statement number that is never referenced should have been, and you must add code to do that. You do those things, make another run against the structural analyzer, and your program gets a clean bill of health.

At least as important as fixing the identified errors, you realize, is the knowledge that no errors of those classes are likely to remain in your program.

REFERENCES

OSTERWEIL76—"Some Experience with DAVE—A Fortran Program Analyzer," *Proceedings of the 1976 National Computer Conference;* Osterweil and Fosdick. *Discusses DAVE, an analyzer that examines multimodule ANSI Fortran programs for uninitialized variables, and variables initialized but unused. Describes its implementation and use.*

2.5.1.4 *Proof of Correctness*

Proof of correctness is the process of using mathematical theorem-proving concepts on a computer program or its design to show that it is consistent with its specification. This is done by breaking the program into logical segments, defining input and output assertions for each segment (an *input assertion* is a statement of what characteristics the input data to the segment must have; an *output assertion* is a similar statement about the output produced by the segment), and demonstrating that, when the program functions, if all input assertions are true then so, too, are all output assertions. It must also be shown that the program successfully terminates.

Showing termination is largely an ad hoc procedure. However, the correctness aspect is a well-defined procedure described as follows: The program is augmented with assertions as described above. The program is broken at the points where the assertions are attached, resulting in a set of program segments. For each program segment, the assertion at the bottom is passed backward through the program statements. The assertion is modified according to the semantics of the program statement through which it passed. The correctness of the segment is demonstrated by showing that the assertion which migrated to the top of the program segment follows from the assertion which was originally at the top.

There are many opinions on the value of program proof. Probably the most universally accepted opinion is that it is at least ten years away from being useful on programs of any significance. In the context of this guidebook, where a menu of reliability tools is being presented for near-term project selection and use, proof of correctness has little value.

The advantages of proof of correctness are:

1. *Provides a rigorous, formalized process.*
2. *Forces analysis.* The proof-of-correctness process forces the programmer to consider sections of the program which might otherwise only get a cursory analysis.
3. *Clarifies computation states.* Writing out the assertions makes the programmer explicitly state heretofore implicit assumptions, which define the state of the computation for specific points within the program.
4. *Clarifies dependencies.* When executing the proof, the programmer becomes aware of what assumptions about the input data are implicitly used by the code in various sections of the system.

Disadvantages are:

1. *Complexity.* Even for small simple programs, the symbolic manipulations can be overly complex.

2. *Errors.* Because of the complexity, it is easy to introduce errors into the computation of the statements to be proven as well as the proof of those statements.

3. *Arrays are difficult to handle.*

4. *Lack of powerful-enough theorem provers.* The proof process could be automated to reduce errors, except that there are no theorem provers powerful enough for most practical problems.

5. *Too much work.* It often requires several times the amount of work to prove a program than was required to write the program.

6. *Lack of expressive power.* It is often very difficult to create the output assertion for what is an intuitively simple computation.

7. *Nonintuitive.* The procedure tends to obscure the true nature of the computation being analyzed rather than providing insight into the computation.

8. *Requires training.* Like programming, the user of proof of correctness requires many hours of training as well as practice in order to use the technique well.

EXAMPLE OF PROOF OF CORRECTNESS

Carried onward by your earlier success in removing bugs from your book-making program, you elect to use proof-of-correctness techniques. In order to learn more about the technique, however, you decide to try it out on a much smaller problem first.

The problem you choose is the calculation of X^n, represented by the code that follows. The facts that you know to be true about the problem—the input assertions—are included as "assume" statements. The output assertion is a "prove" statement.

```
0              Assume (Real (X));      Input assertions
1              Assume (Integer
               (N));
2              Assume (N > I);
3              Real Proc E(X,N);
4              Real X; Integer N,I;
5              Assume (Integer       Input assertion
               (I));
6              E ← X;
7              I ← 1;
8 Loop:        Assume (E = X**I);     Loop invariant
9              IF (I ≥ N) GOTO DONE;
10             E ← E*X;
```

```
11            I ← I + 1;
12            GOTO Loop;
13 Done:      Prove (E = X**N);        Output assertion
              END;
```

First, you break the program into segments which contain no loops, each with its own input and output assertion. Breaking up the program (and the loop), you obtain the following three segments.

Segment 1, the first entry to the loop, is

```
0             Assume (Real (X));
1             Assume (Integer
              (N));
2             Assume (N ⩾ 1);
5             Assume (Integer
              (I));
6             E ← X;
7             I ← 1;
8             Prove (E = X**I);
```

Segment 2, the Ith time through the loop, is

```
8             Assume (E = X**I);
9             Assume (I < N);
10            E ← E*X;
11            I ← I + 1;
8             Prove (E = X**I);
```

Segment 3, the exit path from the loop, is

```
8             Assume (E = X**I);
9             Assume (I ⩾ N);
13            Prove (E = X**N);
```

You elect to start with the second segment, the "general case" for the loop (it covers all cases for $I = 2$ through $I = N - 1$).

The loop invariant is

$$E = X**I$$

That is, the program variables E, X, and I are always in this relation at the top and the bottom of the loop. (Note that "$=$" means mathematical equality, *not* programming assignment.) Passing this expression back through statement 11 (statement numbers are shown to the left of the program listing) produces the expression

$$E = X**(I + 1)$$

Passing this expression through statement 10 produces

$$E*X = X**(I + 1)$$

Passing this expression through statement 9 produces

$$(I < N) \supset (E*X = X**(I + 1))$$

Thus, the condition to be verified for this segment is

$$(E = X**I) \supset [(I < N) \supset (E*X = X**(I + 1))]$$

which can be rewritten as

$$[(E = X**I) \land (I < N)] \supset (E*X = X**(I + 1))$$

[This states that if we know that E is equal to X raised to the Ith power and I is less than N, it must follow that E times X is equal to X raised to the $(I + 1)$th power.] $(I < N)$ is not needed for the proof. Multiplying both sides of

$$E = X**I$$

by X and with a little algebra you get the right-hand side of the implication, and the condition to be verified is shown to be correct.

With only a little knowledge of proof-of-correctness techniques, you feel intimidated by the process. You decide to use the technique only on the highly mathematical and relatively straightforward segments of your bookmaking program.

REFERENCES

DeMillo77—"Social Processes and Proofs of Theorems and Programs," *Proceedings of the Fourth Symposium on Principles of Programming Languages,* 1977; DeMillo, Lipton, and Perlis. *Takes the unusual position that mathematical proofs require an elaborate social process to achieve both rigor and acceptance. Suggests that program proofs are unlikely to be supported in this way, and thus unlikely to ever have practical value.*

Hantler76—"An Introduction to Proving the Correctness of Programs," *ACM Computing Surveys,* September 1976; Hantler and King. *Classic tutorial on early proof methodologies. Discusses the use of automated approaches for simple programs, and inductive assertion for less simple ones. Shows example proofs.*

Howden91—"Program Testing versus Proofs of Correctness," to be published in *IEEE Software,* William E. Howden. *Sees roles for both testing and proofs in software verification; outlines each.*

2.5.2 Dynamic Methods

All the quality processes of all the preceding sections are *still* by no means sufficient to ensure the quality of software. Dynamic checkout methods are needed as well. These dynamic methods are usually called *testing*.

In fact, typically the bulk of software quality work happens in testing, wherein attempt after partially successful attempt is made to get newly produced software to execute correctly. It seems to be human nature to err—and frequently.

It is interesting to note that it is also human nature to expect not to err. A favorite trick played on novice programmers is to bet them that their first program won't work correctly on its first execution. Experienced programmers have been known to gain some measure of wealth preying on the naive expectations of green programmers, whose work is, surprisingly to them, subject to the frailties of us all!

Regardless of the care taken in the earlier phases of development, and in spite of research claims to the contrary, it will be necessary to test—and test hard—to achieve reliable software. No advancement in technology is going to change that situation significantly, although many will chip away at it. Knowledge of testing techniques is an essential part of the programmer's tool kit.

Testing itself may be broken down into several phases or levels of usage. In traditional bottom-up development techniques, individual small program components are tested at the *unit test* level before being assembled into the software whole. *Integration testing,* using the fully joined software product, is the next level of testing; and finally, for embedded computer systems, where the computer is part of a larger system (e.g., the flight computer in an airplane), *system testing* is the final level of test. Even for top-down programming, where the integration phase is largely eliminated, testing proceeds through levels as more and more code stubs are replaced with legitimate code.

Testing is the execution of software to determine where it functions incorrectly. Testing includes deliberately constructing difficult sets of input data designed to maximize the possibility of software failure. What testing should never be is a simplistic application of a minimum number of test cases selected to show only that the software works. Under cost and schedule pressures, it is sometimes tempting to short-circuit the test process in this way. The result is inevitably disaster—unreliable software, unhappy customers, and worse.

The process of going about testing requires planning. In fact, in many environments, particularly U.S. government-sponsored software development, a test plan and test procedures document must be produced prior to the testing itself.

There are two complementary forces driving the testing process. From the software customer point of view, testing must demonstrate that all product requirements are met. Test plans and procedures usually stress the definition of a matrix of requirements versus test cases, sufficient to show that all requirements are covered by at least one test case.

However, from the programmer's point of view, testing must demonstrate that all components of the structure of the software are executed. The construction of odd-ball test cases is usually done to force the test

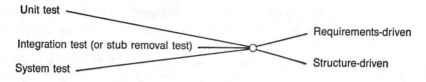

Figure 2.9 Testing involves multiple levels and multiple approaches.

execution of an obscure portion of a program otherwise untestable. As experienced programmers know only too well, it is the exceptional case that often consumes the most programming time, is the most difficult to test, and is the most often wrong. The simplicity of classroom exercises often stems directly from the omission of such exceptions; it is this lack of reality in academic software exercises (the outside world is unfortunately full of exceptions) which gives rise to the expression *real-world programming,* meaning consideration of a problem complete with all its warts and wrinkles, as opposed to *academic programming.* Be warned that a most difficult and important part of testing is the ferreting out of problems in obscure, exception structures.

Thus, we have *requirements-driven* testing, and *structure-driven* testing. Note that neither is sufficient without the other. If a requirement is not satisfied, structure-driven testing may not detect it, since the corresponding software structure may also be omitted. And if a piece of structure is wrong, explicit requirements testing may well not detect it, since requirements are seldom detailed enough to account for all pieces of software structure (i.e., requirements do not dictate, except very indirectly, all the IF_THEN_ELSEs of a program).

Traditionally, then, testing is a blending, as shown in Figure 2.9, controlled overall by a test plan and procedures document. Because there are so many different techniques associated with testing, in this book we divide them into two classes: those techniques which focus on code, and those which focus on test cases.

REFERENCES

ACM88—Special section on "Software Testing," *Communications of the ACM,* June 1988.

COLLOFELLO89—"Evaluating the Effectiveness of Reliability Assurance Techniques," *Journal of Systems and Software,* March 1989; James Collofello and Scott Woodfield. *Looks at design reviews, code reviews, and testing from the point of view of (1) error-detection efficiency and (2) cost effectiveness. Finds testing, though necessary, to be neither efficient nor cost effective!*

DEMILLO78—"Hints on Test Data Selection: Help for the Practicing Programmer," *IEEE Computer,* April 1978; DeMillo, Lipton, and Sayward. *Makes a strong case for the use of an intuitive, ad hoc approach to testing, on the grounds that other approaches reject the truism that most programs under test are "nearly correct."*

HANNAH89—"CASE Focus Shifting to Concern for Quality," *Software Magazine,* November 1989; Mary Alice Hannah. *Popular-press summary of CASE test and debug tools.*

HETZEL88—*The Complete Guide to Software Testing,* QED Information Sciences, 1988; Bill Hetzel. *Describes all kinds of software testing; even includes reviews and inspections in his definition of testing.*

LEVESON87—"A Scary Tale—Sperry Avionics Module Testing Bites the Dust," *ACM Software Engineering Notes,* April 1987; Nancy Leveson. *Informal article that discusses a software vendor said to have asked to substitute fault tolerance at execution time for module testing during development, on the grounds that testing is expensive and boring!*

MORRELL87—"Unit Testing and Analysis," Software Engineering Institute Curriculum Module SEI-CM-9, October 1987; Larry D. Morrell. *Examines the techniques and management of unit testing. For use by an educator wanting to teach the topic.*

MYERS78—"A Controlled Experiment in Program Testing and Code Walkthroughs/ Inspections," *Communications of the ACM,* September 1978; Glenford Myers. *Finds testing to be subject to individual variance, and alarmingly inadequate by itself. Suggests (1) complementing testing with peer code reviews, and (2) use of two independently operating testers.*

MYERS79—*The Art of Software Testing,* Wiley-Interscience, 1979; Glenford Myers. *The classic book on testing approaches.*

PHILLIPS88—"No-Test Software is 'Unobtainable,'" *Software Magazine,* December 1988; Roger A. Phillips. *Popular-press summary (with a strange title!) of commercially available testing tools.*

2.5.2.1 Dynamic Code Approaches

The goal of testing is to identify and remove errors from the software code. Test cases are chosen and constructed to optimize the chance of error detection. Because there are many tools and techniques for testing, we divide them into two classes: those that deal primarily with the *code* (in the next section), and those that deal primarily with the *test cases* (in the section following that).

It is important to keep in mind during any discussion of testing:

1. The ideal in testing is to cover everything that might be tested. That is not possible.
2. The temptation in testing is to cut costs. That is dangerous.
3. Test cases must be carefully chosen to optimize their coverage of the software to be chosen.
4. Knowing whether test results are correct or not is nontrivial. It is

important in choosing test cases to know what oracle will be used to verify the test results.

2.5.2.1.1 Source Language Debug

Source language debug is the process of testing a program using a high-level testing language, rather than a machine-level testing language. Source language debug allows the tester to execute and evaluate test cases in a language well above that of machine dumps. It is often accompanied by interactive capabilities, so that the tester can interact with the program under test, but for this discussion those two concepts are separated. That is, source language debug can happen via an interactive debugger or via a batch debugger.

To make clear what source language debug is, it is helpful to illustrate what it is not. Historically, program testing occurred in a scenario like the following:

The newly constructed program is ready for testing. A test case is constructed, using sample representative input data. The program and its test data are loaded into the computer, and the test run begins.

In the typical situation, the test run aborts: it causes the computer operating system to detect an impossible condition and terminate the job. Even if the run does not abort, it may run to completion with absurd or nonexistent output.

The programmer's dilemma at this point is to find out what went wrong, and where. In the case of an abort, the operating system probably printed out or displayed descriptive information automatically to assist the programmer. However, typically this information in the past has been in machine-code form. Since an operating system supports many different languages, it is difficult for it to know what programming language the programmer understands in order to play back the necessary information in human-readable form. Therefore, its only choice is to print the information in the only form it is sure of—machine code, which, depending on the computer, may be hexadecimal or octal numbers, or character-string equivalents of the numerical form, or both. The information printed will probably include the location in computer memory at which the abort occurred, perhaps a history of the locations of preceding subroutine/procedure calls, and a dump of some or all of computer memory.

Now consider the plight of the programmer. If the run aborted, he or she is confronted with pages of effective gibberish. In order to read this information, one must be able to convert large numbers from hex or octal to decimal, know where in computer memory various components of the program's instructions and data reside, and perhaps even decode numeric data into the corresponding computer instruction or floating-point number or character string or bit string. These are all nontrivial jobs, each requiring an elaborate learning process of its own.

If the programmer's run did not abort, he or she may be in even worse shape. Although there is no gibberish to decode, there is nothing at all to assist in defining what went wrong.

Debugging is like reading a murder mystery. The programmer/reader keeps a sharp eye out for clues which, coupled with knowledge of the program, enable the programmer to realize what portion of the program is the guilty malfunctioner. The problem here is that the clues are either in a foreign language, or nearly nonexistent.

Enter the crime lab of computing! Source language debug transforms the preceding scenario into the one that follows, using debug methodology as modern as the language in which the programmer coded the job.

The preparation of the job submittal takes place largely as before. However, one more pass is made over the program, inserting invocations of source debug capabilities. These are typically computer system dependent but may take the form of (1) special output statements in the program, printing key data in formatted form for debug analysis; (2) abort-triggered calls to a postmortem formatted dump program, embedded in the program or its job control; (3) trace statements in the program, printing program structure points executed and/or data variables as their values are changed, complete with name and value (if any), formatted for ease of readability; (4) calls to formatted snapshot dump routines in the program, where the dump also includes variable names and formatted values and, additionally, prints only those variables whose value has changed since the last snapshot; (5) debug on/off statements in the program which suppress or enable the specified debug actions at compile time so that source language debug statements may be left in a program's source code but turned off until they are needed.

Following the insertion of these debug statements in the program, the program is again executed. The output story, now, is totally different from before. If the run aborts, the abort is preceded by an audit trail of data and logic outputs, saying what has happened as the program executed, in the order in which it happened. The abort itself is accompanied by a human-readable memory dump. If the run does not abort, the audit trail is of course still present, and the programmer may ascertain more precisely what the program did and did not do as it executed.

Now the programmer-sleuth has an effective and usable set of clues to work from. Not only does the computer speak to the programmer, even in times of trouble, in his or her own language; better yet, the programmer has been able to preplan the output clues he or she would really like to have to assist the debug process. Bear in mind that prior to a computer test run, the programmer usually does not know that a "crime" will be committed, or what it will be, or where; but via preplanned source language debug, the programmer can be prepared to research the crime through deliberately implanted clues.

Example of Source Language Debug

The following source language debug invocations show specific examples of the syntactic and semantic forms that source language debug capabilities might take.

```
              Special Output Statements
              PUT NAMED ALPHA, BETA, GAMMA;
              PUT NAMED COMMON_FILE_1;
```

These output requests would result in printouts of the form

```
    ALPHA = 1.2E2, BETA = -12, GAMMA = ABCDEFG
    COMMON_FILE_1:
    ITEM1 = 1.2E0, ITEM2 = 1.6E-1, ITEM3 = 7, ITEM4 = 7A00F
```

where the name of the variable and its value, formatted according to its declaration, are printed at the time the PUT statement is executed.

Note that the PUT request for a data aggregate (e.g., COMMON _FILE_1) produces a printout of each of the components.

Name-directed output such as this is available in a few languages (e.g., PL/1). In languages where the capability for automatic name printout is not available, the programmer may include it in a format statement accompanying a WRITE:

```
    WRITE ALPHA, BETA, GAMMA;
    FORMAT ("ALPHA = ',E, 'BETA = ',I, "GAMMA = ',C);
```

```
                Trace Statements

    TRACE ALPHA, BETA, GAMMA;
```

This executable statement will cause a printout of the form

```
                ALPHA = 1.2E2
```

to occur each time the value of any of the named variables subsequently changes during program execution.

```
        TRACE PROCEDURE1, LABEL1;
```

This executable statement will cause a printout of the form

```
                PROCEDURE1
```

to occur each time the named procedure or label is subsequently entered.

```
        TRACE FLOW;
```

This executable statement will cause a record to be kept at execute-time of the most recent logic branchout statements (e.g., GOTO, CALL), so that they can be printed at the termination of execution, or during execution, or both.

```
DETRACE ALPHA; or DETRACE LABEL1; or DETRACE FLOW;
```

These executable statements will dynamically suppress the named tracing.

Formatted Snapshot Dumps

```
SNAP ALPHA, BETA, GAMMA;
```

This statement will cause the value of the named variables to be printed in a manner completely analogous to PUT NAMED, but only if the value of the variable has been changed since the last such snapshot printout.

```
SNAP ALL;
```

This statement will cause all the program's variables to be printed. It is especially useful if it is specified to be executed on any abnormal halt (e.g., SNAP ALL ON HALT).

Debug On/Off

```
DEBUG ON;
```

This statement takes effect at compile time and causes all subsequent debug statements to be processed by the compiler.

```
DEBUG OFF;
```

The statement causes all subsequent debug statements to be ignored by the compiler.

In any given program, it is unlikely that the programmer would make use of all of these capabilities, since there is some overlap between them. A typical mix might include SNAP ALL ON HALT (for unexpected terminations), TRACE FLOW (for logic flow), and DEBUG ON/OFF (to control the insertion/deletion of debug statements at compile time).

REFERENCES _____

SIGSOFT83—*Proceedings of the ACM SIGSOFT/SIGPLAN Software Engineering Symposium on High-Level Debugging,* August 1983. *Contains articles about vendor-available source language debug products, such as "VAX DEBUG: An*

Interactive, Symbolic, Multilingual Debugger" by Bender of Digital Equipment, *"Multilingual Debugging with the SWAT High-Level Debugger"* by Cardell of Data General, *"DELTA—The Universal Debugger for CP-6"* by Walter of Honeywell and an interesting discussion of the requirements for such a debugger, *"Interactive Debug Requirements"* by Seidner and Tindall of IBM.

2.5.2.1.2 Assertion Checker

Preplanning the debugging process has historically been a problem for programmers. Impatient programmers, hard charging toward what optimism tells them will be their first and last test run, find it very difficult to stop and contemplate the possibility that this first run will, in fact, fail and that they should prepare for it.

Source language debug provides some capabilities for the anticipating programmer. The concept of assertion checking is a more rigorous approach to this problem.

An assertion is a statement of what is presumed to be fact. In a computing sense, it is a statement that should hold true as a program executes. A local assertion is one that should hold true at the point of declaration; a global assertion is one that should hold true throughout program execution.

An assertion checker is a tool that provides for the evaluation of assertions during program execution, and records their truth or falsity. Note that the concept of assertions is also important to the proof-of-correctness process; however, the assertion checker is a dynamic test tool, only mildly related to the static proof process.

Observe the experienced programmer as he or she incorporates the assertion checker capability into careful pretest planning:

Having finished inserting source language debug statements—snapshots, postmortem dumps, and so on—the programmer makes one more pass over the source code, contemplating the assertions he or she is able to make about it.[2] First and foremost, the programmer will specify the legitimate range of all variables in the program; the assertion checker will provide for the detection of any violation of those range limitations. Further, the programmer may specify discrete legitimate or illegitimate values a variable may have. Perhaps the constituents of a data array must possess a certain interrelationship, such as being in ascending order; the programmer will specify that. Or certain constituents of an array have particular limitations on legitimate subscript values; that, too, will be specified. If a subprogram can have (or not have) side effects, they can be stated. The programmer examines the program with a specific set of assertions—those the assertion checker is prepared to deal with—in mind. For each, special assertion code is added to the program.

---

[2] Better yet, the planning for source language debug and (especially) assertions should have occurred in the design phase and will have materialized in the code on that basis.

The programmer now inputs the source code to the assertion checker, just as if it were input data. The assertion checker reads it in and outputs a modified version of the code containing the instrumentation code corresponding to the programmer's assertions. This augmented code is then fed into the compiler. The resulting object code is link-loaded, and in addition to the library routines the program already needed, a few special assertion library routines and an assertion database are linked into the loadable program.

The programmer is now ready to execute the instrumented code. What the programmer has is a version of the program, identical to what has been coded in all other respects but with the added capability of detecting assertion violations (and, for that matter, nonviolations), reporting individual violations, and summarizing the total assertion violation/success statistics for the run.

As he or she runs the test cases, the programmer gets, in addition to normal output and source language debug output, a record of assertion action. Consider the value of any assertion violation messages which the programmer may receive—he or she learns facts that normal debugging techniques might not tell until much later. Unless a variable being out of range causes some other symptom such as an abort, for example, the programmer might not be aware that the program was malfunctioning without the aid of the assertion checker. Thus, the assertion checker is an early warning tool, aggressively seeking out error situations rather than waiting for them to happen.

The assertion checker concept is not yet commonly used. Very few assertion checker systems have been implemented, and no industrial environment usage on a broad scale is known. In one experiment in their use as part of a graduate-level computer science course at UCLA, definite improvements were noted in program testing time, with some surprising fringe benefits in program quality.

Implementation of assertion checkers is language dependent. Since assertions are inserted by the programmer into a program, their form must be compatible with the language being used. Either a preprocessor approach, or an in-compiler implementation, is possible. The latter is preferable (for ease of use, lower implementation costs, and eliminating the separation between the programmer's code and that which he or she is checking out), but it is not commonly done because language specifications rarely include syntax for assertions, and thus compiler implementations do not provide for them.

Local assertions may also be inserted by the programmer using conventional techniques and without benefit of an assertion checker [e.g., IF NOT (.01 < A < 1.0) THEN ASSERTION_VIOLATION(A);]. However, the coding is cumbersome and must occur frequently in the code. There is no convenient corresponding option for global assertions, of course.

Examples of Assertion Checker
The following example data illustrate (1) the form assertion statements
inserted into a program might take, and (2) sample outputs which might
result from those assertions.

Sample Assertion Statements

These assertion statements are coded using a distinctive syntax for ease of
preprocessor recognition; in these examples, each statement is preceded by
an exclamation mark. The assertions are divided into three classes: global
assertions (those which must be valid throughout the program's execution), local assertions (those which must be valid at the point encountered),
and assertion control (directives controlling how the assertions are to be
used).

Global Assertions

!RANGE (list of variables) (minimum value, maximum value)
*Correct values of the list of variables must lie between the stated
bounds.*
!VALUES (list of variables) (list of legal values)
*Correct values of the list of variables are only those in the list of
values.*
!VALUES (list of variables) NOT (list of illegal values)
*Correct values of the list of variables are all those not in the
illegal list.*
!MONITOR (list of variables to be traced)
*Variables in the list are to be printed whenever their values
change.*
!SUBSCRIPT RANGE (list of subscriptable entity, subscript
bounds)
*Correct subscripts for entities in the list must fall between the
stated bounds.*

Local Assertions

!RELATION (expression that must be true)
The stated relationship must be true.
!CALL (variables not to be changed by the following subfunction
call)
*The listed variables must be unchanged following the subfunc-
tion call.*

Assertion Control

!TRACE ALL
Print a record of all assertions executed, violations or not.
!TRACE FIRST n
Print a record of the first n assertion violations to occur.
!TRACE LAST n
Print a record of the last n assertion violations to occur.
!TRACE ON (violation list)
Print all occurrences of the listed violations (e.g., RANGE, VALUES, etc.)
!TRACE OFF (violation list)
Do not check for the listed violations.
!MONITOR ON (list of variables)
Monitor (see above) variables in the list—dynamically executed.
!MONITOR OFF (list of variables)
Cease monitoring variables in the list—dynamically executed.

Outputs resulting from programmer-coded assertions could include the following:

During-Execution Outputs

!!!ASSERTION *(kind)* (VIOLATION) PROGRAM *(name)*, LINE *(number)*
(specifics of the occurrence, such as variable name and value)
!!!MONITOR *(variable name)* = *(value)*, PROGRAM *(name)*, LINE *(number)*

Postexecution Outputs

***ASSERTION *(kind)* SUMMARY, PROGRAM *(name)*, LINE *(number)*
(number) VIOLATIONS, *(number)* OK
***ASSERTION TOTALS FOR THIS RUN-
(number) VIOLATIONS, *(number)* OK

REFERENCES

MILI87—"On the Use of Executable Assertions in Structured Programs," *Journal of Systems and Software,* March 1987; Ali Mili, Sihem Guemara, Ali Jaoua, and Paul Torres. *Proposes a mathematical formalism on the use of executable assertions.*

STUCKI75—"New Assertion Concepts for Self Metric Software Validation," *Proceedings of the 1975 IEEE International Conference on Reliable Software;* Stucki and Foshee. *Describes a specific executable assertion processor. Shows examples of assertions embedded in Fortran programs with resulting output. The classic paper on executable assertions.*

2.5.2.1.3 Intentional Failure

Intentional failure covers a pair of different processes that involve intentionally inserting errors into a program. At first thought, the idea probably sounds absurd since it is hard enough to rid a program of errors, let alone add additional ones deliberately!

There is, however, some method in this madness. There are a couple of hard problems in software testing, and intentional failure is used to help solve these problems:

1. What is the total number of errors in this program? (If we had the answer to that question, we would know roughly how long to continue testing.)
2. How effective is the set of test cases we are using? (If we had the answer to that question, we would know whether we needed to define additional test cases, or perhaps even eliminate some of those being used.)

Two different intentional failure approaches used to seek answers to those questions are *error seeding* and *mutation analysis*.

2.5.2.1.3.1 Error Seeding

Knowing how many errors are in a program is somewhat akin to knowing how many fish are in a lake. The answer is invisible and no amount of peering into the lake (or the program) is likely to find an answer.

In the case of the fish problem, sampling techniques have been devised to try to answer the question. A known number of fish is tagged and intentionally placed in the lake (the lake is said to be "seeded"). Then as fish are caught, the ratio of tagged to nontagged is kept, and the total of nontagged fish can be calculated by

$$\text{nontagged fish in lake} = \frac{\text{tagged fish inserted (known)}}{\text{ratio tagged to nontagged caught}}$$

It is handy for fisheries people that (1) fish in a lake randomly distribute themselves, and (2) since there is no other effective counting system, answers obtained in this way cannot be challenged.

There is a problem with software error seeding, however. Errors in the software "lake" are not distributed randomly, and at the end of testing people do know how many errors were in the software. The first problem especially has been enough to keep error seeding from being used in practice. That is, to be effective, intentionally inserted errors should be of the same kind and distributed in the same way as the other errors in the software. But in general we do not know types and distributions of existing errors. Should we insert errors that

- modify loop variables?
- change initial value settings?
- modify a term in an equation?
- sort in reverse order?

The opportunities for error insertion are unlimited (and, when seriously contemplated, awesome!). The method of choosing is simply unknowable.

One serious attempt to overcome this problem was undertaken about a decade ago by a federal government agency pursuing error profiles for the particular application domain of flight control software. The agency purchased from flight-control software-producing companies data on known errors, intending to construct profiles of representative errors to be used by error seeders for that application. The effort bogged down in details, however, and as far as the author knows it was never completed.

REFERENCES

GILB77—*Software Metrics*, pages 26–49, Winthrop, 1977; Tom Gilb. *Describes bebugging, the author's term for error seeding. Analyzes approaches to use, including automation techniques.*

2.5.2.1.3.2 Mutation Analysis

Mutation analysis is similar to intentional failure in the way it is employed, but the goals are radically different. Mutation analysis involves deliberately introducing errors into the software product also, but the goal in this case is to measure the effectiveness of the test cases.

N versions of a software product are constructed, each with some small deliberately introduced error in it. These versions are called mutations, for obvious reasons. Now all N program versions are executed against the standard set of test cases. If the test case results for each mutant are not different from the standard test case results, then the test cases are considered inadequate to test at least for the mutation introduced into the program.

As with intentional failure, little use is known of this technology and it is not considered a promising one.

REFERENCES

DEMILLO79—"Program Mutation: A New Approach to Program Testing," *Infotech State-of-the-Art Report on Software Testing,* Infotech/SRA, 1979; DeMillo, Lipton, and Sayward. *Describes the initial work on, and motivation for, mutation testing.*

2.5.2.1.4 Performance Analysis

Most of the checkout activities described in this section of the book have to do with error removal. However, as we have already seen, the pursuit of quality software is far broader in concern than just removing errors.

Efficiency is an important attribute of quality software, sometimes *the* most important attribute. There are ways, during the checkout of software, to determine the efficiency of the software, and to do something about it if the software is not efficient enough.

The collection of techniques for doing this is known as performance analysis, which can vary from the extremely simple to the extremely complex. At its simplest, performance analysis is a matter of manually instrumenting a program in order to determine where it is spending its time. All that is needed is a routine which interrogates the computer's clock and another which subtracts a prior clock reading from the current reading.

Upon entry to a section of code whose efficiency is to be explored, the clock routine is called and the reading saved. Upon exit another routine is called which rereads the clock, subtracts the entry clock reading from it, and adds the incremental time spent to a running total for that section of code.

At the conclusion of the performance analysis run, the running totals for the program sections undergoing analysis are printed and the results analyzed. Sections where a lot of time is spent become candidates for optimization. Optimizations might include redoing the underlying algorithm to make it faster, revising the code to utilize known compiler features which are more efficient, or using in-line or subroutine assembly code for that function.

At its most complex, performance analysis is the use of off-the-shelf software and/or hardware monitors which run at the operating system level and develop an execution time profile of the job(s) running over a period of time in a computer system. These monitors may be helpful in analyzing single program behavior but are usually more useful in exploring system-level problems, such as bottlenecks, configuration inadequacies, poor data set placement, and time and space hogging programs.

Performance analyzers are essential in an efficiency-concerned environment. However, there are hazards connected with their use. The method of performing the analysis often interferes with the performance being analyzed. For example, in the simple system just described, suppose the interrogation of the system clock takes a significant amount of time, say the same length of time as one or two entries to the code section being measured. Then the data gathered in this way are perturbed by the time it takes to read the clock, and data which seem to show that one section of code is very inefficient may simply be showing that the reading of the clock dominated the measurement.

An analogous problem exists with the more complicated measurement systems. The performance analysis tool itself uses resources, and the consumption of those resources may affect the measurements being taken. Also, the *installation* of a monitor perturbs the resources, for example, the use of a software monitor may require operating system modifications to make it work.

Performance analysis, then, is a vital function, but one which must be performed carefully by knowledgeable people.

REFERENCES

The periodical *EDP Performance Review* is published monthly by Applied Computer Research, P.O. Box 9280, Phoenix AZ 85068. *It reports on performance concerns and solutions, and publishes an annual survey of performance-related software packages.*

2.5.2.2 *Dynamic test case approaches*

All of the techniques of the previous section had to do with modifying the program source code in order to do better and more efficient testing. The modifications were sometimes debugging statements, sometimes assertions, sometimes the intentional introduction of errors, and sometimes the insertion of code for analyzing software performance.

No matter what the code modification involved, the modification itself was useless if it was not followed by execution of the code, that is, the running of one or more test cases. A test case is a set of input data which, when fed into the software, will cause output to be produced which will help the person executing the test case ascertain whether the software performed properly or not.

In this section, we discuss testing and the generation and use of test cases. There are three phases of this activity: the design of the test cases, the execution of the test cases, and the analysis of test case results. Whole books have been devoted to this activity, and the reader who wants a more in-depth treatment of this subject is referred to Glenford Myers's classic, *The Art of Software Testing.*

By far the most complex part of testing is the design of the test cases. It is important, however, that the software tester caught up in the problem of test case design not lose sight of the fact that the test cases must be easily and economically executed and evaluated. Test cases which are easy to construct but hard to execute or analyze merely defer the complex problem from test case design to a later stage; they do not solve the problem.

There are two fundamental approaches to the design of test cases: requirements-driven testing and structure-driven testing. There are additional approaches which may be used under particular circumstances, such as statistics-driven testing and risk-driven testing. Because each of these approaches seeks to achieve a goal, for example, the testing of all of the requirements or all of the structure, we refer to these approaches as *goal-driven testing*.

Each of these approaches must be considered in the context of the phase of the checkout process where they are most useful. The phases are usually identified as unit testing, integration testing, and system testing. We call this context view *phase-driven testing*.

Each of these test case design approaches is covered in more depth in what follows before we move on to discuss tools and techniques for test case construction and execution.

REFERENCES

HOWDEN86—"A Functional Approach to Program Testing and Analysis," *IEEE Transactions on Software Engineering,* October 1986; William Howden. *Proposes a theory of testing which considers and ties together the functional approaches to testing discussed in what follows.*

LUTZ90—"Testing Tools," *IEEE Software,* May 1990; Mike Lutz. *Surveys a set of research-developed test tools.*

MYERS79—*The Art of Software Testing,* Wiley-Interscience, 1979; Glenford Myers. *The classic textbook on testing from which much of the following material evolved. This book is must reading for the quality concerned software developer.*

2.5.2.2.1 Requirements-Driven Testing

Any software product consists of many artifacts—documents of several kinds (e.g., requirements specifications, user manuals), and code of several kinds (e.g., source, object). Test case approaches tend to focus on those artifacts.

Requirements-driven testing is software testing based on the requirements artifacts. The purpose of requirements-driven testing is to determine whether the source behaves as those artifacts say it should. Most commonly, requirements-driven testing is conducted against the requirements specification. But since the user manual is an expression of the requirements solution to the user of the software, the user manual also often plays an important role in requirements-driven testing.

The act of designing requirements-driven tests is the act of looking at each requirement in the spec (and/or statement in the user manual), and designing a test which, if it executes successfully, will demonstrate that the requirement is met.

Note that requirements-driven testing does not require that the test case designer know anything about the internal structure of the software. Test cases may be designed by looking only at textual documents. For this reason, requirements-driven testing is often called *black-box testing,* since the software internal structure is unimportant to, and unseen by, the tester, a "black" (visually impenetrable) box.

One of the important things about this kind of testing is that although the testing *may* be performed by the software developers, it need not be. No special software skills are required of the black-box test case designer. Often these test cases are designed by the users themselves, user representatives, a separate testing organization, or a quality assurance organization.

Also important about this kind of testing is that it is the minimum required level of testing. Test case design is always an exercise in trade-offs between testing quality and testing economy. There is simply not enough time or money to do a completely thorough job of testing software. And the art of software testing is not only the art of choosing an appropriate set of test cases, it is the art of knowing how many to execute and analyze, and when to stop doing so.

Requirements-driven testing is the minimum required level of testing because (1) it is the surest way of determining that the software does what it is required to do by its user, and (2) achieving thorough requirements-driven testing is more economically viable than its alternatives.

However, the requirements-driven test case designer must still exercise caution to avoid creating an infinite number of test cases. Since test case data consist of sets of input data, and since typically the range of values of even one input variable may be nearly infinite (even a variable which ranges between 0 and 1 may have a nearly infinite number of floating point representations), the test case designer must exercise selection skills. The sections which follow discuss various ways of selecting from this enormous number of possible requirements-driven test cases.

2.5.2.2.1.1 Equivalence Classes

It is immediately obvious that the test case designer need not test all possible values of a data variable which range between 0 and 1. But how can the tester decide which values to use?

From a problem solution point of view, it is quite likely that all of those values between 0 and 1 will have an equivalent effect upon the solution. That is, running a value of .634 will probably be sufficient to represent all the other possible values in that the solution produced will be produced by the same solution methodology as any of the other values.

The same thing may be said about a set of input values, although it may be harder to be sure that the statement is correct. That is, one set of input data can almost always be used to represent an infinite number of variations of the same data items, in the sense that it exercises one facet of the solution methodology.

And, in fact, the same thing may be said about a set of output values. That is, a test case which produces one set of output values may be equivalent to many other test cases which produce a similar set of output values.

A test case which can serve for many test cases in this sense is said to represent those other test cases, and that set of test cases is said to be an *equivalence class* in the sense that running one test case from the set is equivalent to running any or all of them.

The first step in reducing the infinite number of potential requirements-driven test cases, then, is the establishment of equivalence classes of input and output data.

2.5.2.2.1.2 Cause-Effect Graphing

The establishment of equivalence classes of data is a necessary but by no means sufficient condition for minimizing the required number of test cases.

In fact, the task is still a very hard one because it is so dependent on the nature of the application problem which the software is solving. What kind of application-independent advice is there for the test case designer?

One approach taken by Myers in his previously mentioned book [Myers79] is the notion of causes and effects. Each statement in the requirements specification may be considered from the point of view "Does this *cause* something to happen, or is this an *effect* of some other cause?"

When the specification is considered from this application-independent point of view, it may be divided into a set of causes and a set of effects. This kind of analysis is called *cause-effect graphing*.

Once the set of causes and the set of effects are extracted from the specification, they may be used to drive the construction of a set of cases which will (1) enact all the causes, and (2) produce all of the effects. Here, the previous analysis will be helpful. Representative data from the equivalence classes may be used to enact a particular cause, or produce a particular effect. Thus, we have determined a minimal set of representative data (defined by equivalence class analysis) which will drive all the important functions of the software (derived by cause-effect graphing).

2.5.2.2.1.3 Boundary-Value Tests

The preceding discussion describes an apparently thorough application-independent approach to optimizing the number of test cases required to do requirements-driven testing of a piece of software. Unfortunately, experience has shown that it is not thorough enough!

The approach we have discussed to this point might be called *mainstream testing*. That is, its goal has been to establish a set of test cases which demonstrates the performance of the most important functions of the specification.

However, it is the nature of problem solutions in general and software solutions in particular that the behavior of the solution on the boundaries between these mainstreams may be erratic. That is, executing causes A, C, and F and producing effects L and R may be fairly straightforward, but as the data approach the point where an A-C-F-L-R solution becomes an A-D-F-L-R one, the behavior of the solution may change dramatically. Experience with this problem has shown that it is vitally important to supplement the mainstream testing with what are called *boundary-value tests.* These are test cases which intentionally seek out and exercise the boundaries between the mainstream cases.

As a trivial example, consider the mathematical function of tangent. The tangent of 90 degrees, mathematically, is infinity, and choosing a computer algorithm which can accept a 90-degree angle and find its tangent is a difficult problem. Essentially, 90 degrees is a boundary between the data values immediately less than 90 degrees, and those immediately higher than it (both of which, incidentally, have legitimate and noninfinite values).

The tester of the tangent software must be sure to run a test case value of 90 degrees (note that nothing else is equivalent to this boundary value). But the tester must also run test cases involving values slightly under 90 degrees, and slightly over 90 degrees, to see if the chosen solution performs satisfactorily in those delicate areas.

Similarly, the requirements-driven tester for any software solution must identify the boundary values which lie between mainstream cases, and define cases which test the boundary value(s) explicitly, and test very close to either side of the boundary value(s).

The effect of the requirement to do boundary-value testing is unfortunate. We have gone to a great deal of trouble, using equivalence class and cause-effect analyses, to identify a minimal number of test cases. Now we have an explosion of test cases, something like three for every boundary value, in order to verify the performance of these "between the edges" situations.

This explosion is indeed unfortunate, but it is also necessary. Many software solutions which have failed in practice have done so at a boundary value. Boundary-value cases may come up in production execution of the software only rarely, but when they do it is like probing at the weak point in a hardware device and very often that is where latent trouble lies.

2.5.2.2.1.4 Error Guessing
The first tendency of a software tester is sometimes to guess the likely places for problems, and construct test cases which exercise those areas. The whole point of the preceding discussion has been to define a more

organized approach to this practice on the grounds that error guessing is about as effective as playing hunches when betting on the horses.

However, guessing and using intuition are very similar and yet dramatically different activities. Intuition at its best is the unconscious tapping of a body of knowledge stored away in the human brain and forgotten. The person who intuits a solution may very well be using the best powers that the brain possesses, but he or she may simply not be able to articulate how this capability works.

A test case designer who has considerable experience to draw on in the application area in question may very well supplement the test case approaches discussed previously with some intuitively-defined test cases. Perhaps five years ago, a serious problem developed because the then-current solution methodology neglected consideration "XYZ." The test case designer, who may have forgotten why it is important, may be determined to test particularly thoroughly around "XYZ." That determination could be referred to as *error guessing*. And that determination might very well produce the most error-identifying test cases in the test case set. Error guessing, when based on educated and experienced intuition, is an important supplement to the test case methods already described.

2.5.2.2.2 Structure-Driven Testing

When we began the discussion of requirements-driven testing, we talked about the artifacts which make up a software product. Requirements-driven testing, we learned, was based on the requirements artifacts.

Structure-driven testing, in turn, is based on the code artifacts. Specifically, structure-driven testing is testing based on an understanding of the structure of the software as reflected in its source code. The purpose of structure-driven testing is to determine whether the software behaves not just as the customer expects it to, but as the designer and programmer expect it to.

One question that should arise at this point is "If the software solves the customer's problem, why should we care whether it does what the software people wanted it to?" That, it turns out, is an important question, and its answer gives us insight into the complexities of software.

The requirements specification, which is the basis for the requirements-driven testing, must be a thorough and complete document. But it must also not constrain the software engineer (for example, by specifying how the problem should be solved). As a result, there is much detail left out of a requirements specification, and that level of detail is the business of the designer and the programmer.

As a particular set of requirements is fleshed out into a design solution, a whole new set of requirements emerges and is expressed in the design of the software. For example, if we are going to solve Requirement A by the XYZ technique, then in order to use XYZ we are required to do A.1, A.2, and A.3. These requirements are sometimes called *derived require-*

ments or *implied requirements.* They are not a part of the original requirements for the problem, but they are required techniques necessary to achieve a particular design solution.

Every software solution has these implied requirements and they are generally more numerous and may be more complicated than the original, higher-level requirements. Earlier in this book we mention an implied requirements explosion of a factor measured in the hundreds. Requirements-driven testing, which focuses on the original level of requirements, does not and cannot focus on these requirements as well. Obviously, if the software is to be thoroughly tested, it is necessary to include test cases for these implied requirements.

The manifestation of these implied requirements is that they result in sections of code being introduced into the final software. And the most thorough approach to testing all of these implied requirements is through the structure of the final software product. Testing which examines the structure of the software to construct additional test cases supplementing the requirements-driven cases is called *structure-driven testing.*

The goal of structure-driven testing is to test every structural element of the software. But that is easier said than done. The first question that arises is "What constitutes a structural element?"

One answer might be "every module in the software." That is an important answer, an answer that results in a whole different approach to software testing which we discuss later on, the software *unit test.* This answer is necessary but not sufficient. Modules may contain anywhere from 1 to 1,000 lines of code, and software whose modules have each been tested only once is software which may have many latent errors in it.

Another candidate answer is, "every statement in the software." This is a very appealing answer, because it gets down to the elemental level of the units which make up software, the individual lines of code. But that appeal is deceptive because although it is important to test every statement of a piece of software, even that is not good enough.

Examine the following graph. Even in this simple logic structure, path AC between blocks A and C may not be tested even if every statement of the software is tested, if that test only takes path ABC.

Faced with this somewhat surprising dilemma, most software test theorists advocate *branch testing* or *segment testing,* or the construction of

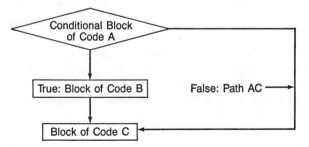

test cases to execute every logic branch in a piece of software. But there is a problem with this approach also.

Even if we test both of the segments in the preceding situation, what if it is immediately followed by a similar structure? Would it be enough to test both segments of the first structure and both segments of the second structure? Or must we test all combinations of the segment choices, which means (in this simple case) not just two test cases, but four?

Both logic and experience tell us that testing each segment is not enough, that many software errors occur because of a particular combination of logic segments. Testing which accommodates all combinations of logic segments is called *path testing*.

Arriving at path testing, although it is obviously very desirable, has painted us into a corner.

Just as input data result in an infinite number of variations on input values, the combinatorics of program paths results in an explosively infinite number of potential test cases. It is simply not possible, for most software of reasonable complexity, to construct enough test cases to test every logic path.

Where are we, so far, with structure-driven testing? We have established that structure-driven testing is necessary. We have defined several levels of structure-driven testing, from module coverage to statement coverage to segment coverage to path coverage. And we have decided that complete path testing is economically infeasible. What is a tester to do?

There is a practical answer to this question. Studies have been conducted which show that most software thought to be adequately tested has been tested at the segment testing level of about 55 percent to 60 percent. In those same studies, cost analyses were conducted on attempting to achieve 100 percent segment testing, and the cost was found to be prohibitive. (Often software contains many exception cases, each with many nuances, where some particular segments are never expected to be executed and are very difficult to formulate test cases to drive them.)

An acceptable compromise was found to be segment coverage at about the 85 percent to 90 percent level. Software which achieves that level of structure-driven testing is likely to be more reliable than today's norm. For some applications, that will be good enough. For others, where lives or enormous dollars depend on correct software function, it will not be. Testing professionals have found that achieving structural testing coverage of higher than 85 percent to 90 percent is often best achieved by thorough static analysis of the untested structure, rather than by forcing test case construction in areas where it is difficult to build the required tests.

The answer to how thorough structure-driven testing must be, then, is an application-specific one. There may be cases where a percentage of path testing, not just segment testing, must be achieved.

Now we have established that structure-driven testing should usually involve executing a high percentage of logic segments and perhaps even paths in a program. How do we do that, and how do we know when we've done it? These, too, are hard questions.

First of all, structure-driven testing is often referred to as white-box testing. Only a software developer is capable of performing this kind of test, because intimate knowledge of the software as represented by its source code is required to construct meaningful test cases. This is the opposite of black-box testing, where the structure of the software could remain opaque to the tester.

Second, it is vitally important to remember that structure-driven testing is a supplement to requirements-driven testing. The first responsibility of the software tester is to evaluate the obvious and visible functions. It is also important to test the structure in order to evaluate conformance to the implied requirements, but this is of secondary importance and should never subsume the first.

There is one other complication that must be dealt with here. We have already mentioned the problem of path testing, where the combinatorics run toward infinity. That is enough to show us that even 100 percent structure-driven testing is not sufficient to find all software errors. There is another similar problem. If logic has been left out of a program, for example, an IF statement including two conditions that should have included three, then no amount of structure-driven testing can detect the error because the appropriate structure is not there to be tested.

Thus, completely thorough structure-driven testing, augmenting completely thorough requirements-driven testing, is still not enough! In fact, a small study conducted by the author over a decade ago suggests that combinatoric and missing logic problems may constitute as much as 75 percent of the errors in some software. That is a depressing finding, indeed; it shows just how bad the problem of thorough testing really is. Nevertheless, we have already seen through practical experience that software solutions to remarkably complex problems have been successful. The warning here should be about overoptimism and not the inadequacy of the testing process.

How can the structure-driven tester construct the necessary test cases? By understanding the conditions which cause every single segment of the program to be executed, and by constructing a test case to satisfy those conditions. This is no small task and requires an impressively thorough understanding of how the software functions. Attempts have been made to automate this process by test case generators which backtrack from a segment and ascertain the conditions which cause it to be accessed, but this is a very hard problem and to date such processors require human guidance to complete their task.

How can the structure-driven tester know what level of segment test coverage has been achieved? One obvious answer is by manual analysis.

Once the effort has been expended to understand a segment and its causative conditions, it is not conceptually much harder to track whether that segment has been tested. But in actual fact, the bookkeeping for this problem is horrendous. Fortunately, tools are available which nicely solve this problem. They are now commonly available commercially, if not commonly in use as yet. This topic is discussed later under the heading "Test Coverage Analyzers."

REFERENCES

NTAFOS88—"A Comparison of Some Structural Testing Strategies," *IEEE Transactions on Software Engineering*, June 1988; Simeon C. Ntafos. *Examines structural testing strategies from the point of view (1) that strategy A includes strategy B, and (2) that strategy A needs more/fewer test cases than strategy B. Finds the latter to be the more useful measure.*

2.5.2.2.3 Other Goal-Driven Testing

Requirements-driven testing and structure-driven testing both focus on testing the software product and are useful no matter what the application, but each has a different viewpoint. There are still other viewpoints which might focus testing efforts. In the sections that follow, we discuss techniques that are not generally useful for all applications but might be applied under certain circumstances. The first, statistics-driven testing, might be used when there is a strong need to demonstrate measurable program correctness to a customer. The second, risk-driven testing, might be used in software with critical reliability requirements, such as software embedded in a system which lives are dependent on.

2.5.2.2.3.1 Statistics-Driven Testing

Both requirements-driven testing and structure-driven testing are necessary and important techniques for detecting and correcting software errors, but there is a problem with them. When the smoke of these kinds of testing clears away, the testers and the customers may have a good qualitative feel for the reliability of the software, but nothing quantitative. That is, confidence will have been built up, especially on the part of the testers, that the software is now in good shape and ready for release, but there is very little they can use to demonstrate that confidence to the customer.

They can, of course, say things like "We have tested 100 percent of the requirements specified in the requirements document," but as we have already seen, that is in fact a fairly weak statement by itself.

They can also say, if they have used a measurable approach to structure-driven testing, "We have tested 87 percent of the logic segments of the program and analyzed manually the other 13 percent," and that is, in fact, a fairly strong statement. Still, the customer who has paid for the software and is waiting to use it might like something stronger, something more understandable, than logic segments, which after all are invisible and not even very comprehensible to the average customer.

One approach to this problem is the independent certifying company, which we discussed in an earlier section of this book. The independent company, by whatever means it chooses, can run a thorough test of the software and pronounce it "usable," perhaps even issuing a "seal of approval." This approach may solve the psychological problems of the customer, but it still begs the technical question "What approach can be used to give a customer a quantitative feel for the testedness of the software?"

What the software customer would really like is an indication that for a typical usage profile the software will tend to run for X productive hours, where X is a large number, before crashing. In the hardware world, this is an MTBF (or mean time between failure) kind of criteria.

As we see later in this book, MTBF presents a problem in the software world. It was invented to describe the hardware situation where we measure time to breakage or wearing out, and of course software does neither of those things. Still, that *is* the criteria that the user of software would like to have a feel for.

Is there a meaningful way that we could define MTBF so that the software customer could get a quantitative feel for its goodness? Research work at IBM [Currit86] has proposed such a technique.

What the IBM paper proposes is what we call *statistics-driven testing*. With this technique, typical usage profiles for the software are developed, using some of the techniques described earlier under requirements-driven testing but focusing on those requirements closest to normal usage of the software.

Using those typical usage profiles, specific test cases are selected randomly, executed, analyzed, and a record is kept of how long the software has run successfully before an error is detected.

Later in this book we discuss *how* test cases may be randomly generated. In this context, it is sufficient to say that it is fairly easily accomplished, and thus this technique does not put a technical strain on the state of the software art or practice. Some IBM authors [Mills86] base a testing methodology on this approach and call it *cleanroom testing* because it emphasizes error prevention rather than error correction.

Currit [86] cautions about this technique, saying "a certain amount of selective testing may still be prudent." (By selective testing, the authors mean the nonrandom kinds of testing we have already discussed in this book.)

That statement is by no means strong enough. The job of the software tester is to conduct a thorough examination of its reliability, poking not just into the mainstream but into all the murky and dangerous nooks and crannies. Only after that job has been completed to some level of qualitative satisfaction should the job of quantitatively satisfying the customer begin.

The IBM report also cautions that "at first glance, statistical testing may seem too inefficient compared to selective testing." The execution and analysis of randomly generated test cases have usually been avoided by traditional testers on the grounds that a rifle-shot approach to test case design requires fewer test cases and thus less cost than what appears to be a shotgun approach. This caution is also warranted, but with the added thought that the purpose of this testing is really to inform the customer, not to do thorough testing, and the acceptable cost of informing the customer must be decided on an application-by-application basis.

REFERENCES

CURRIT86—"Certifying the Reliability of Software," *IEEE Transactions on Software Engineering*, January 1986; Currit, Dyer, and Mills. *Describes and advocates the statistics-driven testing development performed at IBM Federal Systems Division.*

DURAN84—"An Evaluation of Random Testing," *IEEE Transactions on Software Engineering*, July 1984; Duran and Ntafos. *Reports on simulation results which tend to show that random testing may be more cost effective than partition testing approaches.*

MILLS86—"Structured Programming: Retrospect and Prospect," *IEEE Software*, November 1986; Mills. *The first in a proposed series of papers about "Fundamental Concepts in Software Engineering," this paper presents Harlan Mills's view of the history of structured programming and discusses its successes and failures. As part of the paper, Mills discusses his cleanroom approach to testing.*

2.5.2.2.3.2 Risk-Driven Testing

There are many reasons why the proper execution of a software system might be termed critical, but the most common are lives and money. Software which falls into this critical category must use many more quality techniques than software which does not.

One technique that has been explored in the aerospace and nuclear fields is a testing approach called risk-driven testing, based on risk-assessment technology. Using this approach, the software or systems analyst must look at the system from a new point of view, asking "What are the worst things that can go wrong?" There is a fairly well-defined chronology to this technique:

- Determine the most important events in your system.
- Identify any faults that might interfere with the occurrence of those events. Generally, this results in a so-called *fault tree,* where some faults on the tree might directly cause a high-level failure, but other faults might cause a failure in a subordinate component which in turn might cause a high-level failure.

- Identify the software components or paths or even segments associated with those potential faults.
- Identify the data that can cause those software portions to be executed.
- Build a thorough set of test cases to explore those input cases.

In a sense, this approach is structure-driven testing with a new emphasis. We are not trying to test all of the structure, but rather that structure which is critical to the success of the system.

REFERENCES

FRYER85—"Risk Assessment of Computer Controlled Systems," *IEEE Transactions on Software Engineering,* January 1985; Fryer. *Discusses the risk-assessment approach used at EG&G in Idaho Falls for critical systems in the nuclear field.*

LEVESON86—"Software Safety: Why, What and How," *Computing Surveys,* June 1986; Leveson. *Distinguishes between reliability, security, and safety. Assesses ways of achieving and assessing safety. Defines safety in terms of hazardous system states, and risk as the probability of a hazardous state occurring.*

2.5.2.2.4 Phase-Driven Testing

What we have seen so far in this discussion of dynamic test case approaches is that there must be a mix of driving factors behind the selection of test cases. This mix of requirements, structure, statistics, and risk forms the "what" of the test case process. Another important factor in this process is the "when."

Testing is not a single-step process. There is not a point in time where someone says "Now I will run all those requirements-driven, structure-driven, statistics-driven and risk-driven test cases." Instead, the testing process tends to happen in parallel with the coding process. Some code is built, it is tested in some way, and then additional code is built and tested.

This multistep process is what we call *phase-driven testing.* The nature of the testing changes as the software product nears completion. The initial testing in this process, where software components are coded and tested individually, is normally called *unit testing.* As the product components are combined into a software whole, the testing process becomes one of *integration testing* that whole. And, for complex systems where the software is part of a larger system, such as on-board software in a commercial airliner, the software must be tested in that larger context in *system testing.*

In the next three sections, we explore each of these phase-driven testing processes in turn. But before we do, it is important to consider one other overriding factor.

The phase-driven testing process we have described here is often called *bottom-up testing* because the bottom of the software hierarchy, the modules or components or units, are tested first. This approach is taken because it is useful to have well-tested components before the integration process occurs, so that the only errors that remain, it is to be hoped, are at the interfaces of the components. (This is of course often not true. The integration process often surfaces many component errors which unit testing did not detect, but at least the incidence of this kind of problem is minimized by thorough unit testing, and the integration tester can concentrate on the component boundaries rather than their contents.)

An alternative to bottom-up testing is *top-down testing*. As its name implies it is the process of conducting integrated testing of the software from the very beginning of the testing process, bypassing a unit-testing phase. At first thought this may seem a very impractical testing strategy, since the components being integrated will have many bugs in them and the error isolation process will be very complex. But along with this idea of integrating first goes a new definition of integration. With this definition, what is being integrated is a skeletal framework for the top-level logic of the software, a cohesive set of units, and some extra (throwaway) code built only to permit the testing process to proceed.

With top-down testing, then, the integration process is continuous. The top-level framework is built, then a set of components is added to the framework. The throwaway code segments are then put into place. (These are usually called stubs, in that they are stub ends representing more complete code which will be provided later in this evolving integration process.) With this integrated whole, test cases are run, and errors are removed from the code elements present. Next, another set of modules is added to this whole. The necessary stubs for testing these are added, old stubs replaced by new modules are discarded, and the testing begins again. This iterative process is followed until the whole software product is in one well-tested piece.

The advantage of this approach is that there is no single, massive integration test, where everything finally comes together. That is a distinct advantage, because the first stages of integration testing are usually painful for the testers of a large software system. All the miscommunications and errors of the many preceding development months are suddenly barriers to getting that first integration test to execute successfully, and there are difficult technical, political, and social problems to identifying and removing those errors. By finding those errors on an ongoing basis, top-down testing eliminates these problems. The phrase sometimes used for the integration testing that follows a bottom-up process, *big-bang testing,* gives a nice visual image of the problem with that approach.

We have seen that bottom-up and top-down testing each have their advantages. In practice, a mix of the two is often used. Vital modules are often tested first in bottom-up fashion before being placed in the integrated whole in order to eliminate critical errors from the error discovery process. Then the testing proceeds top-down, with the addition of other components and their stubs. This approach tends to yield the best of both worlds. Some authors refer to this approach as *sandwich testing*.

Let us return now with this new insight to a consideration of phase-driven testing.

2.5.2.2.4.1 Unit Testing

Unit testing, we have already seen, is testing done with individual components of software. In order to conduct this kind of testing, an input-output framework must be added to the component (unless it already has one) so that sample input data can be fed to the component, and the resulting output can be examined. This framework is commonly called a *test driver*. (The test driver, like the stub we discussed earlier in top-down testing, is throwaway code that is not useful when the final software integration process is completed. However, it may be useful to keep some of these test drivers for later integration testing or maintenance activity, since it will be necessary to retest the component if it must be changed).

The test driver and the component under test now constitute a tiny program and may be tested like any other program. Test cases are selected to try to force the occurrence of errors. The results of the test run are analyzed to see if any errors have occurred, and a debugging process is undertaken if errors have been discovered. (Software errors are commonly called bugs, and debugging is the process of removing them. One hardware vendor named its debugging package DDT after a bug-killing chemical to symbolize this process!)

Now, looking back to the previous section, are the unit test cases typically requirements driven, structure driven, statistics driven, or risk driven? The answer is related to the purpose of the process.

The goal of unit testing is to remove *all* of the errors from the component under test. The most thorough way to accomplish this is to begin by testing the requirements for the component, which usually include only a tiny subset of the requirements for the whole software product and are thus easily tested, and to move swiftly into structure-driven testing. Structure-driven testing represents the bulk of the time spent in unit testing, and of course it is subject to all the limitations we discussed in the previous sections.

Statistics-driven testing is really not meaningful at this stage, since during unit testing there is no final product to examine. Risk-driven testing may or may not be meaningful.

Recall that unit testing is meaningful in the bottom-up and sandwich testing practices, but less meaningful in the top-down process. However, the early top-down tests are in some sense unit tests, since they are testing a rather small part of the integrated software whole, and so the principles we have discussed here apply to early top-down unit tests as well.

2.5.2.2.4.2 Integration Testing

Once the components have been tested, they are put together to begin the integration testing. This may be a very small number of components in top-down or sandwich testing, or it may be all of the software components in bottom-up testing.

Whereas unit testing is always done by the software development team, it is often true that a new testing team is responsible for integration testing, especially on very large software systems. This integration test team will be responsible for seeking errors, but the responsibility for fixing them will usually continue to rest with the developer responsible for that component.

The technical problems of integration testing, we have already mentioned, are heavily mixed with political and social problems at this phase of the testing process, and it very well may be that a different set of technical and psychological skills is needed to accomplish integration testing. Often during integration an error will occur on the interface between two supposedly thoroughly tested components, and neither software developer will be happy being responsible for the error. The process of each developer believing that the other must fix the error is commonly known as finger pointing, and it sometimes leads to social unpleasantness. It takes a mix of drive and tact on the part of the integration tester to get the problem resolved and the error corrected.

The closer we get to the completed software product, the more the focus shifts from structure testing to requirements testing. During integration testing, structure considerations are important, but the level of structure analyzed has usually shifted to the module level. We are less interested here in testing software paths and segments than we are in testing modules, because the path and/or segment testing has presumably already been done at the unit-test level. But it is important that integration testing be sufficiently structure driven that all modules and many combinations of the modules are tested.

When the module-structure testing is completed, the requirements testing can begin. This may seem backward from our previous discussions, where we said that requirements testing is a minimal level of testing, and that structure testing must supplement it at some percentage level. What is happening here is that we are doing the more rigorous and expensive testing first, and the most vital testing last. The order may seem backward, but it is born of necessity. That necessity, of course, adds to the complexity of knowing when to consider the structural testing sufficient, in order to conclude it while there is still time for the vital requirements testing process.

Statistics testing, if it is to occur at all, must happen after all of the intended requirements and structure testing have been completed. Gathering statistics on a product which is still undergoing frequent change resulting from debugging processes is not very fruitful.

2.5.2.2.4.3 System Testing

Recall that system testing may need to occur if the integrated software product is to be part of a larger system. In one sense, system testing is very much like a huge integration test, where the components are integrated wholes, but not necessarily software wholes.

System testing is almost always conducted by an interdisciplinary group, since the finger pointing which may occur will involve not just software developers but developers of the other components of the system.

The principals of system testing are much like those for integration testing. The system tester seeks errors, the component developers repair them, and the system tester resolves the political and social disagreements which may arise.

Because of the nature of systems, there are many variations of system testing. The different types which follow tend to be independent of the application of the system, but obviously more system-dependent tests would need to be added for particular applications.

Facility tests. The software runs in some kind of facility, perhaps with one or more kinds of computer hardware and other system devices. It is vital to test that the software runs successfully in its intended facility environment.

Data volume tests. The software may nominally expect to service X transactions of size X1, but the range of legitimate quantities of transactions may vary from quantity L size L1–L2 to quantity U size U1–U2. The system must be tested over the whole spectrum of allowable quantities and sizes. If the software is going to choke under heavy usage, it may need serious redesign and it is vital to discover this as early in the implementation process as possible. Sometimes data volume testing will be simulated early in system development in order to prevent this problem from occurring too late to be fixed. Some software products have failed and software companies gone bankrupt because they failed to address this problem adequately.

Stress tests. It is not just the volume of information a system may process which will tax it, it is the rate of arrival of that volume as well. All of the statements made previously about volume testing also apply to stress testing. Performing stress testing is often expensive because people or components sufficient to flood the system with data will be necessary. For example, if the system under test services terminals and was designed nominally for 50 but may occasionally need to service as many as 250, it will be necessary to fire up 250 terminals and run them at high volumes to see whether the system is up to the challenge.

Usability tests. Software developers and systems engineers are one breed of people, and users are another. What seems like a perfectly acceptable user interface to the former group may be a total failure to the latter. Representative users must test and critique the system from a usability point of view. The smart system developer will have been working on this problem since the inception of the system; it is inexcusable to surface major usability problems during the final stages of system testing.

Security testing. The system may be responsible for information which must be protected. If so, the protection and security features require specific testing to ensure that they are working.

Performance testing. Normally the requirements for the system will have specified acceptable performance bounds. For example, "the system will be able to process up to X transactions in Y time units." It is important to verify that these performance requirements have been met. In some performance-critical systems, such as those which perform in real time, performance testing may need to be simulated early in the system development process in order to ensure that the system design will satisfy the performance requirements. A design approach which satisfies all other requirements may still be a failure if it does not satisfy the performance requirements.

Storage use testing. This kind of testing is analogous to performance testing except that performance testing deals with time, and storage use testing deals with space. What is at stake here is whether the system is going to fit the main and auxiliary storage capacities of the facility designed for it. Everything previously said about the importance of performance testing applies in an analogous way to storage use testing.

Configuration testing. Not only must the system run on its defined facility within performance and storage use bounds, but it must run on a particular configuration of that facility. For example, perhaps nominally the system expects disk capacity of X bytes, but it is supposed to be capable of running at a reduced level of functionality if only Y bytes are available. Or perhaps the system is designed to run on computers made by brands X, Y, and Z, and this testing must be conducted on all three of those computers, appropriately configured.

Compatibility testing. Often a system is released to its customer in versions, where a new version may have the same functionality as the old version but with some errors corrected and/or some capabilities added. It is vitally important, before the new version replaces the old, that testing be run to ensure that it is at least as good as and compatible with the old version.

Instability testing. A system should be able to survive and continue to operate even if a user does nonsensical things to it. Part of the system testing process should be the execution of tests deliberately chosen to try to make the system lose stability.

Reliability testing. Earlier in this material, we introduced the notion of MTBF (mean time between failure). For most systems, there is requirement that it be reliable in a measurable way, such as achieving an MTBF goal. Reliability testing is necessary to demonstrate conformance to that requirement. For critical systems, risk-driven testing must take place here as well.

Recovery testing. If a system is unable to continue because of a problem which has arisen, it is important that it be possible to return the system to a useful state as painlessly as possible. Whatever that recovery process is, it is important that it be explicitly tested. This usually means inducing or simulating a failure in the system in order to commence the testing of the recovery process.

Serviceability testing. In some sense, all systems have a need to be serviced on a scheduled or demand basis. For example, a car needs oil changes, and a software system needs maintenance for an error which has been detected. The variety of meanings of serviceability testing is enormous, but whatever meaning it has to a particular system, testing for this ability should be included in the test process. Notice that for a software system that may well include maintainability, a difficult but important thing for a software system to have.

Documentation. Just as a software system is not complete without some kinds of documentation, a more general system must also be accompanied by its documentation. Part of the testing process is assuring that this documentation is necessary and sufficient.

Procedure testing. The system may need to be used in particular ways. If so, it is important that the testing process be conducted according to those recommended procedures, both as mainstream tests (using the specified procedures) and as exception tests (violating the specified procedures to check system stability).

2.5.2.2.5 Test Method Packaging
For the most part in this book, we deal not with packaged methodological approaches to software engineering, but rather with the disaggregation of those packages. For example, when we talk about structured programming, we deal with its several components separately. For example, top-down design was one topic, and structured coding was another, and so on. The reason for doing that is that methodologies are sometimes sold more on sizzle than on substance, and disaggregating the capabilities gets us down to the level of what technology they really employ.

In this discussion, we make an exception to that policy. The several sections prior to this one have presented a collection of ideas on testing that together form an integrated approach. It is the purpose of this section to summarize those ideas to help make them clearer, and to contrast that set of ideas with a different emerging methodology called *cleanroom*.

2.5.2.2.5.1 The Best of Traditional

The testing approaches discussed in previous sections look at both a goal-driven and a phase-driven approach. It is important to package these ideas because it is not obvious which goal-driven approach should be employed in which phase.

Let us examine this issue chronologically. How many of the four goal-driven approaches do we employ in unit testing? In integration testing? In systems testing?

Looking at unit testing first (or its top-down testing equivalent, testing the rudimentary system structure with many stubs in place), this is our chance to wring the errors out of the most detailed level of the software. Here is where structure-driven testing should play its strongest role. For each unit under test, at least 60 percent of the structure at the segment level, and perhaps as much as of 85 percent to 95 percent, should be demonstrably exercised. (The percentage reached should depend on the criticality of the system.) In addition, all of the requirements for that particular unit should be tested. The requirements for a unit may include some explicit (customer-defined) requirements, but will quite likely also include derived requirements that have emerged from the design solution.

What about statistical testing and risk-driven testing? At the level of unit testing, statistical testing does not make much sense. It would be possible to randomly generate test cases focusing on the function of a particular unit, but the result would not help the customer understand the testedness of the system because units are beneath the level of the typical customer's visibility.

But risk-driven testing at the unit level, for those applications where risk-driven testing is being employed, *does* make sense. If the unit under test is particularly critical to the successful functioning of the total system, then extra testing of that unit is called for.

Thus, in unit testing we have the following:

- *Requirements-driven testing:* Test 100 percent of the unit's explicit and derived requirements.
- *Structure-driven testing:* Test 65 percent to 95 percent (depending on criticality of the application) of the unit's segments (branches).
- *Statistical testing:* Does not apply.
- *Risk-driven testing:* Yes, if the unit is a critical part of a critical application.

Now let us look at integration testing (or its top-down equivalent, the latter stages of testing, where most of the pieces have been fit into the overall structure). By now, the structure of the individual components should be pretty well tested at the segment or branch level. At this point, it is important to exercise all of the modules being integrated, but not to repeat all the detail-level structure testing. Structure-driven testing at the integration test level, then, should focus on exercising all of the modules being integrated, not all of the segments of all of the modules. It is not unreasonable to expect 100 percent of those modules to be exercised at this point, and perhaps even all invocations of all modules. Only in this way, for example, can we verify that all module interfaces match.

In addition, all requirements should be tested at this point. It is our first real opportunity to begin a thorough examination of the explicit requirements in an environment where we can really get a customer-oriented view of the result of executing the product.

Statistics-driven testing? Once again, that would be premature. We want to measure the product statistically in its final form (if at all).

Risk-driven testing? Once again, the answer is yes, focusing on critical portions of the integrated whole.

Thus, far integration testing we have the following:

- *Requirements-driven testing:* 100 percent of explicit requirements.
- *Structure-driven testing:* 100 percent of modules.
- *Statistical testing:* Does not apply.
- *Risk-driven testing:* Yes, for critical components of a critical system.

Finally, we arrive at system testing; the entire software product embedded in the final system product is undergoing test. It is time now to focus on the customer-oriented view. Full requirements-driven testing is essential. Statistical testing, if it is employed, should be done at a level that will convince the customer that the product is ready for use, typically somewhere between 90 percent to 100 percent.

Structure-driven testing is still an important concept here, but it means all the pieces of the product puzzle, not just the software. Every component should be exercised. Again, it must at least be verified that component interfaces match.

And risk-driven testing is at its most visible here. Correct performance of the product while handling high-risk situations is a must.

Thus, in system testing we have:

- *Requirements-driven testing:* 100 percent
- *Structure-driven testing:* 100 percent of system components

Phase Goal	Unit	Integration	System
Requirements- driven	100% unit requirements	100% product requirements	100% system requirements
Structure- driven	60–95% segment (branch)	100% modules	100% components
Statistics- driven	—	—	90–100% if required
Risk-driven	As required	As required	100% if required

Figure 2.10   Test method packaging.

- *Statistical testing:* 90 percent to 100 percent
- *Risk-driven testing:* 100 percent of risk areas

Figure 2.10 summarizes this discussion.

2.5.2.2.5.2 Cleanroom

The testing method described in the previous section is based on optimal use of traditional approaches. From a customer's point of view, the software developers play a key role as they do all of the unit testing, perhaps some or all of the integration testing, and sometimes some or all of the system testing. (On large and/or critical projects, test responsibility phases away from the developers and toward system test groups as we move through the process.)

Another philosophy and methodology of testing has emerged in recent years. The cleanroom philosophy, developed at IBM (Federal Systems Division, where government contract software is built), takes an entirely different people view.

In the cleanroom methodology, deliberate separation of the software developers from the testing process is employed. (That is why the approach is called *cleanroom*. The analogy is to scientific activities where humans must not be allowed to contaminate an ongoing process.) The assumption is that disinterested parties are more likely to seek and find errors than those whose reputation may be based on not having made any!

With that in mind, cleanroom employs essentially three error-removal processes:

1. The software developers use formal verification (proof of correctness) to seek and find all errors prior to testing.
2. At the beginning of testing, the software is removed from the developers and given to a separate (product test) organization.
3. Testing is entirely statistical.

At first thought, the methodology seems radical. Remove the developers from testing? Insist that developers use formal verification? Rely only on statistical testing? These practices are so far from current approaches as to be considered radical.

But experimental findings are beginning to appear in the literature suggesting dramatic advantages to cleanroom. Perhaps the most exciting to date finds that over 90 percent of software errors can be eliminated before testing is even begun. This is a strong argument for the use of formal verification practices by software developers. (Note, however, that is says virtually nothing about the merits of separate testing and statistical testing. Few errors are left to be removed using that approach.)

Further analysis of these findings, however, raises additional questions. Although some experiments employed formal verification, in one key experiment [Kouchakdjian89] the experimenters substituted rigorous inspection techniques (i.e., peer code review) for formal verification, and also achieved 91 percent error elimination prior to testing. Thus, it would appear that the most important element of the cleanroom process might be the expectation that developers will remove errors by rigorous, nontesting approaches, rather than specifically using formal verification.

There is another important issue to be dealt with. Randomized (statistical) approaches to testing have been around for a long time. The practitioner community has usually rejected them for these good reasons:

1. In any software application, there are anticipated weak spots in the software product [Grams87]. It is important to focus testing on those weak spots. Traditional testing, especially that employing boundary-value testing and error guessing, has been like firing a rifle at these weak spots. Statistical testing is more analogous to firing a shotgun and hoping that if there is enough shot present it will hit the weak spots.
2. An important part of testing is analysis of test case results for correctness. Using traditional testing approaches, the tester controls the test input and thus can anticipate what correct output will be. Using statistical approaches, since the computer generates the test cases, it is not possible to anticipate the final results. This will strongly drive test result analysis costs up. (Note that for regression testing during maintenance, a standard set of randomly generated test cases could be reemployed, thus alleviating this problem for repeated testing.)

	Thoroughness	Cost	Other
Traditional	Requirements, structural testing like rifle	Probably cheaper	Developer confidence
Cleanroom	Formal verification; very thorough Statistical testing like shotgun; depends on profiles chosen	Formal verification tedious; review less costly! Test result analysis costly	Claims of nearly error-free software; user confidence

Figure 2.11 Testing method packaging comparison.

The issues at stake here are important. Optimal testing approaches are vital to the process of building quality software. The alert software developer will continue to watch this arena for further developments.

Figure 2.11 summarizes the differences between traditional and cleanroom approaches.

REFERENCES

GRAMS87—"Biased Programming Faults—How to Overcome Them," pages 13–23, *Proceedings of the Third International Conference on Fault-Tolerant Computing Systems,* Bremerhaven, September 1987, Springer-Verlag; Timm Grams. *Discusses "biased" faults, those which several software developers working independently might create.*

KOUCHAKDJIAN89—"Evaluation of the Cleanroom Methodology in the SEL," *Proceedings of the Fourteenth Annual Software Engineering Workshop,* NASA-Goddard, November 1989; Ara Kouchakdjian and Vic Basili. *Used a modified cleanroom process in an experiment on a real project using real software developers; found many advantages to the approach, including 91 percent error removal prior to testing. But substituted rigorous inspection approaches for formal verification.*

MILLS87—"Cleanroom Software Engineering," *IEEE Software,* September 1987; Harlan D. Mills, Michael Dyer, and Richard Linger. *The definitive article about cleanroom by its originators. Found that "human verification, even though fallible, could replace debugging in software development" and "human verification is surprisingly synergistic with statistical testing."*

SELBY87—"Cleanroom Software Development: An Empirical Evaluation," *IEEE Transactions on Software Engineering,* September 1987; Richard W. Selby, Victor R. Basili, and F. Terry Baker. *Reports on an experiment using student software developers to develop 800 to 2,300 lines of software in which productivity and quality were improved by cleanroom even among first-time users.*

2.5.2.2.6 Test Coverage Analyzer

One thread left dangling in an earlier section of this book is how to measure the success of structure-driven testing.[3] It was stated that there are now commercially available tools to help provide this measurement. We discuss the concept of those tools here.

Most of the material on structure-driven testing assumes that it is the logic structure of the program that is the basis for the testing and the measurement. Accordingly, the first section that follows deals with that issue.

Because of the prevalence of many systems designed from a data rather than a functional point of view, there has come to be interest in a data-oriented version of structural testing. For the most part, that interest remains at the research level; little use has been made of data test coverage analysis in practice. Nevertheless, we include a discussion of the data-oriented approach to test coverage analysis immediately after the logic-oriented discussion.

2.5.2.2.6.1 Logic

When a program is undergoing structure-driven testing, it is important to know which portions of the program logic have been tested and which have not. A tool that performs the measurement of this information is called the *test coverage analyzer.*

A test coverage analyzer is a computer program which, when applied to another computer program (the subject program), provides for counting each occurrence of the execution of each logic segment of the subject program.

To perform this task, the analyzer program must examine the subject program and divide it into structural members small enough to make the analysis worthwhile and yet large enough to avoid inundating the subject programmer with data. Typically, this division is at the level of logic branches. The code between any two such branch points may be called a decision-to-decision segment; each logic branch in a program causes two or more such segments to begin. A logic branch is a statement such as GOTO, IF, or CASE which causes program flow to divert from the normal sequential process.

Having dissected a program into segments, the analyzer then instruments each one. Instrumentation in this case is the process of adding code to the subject program which provides for tallying each instance of execution of that segment. Those tallies will be recorded (as the program executes) in a small database which the analyzer must also append to the

---

[3] Note that requirements-driven testing success can be measured manually by use of a "requirements/test case matrix," as discussed later.

subject program. At the conclusion of execution, the database must be printed out. An analyzer postprocessor program provides this capability.

Thus, the analyzer is actually a kind of superstructure in which test runs are embedded. The subject program is instrumented by it, its database records the desired information, and its postprocessor operates after the run.

Given all this methodology, what, in fact, does an analyzer do for you?

Suppose that you are a programmer and have just produced a Pascal program which is undergoing test. Suppose further that you have constructed a half-dozen test cases which you believe fairly comprehensively wring out your code. You have carefully tested every requirement levied on you by your customer, but you still have the nagging suspicion that there are byways in your program which remain untested. (If you don't have that nagging suspicion, you are naive!)

Now you consider the analyzer. Knowing that it can relate the structure of your program to execution counts as your program runs, you decide to make use of one. What you intend to do is measure the testedness of your program when your test cases are run against it. *What you are really doing is measuring the effectiveness of the test cases by analyzing the program.*

You input your source code to the analyzer just as if it were input data. The analyzer reads it in and outputs a modified version of your code containing the instrumentation code previously described. This augmented source is then fed into the compiler. The resulting object code is linked, and in addition to the library routines your program already needed, a few special analyzer library routines, and the analyzer database, are linked into your loadable program.

You are now ready to execute the instrumented code. What you have is a version of your program, identical to what you coded in all other functional respects, but with the added capability of measuring itself (and, as a result, your test cases) as it executes.

One by one, you input your test cases. As each runs, your program outputs (in addition to the output you provided for) a table showing each segment of your program and the count of the number of times it was executed.

The most interesting items in this table are the zero-count segments because they are the ones not executed by that particular test case. As each test case runs, you get another table, showing the impact of *that* test case on segment execution frequency counts. If, at the conclusion of all the test cases, there are one or more segments for which the count is zero for all tests, then clearly there is a portion of your program not yet tested.

If there is such a zero-count segment, your work has just begun. Obviously, you would like to either build a test case to force an execution of that segment or at least understand why it was not executed. Perhaps it is an unexecutable, useless code. More likely, it is exception case code for a facet of the program's capability not yet tested. In any case, your job now is to go back to the program source code, find out what the function of the untested segment is, and decide what to do about it.

Analyzer usage, then, may become an iterative process—instrument, execute, inspect results, inspect the program, revise the test, and repeat. The analyzer is, quite literally, a tool by means of which more can be learned about the testedness of a program, in order to decide whether to and how to improve that testedness.

There are other benefits to the use of an analyzer, not all of them reliability related. Since the analyzer relates program segments to test cases that execute them, it is possible to reduce the testing of a revised program to those test cases which test only the revised portions. Also, high-frequency counts for program segments are a clue pointing to portions of a program that perhaps should become candidates for optimization, and thus the test coverage analyzer is like a performance analyzer.

Analyzers are by no means a reliability cure-all, however. Although dissecting a program into its constituent logic segments is a fairly rigorous approach to structural testing, ideally the analysis should take into account *all combinations* of such segments. Frequently, it is not an untested segment, but an untested sequence of tested segments, which hides a latent programming error. Such a level of analysis, however, is infeasible by today's technology. The combinatorial mathematics of a program of any magnitude quickly makes the number of individual sequences of segments astronomical. Thus, the analyzer as we presently know it is a compromise. Note that other compromises are possible. For the integration of large programs, or for programs where the sizing and timing impact of the instrumentation is prohibitive, it may be preferable to segment the program into procedure invocations, for example. The rigor of the analysis is lessened considerably, but the manageability of the resulting data is increased. Such a coarse-grain analyzer might be useful for real-time applications, for example, where instrumentation-caused distortions in program execution time might prevent the program from executing successfully.

Another possible compromise is the computer hardware analyzer, which can monitor the instruction counter of a CPU and can provide statistics at that level without impacting sizing and timing. This technique is especially useful for micro and real-time computing, where sizing/timing may be critical. Statistics at that level, however, are sometimes difficult to track back to the source code level, and a thorough hardware analysis of a class of constructs (e.g., all branches) is hard to implement.

A study was conducted at the Boeing Aerospace Company to estimate what percentage of program errors might be isolated and corrected by rigorous use of an analyzer, forcing the traverse of all segments in the search for program errors. In a population of three fairly mature programs of mixed complexity (one was a compiler) and during the reporting of about 50 errors, the findings were that about 25 percent of the errors would have been found by appropriate analyzer usage; 40 percent would only have been found by an analyzer that examined all combinations of logic segments; and the remaining 35 percent were errors of omission, and thus also not subject to analyzer-aided detection. As stated before, the analyzer is not a reliability cure-all, and this study supports that statement. As with other reliability tools, its use merely increases the chance that the software so processed will be reliable.

The following listings show a simple source program before and after instrumenting and then show the table of segment counts produced when the program is executed. It should be noted that the test coverage analyzer output shown here is quite rudimentary. More sophisticated reporting mechanisms, for instance, showing the source listing with statement execution counts in the margin are more common and much more convenient.

SOURCE PROGRAM

```
RANDOM SMALL, RANDOM_ARGE = 0;
FOR I = 1 TO 1000 BY 1;
BEGIN ""CATEGORIZE RANDOM
NUMBERS''
  GET_RANDOM_NUMBER (RESULT);
  IF 0 ≤ RESULT ≤ .5
  THEN RANDOM_SMALL = RANDOM_SMALL
+ 1;
  ELSE RANDOM_LARGE = RANDOM_LARGE
+ 1;
END ""CATEGORIZE RANDOM NUMBERS''
PUT NAMED RANDOM_SMALL,
RANDOM_LARGE;
STOP;
END
```

SOURCE PROGRAM, AFTER INSTRUMENTATION

```
COUNT_SEGMENT(1);""*ANALYZER
CALL*''
RANDOM_SMALL, RANDOM_LARGE = 0;
FOR I = 1 TO 1000 BY 1;
BEGIN ""CATEGORIZE RANDOM
NUMBERS''
  COUNT_SEGMENT(2);""*ANALYZER
CALL*''
  GET_RANDOM NUMBER (RESULT);
  IF 0 ≤ RESULT ≤ .5
  THEN BEGIN
```

```
      COUNT_SEGMENT(3);""*ANALYZER
CALL*''
      RANDOM_SMALL = RANDOM_SMALL +
1;
      END
   ELSE BEGIN
      COUNT_SEGMENT(4);""*ANALYZER
CALL*''
      RANDOM_LARGE = RANDOM_LARGE +
1;
      END
END ""CATEGORIZE RANDOM NUMBERS''
COUNT_SEGMENT(5);""*ANALYZER
CALL*''
PUT NAMED RANDOM_SMALL,
RANDOM_LARGE;
PRINT_SEGMENT_COUNTS;""*ANALYZER
CALL*''
STOP;
END
```

ANALYZER OUTPUT, AFTER EXECUTION (PROGRAM OUTPUT NOT SHOWN)

```
        SEGMENT NUMBER VS. EXECUTION FREQUENCIES
UNITS     →   1     2    3     4    5    6    7    8    9
TENS    ↓
        0   -   1  1000  475  525  1    -    -    -    -
```

The matrix contents are the number of times each segment was executed. For example, segments 1 and 5, outside the loop, were executed once; and segments 2, 3, and 4, inside the loop, were executed 1,000, 475, and 525 times, respectively.

REFERENCES

FRAKES91—"An Experimental Evaluation of a Test Coverage Analyzer for C and C++," *Journal of Systems and Software*, October 1991; Bill Frakes. *Reports on an experiment examining the value of a particular test coverage analyzer in debugging software. Surprisingly, it did not help the testers find more errors, but it did help in other ways.*

PAIGE77—"Software Testing: Principles and Practice Using a Testing Coverage Analyzer," *Transactions of the Software '77 Conference*, October 1977; Paige. *Defines a test coverage analyzer, shows examples of its use, and proposes testing strategies using such a tool.*

2.5.2.2.6.2 Data
Earlier in this book in the section on design techniques, we saw that there are two fundamentally different approaches to software design: function-driven approaches (discussed under top-down design) and data-driven approaches (data structure design).

The test coverage analyzer which we examined in the immediately preceding section analyzes the testedness of the *logic* of the software. In some ways, this parallels the function-driven approach to design. The question logically arises whether there is a test coverage measurement approach which could be used on problems that are fundamentally data driven. The answer to that question still lies in the research world. However, a technique for measuring data testedness has been defined and is being explored.

Basically, the technique involves treating the data flow diagram (DFD) for such a problem in the same manner as the logic network which formed the basis for the logic test coverage analyzer. That is, a properly tested piece of software should have all *definitions* of data items and all *edges* between nodes tested. A definition is considered to be a point in the program at which a data item is given a value, such as by an assignment statement. An edge is defined as being a data flow arc between two nodes in the data flow diagram, that is, a place at which one or many pieces of data flow from one process to another. Data structure coverage of 100 percent using this definition would be a set of test cases which executed every definition and every edge in the program unit under test.

The research exploration for this approach is discussed in Rapps [85]. At the time of writing of the paper, the authors were building a tool which would take a program and its test data as input, and produce the set of data paths which had *not* been executed by the test cases as output.

Looking ahead, it would seem that this approach could indeed be a successful test measure for programs written using a data structure design approach. However, it also appears that the method might not be as rigorous as every segment logic-driven test coverage, since what is being tested are the data flows between processes. And unless the processes are defined at a fairly low level, they are much like modules. Thus, 100 percent data coverage would be somewhat analogous to 100 percent module test coverage, not 100 percent segment test coverage. Because of the increasing popularity of the DFD approach, this methodology bears watching.

REFERENCES

RAPPS85—"Selecting Software Test Data Using Data Flow Information," *IEEE Transactions on Software Engineering*, April 1985, Rapps and Wayuker. *Describes the research being conducted into data test coverage analysis at the New York University Courant School of Mathematical Sciences.*

2.5.2.2.7 Test Case Management

Given the complexity of the testing process described in the preceding sections, it may have occurred to you that following this process for software that is itself complex could be difficult. That is, of course, the case.

Because of that difficulty, techniques and tools have been developed to help manage this testing process. They range from the simple (test drivers and stubs to represent missing pieces of the product during unit testing) to the complex (managers to control the selection, execution, and result comparison for masses of test cases) to the sophisticated (special tests for software that must run in a complicated environment). Each of these three categories is discussed in the sections that follow.

2.5.2.2.7.1 Drivers and Stubs

We introduced the subject of the test driver program under the topic of unit testing in an earlier section. We return to the subject here because the use of test drivers is an important part of the dynamic testing process.

A test driver is a computer program developed to enable the testing of another computer program or component of a program. In a sense, it is a simulator of the environment in which the component will actually run after the testing is completed. The test driver "drives" the execution of the program component under test. Generally it contains an input mechanism for getting data to the component under test, and an output generator which accesses output from the component and displays it in human-readable form for checking purposes.

Test drivers are usually quite rudimentary. The input format need not be elegant, nor the output format artistic, for the test driver to do its job. For the most part, test drivers are throwaway code for this reason; however, the better class of test drivers may be kept for later repeat testing of individual units during final system testing or maintenance.

The test driver is an essential part of the process of unit testing. It is worth mentioning once more that top-down testing, which avoids the use of unit testing, uses something analogous to the test driver—the skeletal version of the final top-level system structure. In this case, the test driver starts out as a (perhaps rudimentary) version of the final top-level logic and evolves into the final form of that logic.

EXAMPLE OF TEST DRIVER

Suppose that you are a programmer working on a water fountain simulation system and that you have been asked to code a subroutine to be called SQUIRT. (You were chosen for this assignment because the SQUIRT routine might also prove reusable in your elephant simulation.) SQUIRT has inputs of water flow rate and pressure, and outputs the volume of water discharged; SQUIRT (RATE, PRESSURE: VOLUME). Having coded SQUIRT, you then design a test driver:

```
DO UNTIL END-OF-FILE; BEGIN
  READ RATE, PRESSURE;
  SQUIRT (RATE, PRESSURE: VOLUME);
  PRINT RATE, PRESSURE, VOLUME;
  END
STOP
```

Using this test driver is a lot of work, especially in comparing output values with true output values. Being both smart and lazy, you decide to input the previously computed correct volume for each rate/pressure to make the driver self-checking:

```
DO UNTIL END-OF-FILE; BEGIN
  READ RATE, PRESSURE, VOLUME-IN;
  SQUIRT (RATE, PRESSURE: VOLUME);
  IF VOLUME-IN # VOLUME THEN
    PRINT "ERROR', RATE, PRESSURE,
  VOLUME-IN, VOLUME;
  END
STOP;
```

Realizing that you are still testing too small a quantity of input values, you decide to let the driver itself determine a broad spectrum of test cases:

```
FOR RATE = 0 TO 1000 BY .01 BEGIN
  FOR PRESSURE = 0 TO 1000 BY .01 BEGIN
    SQUIRT (RATE, PRESSURE: VOLUME);
    PRINT RATE, PRESSURE, VOLUME;
    END
  END
STOP;
```

(Of course, you now have to go back to manually verifying the output values.)

REFERENCES

PANZL78—"Automatic Test Drivers," *IEEE Computer*, April 1978; Panzl. *Describes three approaches for the construction of automatic test driver builders, including TPL/2.0, a tool under development at the time at the GE Research and Development Center.*

2.5.2.2.7.2   Test Managers

For large and complicated software systems, it is possible for the human tester to manage individual test runs well, but lose track of the full mass of testing for the total range of the product. The test manager is a computer program whose function is the management of the testing process. Test managers include the following kinds of capabilities:

- *Test selection.* Based on a map of test cases versus components to be tested, the test manager will select from a complete test set those tests which are to be run.

- *Test execution.* Using the tests selected previously, the test manager initiates the execution of the test cases against the components under test.

- *Test result checking.* The test manager saves the test case results and compares them automatically with previously obtained and known to be correct test case results. Often these correct results are saved from previous runs of the test cases, but initially they will need to be hand generated.

- *Test report preparation.* Some of the test cases will have run correctly, and some will not. The test case manager prepares a report stating which falls into each category, and what symptoms were identified for those tests which did not run correctly.

Obviously, the cost of such a test manager is large. However, for very large systems or systems which are retested frequently, for example during maintenance, the test manager will quickly pay for itself.

2.5.2.2.7.3 Environment simulator

The *environment simulator* is a special form of test driver. It is particularly useful in real-time software development, where the interfacing of the software with some external device must be tested.

Whereas the typical test driver may be a simplistic skeleton, the typical environment simulator is frequently the opposite. The requirement of an environment simulator to faithfully represent the external world may, indeed, make the simulator more complicated than the program or component being tested. In fact, while the test driver is typically a unit test tool used on a component, the environment simulator may more commonly be used as an integration tool on the total program.

Suppose, as an example, that the SQUIRT subroutine of the previous section is part of a program called FOUNTAIN, which will be used in real time to control an innovative water sculpture in an urban redevelopment area. And suppose, as is commonly the case, that FOUNTAIN and its real-time computer must be checked out and working well before the sculpture itself, or even its water connections, will be complete. Or, if that "suppose" seems unrealistic, suppose instead that the expense and risk of putting an untested FOUNTAIN system into an existing water sculpture (what if it allows the pressure to rise too high and wrecks the sculpture, for example) is too high to be allowed.

Then the FOUNTAIN system must be tested outside its intended environment—at least, initially—and an environment simulator for the water sculpture is needed.

The simulator, of course, need not take the form of the sculpture; it only needs to simulate the interfaces between the sculpture and the FOUNTAIN hardware/software system. Still, the fidelity to those interfaces must be exact; otherwise the test may be too artificial to be of any value.

Because of the complexity of these interfaces and the variety of external stimuli that may be applied to the system under test, a complicated simulation control system called a *scenario* is sometimes needed. The scenario describes what is to happen during the (simulated) test process. It might specify the range of rates and pressures to be applied to FOUNTAIN, for example, including provision for surges of pressure and/or water outages. If the system is sufficiently complex, part of the environment simulator may be a scenario processor, built to allow the user to describe the scenario in human-readable form. A scenario processor is, in effect, a specialized language processor for a scenario input language.

Even more complex environment simulators may include hardware or software components for interface adaptors and/or special simulation consoles. The complexity of the simulator is, of course, totally dependent on the environment being simulated.

One interesting variant of the environment simulator is the *instruction-level simulator* (ILS), a system that allows one computer to simulate another, instruction by instruction. Suppose, for example, that the FOUNTAIN computer is for some reason unavailable when the software is ready for testing. If an ILS for that computer exists which runs on some other computer, the software may be tested there.

Specific complexities aside, the environment simulator is still a test driver at heart—it provides inputs to, and processes outputs from, the software under test.

EXAMPLES OF ENVIRONMENT SIMULATORS

The previously discussed FOUNTAIN system is one example of an environment simulator. For another example, consider the following.

An Avionics computer system is one that utilizes electronic devices such as computers in an aircraft/spaceship environment. Suppose that you are implementing a real-time Avionics flight control system for an aircraft which utilizes digital computers and thus software as a control mechanism. The job your software is to perform is to read aircraft system stimuli, such as speed and altitude and direction, and transmit them to pilot-readable instrumentation. Perhaps this instrumentation is a small TV screen and the pilot can select by a pushbutton mechanism which data he wishes displayed (much like a digital watch). Suppose further that the pilot can act on the data you have supplied him by actuating aircraft controls, and the Avionics computer and thus your software has the job of transmitting those pilot inputs to the proper control systems.

> Obviously, the external world of your fairly simple program is rather populous. There are pushbuttons and TV screens and sensor inputs and flight mechanism outputs. Perhaps not so obviously, it is totally undesirable to test your software in its intended environment. Not only is there enormous cost to flying an airplane around to test a software system (perhaps thousands of dollars an hour), but there are lives at risk. A program malfunction might actually kill someone. An environment simulator is clearly the right answer.
>
> Your Avionics simulator system, at minimum, must contain capability for inputting speed and altitude and direction, and for outputting that information on a simulated pilot-readable system. It must also have the ability to read simulated pushbutton inputs and transmit that information to simulated control systems. Perhaps these inputs and outputs can be simply data entry and display activities. Or, for more reality and confidence in the system, perhaps a mockup pilot cab and simplistic control replicas are needed. Note that what is spent on the simulator is a function of what is at stake if the software is unreliable. With lives and gross amounts of money at stake, the mockup cab system may well be the right answer.

REFERENCES

GLASS82—"Checkout," *Modern Programming Practices,* pages 115–141, Prentice-Hall, Inc., 1982; Robert L. Glass (editor). *Presents discussions of the use of several kinds of simulation systems in the checkout of real-time software, written by the companies that did the work: Computer Sciences Corp, TRW, Boeing Computer Services, Sperry Univac, and Martin-Marietta.*

JACKSON71—"Software Validation of the Titan IIIC Digital Flight Control System Utilizing a Hybrid Computer," *Proceedings of the 1971 Fall Joint Computer Conference;* Jackson and Bravdica. *Describes an elaborate test system built to validate real-time flight control software. Covers the total mission of the system as well as the testing strategies.*

2.5.2.2.8 Test Data Generator

The problem of building an adequate set of test cases is nontrivial. Although the initial test cases fired at a new piece of software are usually simple subsets of the population of possible program inputs, the time must come during the testing process when the test inputs must probe all the obscure nooks and crannies of the program. Manually constructing those test cases becomes harder and harder. The discussion of test case analyzers elsewhere in this section, while exploring means of identifying inadequacies in test cases, leaves open and in fact begs the question of generating adequate test cases.

In the past, test cases have been hand-hewn, specially tailored to the software to be tested. A *test data generator* is a computer program that automatically and systematically constructs test cases.

The problems confronting the generation of test cases, whether manually or automatically, are many. On the one hand, it is desirable to maximize the number of test cases used in order to increase the chance that the program is thoroughly tested. On the other hand, since the construction, execution, and analysis of test cases cost money, it is also desirable to minimize the number of test cases. These two opposing goals can only be met by a carefully chosen set of test cases which covers the necessary ground without needless redundancy.

This is both a positive and a negative factor in doing automated test case generation. It is positive because it involves a complex optimization problem at which computers on occasion excel. It is negative because the very complexity of the problem has so far eluded practical solution except in relatively straightforward cases.

Early test data generators were nothing more than sophisticated random-number generators. Although they were able to produce a broad spectrum of inputs, the inputs so produced were not adequately tuned to the problem at hand. As a result, such programs, even when available, were seldom used.

More recent attempts at test data generation have been driven from the content of the program under test itself. Either from structural analysis such as that performed by a test case analyzer, or from programmer-inserted test case generation clues (a "test pattern"), the generator deduces test cases which satisfy the specific test needs of the program. Obviously, there is a great deal of promise in this approach, but it is technologically difficult.

The concept of statistics-driven testing, discussed earlier, is based on a revival of interest in the random test approach. Here, a profile of typical operational usage is defined, including legitimate ranges of input data. Test cases are constructed by repeated application of random-number techniques that obtain a data input value of the desired type within the desired range.

EXAMPLES OF TEST DATA GENERATORS

Let us suppose that you have a fairly straightforward report generator with one structured data file as input to check out. It is part of FOUNTAIN simulation system.

You elect to use a random-number-type test data generator. Looking at the required data file structure, you describe to the test data generator the form and content of each data field. INPUT-PRESSURE, for instance, might be a numeric field of two digits on each side of the decimal point with a range of 0 to 99.99. SCULPTURE-NAME might be a 30-character field with effectively no constraints on content. The test data generator, given these field definitions and the others adequate to define the program input, would construct one or more test cases satisfying the specified definitions.

As checkout progresses, you elect to use a test coverage analyzer program to see if your automated test cases have adequately covered all program segments. The analyzer you choose has the additional capability of providing logic flow diagrams which show how particular program segments may be reached. Use of the analyzer shows that three segments remain untested. Via use of the flow diagrams, you deduce those values of input variables that will force the testing of the untested segments.

You have used two types of test case tools—the first, a test data generator, produced test cases but not comprehensively; and the second, an augmented test coverage analyzer, produced no test cases but provided in an automated fashion information which assisted you in completing the comprehensive test process.

REFERENCES

CURRIT86—"Certifying the Reliability of Software," *IEEE Transactions on Software Engineering,* January 1986; Currit, Dyer, and Mills. *An IBM study advocating statistics-driven testing.*

DURAN84—"An Evaluation of Random Testing," *IEEE Transactions on Software Engineering,* July 1984; Duran and Ntafos. *Takes the position that random inputs from an operational profile should take precedence over other testing approaches.*

MILLER77—"Generation, Processing and Application of Program Test Patterns," *Proceedings of the AIAA Computers in Aerospace Conference,* 1977; Miller. *Defines a method for programmer insertion of test patterns that an automated test generator could use to deduce test cases, where a test pattern is the set of I/O relationships that apply to a program segment.*

2.5.2.2.9 Standardized Testing

The concept of *standardized testing* is analogous to that of generalized programming: Wouldn't it be nice if you didn't have to construct tests at all in order to wring out a new piece of software? Wouldn't it be nice if there were a library of available tests to draw from?

In most situations, that is not possible. If the requirements for the program you are writing are sufficiently unique to require it to be written at all, there probably is also a unique requirement for test case construction.

However, such is not always the case. Suppose that your problem is to implement an Ada compiler for a new line of computers. There already exists a standard set of test cases for all such compilers, called the Ada Compiler Validation System (ACVS), that can be used virtually unchanged to comprehensively test your compiler when it is complete.

Standardized testing, then, is the process of using a set of application generalized test cases (usually developed independent of a particular project) to test software.

An analogous situation is the *benchmark test.* A benchmark is a standardized test designed to exercise one or more competitive systems in order to evaluate them. Whereas the goal of standardized testing is normally to assist in program debugging, and, perhaps, to use as a basis for sanctioning or certifying the program as a correct and acceptable implementation, the goal of the benchmark system is to evaluate, with an implied decision regarding program usage at stake.

The standardized tests for the Ada compiler consist of many thousands of Ada statements that must be compiled and executed to test any new compiler system, and in fact to revalidate old ones that have been revised. The statements that make up the tests are chosen to span the spectrum of allowable inputs (in this case, Ada statements). Each statement (or series of statements) is followed by some conditional code in which the result of executing the statement is compared with its correct result; in this way, the tests are self-checking. Machine-dependent parameters (e.g., word length, number of bits per character) are isolated and flagged for ease of change for each new test situation.

To generalize this concept, forgetting for the moment that an Ada compiler is being tested, the standardized test contains

- a comprehensive set of inputs
- a simple mechanism for making the standardized test specific to a particular situation
- a mechanism to simplify test result analysis

These concepts should characterize any standardized test.

REFERENCES

BAIRD72—"The DoD COBOL Validation System," *Proceedings of the Fall Joint Computer Conference, 1972; Baird. Describes the need for, history of, and implementation of a COBOL compiler standardized test system called CCVS (COBOL compiler validation system).*

NG73—"Mathematical Software Testing Activities," *Program Test Methods*, Prentice-Hall, Inc., 1973; Ng. *Certification of mathematical software, such as Fortran libraries, is discussed. A variety of test methodologies is described, and favorable results cited.*

2.5.2.2.10 Mathematical Checkers

Programs with a heavy mathematical flavor need special test tools. Not only is it difficult to determine whether a minor error in the second decimal place of a coded constant has been made, but it is also possible that because of such computing artifices as word length, even a correctly coded algorithm may behave incorrectly.

The *mathematical accuracy checker* is a process by which the accuracy of a computerized mathematical solution is evaluated. The accuracy checker accepts as input previously computed values (perhaps obtained by hand, perhaps via a simulator), and outputs a comparison of the computed and "correct" input results.

The *mathematical significance checker* is a process by which the significance of a computerized mathematical solution may be monitored. A special processor, perhaps an interpreter for a commonly used algorithmic language, keeps track of the significant digits or bits of accuracy in each equation as it is executed. The significance of each variable is also maintained in a symbol table or name list. As results are printed or displayed by the program, the significance of those results can also be shown. At the conclusion of execution, the final significance (and value) of each variable may also be shown. Loss of significance due to round off, word length, or algorithmic ineptitude may thus be tracked by the user of the significance checker.

EXAMPLES OF MATHEMATICAL CHECKERS

As the result of past painful experience in the use of mathematically-oriented programs, you are gun shy about the results of your nearly complete FOUNTAIN simulation program. You decide, based on the fortuitous in-house availability of a mathematical checker package, to subject your program to further analysis.

Adding to your good fortune, you have saved the computed results used to test out the mathematical aspects of your flow algorithm prior to putting it into code. Therefore, you prepare these results as input to the mathematical checker, turn on a significance option, and launch the execution of your job.

When the results come back, your suspicions are justified. The significance, you are gratified to see, is tolerable at each step of the process. However, miscoding of a sign on a simple assignment statement has led to a minor distortion of the final results.

You correct the error, rerun the job, and now find both significance and accuracy acceptable. (Happily-ever-after stories appear in books in every field!)

REFERENCES _____

BRIGHT73—"A Method of Testing Programs for Data Sensitivity," *Program Test Methods*, Prentice-Hall, Inc., 1973; Bright and Cole. *Describes a system for doing mathematical significance checking.*

NG73—"Mathematical Software Testing Activities," *Program Test Methods*, Prentice-Hall, Inc., 1973; Ng. *A variety of mathematical test methodologies are described, and results cited.*

2.5.2.2.11 Symbolic Execution

All the testing methodologies described in this section deal with exercising a program on data selected to be similar to operational input data. *Symbolic execution,* a radically different concept, involves the algebraic execution of the symbolic version of a program upon symbolic input data. A special symbolic execution tool is required. The source program to be symbolically tested is fed into the tool, along with a set of input data classes. Each statement of the program is "executed" in normal go-time sequence, but the result of execution is the algebraic symbolic substitution into the expression in the statement of the input and any previously "computed" data.

Obviously, the result in a program of any size will be a dramatic increase in the complexity of expressions as program execution progresses. In addition, as conditional statements are encountered, the symbolic execution tool will likely find it impossible to determine which path should be taken. Therefore, some symbolic execution tools are built to interact with the programmer user, so that human decision making can steer the program in simplified and promising directions.

It is difficult to grasp the potential of a tool of this type. On the one hand, there is enormous promise to the symbolic test concept, since a single symbolic test case is equivalent to an infinite number of traditional numeric test cases. On the other hand, the complexity of the symbolic process may make that promise unreachable in a practical sense. In addition to the previously mentioned conditional statement problem, there is a serious problem in the symbolic execution domain involving subscript and pointer-type variables. They are essentially unserviceable, since the result of using such a variable negates the ability to develop a meaningful symbolic expression (e.g., what previously obtained expression does A[I] point to?). Until this problem is solved (if ever), symbolic execution cannot have broad usefulness. It may be useful in a local domain of a complex computational program, however, to help clarify the occurrence of a problem. In that sense, symbolic execution is a formalization and generalization of desk checking.

Symbolic execution may also be useful in proof-of-correctness techniques, by symbolically executing assertions to demonstrate correctness.

EXAMPLES OF SYMBOLIC EXECUTION

Suppose a highly mathematical part of the FOUNTAIN system is not providing correct answers to the input data fed it. Visual inspection of both the code and the algorithm give you no clues as to the problem. Therefore, you elect to try symbolic execution. An interactive symbolic execution system is available on your company's timesharing computer.

You define a set of input data in algebraic terms. INPUT-FLOW-RATE, for instance, may be defined as the result of a quadratic equation; the gate BY-PASS-VALVE may be defined as "even" (all even values represent "open"). These expressions, and the expressions of the algorithm itself in the form of the program's source code, are input to the symbolic executor. Using algebraic substitution, the tool proceeds through the algorithm code statement by statement, making appropriate substitutions from the preceding algebraic manipulations into the current one. The execution pauses after each statement, giving you the opportunity to inspect and mull over the results, and select (where necessary) the appropriate branch of a conditional statement. You can also guide the meaning of subscript and pointer variables, to the extent that you are able.

Watching the algorithm behave as symbolic execution proceeds, you spot an anomaly in the behavior. The simulated BYPASS-VALVE has become stuck shut. Upon further inspection, the error—failing to set a flag to signify that the valve is to open—becomes apparent to you (because a mathematical subexpression that should have dropped out in the evaluation of a variable did not), and you correct it. Reexecuting the program symbolically, your FOUNTAIN program now behaves properly.

REFERENCES

CLARKE85—"Applications of Symbolic Evaluation," *Journal of Systems and Software*, February 1985; Lori A. Clarke and Debra J. Riohardson. *Presents symbolic execution as a useful tool in (1) formal verification, and (2) path selection for testing.*

KING76—"Symbolic Execution and Program Testing," *Communications of the ACM*, July 1976; King. *Describes a specific symbolic execution tool.*

2.5.2.2.12 Organization of Testing

The technology of testing is difficult, as we have already seen. Most of the preceding sections have dealt with things the tester could do to improve the results of testing.

But what can management do? There are organizational approaches to testing that can help, as well. In this section we discuss several options that have organizational implications. Who does the testing? How do we do phase testing? When do we formally include the customers and users? How do we document before and after testing processes? These questions are dealt with in the following sections.

2.5.2.2.12.1 Independent Testing

Objectivity is a serious issue in testing. The software developer *should* be interested in finding errors during the testing phase, not in demonstrating that the program executes correctly. But the tendency of all human beings is to exhibit how good we are, not what flaws we have.

Because of that, in many situations outside testers are brought in to supplement the work of the software developer. There are three common labels for these outside testers: product testing, independent verification and validation, and independent testing.

Product testing is done by an internal organization devoted to providing objective testing of products built by the organization's software developers. It is discussed again in more depth under management organizational approaches to software quality.

Independent verification and validation (IV&V) is done by an outside company that specializes in the service of verifying the software of others. Testing is just one of the services provided. The range of the services is fairly analogous to the content of this book in that IV&V companies typically are full life-cycle quality assurance companies. Their use is common on supercritical space and military applications.

Independent testing is done by an outside company that specializes only in *testing* the software of others. These companies offer such services as test development, test conduct, test result analysis, and test report generation. How individual companies do this is dependent on the company involved; one company claims to use as many as 70 test tools, and another offers a "seal of approval" when it successfully completes testing. These companies typically are employed for use on microcomputer mass-market software.

2.5.2.2.12.2 Beta Testing

Sometimes there is not a single, crisp moment when software passes its acceptance test. Sometimes instead the software bypasses the whole acceptance test process for one reason or another, and moves out into the field for use.

One common way to cushion the blow for the first users of such software is what is called a *beta test* process. Beta testing is the use of software by real users in a setting where everyone knows that the software is just past its development cycle and may still be buggy. Usually only a few users are selected to be beta testers—users who perhaps need the software immediately, but in any case are known to be tolerant of early release bugs and cooperative with the programmers who must remove them.

Beta testing is commonly used by vendors of mass-market software. It is essentially an insurance policy. In-house testing (*alpha testing*) has completed its work, but the software vendor knows from past experience that heavy product usage by real users will detect errors the alpha testers have been unable to find.

It is interesting to correlate this process with statistics-driven testing, discussed earlier. Recall that in statistics-driven testing, a user profile is created and a randomly drawn set of test cases which fits the profile is executed. Beta testing may be viewed as a human approach to statistics-driven testing because the test cases are generated by real users rather than by random-number processes!

2.5.2.2.12.3 Acceptance Testing

The time must come to show-and-tell the newly developed and checked-out software to the user world outside. This exposure is usually conducted through the formality of the acceptance test.

An acceptance test is the checkout of software via a formally defined and conducted test in the presence of and requiring the approval of the software customer.

Acceptance testing typically takes place as part of the delivery and installation of the software at the customer's site (if the customer is the development organization, of course, this fact is of no consequence). The process will usually consist of an installation by the development team, conduct of the acceptance test, and, following approval of the test results, formal delivery.

Considerable thought has generally gone into the acceptance test well before it occurs. It may well have been defined by an acceptance test plan, and that document may have been reviewed as early as the software critical design review. As discussed in the management section of this book, the test plan probably describes the methodology of the test, the specific tests to be conducted, and the acceptance criteria for each test. Additionally, the test plan often contains a matrix relating all the requirements in the software specification to the test which shows achievement of that requirement.

Even if a formal test plan document does not exist, an alert customer will still insist on reviewing, in advance, test methodology, the manner of determining that the test performs satisfactorily, and the adequacy of the testing.

For small software projects, acceptance tests may end up being a simple and straightforward process. Even for large projects, the test should in general be straightforward, since presumably the development organization will have run the test previously at its own site. However, the realities of large software delivery seldom work out that way. Schedule constraints often force the developer into the acceptance test phase prior to the completion of in-house testing. As a result, the acceptance test is sometimes a traumatic process. Major software acceptance tests may frequently require 30 to 90 days of calendar time to complete, and failure of software to pass an acceptance test is not unheard of (the developers fall back to their lair to regroup, and the test is rescheduled for a time when the software has hopefully gotten well).

Not the least of the problems of the acceptance tester is the installation itself. Company A's Marketronics computer may behave rather differently from Company B's Marketronics, and an expert on the vagaries of the

Marketronics command language and operating system is a vital part of the installation team. When available, standardized tests are an important part of the acceptance test process.

EXAMPLE OF ACCEPTANCE TESTING

Your bookmaking program, defined in an earlier section, has finally achieved a sufficient state of readiness to be delivered to your customer. You catch a flight to Reno, along with a development teammate who is an expert on the customer's Quadranova computer operating system, and arrive at the customer's installation with a briefcase full of documents and a floppy disk containing the program.

Although the customer is happy to see you, his computer is not. It is being used to capacity two shifts a day, and your testing is relegated to a time slot that you had forgotten existed on a 24-hour clock.

Bleary-eyed, you, your companion, your program, and your test cases arrive at the Quadranova at 2 A.M. The first night is spent wrestling with the uniqueness of the customer's installation. At last, your program takes hold and runs. Your companion catches a plane home.

On subsequent nights (the customer is generous enough to let you work first shift on weekends), you run a set of tests, then meet a member of the customer's technical team to review the night's results at 8 o'clock the next morning. The customer, fresh and alert, runs mental circles around your off-hours-tired brain, but he also, one by one, signs off as accepted the tests you have been running.

The blackjack test, in spite of all your previous effort, still has a bug related to the value of the ace of spades. You correct the bug the following night, rerun the test, and that result, too, is signed off.

After so long away from home, working undesirable hours in an environment your mother would find difficult to understand, you are happy to climb aboard a plane a week and a half later, an approved acceptance test report in your briefcase, and head home.

2.5.2.2.12.4 Postdelivery Review

During much of the early history of software, practitioners have been more interested in getting a high-quality product out the door on time than in ruminating after the fact on what went wrong and what went right.

That is a shame. Many lessons have been learned and forgotten and relearned by software practitioners over the years. Without any attempt to record those lessons in any formal way, all of that valuable experience has simply been lost. (A most wonderful exception is Brooks's *The Mythical Man-Month,* the story of what happened on the gigantic OS360 project of the 1960s.)

Fortunately, that is beginning to change. After all the smoke of delivery and early usage has cleared away—certainly after the independent testing, beta testing, and acceptance testing are long past—some companies are beginning to employ a postdelivery review. Fundamentally, two things happen at a postdelivery review:

- A wrapup of the *total project* is made. Users and customers talk about their reactions to the delivered and now-used system, and developers and users share a discussion about the process of getting that product.
- And a wrapup of the *development process* is also made. Developers talk among themselves about what worked and what didn't, and what should be tried next time and what shouldn't.

According to Kumar [90], only 18 percent of software sites surveyed are using this kind of process. Those who are using it focus on these issues at the review:

- product quality
- documentation quality
- process effectiveness
- lessons learned

Findings are saved in a "lessons learned" database [Fenick90].

Early findings indicate that the optimal time for a postdelivery review to take place is 3 to 12 months after cutover of the system to its users, giving everyone enough time to *really* understand how well the process worked and the product has been accepted.

REFERENCES

FENICK90—"Implementing Management Metrics: An Army Program," *IEEE Software*, March 1990; Stewart Fenick. *Defines the history and practice of a software metrics program in the U.S. Army. Identifies metrics collected, uses made of them, the process of collection and use, and talks about a "lessons learned database" for saving the results.*

KUMAR90—"Post Implementation Evaluation of Computer-Based Information Systems: Current Practices," *Communications of the ACM*, February 1990; Kuldeep Kumar. *Advocates and describes postimplementation review, but says the largest benefit is project closure and not project improvement. Suggests that "evaluation should be managed and performed by people other than the members of the development team."*

2.5.2.2.12.5 Test Documentation

We cover documentation needs for software quality in some detail in a later section on software quality management. However, it is worth mentioning in context that there are special documentation needs in most of the life-cycle phases. Test documentation usually consists of three parts: the test plan, the test procedure, and the test report. They may be three separate documents, or the first two may be combined.

The *test plan* is the definition of what tests will be run. The opening part of the test plan should indicate the testing philosophy to be employed, and the degree to which the philosophy will be satisfied. (" . . . Following complete requirements-driven testing, structure testing will be performed at the 85 percent segment coverage level . . . ").

The test plan should include a matrix of requirements identified by paragraph in the requirements specification, and the test case or cases which will test each requirement. For example:

Requirement	Test Cases													
	1	2	3	4	5	6	7	8	9	10	11	12	13	14
. . .														
1.3.2.2	X		X	X									X	
1.3.2.3	X			X								X	X	
. . .														

In the preceding example, the first requirement identified (1.3.2.2) will be tested in test cases 1, 3, 4, and 13. A quick scan of such a matrix allows the reader to see that either requirements-driven testing is complete, or that some requirements are not being tested. The remainder of the test plan should be a list of the test cases, each accompanied by a description of what it does and why it does it.

Generally a test plan will discuss the whole testing process, not just the final acceptance test. However, the list of test cases will usually be limited to the most significant tests. Unit tests, for example, are too numerous to be listed. The test plan may discuss the method of approach to be used for unit testing, but it will not contain the complete test set.

The *test procedure* document tells how the testing will be conducted. Generally it is provided only to describe formal testing, such as the acceptance test. It answers such questions as

- What facilities are needed for the tests?
- When will the testing happen?
- Who must be present for the tests?
- What role will each person play?
- What steps are involved in the testing?
- Who performs which steps?
- What is the approval criteria for the tests?
- Who is authorized to provide approval?

- How is approval indicated?
- What happens if some or all tests fail?
- What are the circumstances surrounding retest?

The *test report* summarizes the test results. Sometimes it will report on all testing, from beginning to end. More often it will discuss only the results of acceptance testing.

Usually the test report is an exception report. Since the norm should be successful execution of test results, only test anomalies (failures to pass a test) are noted here. The report must include a description of what went wrong and what was done about it. Often tests may be rerun under certain controlled conditions after a first failure. The test report may be an incremental document, being updated each time one or more tests are rerun, never becoming complete until the final acceptance test case is successfully run. The test report then becomes an archival document, providing a historic record of how the tests went.

2.5.2.2.12.6 Test Review

The testing for a large software system, as we have seen, may be a quite complicated process. It is often true that an objective look at the definition of the testing process is vital to ensure that the testing will be adequate. The test review is the event where that happens.

The function of a test review is to reach agreement on the testing process. If there is a test plan and/or a test procedure, this agreement may be signified by signing the appropriate document. If there is not, then the agreement will be stated in minutes of the review.

The review may happen remotely or in a meeting. If it happens remotely, the proposed test plan/procedure is presented to the concerned parties (software developers and quality assurance specialists, for example). The concerned parties read it, critique it, and either ask for changes or sign it.

If the review happens in a meeting, generally the attendees at the meeting will have read the documents beforehand and the purpose of the meeting will be to resolve any problems which the readers have identified. Sometimes new wording will be created at the meeting, and the completed version can be signed as soon as the clerical updates are made. At other times, agreement in principle on changes will be made, and the authors of the document will revise it and present the revision for one last review process.

If there is no written document, the test planners will use a lecture mode of presentation and ask for either agreement or revision suggestions. Once agreement has been achieved, the testing may begin as soon as the testers are ready.

2.5.2.2.13 Innovations in Testing

If you were to slip back in computing history two or three decades, you would find a fairly primitive testing environment. Heavily-loaded mainframe computers gobbled up batch test runs, and sometimes didn't give the results back for a week or more. Heavily-loaded minicomputer installations required testers to schedule their test sessions and operate the computer themselves, often at odd hours of the day or night. Clearly, in those days priority on computers was given to executing production software, not testing.

Fortunately for all of us, that has changed. Through the years, a lot of innovations have served to move testing into an environment just as favored as anything else. This section discusses some of those innovations, past and future.

Innovation sometimes involves people doing things in new and interesting ways. For example, a few years ago Microsoft found 185 errors in a prerelease version of some of their software by offering instant cash prizes to computing conference attendees who would sit at a micro and "break" the product!

But more often innovation means new technology. In the first section that follows, we talk about interactive debug, a technique that required new technology to make it possible. Interactive debug is now so solidly entrenched that it is hard to think of it as an innovation. But it was this technology that rescued testing from the ugly scenes described previously, and because of that historical significance we cover it here.

The next two sections talk about technology-dependent advances of the future: visual debug (the use of graphics and animation, not just text, to do testing); and knowledge-based debug (the application of artificial intelligence expert system thinking to the debug process).

Whereas it is clear what benefits have emerged from interactive debug, it is not at all clear yet whether there will be payoff to these newer ideas and, if there is, how much. That makes them important areas for the dedicated software professional to watch.

2.5.2.2.13.1 Interactive Debug

There are two distinct methods of using a computer to test a program: *batch* processing, where the programmer submits a job to the computer with the understanding that it will be placed in a queue to be run when the computer is ready for it; and *interactive* processing, where the programmer launches a job expecting instant and ongoing response from the computer. All the other discussions of this section deal with techniques that are applicable to either batch or interactive mode; this section deals with techniques and capabilities of the interactive approach alone.

Interactive debug is the process of seeking and correcting errors in a computer program while communicating with the computer executing the program. Typically, the communication takes the form of monitoring program progress, inspecting intermediate values, inserting data correction as needed, and in general controlling program execution.

This interaction sometimes is facilitated by a special language processor, an *interpreter,* which takes the place of a compiler and an execution environment. The interpreter keeps control of the program while it is being tested, allowing the programmer user to communicate with its new execution environment in the ways just described. It is often true using this mode of operation that the interpreter and a text editor are interlinked, so that once an interactive test run identifies an error, the text editor can immediately be invoked to repair the source code, and the testing is resumed without the programmer ever knowingly exiting from the interpreter.

Interactive debug may be accomplished either through a timesharing system on a relatively powerful computer, or through a single-user system such as a personal computer or workstation.

EXAMPLES OF INTERACTIVE DEBUG

Suppose that you have just walked up to your favorite timesharing system terminal, logged on, done a little housekeeping of your files, and are now ready to make a debug run of your FOUNTAIN simulation program. You invoke an interpretive compiler with interactive debug capability, and sit back to monitor the results.

Owing to your source language debug preplanning, fairly soon your program begins displaying a series of trace outputs, showing the values of several key variables as they change.

Then you notice it. One of the variables, output volume, is going sour—its values are clearly beyond tolerances. (Note that you have just performed the role of a human assertion checker.) Quickly, you signal an interrupt to the executing system before it goes too far and obliterates the immediate evidence of the problem. Via the system's interactive debug capability, you probe through your program's database, keying in the names of program variables and monitoring the responses as the system displays the values of those variables. Narrowing the problem, you see that one intermediate variable in a complex calculation leading up to obtaining output volume is totally wrong. Referring to your source listing, you see that the arithmetic expression for that intermediate value is coded erroneously.

Using another function of the interactive debug system, you rewrite the erroneous expression and substitute the new correct source code for the old in your program. You direct the interactive debug system to start up your program again at the point of the revised statement, rather than where you interrupted it.

The system returns control to your program, and off it goes again, executing and displaying trace outputs. Your correction appears to have been a good one; the variable that had gone sour now looks reasonable, and you allow the execution to proceed to completion.

REFERENCES _____

SACKMAN68—"Timesharing vs. Batch Processing: The Experimental Evidence," *Proceedings of the 1968 Spring Joint Computer Conference;* Sackman. *A classic paper that summarizes the pros and cons of timesharing usage via five experimental studies.*

2.5.1.1.13.2 Visual Debug

Some interactive debuggers have the capability of displaying one or more parts of the program as it executes. These tools are called *visual debuggers.*

The goal of a visual debugger is to display as much meaningful execution-time information to the programmer, in as convenient a format, as possible. Recall that the source language debugger presented the debug results to the programmer in a form similar to that of the original source program to maximize debug result readability. The visual debugger takes this philosophy one step further in that it uses graphic techniques for the presentation of the information.

Visual debug tools use a multiwindowed screen capability to display several useful things to the programmer simultaneously, as the program executes. Windows may include such things as:

- values of data being manipulated by the program
- behavior of complex data structures being used
- the program source text currently being executed
- any special information requested by the programmer
- any interactions between the programmer and the debugger

Some of these techniques have been called *program animation,* in that they allow the programmer to see program execution in a moving, graphical form. Data structure behavior, such as the creation, expansion, and contraction of a tree structure, is especially interesting to see in animated form.

A visual debugger must slow down program execution in order to allow time for the programmer to see and understand the artifacts of the execution. Because of that, visual debuggers are run in interpretive mode, and often include an additional slowdown factor, such as a dummy vacuous loop, to bring computer execution speed down to human reading speed. One visual debugger [Isoda87] even has an *accelerator* window, in which the programmer can adjust the current execution speed of the program to match his or her comprehension speed.

Visual debug capability is not yet in common use, but with the advent of high-resolution graphics screens that permit multiwindow displays, and the increasing interest in productivity during the debug phase of software development, they will likely become much more common in the near future.

REFERENCES _____

Isoda87—"VIPS: A Visual Debugger," *IEEE Software,* May 1987; Isoda, Shin-imura, and Ono. *Describes a visual debugger which runs on a PERQ workstation connected to a Japanese NTT mainframe and executes the Ada language. Shows and explains examples of content for each of several window types. Contains a good set of references for other work in this area.*

2.5.2.2.13.3 Knowledge-Based Debug

Debugging is much like solving a detective mystery. There is a crime, a failure of the program to execute correctly. There are clues, artifacts left behind by the program as it executes which indicate that all is not going well. And there is the detective, the programmer-debugger, pouring through the clues to try to identify the criminal (the offending program part).

This analogy naturally leads to the thought, "Is it possible to auto-mate the debugging process?" Until the advent of artificial intelligence expert system techniques, the answer was fairly clearly "No." The skills and actions of the experienced debugger were simply too complex to be built into a computer-driven system.

That negative answer is now being rethought. Suppose the skills and experience of a knowledgeable debugger-detective could be built into a knowledge base? Then could we not have AI-controlled, automated debug-ging?

There are those exploring this issue [Seviora87]. Knowledge bases with limited debugging skills have been built. Experimental debug ses-sions have been run with sufficient success to continue the work. The investigation is still in the research stage, and present-day debuggers should not expect to be obsoleted soon! Fundamental problems lie in these areas:

- Human debuggers use a variety of intertwined techniques.
- Debugger knowledge must not only include debugging techniques, but also the characteristics of the program under test.
- Knowledge of the program under test must be both global and local.
- Isolating a bug is one problem; repairing it is yet another.

REFERENCES _____

Seviora87—"Knowledge-Based Debugging Systems," *IEEE Software,* May 1987; Seviora. *Reports on the state of the theory of knowledge-based debug. Says that the technique has been used successfully on tiny programs, with execution speeds (on these experimental systems) of "tens of seconds to tens of minutes on a VAX 11/780-class machine."*

2.5.3 Reprise: Testing versus Review[4]

What's the most effective way of getting errors out of software?

What's the most *cost*-effective way of getting errors out of software?

Those are big-ticket questions. If you look at how the dollars are spent on software development, error removal is generally seen as *the* most expensive part of the software life cycle, beating systems analysis and design and coding each by a factor of something like 2 to 1.

Because those are big-ticket questions, let's explore what we know about answers to those questions. What I'd like to be able to say is that we know Fact A, and Fact B, and Fact C, and because of that your best way to spend your software error removal money is to use Strategy Z. But it's not that simple.

Why isn't it that simple? Well, for one thing, there are a lot more opinions about the effectiveness of various things in software development than there are pieces of real and useful data. Perhaps even worse than the prevalence of opinions over facts, we have a lot of advocates in the software engineering business.

Because of all these opinions and all that advocacy, not only do we not have quantitative information with which to answer big-ticket questions like the preceding ones, but the whole atmosphere is emotionally charged. The advocates tend to grind a particular ax so thoroughly that either people flock to their side or are turned off by them. There is a large loss of objectivity when opinions and advocacy enter a picture.

But the solution to opinions and advocacy is objective data, right? Well, are there data to allow us to answer those big-ticket questions? The overriding answer to that question is *no*. It takes careful, controlled experiments to get facts and data, and hardly anyone is doing those experiments. Why isn't someone doing them? As we try to answer that question, things get even muddier.

One answer is that it costs a lot of money to do careful, controlled experiments. More money than the average researcher has. So much money, in fact, that hardly anyone is doing software experiments, especially where it counts most, in the world of large-scale software created by software practitioners. Not even those places where you might think these experiments *should* be done, like the government-funded Software Engineering Institute, or the industry-funded consortia like the Software Productivity Consortium and the Microelectronics and Computing Consortium (MCC).

---

[4]Reprinted from "An Experimental View of Software Error Removal," *Software Conflict: Essays on the Art and Science of Software Engineering*, Yourdon Press, 1991; Robert L. Glass.

But another answer is that there's a strange climate in the computer science and software engineering worlds, a climate in which the experimental component that is present in most other sciences and engineering is simply not present. The researchers who ought to be best qualified and most motivated to do software experimental research are simply not doing it.

There are Experimental Findings About Testing. Now all of that is a pretty depressing prelude to what I *really* want to say. Because in spite of all this gloom and doom about software experimentation, some of it has been done. And some fairly important experiments have been done in an attempt to answer questions about testing. We, in fact, have some experimentally-obtained answers to those questions. They aren't totally conclusive answers, but they're consistent enough that practitioners and their managers can probably start making decisions based on them. You *can*, in this case, use Facts A and B and C to choose Strategy Z.

And what makes this worth reading, if you're still with me at this point, is that the findings of those experiments are not only relatively consistent, they also point us in a different direction for software error removal than the one we currently tend to pursue.

What do we currently tend to do? Test the software hard, and then test it some more, and then test it again.

What do the experiments say we should do? Well, if our goal is to find the most errors and/or to get the lowest cost per error found, experimenters tell us that we should emphasize review processes more than testing. Design review, code review, test review—that sort of thing. As we will soon see, those approaches tend to unearth more errors faster and cheaper than does testing.

But wait! Don't go out and fire your independent test group and cut off the machine budget for your developers during checkout. The findings *don't* say to stop testing, period. They just say that testing isn't enough, and that reviews need to supplement testing. That's *still* a big deal finding, because in my experience not very many software developers do much design and code review work before throwing the new program in for testing.

So, enough preliminaries. Who are the researchers doing this experimental work, and what have they learned?

The Experimental Findings. I'm going to tell you about three different sets of people who have done experimental research in this area, all of them pretty much independent of each other except that the latest researchers have seen the published results of those who've gone before them. The people I'm going to talk about are:

- Glenford Myers of IBM Systems Research Institute, who published his findings in an article called "A Controlled Experiment in Program Testing and Code Walkthroughs/Inspections" in *Communications of the Association for Computing Machinery* in September 1978.

- Victor Basili of the University of Maryland and Richard Selby of the University of California at Irvine who did their work in conjunction with the NASA/Goddard Space Flight Center and published their findings in "Comparing the Effectiveness of Software Testing Strategies" in the *IEEE Transactions on Software Engineering* in December 1987.

- Jim Collofello of Arizona State University and Scott Woodfield of Brigham Young who did their work at an unnamed company and published their findings in "Evaluating the Effectiveness of Reliability Assurance Techniques" in the *Journal of Systems and Software* in March 1989.

There's the answer to the question of who the researchers are who do experimental work in this area. Now for the second question, "What have they learned?"

In order to answer that question, let's look first at what they did. Each set of people put slightly different English on their approach to the question.

Myers and Basili/Selby compared what some people call *functional testing* (testing to see if all the requirements are satisfied) with *structural testing* (testing to see if all parts of the program have been tested) and with code review. They performed their experiment on one or more relatively small programs using largely experienced practitioner subjects, having them look for errors known to be in the software.

Collofello/Woodfield broadened the base of the exploration and narrowed it at the same time; they used data from a massive real-time software project rather than conducting controlled experiments. And they did their analysis on design reviews versus code reviews versus something generically referred to as *testing*.

Each of the three sets of researchers was looking for the same kind of answers, but they each took a slightly different approach to measuring for those answers. All three, for example, wanted to get a handle on the *number* of errors removed and the *cost* of removing them, but Collofello/Woodfield designed new metrics for measuring counts and costs, which they called *error detection efficiency* and *error detection cost effectiveness*.

Now I know you're eager to get on with what these three sets of people found out specifically, but bear with me for one more detail. It turns out that, much as we wish it weren't so, the *way* you conduct research can have a major bearing on what you learn from the research.

To a certain extent, these findings compare some varieties of apples with some varieties of oranges. For one thing, whereas in a review process the reviewers tend to not only identify a problem, they also isolate where the solution to the problem lies; in testing (as conducted in these experiments) independent testers only identify that there is an error without isolating where the error can be fixed. Therefore, as experimentally measured here, the reviewers were doing more of the job than the testers were.

For another thing, in the Collofello/Woodfield research, which used project data, the testing took place after the review processes had removed a fairly large percentage of the errors, so that the testers were (1) looking for a different class of errors from the subjects in the other two experiments, and (2) possibly the errors remaining after the review processes were tougher errors to identify than those caught earlier.

Those kinds of differences may have an effect on research findings that ranges from trivial to profound. I only mention those here as an example of the difficulties involved in doing these kinds of experiments, and (more to the point) as reasons why using "facts" to choose "strategies" still should be done with caution.

And now (ta-ta!) specifically what did these researchers learn? First of all, regarding testing versus reviews, Basili/Selby found strong evidence that code reading was considerably better than both kinds of testing that they examined, and Collofello/Woodfield found that both kinds of reviews they examined were considerably better than testing. Oddly, the Collofello/Woodfield data were more conclusive in cost considerations than in count considerations and the Basili/Selby findings tended in the opposite direction. But nevertheless, these two sets of researchers came to the same overall conclusion—reviews beat testing.

Myers's findings are only partly in sync with the others on this matter. Myers found reviews and testing equally effective; and reviews more expensive than testing.

What about kinds of reviews, and kinds of testing? Well, there were more data gathered on kinds of testing. Basili/Selby found functional testing discovered more errors than structural testing, while Myers found them nearly equivalent. Regarding kinds of reviews, only Collofello/Woodfield looked at that, and they found design reviews much more cost effective in error removal than code reviews, but code reviews are somewhat more effective in errors removed than design reviews.

Now all of these words tend to muddy the picture of what we're learning here. Table 2.1 summarizes the findings of the three sets of researchers. In simplified form, here's what they seem to have learned, using a kind of majority rule argument:

1. **Reviews are more effective than testing in error removal, and they tend to be more cost effective as well. The data here are not unanimous, however.**

TABLE 2.1   RESEARCH FINDINGS ON ERROR-REMOVAL STRATEGIES, REVIEW *VS.* TEST

Researcher	Myers	Basili/Selby	Collofello/Woodfield
Error-finding effectiveness	equal	1. code reading 2. function testing 3. structural testing	1. code review (best) 2. design review 3. testing
Cost effectiveness	code review most expensive	code reading least expensive	1. design review 2. code review 3. testing (least)

2. In kinds of testing, functional testing tends to find more errors than structural testing, and to find them more cheaply.

3. In kinds of reviews, design reviews are far more cost effective than code reviews, but code reviews tend to find more errors.

What does all that mean in terms of error-removing strategies? Probably something like this:

- Reviews *must* supplement testing.
- Testing must emphasize functions but not ignore structure.
- Reviews must cover both design and code.

Some Loose Ends. There are a few loose ends still to be tied up here. For example, what exactly did the researchers mean by functional testing and structural testing and code reading and reviews? It would be dangerous to go too far with strategies based on these findings unless we have a clear notion of what the findings are about.

Functional testing: uses the requirements specification of the program to define what needs to be tested. Myers gave the experimental subjects the specification and let the subjects decide how to use it for testing. Basili/Selby's subjects were asked to use equivalence partitioning (one test case representing a class of similar test cases) and boundary value analysis (emphasizing test cases at points where algorithms or methods change) as their way of developing test cases from the specification.

Structural testing: uses the internal working of the program to determine how to build test cases. Myers's subjects were given both the specification and the program listing from which to derive test cases in whatever way they wished. Basili/Selby's subjects were asked to make sure that each statement of the source program was tested by at least one test case.

Code review: is a static process (the software is not executed) in which participants examine the source listing looking for errors. The Basili Selby subjects used a process they call *stepwise abstraction,* in which the prime subprograms of the software are identified, their function determined, and a composite picture of the whole software is determined from these individual functions so that these derived functions can be compared against the specifications. Myers's subjects, on the other hand, used *walkthrough/ inspection* as their method of code review; it included individual code reading prior to the review, and some use of mentally walking test cases through the software's logic.

The Collofello/Woodfield paper did not specify the processes used in testing and reviews, but the description of the project in question (700,000 lines of real-time code developed in a modern high-level language by 400 developers, with quality assurance activities associated with each major phase of the life cycle) suggests that it either was a military project subject to the Department of Defense standards for reviews and testing, or one using similar standards.

Other Fascinating Miscellaneous Findings. For those of you who enjoy poking around in the dusty artifacts of experiments, there were other interesting findings, not previously summarized.

Basili/Selby found these tidbits of information:

1. The "number of faults observed, fault detection rate, and total effort in detection depended on the type of software tested." In other words, perhaps the choice of testing methods should be application dependent.

2. "Code reading detected more *interface* faults than did the other methods;" "functional testing detected more *control* faults than did the other methods." In other words, perhaps the choice of checkout methods should be dependent on the kinds of errors sought.

3. "When asked to estimate the percentage of faults detected, code readers gave the most accurate estimates while functional testers gave the least accurate answers." In other words, poking around in the code seems to give people a better perspective on what they've done.

Myers found these additional tidbits:

1. "There is a tremendous amount of variability in the individual results." In other words, *who* does the checkout may be more important than how it's done.

2. "The overall results are rather dismal." In other words, none of the error-removal processes, and in fact even combinations of the processes, was very good at identifying all the errors that were present.

3. There was "a negative correlation . . . between subjects' prior walk-through/inspection experience and their performance . . . " In other words, code reviewers may get tired of the experience over time.

Collofello/Woodfield also found additional information:

1. "Unfortunately, much of the data was inconsistent and unreliable. . . . The low number of data points seemed to mirror the disinterest of the developers in recording data. . . . No one checked the quality of the quality assurance data." In other words, even the use of project data is prone to problems in research analysis.
2. "The high [success] associated with the design review was surprising." In other words, a lot of errors were found very cheaply at design review time.
3. "Interestingly, one reliability assurance technique—testing—was not cost effective." In other words, testing, though necessary, is a pretty expensive way of doing business.

The bottom line of this essay can, in fact, be taken from the bottom line of the Collofello/Woodfield paper. "Testing must always be done, but organizations must recognize that the traditional emphasis of testing instead of reviews is not a cost effective approach."

In other words, the answer to those two questions we asked at the beginning of this article:

- What's the most effective way of getting errors out of software?
- What's the most *cost*-effective way of getting errors out of software?

is something of a surprise. It's not that we've been doing a bad job of answering them in the past; but there are some new answers that may cause us to revise the way we've been doing business.

And those answers are coming from the folks who, at last, are beginning to apply experimental techniques to the science of computer science and the engineering of software engineering.

2.6 MAINTENANCE

The software development team has finished its work. There is a feeling of creation, of giving birth, of changing a bunch of characters keyed to a text editor into a living and breathing problem solution, one that makes a computer do things it could not have done by itself.

It is a euphoric feeling when it comes out right. The developers are ready to move on to the next task, to tackle the world if it comes to that.

But there is something false in this picture. For all the euphoria, in fact the software task is far from done. There is maintenance ahead.

What is software maintenance? It is the act of taking a software product that is being used by a customer, and keeping it working satisfactorily.

What does that mean? It means fixing software errors left in the product by the developers. It means making changes that the customer finds will strengthen the product. It means adapting the software to environmental changes, like new releases of the computer operating system, or a newly added device.

Some people think *maintenance* is the wrong name for this activity. After all, in other fields, maintenance is the act of repairing broken and worn-out components. But software does not break and software does not wear out. If it fails to work, it is probably because those euphoric developers overlooked something. If the customer wants a change, it is probably because the insight gained by using the product allowed the customer to see new potential. "Unfortunately, the nature of hardware and software errors differs in at least one fundamental characteristic—hardware deteriorates because of lack of maintenance, whereas software deteriorates because of the presence of maintenance."[5]

People who don't like the term *software maintenance* have long cast about for a replacement. Currently, *software evolution* is the most popular. Evolution denotes the process of inevitable change which happens to a software product better than maintenance.

However, in this book we continue to call it maintenance. Too many programmers have spent too many years doing something they call maintenance to allow a change to be effective.

It is important to highlight something said a couple of paragraphs back. Change in software is inevitable, we said there. That may strike you as an unusual thing to say, particularly if you are used to thinking of software maintenance as fixing errors. Can't we just produce error-free software and forget about maintenance?

Well, no we can't. There are two reasons why we can't, and the second is far more important than the first.

1. It is regrettably true that we simply don't know how to produce error-free software.

2. Software change (not error correction) is the major component of software maintenance. That change, as we mentioned earlier, often comes about because the customers of a software product have new

---

[5]From "Initial Thoughts on the Pebbleman Process," Institute for Defense Analyses, Jan. 3 1979; Fisher and Standish.

vistas opened for them at product delivery, and come to understand new software capabilities they would like to have which they had not envisioned before. Therefore, the majority of software maintenance comes about not because someone did something wrong, but because someone did something right, that is, built a software product which (1) enlightened someone, and (2) did it in such a way that the software could be easily modified.

Maintenance was performed but largely ignored in the early days of software. There were few studies into what it was about; there was little research into how to do it better; there were few tools to help the maintainer. All of that is changing.

First came an important study conducted about 15 years ago [Lientz78]. In a survey of (largely data processing, COBOL) computing installations, three people from UCLA found that maintenance was 60 percent perfective (making customer-defined enhancements), 18 percent adaptive (making changes required by the environment, such as to match reconfigured computing equipment), and only 17 percent corrective (fixing errors). (The remaining 5 percent was "other.") See Figure 2.12.

The importance of that data is still being absorbed. Basically, it says that 78 percent of software maintenance activity is in a sense inevitable, due to the wishes of the customer and the needs of the setting, and only 17 percent is due to problems (errors introduced by the developers).

About the same time other data were being gathered on how the software dollar was being spent [Boehm75]. There were two surprises in those data. The first had to do with development. Over twice as much time was typically spent in checking out software than was spent in either requirements gathering, design, or code. The second was that half or more

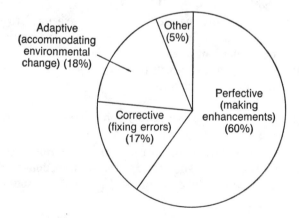

Figure 2.12 Kinds of software maintenance. Most software maintenance is *not* repairing errors, but rather enhancing functionality.

of the software dollar was being spent on maintenance (the percent actually ranged from 40 percent to 80 percent depending on who was surveying what). (See Figure 2.13.) The initial reaction to those data was concern—why are we spending so much money on maintenance?

Somehow the two sets of data were never really blended. As time has gone by, the percent of the dollar spent on maintenance has gradually increased. In some organizations, there remains no new software development. *All* work is maintenance, and the concern has increased into a cause. "Let's eliminate software maintenance costs" was a cry heard in some organizations.

The cry was, of course, doomed to failure. Since most software maintenance is not only inevitable but probably desirable as it is a positive service to customers and users to allow them to enhance what the software product does for them, software maintenance both cannot and should not be eliminated.

In more recent years, the concern has shifted from "Why are we spending so much time on software maintenance?" to "Just what are those maintainers doing?" Fortunately, there is also data available to answer that question. In a study conducted at IBM some years ago [Fjelstad79], it was found that two types of tasks dominate the maintainer's time: understanding the existing software, and testing the changed software. (See Figure 2.14.) What is interesting in these data is what was *not* stated. Making the required change in the software is *not* one of the significant tasks of software maintenance. The important message here is that what the software maintainer needs most, over and above what the developer needs, are techniques and tools for *understanding* existing software (note that testing, the other leading consumer of a maintainer's time, varies little from the testing that must be done by developers). As we discuss later

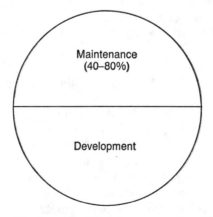

Figure 2.13 Cost of maintenance. Maintenance accounts for over half of software costs. The percentage is increasing in more recent years.

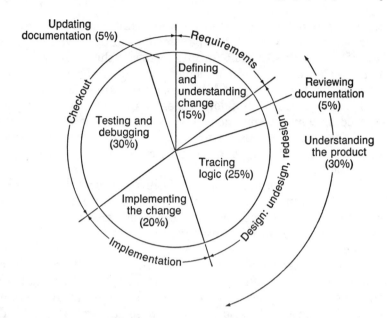

Figure 2.14 Tasks of maintenance. Product understanding, and testing/debugging, dominate maintenance tasks. Notice that the maintenance tasks correspond to development life cycle phases.

what the developer can do for the maintainer, and what tools are available for the maintainer, keep in mind what the area of greatest need is.

What kind of a job *is* software maintenance? It's interacting with customers to identify changes and corrections; it's reading someone else's program to understand what it does; it's changing that program to make it do new or different things; it's testing that program to make sure it does both new and old things right; and it's releasing a new version to the customer with sufficiently revised documentation to support the customer and the product.

If you've never done maintenance, you may not realize from that description that maintenance is both different from and the same as development.

It is different because one key element is reading existing code to understand it, and solving a problem within the framework of an existing solution. This is a challenge, but it is a constrained challenge, since the maintainer is constrained to analyze the problem within the envelope of the existing solution. It is the same because it is to some extent a life-cycle activity. That is, the maintainer must perform some of the same tasks as the developer such as formulate the requirements for the problem, design a solution (within the constraints of the existing solution), convert that design into code, and test the resulting revised solution. The life cycle of software maintenance is like a miniature of the life cycle of software development.

Software maintenance is not a universally popular activity. Most software people want to be developers. That euphoria of creation that we mentioned earlier is a potent lure. And then there are those constraints—creating within constraints is far harder than creating a new product. As a result, most software engineers avoid maintenance if they can. The task is often left to the few who enjoy it, and the newcomer who doesn't have the clout to avoid it. This is unfortunate because maintenance is often a computing installation's most important activity in terms of customer satisfaction and therefore political power.

Let us return to the word picture at the beginning of this section. The euphoria of the developers is ebbing, and a maintenance team shuffles onto the scene. Their enthusiasm does not match that of the developers. They know that, for all the joy the developers feel, there are problems in the software they are about to take over. It will need change. It will have bugs in it. It will have been created in a way neglectful of the needs of the maintainers.

The maintainer's euphoria will come later, when they find a way to satisfy a customer's change request that taxes their ability to create within constraints. Then, as with the miniature life cycle within which they function, they will feel a mini-euphoria for the changes they have made.

Embedded in the preceding paragraphs are two different facets of software maintenance: the developer's job of producing software that can easily be maintained, and the maintainer's job of doing the maintenance. They are rather different topics, but they are both vital to software maintenance. We deal with each in turn in the sections that follow.

REFERENCES

FJELSTED79—"Application Program Maintenance Study: Report to our Respondents," *Proceedings of GUIDE 48,* The Guide Corporation, Philadelphia, 1979; Robert K. Fjelsted and William T. Hamlen. *Analyzes how maintainers spends their time. Provides data that show that 30 percent of the time is spent on product understanding, 30 percent on testing the change, and considerably less on actually making the change.*

IEEE86—Special issue on software maintenance, *IEEE Software,* May 1986.

IEEE87—Special section on software maintenance, *IEEE Transactions on Software Engineering,* March 1987.

IEEE90—Special issue on maintenance, reverse engineering, and design recovery, *IEEE Software,* January 1990.

LIENTZ78—"Characteristics of Application Software Maintenance," *Communications of the ACM,* June 1978; Lientz, Swanson, and Tomkins. *Surveys 69 computing installations to identify the characteristics of software maintenance. Describes what maintenance is like in a typical data processing computing shop.*

Software Maintenance News, periodical devoted to the practice of software maintenance, 114 St. Marks Pl. #5F, Staten Island, NY 10301.

2.6.1 Preventive Maintenance

What can the software developer do to ease the task of the maintainer? The answer to this question is *preventive maintenance.* It is preventive maintenance because it is a "do the job right the first time" kind of activity.

In the last section, we already dismissed the notion that building error-free software would do away with software maintenance. Well, then, if preventive maintenance isn't building error-free software, what is it?

There is a whole collection of actions the developer can take to pave the way for the maintainer. They focus on the general notion that maintainers must read and modify code, and their intent is to make that reading and modifying easier. That collection is dealt with at length in the sections that follow. But before we do, let us tackle one more terminology problem.

We have already seen that the term *maintenance* is controversial. So is the term *preventive.*

In other fields, preventive maintenance is the activity that the maintainer performs to lessen the likelihood that maintenance will be needed soon. That is, preventive maintainers fix things that aren't yet broken.

Once more, software doesn't break and software doesn't wear out. The person who does *software* preventive maintenance is not the maintainer, but the developer.

With the same degree of stubbornness that we display in the previous chapter, we continue to use the term *preventive maintenance* in this new way for software. Although the meaning is not the same as in other fields, the analogy is still valid. Preventive maintenance is what the software developer does to lessen the tasks of the maintainer.

Now, what can the developer do that constitutes preventive maintenance? The answer to this question lies in two main areas; single-point control and defensive programming.

2.6.1.1 Single-point control

Single-point control is taking something that must be done in several places, and doing it in one place while referencing it from the others. The advantage of this technique is that if other changes are necessary, it need only be changed in the one place. Not only is the change easier, but there is no possibility of a broadly-reaching change being done inconsistently.

Probably the best and most common example of single-point control in software is the *module.* If software developers anticipate needing to perform the same task several places in a program, they create a callable module for the task. Wherever the task is to be executed, it is invoked through a module call mechanism. Subroutines, procedures, and functions are all examples of the module concept. All leading programming languages, including assembly language, have a mechanism for module definition and use.

Modules are good preventive maintenance because if the function of the module must change, it need only be changed in one place, not many. This is also true because enhancements can often consist of new invocations of existing modules.

The second most commonly accepted instance of single-point control is *data abstraction*. In data abstraction, there is a single, central definition of a data entity, coupled with a definition of the operations that act on the data, such that all access to the data must be to the central definition through the centrally defined operations. Once again, changes to the data, or enhancements requiring new uses of the data, may be handled centrally at the single point of control.

A third popular example of single-point control is *object orientation.* Here we have the use of data abstraction but with the added idea of inheritance of attributes of one collection of data by another. New variations of old objects can be invented simply by inheriting what is to be kept, and adding new attributes where a change is desired.

Another example is *named constants,* where a frequently used constant is given a name in addition to its value and then is always referenced through its name. If the value of the constant must change (as might happen, for example, to the size of an array of storage if an enhancement required more capacity in the array), then only the definition of the name must change, not each reference to the constant.

Bit strings and *byte strings* can be declared in most programming languages as named data items. (The alternative in some other languages is to refer to the string by a function call, such as to bits 3 through 7 of item ALPHA.) If the string declared by a name must change (e.g., a change to its starting or ending position), only the definition of that name need change. Note that if function calls had been used, every call would have to be changed to accommodate the new starting and/or ending positions.

Table-driven code is a way of attaching decision criteria or other information to data in a table rather than to executable statements in the procedural logic. If the criteria needs to change, one or several values of the table need to change, but program logic need not be changed. Note, for example, that program changes can be made in this case by inputting a whole new table during execution, thus allowing for program changes without even requiring recompilation, let alone complicated logic changes. (As an example, consider an application where at various altitudes differing actions need be taken. The actions could be handled in standard program logic, but the decision criteria could be based on the easy-to-change content of a table rather than a collection of hard-coded IF statements.)

File-driven code carries table-driven code one logic step further. Recall the previous example that a new table could be input to a table-driven logic program, allowing significant program changes without any reprogramming. File-driven code is this idea, extended to even more comprehensive collections of data. For example, suppose you have built software for a popular line of microcomputers that is so successful that you want to market it internationally. How do you handle the problem that the user interface must be represented in many different languages? One solution is to put all the text for the interface into a single file, construct a different file for each language to be supported, and simply read in the appropriate language file at the beginning of execution of the program based on the language needs of the user.

Documentation can employ single-point control in analogous ways to programming. For example, the description of a particular function can be kept in one place in the documentation rather than scattered throughout the document at points of usage.

Note here that there is a trade-off in single-point control. In the example of documentation, let us think for the moment about the user document for a program. Perhaps a particular function can be invoked by the user in several different contexts. Should the description of the function be included in each context, or placed in one with a reference in the others? In this case, the answer is not obvious. Single-point control and maintainability argue for a single definition and references. But perhaps users will be annoyed at having to flip pages in a document to find the single-point definition for a particular function they wish to use. It may well be true that the needs of a friendly human interface will cause single-point control to be rejected in some circumstances.

The same argument, in fact, might be used for the software maintainer. To find a single module from every point of reference to it, the maintainer may need to keep multiple fingers stuck as placeholders in a paper listing, or flip screens on a text editor back and forth between contexts. The finger gymnastics here are accompanied by an equivalent need for mental gymnastics!

There are two arguments that support modularity for maintainers here, even if not for users:

1. The maintainer is expected to gradually become an expert in the modification of the software being maintained. Once a module's function has been absorbed, understood, and remembered by an experienced maintainer, the paper or screen flipping exercise goes away. Users may never become that expert in *using* software.

2. Multiwindowed text editor interfaces now allow the screen flipping to be contained in one screenload simultaneously. Even a maintainer

learning a program can readily switch back and forth between areas of interest without the previously described physical and mental gymnastics.

The point here is that single-point control, for all its benefits, requires consideration of certain trade-offs. Generally in issues related to software maintenance, the benefits will well outweigh the costs.

2.6.1.2 Defensive programming

Single-point control, looked at it one way, is the use of good *design principles* to perform preventive maintenance.

Defensive programming is the use of *anticipative design* to accomplish the same end. In anticipative design, the software developer anticipates specific problem areas that a maintainer may encounter, and designs solutions into the software for them. It is analogous to defensive driving, where a driver looks ahead and tries to see potential problems and react to them before they become real problems.

What forms can defensive programming take? *Exception handling* is one of the most common ways. The designer creates logic to handle as many potentially harmful situations as he or she can anticipate. What would happen if input data being fed into an array might exceed the capacity of the array? Build a test into the software to detect this problem and report it to the user. Now the maintainer will not get calls from an irate user asking "Why did your program blow up?" The user will have been told by the program, through defensive programming, what is going wrong. In many production programs, this kind of exception handling—dependent, of course, on the application problem being solved—will make up more than half of the code.

Another example of defensive programming is the use of *assertions*. We have already seen assertions discussed as a checkout idea, as an early warning system for error detection. Here, they can be an early warning of possible user problems. Assertion reports will give the maintainer information about what was going wrong even before the software finally blew up, such as:

- erroneous or improbable data
- improper logic flow
- undesired function side effects
- data storage overflow
- subscripts out of range
- uninitialized variable usage

Here, the designer builds in assertion mechanisms that the maintainer can use as clues to explore a potential or real failure.

Margins are another way of anticipating problems. You are pretty sure that an array will never be asked to hold more than 100 items, but you design the program allowing 150 anyway. Margin techniques are simply "overengineering." That is, you build the system stronger than you think it needs to be so that it is less likely to break under stress. Good overengineering of a task does away with the need to perform that task under maintenance later on.

Another common use of the margin concept is the selection of the computer hardware itself. If this year's version of the program will fit into a 256K memory but next year's may not, spare the maintenance programmer the pain of making the change next year. Choose the hardware and design the software to solve the problem now. During maintenance it costs more to shrink a program, instruction by instruction, than it does to expand it. Eliminating this kind of task is important.

Audit trails are also useful to build into a program. If the program, as it executes, saves pertinent data in a sort of "software cockpit recorder," and if the program aborts, there is a trail of past events which may help point to the cause of the failure. Some real-time programs may not be able to afford the time and space this process requires. (Of course, other *critical* real-time programs may not be able *not to* afford to do this!) But on the whole, most programs can spare the cycles and space necessary to carry these data along because of the benefits to the maintenance programmer when a problem occurs.

Another interesting category of defensive programming is the placing of *limits on unsafe programming practices*. About 99 percent of the time, programmers can play by the rules of their language and need not resort to trickery. But occasionally, in special kinds of situations, the programmer may have to violate a fundamental rule of programming in order to get the job done.

For example, there are several occasions where a programmer may need to escape from the tight confines of strong type checking. Type checking is the process of not allowing programs to perform certain kinds of operations on certain types of data, like adding a character string to an integer.

Suppose you are writing a solution to a hash code algorithm that requires you to take the character string which represents a key field and manipulate it arithmetically in order to use it as a numeric index. The process may sound distasteful, but it is necessary to accomplish the algorithm in question.

Most programmers in most languages have found ways to accomplish this sort of thing, such as using the equivalence statement in Fortran to overlay an integer declaration over the character string. Using this integer "alias," then, the program may perform the required arithmetic.

But this is a deceptive way to perform the dastardly deed, one which may cause the maintenance programmer no end of grief as he or she attempts to fathom the peculiar coding which results.

More modern languages are adopting the idea of explicitly declared unsafe practices which are (1) clearly identified as intentional deviations from standard practice so that the maintainer may know what to do with them, and (2) reported to software management so that the unsafe programmers may be held accountable for their actions.

When the requirements for the programming language Ada were being defined, I was active in the definition process, representing the Boeing Company.

There was strong backing for the language to be strongly typed. Most advanced concept languages of the day were strongly typed, and the accepted philosophy was that programmers must be protected from writing unsafe programs.

I acknowledged the wisdom of the philosophy, but I had also been victimized enough times by strongly typed languages (they had prevented me from solving the problem at hand, forcing me to drop into assembler code) that I knew a carefully drawn escape mechanism was needed.

I held firm, and as the language took form it included the function UN-CHECKED—CONVERSION. Using it, a programmer can manipulate a variable of one type as if it were of another. But in fact, the function does nothing whatsoever. It is just a semantic device to trick the compiler into allowing type violations!

Now for the question: Should I be proud of the fact that my strongest contribution to Ada was a language feature which does nothing?!

Another form of defensive programming is *complexity limitation*. Since reading the program is a major part of the maintainer's task, anything which simplifies that reading is beneficial. Software complexity, although sometimes necessary to match problem complexity, is to be avoided whenever possible. The whole structured programming movement, especially that part which stresses the elimination of GOTOs, is a form of complexity limitation. So are rules which cause the development programmer to avoid other error-causing practices, such as the assigned GOTO statement in Fortran. These kinds of rules, which often take the form of standards or guidelines, help the maintenance programmer maintain a cleaner product.

Most of the collection of practices mentioned previously may be used in most any programming language. Some, however, may not. In general, these practices are sufficiently valuable that it is worth choosing a programming language which offers them. If you do not have that choice, of course, your usage of these practices will have some language-specific elements to it.

2.6.1.3 Documentation

If there is one thing which is ultimately predictable in the business of software maintenance, it is that the software documentation will be inadequate for the maintainer's purposes. The fact is, this will be true even if the developer prepared maintenance documentation, because the maintainer's appetite for such information is enormous!

But more to the point, adequate documentation is rarely prepared by the software developer. In class after class of software maintainers, I have asked the question "Do you have *any* software maintenance documentation to work with?" Time after time, the answer comes back "no." The state of the practice, for whatever the reason, is that maintenance documentation is not prepared.

There is one exception to this rule of thumb, and interestingly enough the exception is about as bad as the rule. In the world of the U.S. Department of Defense, the software developer is required to produce a software maintenance manual to exacting specifications. The problem here is that the information is so detailed that it rapidly grows out of date and becomes untrustworthy. Clearly, one of the great unsolved problems in software maintenance is the problem of maintenance documentation.

The problem is genuine, since there is cost attached to building the required materials, and managers are reluctant to undertake the cost while developers don't really want to do the job anyway (documenting an existing program isn't "creative"). However, there are known solutions which minimize the pain of the problem.

The first solution is to *do all detail-level maintenance documentation as comments in the listing of the program.* That is the place where the maintenance programmer needs it (to understand "what is going on here?"), and that is the place where the maintenance programmer is most likely to keep it up to date as the code evolves.

The second solution is to *present sufficient levels of overview documentation to allow the programmer to understand the program down to the detail level.*

With these two solutions, good maintenance documentation becomes

1. a top-level document, containing
   a. overall product design
      • logic structure
      • database structure

    b. midlevel product design to as many levels as necessary
    c. pointers to detail-level information in the listing
    d. design philosophy and decision processes
  2. detail-level listing commentary, containing
    a. logic structure and meaning
    b. data structure and meaning
    c. code anomalies
  3. readable listing, including
    a. structured, indented code
    b. meaningful naming conventions

The task of preventive maintenance, measured in the words of this section, may seem large. In actuality, however, the task is not. Furthermore, most experienced programmers know how to do all of these procedures. The problem is not the need for a learning experience; the problem is the need for a commitment. Most development programmers are simply not heavily motivated to make the maintainer's job easier. It is not a malicious decision, just one born of the frustrations of developing software and putting it into production use under cost and schedule constraints.

What is needed here is a commitment at both the technical and management level to make one last pass over the developer's "completed" product to make sure it is ready for maintenance. The added cost of getting it ready, if this approach is taken, will nearly always be minimal. The cost of *not* doing it, on the other hand, is guaranteed to be more than minimal.

2.6.2 Doing Maintenance

No amount of prevention, we have seen, can eliminate the need for doing maintenance. The softness of software, its ease of malleability, ensures that customers and users will invent lots of changes to keep the software maintainer busy. Given that, what are the techniques, tools, and organizational strategies that can be used to improve the job of doing maintenance?

It is popular in the 1990s to speak of maintenance as a collection of ideas—reverse engineering, restructuring, and reengineering. We start with those ideas, then move on to discuss the tools and processes of maintenance.

2.6.2.1 The "R" words: reverse engineering, restructuring, reengineering

Maintenance has at last been discovered! The tasks and traumas, long known to software maintainers, have become hot items of interest among corporate managers, vendors of software products, and researchers. Because of that, a whole new collection of maintenance-relevant buzzwords has been invented.

As with most buzzwords, these were bandied about a bit before someone got around to giving them a good definition. Fortunately, in Chikofsky [90] we find a collection of definitions that is well thought out. The words that follow and Figure 2.15 are adapted from that paper.

Reverse engineering is the process of examining a completed software system to abstract out its design and underlying requirements. It is the opposite of *forward engineering,* which is the traditional software development process.

Restructuring is the process of reorganizing the syntax of a completed program while leaving its semantics intact. Most commonly, restructuring is the act of taking a (perhaps unstructured) program and adding structure (in the sense of the structured programming constructs).

Re-engineering is the process of revising a program semantically as well as syntactically in order to improve its operation. It may involve adding function, but most commonly it is restricted to improving the maintainability of the software.

Thus, restructuring and re-engineering are activities used to help make existing software better, not necessarily connected to any particular

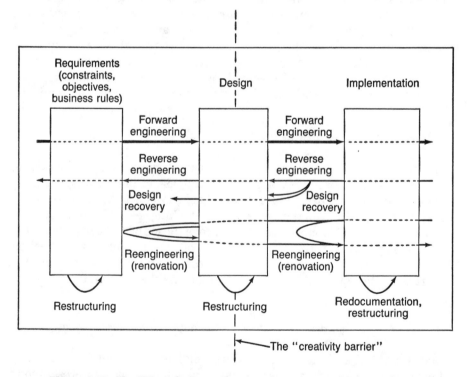

Figure 2.15 The "R" words. Reverse engineering, restructuring, re-engineering and related terms are illustrated here graphically (adapted from [Chikofsky90]).

perfective, adaptive, or corrective task. They constitute an acknowledgment that old software may be structurally ugly, or get brittle after repeated changes, and need change purely for the sake of internal improvement.

And reverse engineering is the end-to-beginning process used to understand existing software well enough to make changes in it. Note that reverse engineering is simply the *examination* of the software, and not any act of change.

What brought these terms to the forefront of the software maintenance arena was the thought that the underlying processes could be improved, formally described, and perhaps automated. In fact, early on automated restructurers came into the marketplace, tools that claimed to convert "spaghetti" (unstructured) code into structured programs. These tools do, in fact, succeed admirably in doing that task, although there is some debate about whether the resulting program is truly easier to maintain, since in the process of adding structure a restructurer may lose some original context information.

The automation of re-engineering and reverse engineering is much more problematic. Various tools chip away at the fringes of the job, such as reorganizing data structures and assisting the maintainer in understanding various facets of the existing software, but end-to-end automated support is not available. It is interesting to speculate on whether it can *ever* be done. Recall that both these processes involve not just syntax but semantics, and thus call for a considerably more complex tool. Further, both processes involve reconstructing design from code, and just as the forward design process involves creativity—something very hard to automate—this reverse design process involves both creativity and a recreation of the application problem requirements. Automating undesign seems very difficult, and automating the recreation of application requirements from code is probably impossible, since the requirements are not present there in any form.

Thus, the attention focused on the "R" words is appropriate, given that they are at the heart of the maintenance process, and yet to some extent inappropriate, since those doing the focusing have (at least implicitly) promised an automated process which is not likely to come into existence in the near future.

REFERENCES

CHIKOFSKY90—"Reverse Engineering and Design Recovery: A Taxonomy," *IEEE Software*, January 1990; Elliot J. Chikofsky and James H. Cross II. *Sets the context for and defines the software maintenance "R" words.*

YOURDON89—"RE-3," *American Programmer,* April and June 1989; Ed Yourdon. *Takes a product-oriented look at tools for re-engineering, restructuring, and reverse engineering.*

2.6.2.2 Tools

If the automation of the "R" words is difficult, are there then *any* tools for the software maintainer? The answer, happily, is a resounding "yes." A strong collection of tools for the maintainer has been defined and constructed over the last decade. Not as many tools as, for example, are available to assisting with front-end requirements and design processes, but still. . . . Companies building CASE (computer-aided software engineering) tools for the maintainer offer useful products, and there are many to choose from. The concepts behind those tools are discussed as follows.

First, of course, there are the tools needed by the maintainer but originally constructed for the developer. We mention those, albeit briefly, in passing. But what is really interesting here is the collection of tools built purely to support maintenance. We spend more time looking at those.

2.6.2.2.1 Developer Tools

Almost anything used by the software developer is useful to the software maintainer. Recall that the software maintenance process is in some ways a miniature of the software development process.

Some, in fact, take the position that all software maintenance is really just software development with a different starting point. But others, at least as convincingly, argue that all software development is software maintenance, especially since more and more new problems are being solved by reusing old software (in whole or in part).

That discussion, though interesting (it is software maintenance's equivalent of the chicken and egg problem!), is something of a digression here. The following tools of development are essential to the maintainer, and it does not matter so much who they primarily support.

Maintainers need:

- The *text editor* and *database/data dictionary* used by the developers, for system modification.
- The *language processor(s)* and *linker/loader* used by the developers, for system rebuilding.
- The *operating system* used by the developers, for system execution.
- The *verification aids* and *debugger* used by the developers, for system testing.
- The *status reporting* used by the developers, for progress tracking.

But notice what is *not* present in the preceding list. There is nothing to support the understanding of the existing system. That is the prime area where the maintainer needs (and fortunately has) unique tools.

2.6.2.2.2 Special Maintenance Tools

Not long ago, a list of tools to support software maintenance would have been short, indeed. Glass [81], for example, listed barely over a half-dozen. Now there are more than a half-dozen *categories* of such tools, with many tools in each category. In fact, in the sections that follow we discuss these tools by category.

REFERENCES ———————————————————————

GLASS81—*Software Maintenance Guidebook,* Prentice-Hall, Inc., 1981; Robert L. Glass and Ronald A. Noiseux. *An early book on software maintenance with a complete (for then) but very short list of tools for the maintainer.*

2.6.2.2.2.1 Code Analyzers

Recall that the big gap left by developer tools concerns tools to help the maintainer understand the existing software. Recall that this job is the hardest and most time consuming of the software maintainer's tasks. The first several categories of maintainer-unique tools are designed specifically to assist with that problem.

Cross reference/browser. Suppose in the software modification you are making, a change is necessary in the use of data items Net-pay and Year-to-date-pay. It is important to find out exactly where those data items are referenced, so that the change can be made consistently.

There are two entirely different kinds of tools that can be used to perform this task. The cross-reference list, prepared normally by the compiler and available for static examination, which will show for each named item a list of lines where it is referenced. The second tool is the text editor find-all capability, which can be applied to the source text to find all references in context (one at a time) interactively.

The choice of which tool is used, interestingly enough, derives from an apparently fundamental difference in approaches to developing software. Some people are planners and analyzers by nature, and prefer static processes based on pencil and paper. Others are on line and dynamic by nature, and prefer to work on line with their terminal. The first might be called *analyzers,* and in this situation they tend to use the cross-reference list. The second are often called *hackers* (in this case, with positive connotations), and their tendency would be to use the text editor approach.

No matter which approach is used, the goal is to find all references to named items to be changed so that the change may be made consistently.

Note that named items need not be restricted to data items. Named logic items, such as procedures and labeled statements, can also be analyzed in this way.

The term *browser* in the section title refers to a tool specifically built to allow the maintainer to dynamically browse through a source program looking for these kinds of information.

Call structure generator. Suppose that your program has been built as a very large whole, and changing circumstances at your institution demand that it be modified to run on a new distributed system. How can your program be broken apart in such a way that each subdivision is complete within itself? Obviously, a program subdivision must be an aggregate containing a collection of functions and all the modules called by those functions. The call structure generator identifies the binding that must be honored during the aggregation process.

This is just one of the uses for a call structure generator. This tool shows what portions of a program call, or are called by, other programs. A distributed subdivision of your program must include all the modules called by the portions you are separating off.

There are several other possible uses for a call structure generator. For instance, on a computer with virtual memory, sometimes execution time is unnecessarily high because a program "page faults" frequently, bringing in modules from external memory more often than necessary. Although users of a virtual memory computer should not need to worry about this problem, sometimes for performance reasons it is important to group portions of a program in such a way as to optimize this process. Aggregating program portions that are mutually dependent, in the same way discussed earlier for a distributed system, can solve this problem as well.

In the opposite situation, where a computer has extremely limited memory size, sometimes program portions are "overlaid," brought into memory as needed but not left resident there. Aggregating program portions using a call structure generator as described previously, may be essential, to allow an overlay to be a unified whole.

In programming languages that do not support recursion, sometimes a programmer accidentally does it anyway. (For example, module A calls module B which in turn calls module A.) This is a difficult error to find. The call structure generator can identify such problems in advance, since it must detect such recursions in constructing the calling trees it produces.

Some programming methodologies call for the documentation to contain these call structures. It may be easy to construct them manually the first time, but during maintenance, as the software is repeatedly changed, if this process is not automated it will simply be abandoned.

Performance analyzer. Suppose the program you are maintaining runs abominably slowly, and your most important maintenance task is to diminish its running time. There are many tools to assist in identifying those program portions that consume the most time, so that optimization efforts can be focused there. (In most programs, the "Pareto effect" which states that 20 percent of causes produce 80 percent of the effects comes into play here. That is, 20 percent of the software probably accounts for 80 percent of the running time. It is that 20 percent that must be identified and improved.) Techniques for doing performance analysis are discussed in depth in a later section of this book.

Metrics analyzer. Over the years, numerous algorithms have been developed for measuring as-built software for a variety of reasons. The most common reason is to calculate complexity, to determine which portions of a program are more complex than some norm. Tools automating these algorithms are now plentiful. There is considerable debate, however, as to their value. Some use them to identify program portions where simplification could be important. Others say that such complexity analyzers are more alchemy than science, and that some program portions are complex simply because the underlying problem to be solved was complex. We return to this debate in a later section of this book on software metrics. Meanwhile, let us simply say here that if it is important to identify program portions that are complex, there are certainly tools available that can do it.

Code auditor. Most programs are written to coding standards. It is important to determine whether those standards have been followed, whether it is during development or during maintenance. Code auditors assist in that process by checking for standards conformance for those standards where automated checking is possible.

The last clause in the preceding sentence is an important caveat. Although some standards can be checked for automatically, many cannot. (A conservative estimate is that perhaps 40 percent of standards violations can be so detected.) Consider, for example, a naming convention standard. Suppose it has a structure component (e.g., data names must reflect the name of the structure in which they reside, if any) and a mnemonic component (data names must reflect the meaning of the variable named). The first component can probably be automatically checked by a code auditor, but the second cannot. In general, syntactic standards can be automatically checked, and semantic ones cannot. (As another example, consider commentary. It is easily possible to automatically check the standard "comments shall constitute 40 percent of the source code," but it is not possible to so check "comments shall amplify the meaning behind the code.") Thus, code auditors can be an important part of, but not the whole of, standards conformance checking.

Ripple-effect detector. Suppose you are modifying a program, and you change a particular function, only to discover that although you changed 99 percent of the code related to the function, there was a difficult-to-spot side effect in a remote section of code that should have been changed but was not. This is a so-called *ripple effect* when there are hidden connections throughout a program such that a change in one part ripples into several other parts unexpectedly. There are tools which statically identify such ripples. (Note that the cross-reference lister falls into this class of tool; but ripple-effect detectors do sufficient static analysis on a program to automatically find the linkages, rather than leaving it manually to the maintainer-user, as with the cross-reference list).

Requirements tracers. In an earlier section of this book, we discuss the trials and tribulations of requirements tracing. Recall that it is a really great idea where all requirements are traced downward through the artifacts of the as-built code and upward again, so that a maintainer can immediately see the effect of changing a particular requirement. However, there are problems as the "requirements explosion" makes the bookkeeping difficult and visibility nearly impossible. Tools to support this activity are still rudimentary (most are driven by a U.S. Department of Defense methodological requirement to do this kind of tracing), but the subject area is worth watching. Better tools may make this technology area worth pursuing.

2.6.2.2.2.2 Data Analyzers

Just as the maintainer needs tools to help understand the existing software code, help is needed with the existing data as well. The following tools assist with that.

Data layout. Suppose you are maintaining a program whose data interrelationships are at best obscure. The data layout tool will abstract out the relationships between data items and show them graphically.

Data name standardization. Usually there are data naming conventions to be followed during development and maintenance. This tool can perform such standardization-supporting tasks as replacing all instances of a particular (presumably nonstandard) name with another; add record prefixes to all data names within the record (to support structured naming conventions); alphabetize scalar data items (to help the maintainer be able to find them); standardize data representations in a language such as COBOL that allow multiple types of representations (e.g., textual or pictorial representation); note all instances of data items that are initialized with values that do not reflect their type; and many other similar detail-level data tasks.

Data extraction. Sometimes data for a program may be extracted from a database that already exists. These tools support obtaining such data. One common use of such a tool is to extract artificial test data from "live" data files.

Data normalization. Database theory identifies proper and improper ways of entering and relating data within the base. A database normalizer checks a database for conformance to such rules, and identifies data items that need changing.

2.6.2.2.2.3 Change Analyzers

All of the preceding tools, in one way or another, support the maintainer in *understanding* the existing software. The tools in this section move beyond that. Their purpose is to assist the changing of the software once it is understood well enough to make the change possible.

Comparator. This is a multipurpose tool, used to compare two data files and identify differences between them. Maintainers can use it for two dramatically different activities. In the first, it is used in version control to check differences between one version of the software and another. For example, suppose you have made a change in some software such that a function that used to work correctly is now failing, and you are not aware of any change you made that could account for this problem. Using the comparator to identify differences between your new version and the old, you can check for places where a change you did not intend to make was in fact made.

"That program never did run right," said the maintainer. He had just finished putting a change into a program, and the test results were abominable.

"It did, too" said the developer. "All the test cases ran correctly before you put that change in."

Clearly it was time for a little impartial, perhaps even automated, adjudication.

The maintainer's version of the source and the developer's version of the source were supplied to the file comparator. Out came the list of file differences.

All but one were predictable—they were changes clearly related to the modification the maintainer had done.

But wait—what is this difference down here? Unexpectedly, there is another change in the program. Somehow, the word "ELSE" has been dropped out of the middle of an IF test unrelated to the change the maintainer made.

Somehow, perhaps no one will ever know how, that ELSE had been edited out of the developer's source along with the changes the maintainer had intended to make.

The comparator found the problem. No amount of human inspection had been rigorous enough to catch it.

In the second use of a comparator, test case results from a current test run can be checked against past correct results from the same test case to provide automatic detection of anomalies, alleviating the need for human checking of the test results.

If test inputs are created at the keyboard, keystroke capture programs can be used to "remember" what the input was, so that it can be reused later on.

Change tracker. This is a clerical tool, which can be used to do status reporting of modifications caused by software errors and changes during maintenance. We return to this concept in a later section.

Documentation manager. This is another clerical tool to help in constructing new versions of software documentation from old. For example, things in the new version that differ from the old can be marked in the margin with change bars, so that those who use the documentation can see at a glance how the new version differs from the old. This is especially important for reference documentation, such as user manuals or maintenance documents, where users taking delivery of the new document may wish to know immediately what is new about it.

2.6.2.2.2.4 Constructors

Once a change has been made in the software, it is necessary to insert the changed portions and rebuild the whole. It is the purpose of constructor tools to assist in that rebuilding.

Conditional compilation. Suppose the software you are maintaining is actually several pieces of software: a version for the IBM PC and its compatibles, a version for the Macintosh, and a version for the IBM mainframe. Suppose further that it exists in a debug version and a production version. The principle of single-point control suggests that it would be best to keep all these versions as one version with variants, so that when changes are made all changes can be consistent across versions. Conditional compilation is a tool capability that allows identifying, within a single source file, the various variants in the file, so that when the time comes to extract out and compile a particular version from the whole, the extraction can be done automatically. Conditional compilation tools come in several variations. Sometimes they are built into a compiler, and sometimes they exist in a separate preprocessor run before the compiler. But either way, their job is to allow a means for identifying and selecting versions.

Reformatter. Most software developers and maintainers believe that software with certain standards of readability is better than software that does not meet such standards. Readability is generally thought to include rules for indentation (such that source statements at like levels or of like kinds are aligned), and rules for appropriate use of white space. A reformatter, sometimes called a *prettyprinter,* transforms a source program into its indented, white-spaced equivalent.

Restructurer. Going one step further than a reformatter, which pretties but does very little code rearrangement, a restructurer will actually move and reorder code in order to make it structured (in the sense of structured programming). This capability was discussed in the earlier "R" words section.

Configuration management/version control. The worst nightmare in the software world is the one in which a carefully crafted program, in its *n*th incarnation, is lost, and there is no backup version from which to reconstruct it. Configuration management is the insurance policy that prevents that nightmare from happening. Version control is the capability that simplifies the tasks of configuration management.

The theory of configuration management is simple: Baseline versions of the product are saved and protected in such a way that they will exist even if something happens to the current version. But the practice of configuration management is more complicated than its theory. A software product typically consists of multiple artifacts such as source code, object code, documents of various kinds, with multiple versions such as the most recent experimental version, the most recent production version, the version used by most customers, the version(s) used by other customers, and so on. The task of configuration management is to extend that baseline insurance policy to cover all these multitudinous artifacts, and to do it in such a way that while the baselines are protected, the maintainer can still move forward in the necessary tasks of maintenance. Version control tools ease the task of reconstructing and/or rationalizing the various product versions being kept.

When John Harris, author of best-selling computer games on the Softsel "Hot List," headed off for Software Expo to show off his wares, he took a caseload of software with him. Key in the collection was his Atari computer version of "Frogger," the video arcade game, which was not quite complete yet, but ready for demonstration.

Not only did he have the unreleased Frogger with him. In his traveling case he also took a backup copy of Frogger, in case something went wrong with the original.

It was the only backup for Frogger.

Somewhere in San Diego, at one of the social events surrounding Software Expo, the inevitable happened. John's case vanished (as he learned later, it vanished into the hands of a competitor!). With it went not only the months of work which had gone into Frogger, but all the software tools and parts John had ever created for his other game efforts.

It took several months of despondency before John began again. Eventually, he overcame his configuration management calamity, rewrote Frogger, and saw it go to the top of the best-seller lists.

But not without enormous pain.

—*Adapted form* Hackers, Dell Books, 1984; Steven Levy.

Translator. Recall that one of the attributes of software quality is portability. Porting software from one setting to another is often a nontrivial task. Translators are tools to convert a software product from its current version into one acceptable in a new setting. There are translators from one variant of a language to another (e.g., old COBOL to new COBOL), from one machine setting to another (IBM mainframe to IBM PC), from one form of data to another (PC compatible to Macintosh compatible). The task of some translators is easy, but in the more difficult cases (e.g., one machine language to another) the automated tool can translate only a certain percentage of the source, flagging the rest for manual translation (for example, converting the easy 80 percent automatically but leaving the hard 20 percent to be done by hand).

Documentation extractor. Often the maintenance documentation consists of material originally written for another purpose, most commonly for design representation during development. Because maintainers may need that material in a new format, there are tools that extract from the original form the information wanted, and create a new version for the new usage.

Sometimes these tools are used to collect maintenance-relevant commentary from the source code and place it in a new maintenance document. It is the philosophy of this book that that level of maintenance documentation should be in the listing, not in a separate document, so this particular use of a documentation extractor is viewed here as counterproductive.

2.6.2.2.2.5 Testers

The software has been analyzed, changed, reconstructed, and now it is ready for testing. Most of the test capability needed by the maintainer is the same capability needed by the developer. But there is at least one additional tool the maintainer needs.

Regression tester. One of the surprises in software maintenance is the frequency with which a software change made for one purpose causes something else that used to work to fail. (Most commonly these problems are caused by ripple effects, discussed earlier.)

Because this problem happens frequently, a technique has been devised to protect against this class of problems. Regression testing is the act of running a standard baseline of test cases against each new version of the software, even when the code change is thought to have not affected most of the test cases, just to verify that everything that used to work still does.

Largely, regression testing is a technique rather than a tool. However, because of the repetitive nature of the technique, several tools already discussed can help in accomplishing its goals. Test managers are handy for setting up and executing the test cases. Comparators are useful in checking the test results against a baseline of correct answers.

However it is done, most maintainers learn early in their maintenance career (and the hard way!) that regression testing is an essential final step in preparing to release a new version of a software product.

2.6.2.3.1 Change Review

Just as there is a review process for software development, so, too, is there review of maintenance. *Change review* includes not only a decision-making process on what changes to make and when to make them, but also tracking the background information necessary to those decisions.

Change review, then, may be considered a multifaceted process. Records should be kept of all software error reports, software change requests, and their status. Status will include date of origin, priority assigned to the change, and estimated completion date. The records themselves should be reviewed to determine whether maintenance activities are keeping up with changes and thus whether manning is adequate, and to make sure that no change falls through the crack and is forgotten until some potentially embarrassing point in the future.

Change review also includes the process of deciding whether a change is appropriate and, if so, what priority to assign to it. Such a decision process must be both dependable and responsive; provision must be made for consideration of emergency changes, for example.

Usually, maintenance is an ongoing or "level-of-effort" activity. One or several programmers are assigned to maintain one or several pieces of software on a continuing basis, perhaps even interspersed with other development activities. Changes are scheduled dependent on both their importance and maintenance programmer availability. However, some computing installations with a heavy production-run orientation are using the concept of scheduled maintenance—changes are aggregated until a date defined in advance independent of the changes, and then all are put in at once. This technique will minimize the frequency of perturbances in the stability of the production program.

2.6.2.3.2 Change Reporting

During the time a software change is underway, there are a lot of interested parties who want to know how that change is progressing.

There is management, wanting to know if the change will be done on time, wanting to know if personnel levels are adequate, wanting to understand the status of the software product.

There are the maintainers, wanting to know how soon the change will become a part of the software they are maintaining, wanting to know if a change they are to make can begin without getting tangled up in another related ongoing change.

There are the users, wanting to know when they will have the capability they have requested, wanting to know when a failed part of the product will be well again.

And there are the customers, wanting to know when they will get what they are paying for.

It is for all of these players that the change report is made. The change report is simply a status report of all ongoing changes, showing (for each change) such things as

- who is working it
- how far along it is
- when it should be completed
- what version it will be in

The change report can be more than simply a status report, however. At its best it will include, probably in a separate report, trends information of interest to management:

- charts of the number of new changes versus time (to answer the question "is the change activity increasing or decreasing?")
- charts of the number of new errors versus time (to answer the question "is the product getting better or worse?")
- charts of the number of in-work changes versus time (to answer the question "are we keeping up with the changes?")

Thus, the change report is both a communication device, to keep all the players informed, and a decision-support device, to provide necessary information to the planners in software maintenance management.

2.7 AN ATTRIBUTE APPROACH TO QUALITY

Looking back over the pages of this book, we can see that up until now we have taken a *chronological* view of building quality software. That is, we have talked about the kinds of things a software person can do at each phase of the software life cycle.

There is another way to view the same material. Recall that we define quality as a set of attributes. A legitimate question to ask at this point is "Which of these techniques are useful to achieve which of these attributes?" After all, we have said that any software project should begin with a prioritization of the quality attributes in their order of importance. Once we have done that, the next question could very well be "Now that I have said that X is highest in priority, how do I go about achieving X?"

It is the intent of this section of this book to answer questions of that kind. In the sections that follow, we discuss each of the attributes in turn. And, when we finish with that, we talk about one other important approach to building a quality software product—satisfying the user of the product.

This, then, is the portion of the book that takes an *attribute-oriented* look at building a quality product. First we talk about the seven quality attributes as attributes of the *product*. Then we talk about user satisfaction, a *service attribute*.

2.8 PRODUCT ATTRIBUTES

> The testers gathered around the terminal.
> Project Spiffy, the software system whose bugs they were trying to remove, had done it again. The tester had keyed in what seemed like a fairly straightforward command, and the computer, in response, had apparently gone to sleep.

> The testers shuffled uneasily, stepping from one foot to the other. It wasn't the first time the system had done this.
>
> Then, just as before, after 35 or 40 seconds had gone by, a reawakening happened, and a response to the command appeared on the terminal screen. It was a good response. But that wasn't the point. The system response time was inadequate, and the response mechanism were unfriendly. Unless Spiffy's developers could overcome these problems, it was a dead system.

Quality, we saw earlier in this book, is made up of a lot of attributes. Spiffy's testers nominally were examining the system's *reliability,* but in the process of doing so they had come across a very serious problem of *efficiency.* And to make matters worse, it was badly *human engineered,* because while it was being inefficient it didn't warn the user that it was *not* asleep.

Quality is a mix of many attributes. We name and define them in a previous chapter: portability, efficiency, human engineering, understandability, testability, modifiability, and reliability. We talk about the fact that achieving all of them is difficult because they conflict with each other. And we talk about the need for prioritizing the attribute goals for a particular project at its inception because different projects demand emphasis on different attributes.

It should not have come as a surprise during testing that efficiency was an important quality attribute for Spiffy. Early on, during requirements specification, a requirement for appropriate response time should have been included in the system performance requirements. And that requirement should have served as a red flag to the developers, one among all the other requirements to be met, but one requiring special attention throughout the software development process. The design alternative studies should have examined ways of optimizing response time. Perhaps a model should have been constructed specifically to simulate the timing of the user interface. The as-built code should have been subjected to early timing studies. If file access was identified as a problem, quicker access structures should have been substituted even if coding them was a harder job. And as a last resort, if the function in question simply took too long and there was no help for it, human engineering techniques should have been employed to warn the user that a time-consuming task was about to be undertaken, and to keep the user posted as the task progressed.

Achieving just one of the quality attributes, in other words, may require a lot of focused work. And this work is over and above the normal, attribute-independent task of building a quality product. Of course we want an understandable, testable, modifiable, and reliable system. Perhaps it even needs to be portable. But while accomplishing all of this, we must also achieve the proper level of efficiency and user friendliness.

The story of Spiffy is just one of the stories which could be told about quality attributes. For another system, one which is expected to undergo frequent revision such as a tax system dependent on the latest tax laws, modifiability and understandability may be the key problems, and efficiency and human engineering may not be problems at all. For yet another system, microcomputer software that must run on every chip made and must be superbly user friendly, portability and human engineering may be so important as to dwarf all the other quality requirements.

The point is that the software developer must be concerned with a certain minimum standard of quality, and *in addition* must employ special techniques to ensure successful achievement of the highest-ranked quality attributes.

What special techniques? That's what this chapter of the book is all about. What we do here is look at each of the quality attributes, and for each of them provide a list of special techniques that will help achieve them. Fortunately, that does not mean that we must proceed through yet another several dozen techniques for achieving quality. All the special techniques we discuss here were already defined in the previous section when we talked about a life-cycle approach to quality. Here, acknowledging that not every project will be able to afford the use of all of those techniques, we simply focus on the ones most relevant to particular quality attributes.

The contents of this section, then, are presented in this form: an attribute followed by a list of the techniques that can help achieve it with each technique referenced to the life-cycle section where it was first discussed so that you can easily refresh your memory.

2.8.1 Techniques Useful for All Attributes

Certain quality techniques are so important that they transcend individual attributes. In this section, we deal with the set of techniques which should be used on nearly all software projects, regardless of each attribute's priority.

Reviews. (requirements reviews, 2.2.2.6; design reviews, 2.3.4; peer code review, 2.5.1.2; change review, 2.6.2.3.1; test review, 2.5.2.2.12.6; post-delivery review, 2.5.2.2.12.4). The review is a fundamental quality technique. The question should never be whether reviews are necessary. The only legitimate question is "What reviews shall we use on this project, and how formal should they be?"

A large or critical system might hold the complete spectrum of reviews: requirements, preliminary design, critical design, peer code, test, change, and probably a final delivery review as well. A small, noncritical project might have as few reviews as an informal requirements review, a single informal design review, and a final delivery product examination review.

Single-point control (2.6.1.1). For years, software engineers have sought to define a fundamental set of principles which could form the foundation of the discipline. The identification of those principles is still elusive as software development remains more of an art than a science, even though we might wish it otherwise. But one leading candidate for such a principle is single-point control. Recall that single-point control is the notion of taking an action which must be done in several places, doing it once instead, and referencing that one occurrence from the several places it is needed.

We previously discussed single-point control as a preventive maintenance technique and applied it largely to code. But the principle is more pervasive than that. It applies to any artifact of any technical problem. For example, in documentation we strive to describe something only once, and in databases it is considered most useful to have one occurrence of a set of data.

Single-point control is not only beneficial, it is nearly without cost as well. It is at least as easy to use as its alternatives. Thus, in single-point control we have one of those nice and rare occasions where quality and productivity go hand in hand!

High-Order Language (2.3.4). Recall that high-order language is a spectrum, and that quality is usually enhanced by using the highest-level language that solves the problem at hand. (Here again, productivity and quality go hand in hand.)

This particular attribute-independent technique, however, *does* have a small amount of attribute dependency. On those rare occasions where efficiency would be too seriously degraded by the highest-order language that would solve the problem, it is necessary to move down the language ladder until an appropriately efficient language is found.

It should be noted that efficiency is at least as much a function of language processor as it is of language. For example, a Pascal compiler will be considerably more efficient than a Pascal interpreter (probably 100 times more efficient!), and a bad COBOL compiler may produce object code ten times as inefficient as a good one. In other words, the pursuit of efficiency through language choice is a complex, multidimensional activity. Good design is always the best and easiest first approach to efficiency.

Standards and enforcers (2.3.5). A minimal set of standards with a mechanism to guarantee that these standards are used is vital no matter how big or small the project is. For particularly large projects with attendant communication problems, a larger set of standards may be needed to ensure that not just code but communication is well defined and predictable.

Structured coding (2.5.3). This is another technique like single-point control that is usually as economical to use as not to. Its benefits are attribute independent and it is useful regardless of the size of the project.

2.8.2 Portability

If you create a piece of software in one environment but you want to be able to use it in many, that software must have the attribute of *portability*. Portability has been a desirable quality attribute of software since the very beginning. In those days, computer hardware was improved so frequently that transferring software from one computing system to a newer one was the norm.

Now portability has taken on new dimensions. With a mass computer hardware market in place, software that is portable can tap into more of that market than software which is not. On the other hand, a lot of software not destined for this mass market need not be portable at all. But still, to the extent that software is made up of reusable parts (still more of a dream than a reality), those parts will have increased value if *they* are portable.

Portability, then, is a rather special quality attribute. Whether it should be a concern or not is almost entirely a matter of the case at hand. When it is needed, it is vital. When it is not, it can be ignored. Most other quality attributes are colored in shades of gray; portability tends to come in black and white.

A word of warning is appropriate here. Portability is deceptively difficult to achieve. Software which is to be portable must be developed independently of any single environment in which it will run. But differences between environments are often subtle. To achieve portability, it is vital to select a method of approach early in the software construction process (preferably, that approach should be specified in the requirements), and then enforce that approach with all the discipline of the dedicated. The following approaches can help achieve portability.

Standardization (2.3.5, 2.3.6, 2.5.2.2.9). The use of standardization is the most important way of achieving portability. But standardization takes on special meanings in this context.

Given that the software will run in multiple environments, it is necessary to define a common underlying environment that the software may rely on. There are several levels of environment which might be chosen to help achieve portability, and we discuss each of them in turn.

Standard Programming Language: The usual approach to achieving portability is the use of a common high-level programming language. By this, we mean not just a language which is commonly available, but one which can easily be subsetted if necessary to eliminate variations unique to particular environments.

The problem of choosing and using a common language is more complicated than it sounds. First of all, it must be true that acceptable-quality compilers for the language in question are available in all the prospective environments. Secondly, it must be true that language variants and compiler variants must be identified. Language and compiler variants are sometimes subtle, and sometimes only discernible through experience with the environment in question. Thus, the correct choice of a standard language requires both intelligence and experience.

Once the common language has been chosen and defined (that is, the common subset of the chosen language has been documented), it is not enough to turn the software developers loose on the project. Discipline must be used to ensure that the chosen language subset is not sidestepped; standards enforcement is vital. It is all too easy, in the heat of coding, to slip in the use of a nonportable element because the alternative is hard. That short-term decision will cause long-term pain for the people responsible for porting the resulting software to all its new environments.

Common choices of portable languages are the following:

- *C.* This language is frequently chosen because it runs on a portable operating system (Unix) and utilizes a portable compiler. Thus, the number of variants possible in both the language and its processor is nearly zero.
- *Ada.* The U.S. Department of Defense has worked very hard at ensuring that Ada is portable. They have standardized the language, built a standard set of tests for compilers that must be passed before the compiler can be used, and disallowed subsets. Ada is the epitome of the notion that it takes will and forethought to make a language portable.
- *Fortran.* This language has been chosen over the years because compilers are available for it nearly everywhere. The compilers are different, and language variants have been allowed, but it is common to define a machine-independent subset of Fortran and use that.
- *COBOL.* The same tends to apply to COBOL as to Fortran.
- *Basic.* The same tends to apply here, as well, especially in the microcomputer world.
- *Pascal.* This language was popular for portability in the late 1970s because of its common availability, especially through the existence of a portable operating system and compiler known as the UCSD Pascal system. (UCSD refers to the University of California at San Diego, where the system was conceived and implemented.) The users of this system had all the benefits of the C approach mentioned earlier.
- *Other languages.* These are by no means the only choices for portability; they are, however, the ones most commonly used by software

practitioners. The language Forth is popular among some microcomputer software developers because its interpretive system minimizes memory requirements for the application software, and because it is somewhat commonly available on micros.

Standard Computer: The second most common way of achieving portable software is the use of a standard computer. (Note that this is analogous to using a standard programming language in the sense that the machine language of the standard computer, or a compiler that generates that language, becomes the standard language.)

Early in software history, using a standard computer meant building software for the most commonly available computer, usually an IBM system, and insisting that all users acquire that computer. But more recently, more choices in standardized computers have become available.

First of all, most computer hardware vendors are trying very hard to standardize on a common hardware base for their software. The Digital Equipment Corp. VAX computers, for example, are available in sizes ranging from a micro version to a maxi version.

Second, some de facto standardization has occurred among chip makers in the micro world. Most microcomputers now manufactured are based on a chip purchased from one of the half dozen or so chip makers, so that computers from different manufacturers may be software compatible simply because their underlying chips are the same. The practice of building computers compatible with the IBM PC in the 1980s was a dramatic (and deliberate) example of chip-level compatibility.

Third, there are attempts being made to standardize the software interface of computer hardware so that computer vendors can build their hardware in whatever way they want, but the computers will appear the same to the software builder. This is a lot easier than it sounds. The instruction set is the heart of the computer from the programmer's point of view, and machines built with the same instruction set (list of instructions they will execute) will behave much the same way no matter who builds them. This is, in fact, an explicit standards approach to the de facto standardization which has occurred in the micro world. The U.S. Department of Defense has taken the lead in this area with its MIL-STD-1750 16-bit architecture and its MIL-STD-1862 32-bit architecture.

The progress of software portability in the future may very well depend on computer users organizing politically and insisting that hardware developers adopt such a standardized approach. The problem in the past has been that many computing standards are proposed, even by internationally recognized organizations, but the standards are ignored by enough vendors that they are effectively valueless. However, some users have joined in organizations such as the Corporation for Open Standards; the goal of such organizations is to ensure that everyone conforms to appropriate international standards. To date, they have not been notably successful. Note that software built for a standard computer needs no special attention to make it portable; by definition it will run wherever the standard hardware is available. This is the *best* approach to portable software.

Standard Operating System: Even if a standard programming language is used to achieve portability, there will be places in the program where it interacts with the operating system which cannot be made machine independent. This level of nonportability can be solved using a standard operating system.

Early in the history of computing, all hardware vendors defined their own operating system and interface. That is changing. First the Unix operating system came along and attracted such a strong phalanx of followers that it was made available (usually as an optional second operating system) on a large number of computers built by different vendors. Then, in the micro world, where standardized chips were already the norm, it became obvious to the new breed of hardware vendors that they could eliminate the tremendous cost of building their own operating system by buying one. CP/M was an early success in this area, and MS-DOS and then OS/2 came along later to usurp its popularity.

Because of these trends, it is frequently possible now for the software developer to write software whose operating system interfaces are standard. Recall that the popularity of the C language comes partly from the fact that language variants were eliminated by the common compiler, and operating system interface variants were eliminated by the common operating system (Unix).

Single-point control (2.6.1.1). The goal in making software portable is to write it in such a way that changes for alternate environments are nonexistent. Since that is often not entirely possible (you may, for example, need to write software for both the OS/2 and MS-DOS operating systems and the Intel and Motorola chips for marketing reasons), a secondary goal is to minimize and isolate the areas which may need change. These areas of change are commonly known as machine dependencies, and the method of isolating them is that of single-point control.

Things that are machine dependent must be defined once in a single point of control, then referenced wherever they are needed. Furthermore, these single points of control must be gathered together so that revising them for a new environment is made convenient.

What this means in practice is that portable software should have a large number of machine-independent components, and a small number of components isolated into clearly identified machine-dependent modules. It is especially important, of course, that these machine dependencies be heavily annotated, so that the software developer who must port the software to a brand-new system has a clear definition of what changes must be made. Examples of such machine-dependent components are:

- operating system interfaces, if a standard operating system is not used
- hardware dependencies (e.g., word length), if a standard computer is not used
- language variant usage, if a standard subset of a common language was not possible
- timing dependencies, where the execution of the software depends on the timing characteristics of a particular hardware or operating system

Conditional compilation (2.6.2.2.2.4). It is not uncommon that portable software does have isolated points of system dependency. Given that, it is useful to have a mechanism by means of which the right system-dependent components may be selected for a particular system creation of the software.

For example, suppose software system TOP-SELLER must run on both the Intel 486 and the Motorola 68000 chip. It would be possible to have two complete versions of the software with one for the Intel with its system-dependent components, and one for the Motorola with a different set. But now maintenance becomes something of a nightmare, because all changes must be made consistently in both versions, or they will begin to differ.

A preferable approach is to have one version of the software with special components for each of the environments in which it will run. For example, the random-access interface for the Intel version would be immediately followed by the comparable interface for the Motorola version, each identified with its own version selection code. Then, when the Intel version is to be compiled, for example, the compiler can be told to select only those components that are coded for it.

Conditional compilation, as we saw in an earlier section, is a powerful and simple way to accomplish this. It defines the version encoding scheme and provides the automatic selection mechanisms needed. For portable software containing multiple version definitions, this is an essential piece of technology.

REFERENCES

CASHIN89—"NIST Standards Expanding," *Software Magazine,* January 1989; Jerry Cashin. *Popular-press article on the role of the National Institute for Science and Technology (formerly, National Bureau of Standards) in applications portability facilitation.*

MOONEY90—"Strategies for Supporting Application Portability," *IEEE Computer,* November 1990; James D. Mooney. *Good, academic treatment of what is needed to achieve portability: languages, operating systems, environments, standards.*

STONE88—"We All Live in a Converting World," *Software Magazine,* December 1988; Benjamin Stone. *Popular-press summary of commercially available porting/conversion tools.*

2.8.3 Efficiency

Efficiency is the measure of the timing and sizing characteristics of a program. All software must be at least somewhat efficient. That is, it must not use too much of the computer's time or the user's time or the computer's storage resources.

With today's superfast computers, however, efficiency is something that most software developers for most applications rarely need to worry about. Of course, during design, algorithms and data structures are chosen so that resources are conserved, but generally these are almost automatic decisions.

For some applications, however, it is not that easy. In these cases the struggle to select the best algorithm or choose the best data structure is difficult. These applications are usually characterized by severe interface constraints such as the software must interact at just the right moment with nanosecond-fast hardware, or the software must interact within severely constrained response times with a human being. Or, if the problem is one of storage space rather than timing, the computer's main memory or secondary storage is severely strained by the quantity of data being processed or the size of the processing program.

There are some ways of achieving efficiency that are considerably better than others. Because of that, we not only list the techniques which promote efficiency, as we do in the other attribute-oriented sections, but we organize them into an optimum approach.

It should be noted that the quest for efficiency may not end with the development phase but may go on into maintenance. Programs which are efficient enough under test loading may not be good enough under production loads; or programs which were successful under last year's production loading may fail with increased activity. For some programs, analysis and adjustment may be a never-ending activity.

Design for efficiency. The place to start achieving efficiency in software is during design. If the effort is postponed to the coding phase, it may well be too late to achieve the desired efficiency.

The first level of concern in an efficient design is to minimize *input/output activity* within the program. The operation computers do least rapidly is access secondary storage devices; the design goal here is to minimize the number of accesses. If possible, for example, five pieces of information should be fetched in one access rather than in five. This may mean information should be grouped for speed of access. Often it means using an access scheme which goes directly to the desired information, as in random access, rather than working through a lot of other data looking for the desired information, as in sequential access.

Recall that sizing as well as timing is an efficiency concern. A choice of data organization which optimizes access time may or may not optimize storage utilization. It is important, therefore, when optimizing either sizing or timing to make sure that the other is not being seriously degraded.

As we have seen, minimization of input/output means making careful choices of data and file structures. Fortunately, coursework in these areas is now a standard part of the computer science academic curriculum, so most programmers are well armed with knowledge in this area.

In some applications there is huge potential for waste of time in certain interfaces, such as where the software polls a hardware device for information. Generally there is a best way of coding such an interface, and it is important to make use of that way. If it is not, and the interface is accessed frequently, a few milliseconds lost at each interface execution can add up to minutes or even hours of computer time during a lengthy application run. Here is an area where the designer may need to commit to using machine language code segments to achieve the necessary timing characteristics.

Some applications do not have data concerns to worry about but have complicated or frequent use of algorithms. It is important first to choose the optimum form of such an algorithm, and second to code it as tightly as possible.

The timing analysis of the software for the radar airplane showed that the program, which at this stage of development was too slow to keep up with the hardware from which it received data, was spending most of its time in a tight and small loop.

The software developers focused their attention on the loop. Most of the code in the loop couldn't be reduced or eliminated; it was essential to the function of the system. There was, however, one call to the trigonometric SIN routine. The call looked innocent enough, but in fact it accessed an algorithm which used a series expansion. Quite a bit of code was involved. Was it possible to make the SIN algorithm more efficient?

In this case, the developers realized, the SIN being calculated did not need the full seven digits of accuracy that the series algorithm gave them. In fact, for the purpose of this approximation, about three or four digits would do. With that in mind, they built a new SIN routine which used a table lookup and a linear interpolation rather than the series expansion. The new method took around a

> dozen instructions rather than the several dozen of the standard algorithm; it
> was enough to allow the program to meet its timing constraints.
>
> The table used in the new algorithm, of course, caused it to take up
> considerably more space than the other algorithm. It is not unusual that to
> optimize time you end up degrading space, and vice versa. But in this applica-
> tion, the problem had been timing. By appropriate (and unusual) algorithm
> substitution, the problem had been solved.

Since there are so many diverse ways of designing for efficiency, and
since achieving efficiency for a particular application may be so complex, it
is sometimes necessary to simulate or prototype a proposed design in order
to get an advance measure of whether it will be good enough.

This simulation can be on paper, simply looking at transaction rates
and average access times: "Suppose we have 5,000 transactions an hour,
and suppose each takes an average of 3 seconds, will the proposed system be
able to keep up?"

But at other times simulation software may be needed. Suppose the
transaction rates are variable, or access time depends on machine loading,
or simultaneous requests come in from many user terminals. Then the
designer will build a simplistic version of the final product, in order to
conduct timing studies to determine if the design is feasible. Real-time
systems for application problem areas which have never been solved before,
such as space missions, often involve the construction of design prototypes
which are almost as complete as the final software itself.

Code for efficiency. Only after all design efforts for optimization have been
utilized should coding solutions be employed. There is a good reason for
that. Software productivity and quality are generally both dramatically
improved by the use of the highest-level language possible. Techniques for
making code more efficient often involve moving away from this highest-
level language. This is a step to be taken reluctantly.

In fact, the first step to be taken to code for efficiency is to use an
appropriately *optimized compiler* for the high-level language. This generally means, for openers, avoiding interpretive compilers if timing efficiency is a concern. Interpretive code usually takes at least 100 times
longer to execute than compiled code. (However, if space is a concern,
interpreters generally produce a smaller object program than compilers,
and so interpreters may actually be the optimization choice if main memory space is the problem!)

Assuming that an interpreter is not being used and there is still a
timing problem, it may be that the code being produced by the compiler is
less efficient than it ought to be. Some compilers use complex optimization
schemes to produce faster object code; code produced by these compilers

may be 50 percent to 100 percent faster than code produced by a simpler compiler. If timing efficiency is known in advance to be a problem, it may be essential to run some compiler benchmarks (execute the same algorithm on several different compilers and measure the execution time for each) to select a compiler which produces the best-quality code for the application domain in question. This kind of analysis may even affect the choice of high-level language to be used. (Obviously, this analysis should be done well before the coding phase begins.)

It should be noted that there is almost no way other than through benchmarks for the average software engineer to determine the efficiency of code produced by a compiler. Compiler builders may claim to have performed certain kinds of optimizations, but it is easier to claim an optimization than to perform it.

With or without an optimizing compiler, code produced by a compiler is sometimes erratic. For an algorithm whose timing is critical, the programmer may want to code it in several different but comparable ways and measure the execution efficiency of the compiled code for each.

In addition, certain optimizations that compilers may perform can also be performed relatively easily by the programmer. For example, code whose effect does not change during the execution of a loop should never be present in the loop. A high-quality (and expensive) optimizing compiler can perform this optimization, but so can a programmer. These kinds of optimizations, where the programmer continues to use a high-level language but seeks to improve the code, are called *hand optimizations.*

One of the most famous optimization studies of all time was really a competition. It happened on the Space Shuttle project.

There was a strong debate between the backers of high-level language (in this case, NASA's HAL/S) and the backers of assembler code as to which was appropriate for the system code. The contestants decided to settle the issue with a code-off.

The ground rules were simple. The backers of each language could code their solution and revise it as often as they wanted. When it was as good as they felt they could make it, the two products would be compared. The fastest code would be the winner, but because the other benefits of high-level language are so large, it was acknowledged that the assembler code would have to be significantly better for it to win.

The skilled assembler programmers took their best shot and turned in their code. But the high-level language programmers coded a first solution and then began a series of hand optimizations seeking the most efficient code. It was easy for them to perform these hand optimizations, just a matter of substituting one or two statements here and there. The assembler programmers, on the other hand, did not do hand optimizations. Assembler code is much more difficult to tinker with without destroying its correctness.

When the time came to measure the final versions, the result was a surprise to everyone. The high-level language code was always within 5 percent to 10 percent of the assembler code in efficiency; sometimes it was even better. Hand optimization had been good enough to make high-level language a viable option even when superefficient code was needed.

If automated optimization and hand optimization still don't produce the necessary efficiency, it may indeed be necessary to resort to *assembler code* in certain timing-critical sections of a program. This is most often done by writing an assembler language subroutine and calling it from the high-level language, but for some compilers (e.g., Ada compilers) the programmer may actually insert machine language code in line amid the high-level language code. The latter solution is dangerous in that it reduces code readability and modularity and scatters machine dependencies (undesirable from a portability point of view), but the elimination of the subroutine call overhead may on rare occasions be the difference between a successful optimization and an unsuccessful one.

Analyze for efficiency. In the preceding two sections we discuss design and then coding optimization schemes. Design optimization, we saw, should be performed up front in the project. When should coding optimization be performed?

The obvious answer, "during coding," is incorrect. The problem here is that during coding the programmer simply doesn't know which portions of the code are worth optimizing and which are not. The proper solution is to code the carefully chosen designs in the high-level language of choice, and then conduct performance analysis of the resulting code to see if it needs additional optimization. Code optimizations should only be performed in portions of the program where it has been found that help is needed.

Performance analysis tools, which monitor the execution of code, are discussed in Chapter 1.5.2. Appropriate use of a performance analyzer should allow the programmer to identify timing-critical sections of code, and begin code optimization work in that area.

Fine tune for efficiency. Sometimes program performance can be improved without changing the program at all! We have already seen one example in the discussion of the impact of compilers on code efficiency. Another place where such improvements can be made is in the computing system underlying the program. Sometimes the hardware configuration, or the database/file organization, or the operating system options can be modified to produce impressive improvement of program performance. This is the fine-tuning process, and it can best be performed by those responsible for the artifact in question—the systems programmers, if tuning of the operating system or hardware configuration is involved, or the data administrator, if data organization is involved. Many tools are available to support these people in this kind of work, some from the computer hardware vendor, others from performance analysis software vendors.

Wizards. Key, knowledgeable people are important to all software processes. This is especially true in matters of efficiency. We have already seen that compiler gurus, systems programmers, or data administrators can be helpful in obtaining a more efficient problem solution. In most software development organizations there are also applications specialists who are particularly helpful in these matters. Often called *wizards,* they are the people who have particularly well-honed optimization skills. The consultation support of one good wizard may be worth more than all the other efficiency approaches mentioned here put together! There is, however, one appropriate warning in this regard. Sometimes wizards are so involved in optimizations that they optimize things that need not have been optimized. A little wizardry can go a long way!

Summary As you have seen, this whole process of performance analysis and optimization can be complicated. Fox [89] offers an excellent discussion of the intricacies of performance engineering for those applications where efficiency is of the essence. Figure 2.16 is taken from that paper and shows the various activities that may be undertaken on a project life-cycle framework.

REFERENCES

ARMENISE89—"A Structured Approach to Program Optimization," *IEEE Transactions on Software Engineering,* February 1989; Pasquale Armenise. *Proposes a "paradigm for program optimization" to overcome software engineering's "neglect" of optimization.*

ESTOCK89—"The Inside Scoop on Execution Analysis," *IEEE Software,* January 1989; Richard G. Estock. *Product review of a tool called "Inside" that helps identify and isolate inefficiencies in programs written in certain versions of C, Pascal, Basic, Fortran, and Modula-2.*

FOX89—"Performance Engineering as a Part of the Development Life Cycle for Large-Scale Software Systems," *Proceedings of the 11th International Conference on Software Engineering,* May 1989; Gregory Fox. *Describes an approach to performance evaluation that begins with system modeling early in the life cycle and continues with performance checkpoints scheduled throughout the software development process.*

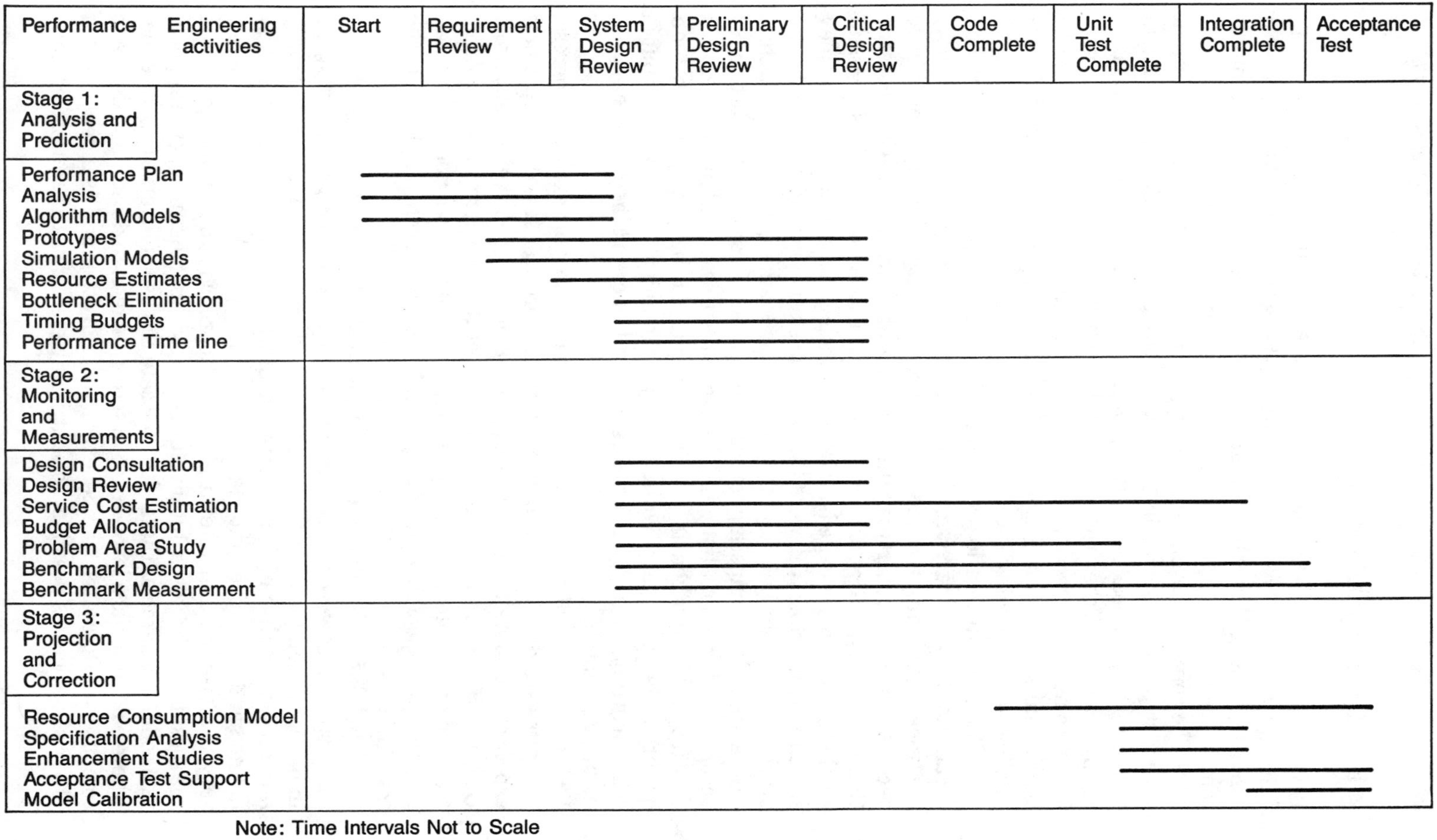

The chart is organized as a table with the following structure:

Performance Engineering activities	Start	Requirement Review	System Design Review	Preliminary Design Review	Critical Design Review	Code Complete	Unit Test Complete	Integration Complete	Acceptance Test
Stage 1: Analysis and Prediction									
Performance Plan									
Analysis									
Algorithm Models									
Prototypes									
Simulation Models									
Resource Estimates									
Bottleneck Elimination									
Timing Budgets									
Performance Time line									
Stage 2: Monitoring and Measurements									
Design Consultation									
Design Review									
Service Cost Estimation									
Budget Allocation									
Problem Area Study									
Benchmark Design									
Benchmark Measurement									
Stage 3: Projection and Correction									
Resource Consumption Model									
Specification Analysis									
Enhancement Studies									
Acceptance Test Support									
Model Calibration									

Note: Time Intervals Not to Scale

Figure 2.16 Performance engineering and the software development life cycle (from [Fox89]). © 1989 IEEE.

2.8.4 Human Engineering

It is not enough in the 1990s to build software that does its job well. Software must also be convenient and comfortable to use. Working toward achieving this goal is called *human engineering*. And there is one thought that is the essence of all of human engineering: "think user."

The software developers striving for a well human-engineered product must put themselves in the place of the user, and develop a system according to the needs perceived from that point of view. Some go so far as to say [Heckel84] that the software developer must *start from* the user interface needs and work into the technical solution, rather than the more traditional software engineering approach of starting with the technical problem and troweling the user interface on later.

The most dramatic progress in the software world during the last decade has been achieved in the field of human engineering. *User friendly* has gone from being a buzzword to being a reality. User interfaces have become innovative, starting with the work at Xerox's Palo Alto Research Center (Xerox PARC) and evolving on to the commercially successful Apple Macintosh. So-called *windows* technology, where the user's display screen is treated as if it were the user's desktop and information can be overlaid over other information there, is now available for most computers from a number of competing software companies. Graphics interfaces have become much more realistic and the user can interact with pictures as well as with words and charts. Auditory output can be achieved with high quality if the customer is willing to pay for it, and although audio input is still fairly constrained, it has been successful where a constrained environment is acceptable.

It is important to note that there is a price for this exciting progress. The software developer who wants a successful user interface must now expect to spend half again or perhaps even double the development time. User interfaces are becoming a specialty of their own; for products to be marketed to the general public, it may be necessary to bring in a human engineering specialist to design and perhaps even implement the interface.

Modularity is of course important in good interface design, but in some special new ways. Some advocate a *dialog socket* [Coutaz85], an implementation technique where the interface implementation is totally separated from the application implementation except through a carefully defined and minimized interface. With this approach, should it be necessary to revise the user interface, the old approach can be unplugged from the socket and the new solution plugged in, without disturbing the application code. The same authors also advocate the use of layers of abstraction, where each interface level—user to screen, screen to device, and device to computer—are treated as independent of each other and as independent of physical devices as possible, so that if any element of the interface must change (e.g., we choose to support another device) there is minimal perturbance to the rest of the code. The goal and the hope here is that a standard library of interface construction parts, a *user interface toolkit,* would eventually be developed. Some of these toolkits are now available.

However, implementing the user interface is not the hardest problem; designing it is. As we mentioned before, the key to good interface design is for the designer to think like a user. Heckel [84] advocates that the designers consider themselves as artists, not technologists, and treat the problem as one of communication. He suggests studying some traditional art disciplines, such as movie making and entertainment, to find analogies to help the designer be more effective at thinking like a user.

"Think user" can take on many dimensions:

- *Market research.* Know your users and what they want and need. (Note that what they want and what they need may not be the same thing, but be careful about ignoring wants.)

- *User participation in reviews.* Let your user give feedback as the design evolves.

- *Prototyping.* If the users don't have a clear picture of wants and needs, build a sample and let them experiment with it.

- *User education.* Help the user get comfortable with the interface you eventually choose. Offer courses in product use.

- *Levels of user support.* Make the software self-instructional through a carefully constructed tutorial interface. Provide optional access to help files. Give the experienced user a faster interface option. Provide good user documentation to use when all else fails. Produce meaningful diagnostic messages.

- *Use established guidelines for user interfaces.* Every publication on user interfaces (see the reference list) includes a set of 10 to 100 guidelines for building good interfaces. Admonitions include simplicity, consistency, predictability, and so on. Find a set of guidelines appropriate for your application and follow them.

It is important for the software specialist to keep abreast of both research literature and industry progress, especially in the microcomputer world, in this area. It is evolving so rapidly that the unaware specialist runs the risk of becoming obsolete.

REFERENCES

ABLEX—This publishing company (Ablex) publishes a series of books on the theme of human/computer interaction, with such titles as *Advances in Human-Computer Interaction, Human-Computer Interface Design Guidelines, and Directions in Human/Computer Interaction.*

COUTAZ85—"Abstractions for User Interface Design," *IEEE Computer,* September

1985; Coutaz. *Discusses ways of implementing good user interfaces. Stresses layers of abstraction and a user interface toolkit.*

GRUDIN89—"The Case Against User Interface Consistency," *Communications of the ACM,* October 1989; Jonathan Grudin. *Finds the arguments in favor of consistent user interfaces dissolve upon closer inspection; it is the user's needs, rather than consistency, that should drive interface design.*

HECKEL84—*The Elements of Friendly Software Design,* Warner Books, 1984; Paul Heckel. *Says that good interface design is an art form, not a technology, and suggests that software engineers must study the techniques of such artists as movie makers. Lists guidelines for good interface design.*

IEEE89—Special issue on "User Interfaces," *IEEE Software,* January 1989. *Contains nine papers on user interfaces, including "User Interface Tools: Introduction and Survey."*

IEEE90—Special issue on "User Interface Design," *IEEE Software,* July 1990. *Describes graphical user-interface specification techniques, constructing graphical output, and a tool to handle user interface design within an application system.*

SHNEIDERMAN86—*Designing the User Interface: Stategies for Human-Computer Interaction,* Addison-Wesley, 1986; Ben Shneiderman. *Concepts of interface design by one of the activists in the field.*

SMITH82—"Designing the Star User Interface," *Byte,* April 1982; Smith, Irby, Kimball, Verplank, and Harslem. *Popular-press article on the pioneering user-friendly system that evolved to become the Apple Macintosh interface, written by the Xerox PARC system developers.*

2.8.5 Understandability

When computing was new, it was so difficult to write a program that no one thought about making it readable. After all, who would ever want to read a program?

The answer came along all too soon. *Maintainers* need to read a program. A whole new outlook on programming came into being; that is, programs must not only be easy to write to increase productivity, they must be easy to read as well.

By the later 1950s, when high-level programming languages were first being defined and used, the creators of COBOL not only knew that reading code was important, they believed it to be more important than writing it. The result was the verbosity of COBOL, with verbs like MOVE CORRESPONDING that take a long time to write but add to the readability of the result. The hope at that time was that with a "self-documenting" language anyone, including the managers of software developers, could and would read code.

We have gotten smarter since then. It is generally accepted now that programming must balance ease of writing with ease of reading, and that neither can be sacrificed to the other. It is also generally accepted that, no matter how palatable the code is, it takes a technically knowledgeable person to read it.

That is the history of *understandability* as a quality attribute. It is vital that a program be understandable because a maintainer will inevitably need to understand the code in order to revise it. Experience has told us that the hardest part of the maintainer's job, in fact, is *not* making changes but understanding the existing code well enough to find where to make the changes.

Fortunately, understandability as a quality attribute is easy to achieve and most professional programmers know how to do it. Unfortunately, however, the pressure to write code still causes programmers to sacrifice understandability in the pursuit of productivity. The following guidelines are reminders of what must be done to make a program readable. It is up to the programmer or the programmer's manager to apply discipline to achieve the necessary result.

Readable code. There are very specific guidelines for making code more readable. Choose *naming conventions* for data items and logic structures that reflect and reinforce the meaning of what they do. For example, some programmers use nouns to name data items (the objects of actions) and verbs to represent subroutines or procedures (subroutines perform actions on data items). Other programmers, especially on massive software systems, let the names of data items reflect their encompassing structure. A field of a record, for example, might contain a key to its record in its name, or a data item in a component of a system might contain a key to its component in its name.

Make the code itself simple, structured, and modular. Use indentation and white space both to clarify logic organization and to make the code visually interesting and appealing. Organize the code logic to facilitate ease of reading and reference. (Some programmers place internal subroutines in alphabetical order, for example, to make it easier to look them up and find out what they do.) Use a consistent and easy-to-understand style. (Some software houses have one person on a project responsible for style; that person has the authority to revise style to match the norm or the corporate standard.) Provide assertions 2.5.2.1.2 which indicate to the reader what results are to be achieved by particular collections of code.

Commentary. There is no such thing as a self-documenting programming language. No matter how much we wish there were one, and now matter how much care a programmer puts into making the code readable, it *must* be supplemented by commentary. There are well-known guidelines for where and how to comment:

- At the beginning of each module, place information that defines the module's fundamental function and possible anomalous results.
- At each subfunction (begin-end block, logic branch, straight segment of code) define the function it performs.
- At each complex section of code, define what it does and why it is complex.
- At each interface, define the interface.
- At each collection of data items, define the purpose, possible values, and meanings of those values.
- For each individual data item, do the same.
- Provide appropriate overall historic information, such as a record of changes, with dates and names of programmers.

There are several rather different ways of achieving this level of commentary information. The coder may simply follow these guidelines explicitly and add the commentary to the code, either at creation time or later. *Or* the programmer may save the appropriate level of design representation, and insert it into the code to become the commentary. *Or* the programmer may write an English prose description of the problem, as might appear in a maintenance document, and embed the code itself within the prose, treating the prose as big chunks of commentary. (See examples of this latter approach in the material on *literate programming,* such as Knuth [84] and Bentley [86].)

Documentation (2.6.1.3). The documentation which should be created to aid understandability is maintenance documentation. It is important here to prioritize these understandability tasks. Only after a thorough job is done of making the code readable and well commented should the software developer undertake the written documentation. That is not to play down the importance of the document to the understanding of the software; it is just that in-place explanations have far more value than separate explanations. The role and content of maintenance documentation is discussed in the previously referenced section.

Code analysis. Analysis is important to understandability in two ways. The first is simple; it is important that a process be defined whose goal is to check the code for understandability. This might be one of the functions of the peer code review, or it might be a separate pass over the code by the developers or by an overview organization just to assure that understandability is present.

The second part of analysis is the need to extract meaning from the code once it has been created. The cross-reference capability and the call structure generator (see 2.5.2.2.2.1) are narrow but useful analytic tools. Commercially available products to support other aspects of understandability are beginning to be available. For example, several companies market programs which restructure spaghetti code into structured code, and a product called Via/Insight analyzes a program for meaning, then interacts with the maintainer who may obtain information about logic paths.

Analysis is the capstone of all the other understandability actions. It is the necessary supplement to the vital foundation of making the code readable in the first place.

Pointers to the authors. If analysis is a capstone, identifying the author is a court of last resort. Some code is so obscure that even with a good foundation and useful analysis, the maintainer may still not be able to understand it. It is important that the program be linked in some way to the programmer who originally wrote the code, so that the maintainer may make contact and obtain a firsthand explanation. It is vital to note that, after time passes, the author may be only slightly better prepared than the maintainer to recall and understand the code. That is why it is vital for the author to put the foundation firmly in place at the outset, while he or she is still able to do so.

REFERENCES

BENTLEY86—"Programming Pearls" columns on literate programming, *Communications of the ACM*, May and June 1986; Jon L. Bentley. *Advocates and illustrates the use of Knuth's literate programming. See Knuth [84].*

KNUTH84—"Literate Programming," *Journal of the ACM*, 2 (1984); Donald E. Knuth. *The seminal work on literate programming, a focus on creating readable programs through heavy emphasis on explanatory text in the program.*

2.8.6 Testability

In an earlier section of this book we spent quite a bit of time on how to construct test cases. There is another facet of this testing process; that is, not only must the test cases be necessary and sufficient, but the software itself and the process of creating it should facilitate good testing. This is the quality attribute of *testability*. It is vitally important to software which will undergo intensive initial testing, or frequent change and thus frequent retesting.

To build testable software, start with testable requirements that can be expressed with a method of demonstration in mind. The test plan should link each requirement to one or more test cases which can demonstrate it.

In designing for testability, exception processing and diagnostic handling must be clearly thought out and explicitly handled.

Techniques for coding for testability include:

- Source language debug capability (2.5.2.1.1) should be created and left in the code, selectable via conditional compilation (2.6.2.2.8.4).
- Self-checking code, such as assertions (2.5.2.1.2), should be used to ease the task of understanding anomalous results when the code is executed.

To facilitate testing itself:

- Test planning should include preparation of test documentation (2.5.2.2.12.5) and the use of test reviews (2.5.2.2.14.6).
- Test drivers (2.4.2.2.7.1) or environment simulators (2.5.2.2.7.3) should be constructed and saved where appropriate (along with the code) for reuse. If the system is complex, an automated test manager (2.5.2.2.1.2) may be vital.
- Correct test results should be saved for comparison with new test results, preferably using an automated comparator (2.6.2.2.2.3).
- To the extent practical, test cases should be created by a test data generator (2.5.2.2). No matter how created, a test bank of good tests should be saved for regression testing purposes (2.6.2.3.2.5)
- Testing should be measured for thoroughness by a test coverage analyzer (2.5.2.2.6).
- Order for the whole process of testing and revision must be maintained through configuration management (2.6.2.7.2.4), change review (2.6.2.3.1), and error reporting (2.6.2.3.2).

Testability is not just a matter of attention to the code. A testable system considers code, documentation, support tools, and methodologies as an integrated whole.

2.8.7 Modifiability

The maintenance of software involves two key quality attributes; understandability and modifiability. We discuss understandability in Section 3.2.5. Here we discuss modifiability. Software which is *modifiable* has been built with change in mind.

Given some software and a request for change, once the software in the area of the change is reasonably well understood, the maintainer will soon learn whether or not the software is modifiable. Most software is built for long-term usage, and thus will undergo frequent or at least occasional modification: Modifiability should be a nearly universal quality attribute.

Because of that, the techniques discussed in section 2.8.1, as the techniques useful for all attributes are especially important here. In particular, *single-point control, high-order language, standards and enforcers,* and *structured coding* are vital.

For software to be modifiable, it must also be understandable. All of the techniques discussed in Section 2.8.5 are applicable to modifiability as well.

Once the software is modified, it must be testable. All of the techniques discussed in Section 2.8.6 are also applicable here.

Consequently, making software modifiable is a tall order. It is no wonder that modifiability is an often neglected quality attribute. In fact, in many software projects where maintenance is a contractual add-on, software managers will specifically object to efforts to make the software more modifiable during development. "Why do something free that you can get paid for later on?" is the objection here.

Nevertheless, the quest for software quality must include consideration of at least the desirability of modifiability, and quite likely the implementation of it as well. What other techniques are there for making software modifiable?

It should be written where possible to anticipate change. The techniques of preventive maintenance (Section 2.6.1) are useful here; so is the use of designed-in *stubs,* sections of code which go nowhere initially but may lead to code added if an anticipated change occurs. It is particularly important, of course, to comment or document these stubs are for, and how they can become useful.

As software is modified, *version control* and *configuration management* 2.6.2.2.2.4 become vital. Without baseline and backup for elements of the software being modified, a whole system can be lost.

Requirements traceability (2.2.2.4) can be particularly useful here. If a requirement changes, the thread of design, code, and test which flows from the requirements can be followed to find the parts of the software and its support materials which must be changed.

From a technical point of view, the problem of modifiability is relatively straightforward and the techniques for achieving it are well known. The problems for this particular quality attribute fall more into the political and economic realm. That is, we know how to do it, but we are not always convinced we want to!

2.8.8 Reliability

The most universal of the quality attributes is *reliability.* No matter what other aspects of quality are important to the software, reliability always is. Of course, for some software with lives or large amounts of money depending on it, reliability becomes more of a focused concern than for other kinds of software.

Slicksoft, a software house, was sponsoring a programming contest. The person who wrote the shortest and fastest program to a given set of requirements would be acknowledged as the best programmer in the house.

Everyone talked about the contest. Programmers are generally not bashful about their own abilities. Nearly everyone thought they had a chance to win.

But when all the results were in, one programmer was so far ahead of the others that it was embarrassing. The programmer had solved the problem in one programming language statement!

The judges scratched their heads and looked at the program. It was, to be sure, the shortest and fastest submitted. But it also didn't even begin to solve the problem. "Why did you do this?" the judges asked the responsible programmer.

"Well, it is the shortest and fastest," said the programmer. "You didn't say it had to be reliable, too."

Reliability is the ability of the software to satisfy its requirements without error. The task of producing reliable software, then, is to minimize errors during development and eliminate them as far as possible during checkout. The techniques that follow are designed to help accomplish that task. (It should be noted that there is an alternate use of the word *reliability*. It is used by some people to discuss the statistical measurement of how error free a product is. This book focuses more on the achievement of quality than its measurement; except for a later section on metrics, we do not treat reliability as a statistical concept.)

Rigorous requirements approaches (2.2.2). All of the techniques for requirements are vital to producing reliable software. If the requirements are not right, the software cannot possibly be right. The most common cause of *major* software development problems is erroneous or unstable requirements. The developer must use all means necessary such as appropriate requirements languages, modeling and simulation or prototyping, traceability, and reviews to eliminate any chance of a requirements problem. Economics may dictate that not all of these approaches be used; it is then the job of technology to choose the best cost-effective subset for a particular application.

Correct design approaches (fault-tolerant software, 2.3.2, automated design checking 2.3.3, design reviews 2.3.4). Design is another make-or-break phase of software development. We have seen that most software errors happen during design. It is vital that careful design techniques be used to minimize or eliminate those errors. Again, the choice of techniques must meet logical cost-benefit criteria. Design reviews are nearly always used. Automated design checking may be used if the appropriate tools are available, but fault-tolerance techniques may only be used in software with a particularly high reliability requirement.

Error-inhibiting implementation techniques (high-order language 2.4.4, standardized elements 2.4.6). By the time the coding phase is reached, the most important opportunities for eliminating devastating errors have passed. Many of the implementation techniques discussed in Section 2.4 are focusing more on other quality attributes and on productivity. But the use of high-order language eliminates the possibility of whole classes of errors, and the use of standardized parts means using bug-free software instead of starting from scratch. There is still the potential for introducing lots of errors into the software at this stage; that is one reason why checkout will always be a necessary part of the software development process.

Thorough checkout techniques (2.5). The whole purpose of the checkout phase of software is error removal. All of the techniques of that earlier section are vital in the context of producing high-reliability software. Because of the plethora of choices, once again, the developer must make difficult but vital cost/benefit trade-offs.

Careful maintenance (2.6.2.2.2.4 configuration management 2.6.2.2.2.5, regression testing 2.6.2.3.2, error reporting 2.6.2.2.2.3, comparator). More errors than we wish are removed from software during the maintenance process, but probably the more serious problem here is the reintroduction of errors, those which are caused by the changes being made. Reliability concerns do not end with product delivery, then; it is necessary to pursue reliability as carefully in the mini life cycle of maintenance as it was during the original development process. Because of that, all the techniques of all the life-cycle phases come into play here, and then maintenance-phase reliability techniques as well. Configuration management wards off the ultimate software error, losing the whole system; regression testing is designed to keep the software from backsliding; error reporting ensures that errors, once detected, are not forgotten; and the comparator is a handy tool for detecting errors in a new version of software run against a baseline set of correct answers. Most of what we have seen so far in this book is applicable to producing high-reliability software.

2.9 SERVICE ATTRIBUTES

It is not just the software product that must have quality; the service performed on that product must be quality oriented as well.

From a computing installation point of view, good service can be measured by several attributes: timeliness (response time per interaction, turnaround time for complete results), reliability (availability of service on demand), accuracy (correctness of results), and cost (price per unit of solution, resource usage).

Software plays a role in each of these service attributes. Timeliness is dependent on the efficiency of the software; reliability is dependent on the reliability of the software; accuracy is dependent on the correctness of the software (and thus, again, its reliability), and cost is dependent on the efficiency of the software.

However, software's role in these service attributes, although important, is not key. Service attributes are usually a part of the discipline of computer installation management. And as can be seen from the preceding paragraph, software's role in giving good service can be fulfilled by building a quality product via key attributes (in this case, reliability and efficiency).

There is one additional topic that software people should consider that is key to these services, however; that topic is user satisfaction. We discuss ways of producing satisfied users in the section that follows.

2.9.1 User Satisfaction

It is no wonder that software quality is a difficult topic to talk about. Key players in the field disagree on what it really means.

Probably the most popular school of thought says "quality is meeting requirements." However, it has a major flaw. Even if the requirements for software specify such important quality attributes as modifiability and testability, in some way—and generally, in today's state of the practice, they do not—there is still the dilemma that if the requirements include cost, a Hyundai may be considered of higher quality, using this definition, than a Rolls Royce.

Well, then, if "quality = requirements" is flawed, how about taking a step backward and saying quality is the same as user satisfaction? After all, satisfying the users is what requirements are really all about. Why not get right to the heart of the matter?

That school of thought has a problem, too. Ives [83] states it succinctly: "A 'good' information system perceived by its users as a 'poor' system is a poor system." But perhaps that's too succinctly. Let's look at it a little more colloquially. Suppose I can build a software product with one of two people—rude Rudy, a technical whiz who knows computing and software inside out but has (shall we say) rough personality edges, or slick Sam, who has a personality that would charm an iceberg but whose technical knowledge is a cut below MIS 101. If we choose rude Rudy, we will likely get a quality product but an alienated customer; if we choose slick Sam, we will get the opposite.

Clearly, then, both Ives [83] and rude Rudy show us that quality and user satisfaction are two rather different things. Something is wrong with the "quality = satisfaction" school of thought, too.

The problem here is that we are casting about in the world of goals, and coming up with the wrong catch. Certainly, meeting requirements and user satisfaction are important goals. But neither of them is really quality. And quality is an important goal as well.

The clearest exposition I've seen on this topic was in an article called "Beware the God of Quality" [Redenbaugh90]. In that article, the author took a surprising view. "Customers do not buy quality," he said. "Customers buy satisfaction. The two are dramatically different." Then he went on to say that companies that pursue quality to the exclusion of satisfaction will probably fail.

That is a depressing thought for an author who has spent many months putting together a book on software quality! But it also is an important thought. We have several different important concepts to define, and we are trying to put the same name on all of them. No wonder, in Pirsig's wonderful book *Zen and the Art of Motorcycle Maintenance,* the main character was driven crazy by the pursuit of a definition of quality!

But that also leaves this author with a dilemma. If in fact user satisfaction may be more important than quality, is there anything we can say here about user satisfaction to augment the rest of the material on quality? Fortunately, the answer is yes.

The discussion of rude Rudy and slick Sam gives us a clue as to what is unique about user satisfaction. It involves a good product that meets its requirements, for example, but it involves more than that. It involves servicing the product, both its development and its use, in such a way that the customer feels valued. As with most feelings, the feeling of being valued stems most honestly from a reality of being valued.

What can the software manager do to build this feeling and this reality? Building a quality product by achieving requirements satisfaction is a first and minimal step toward doing it. The second step involves actions whose goal is to facilitate a positive relationship with the customer.

If your software product services a lot of users, put user service high up on your organization chart and staff it with helpful, knowledgeable, friendly people. (Software end-product companies like Microsoft and Lotus have vice presidents responsible for this function.) In your organization, establish an information center where users can expect to get the information they need. Form user groups, so that user concerns can be expressed and heard in a mutually supportive environment. Form user advisory committees to help steer the direction of future products and their quality. Publish a newsletter and/or use electronic mail to communicate with your users so that they can be informed. Distribute user directories and/or establish user bulletin boards, so that users can network with each other. Conduct user surveys to gather information about how users *really* feel.

In the development organization, make sure that the quality attribute of human engineering is facilitated. Add skills in interface design if you do not already have them. Analyze HELP mechanisms, and use the ones that make most sense from your user's point of view. Produce user documentation that is not only accurate and complete but readable and understandable by its intended audience as well.

And above all, *listen*. Users need and want to be heard, and you need and should want to hear them. They have a view of your product that no one else has, and because of that they are an important resource. If you utilize that resource, and acknowledge its importance, you will have taken a huge step toward making your users feel valued.

And remember, that's an essential part of this idea of user satisfaction.

REFERENCES

GLASS91—"User Support: There's More Here than Meets the Eye," *Software Conflict,* Yourdon Press, 1991; Robert L. Glass. *Suggests via anecdotes ways of improving user support in a software organization.*

IVES83—"The Measurement of User Information Satisfaction," *Communications of the ACM,* Oct. 1983; Blake Ives, Margrethe H. Olson, and Jack J. Baroudi. *Surveys attempts to measure user satisfaction, and proposes a new assessment mechanism.*

PIRSIG74—*Zen and the Art of Motorcycle Maintenance,* Morrow, 1974; Robert M. Pirsig. *A book to be read on many levels. At one level, the main character is an academic who is attempting to define quality, and becomes insane.*

REDENBAUGH90—"Beware the God of Quality," *Business Month,* June 1990; Russell G. Redenbaugh. *Distinguishes between quality and user satisfaction. Sees the latter as being the more important of the two.*

2.10 QUALITY AUTOMATION ADVANCES

Much of this book on the technology of quality has been about tools that automate portions of the process of building quality software. In this chapter, we focus on two particular classes of tools because in these classes important progress has been made in the marketplace; there is a plethora of these tools commercially available.

The two classes are fourth-generation languages (4GL), and computer-aided software engineering (CASE). There are enough products available in these categories to fill a catalog, and in fact catalogs of them do exist ([Knutson90], [ACR90], [Datapro90]).

Fourth-generation language tools are language processors for problem-focused languages, generally in the database/report generation application domain. CASE is an umbrella term for any tool supporting the construction and maintenance of software, although it is often used to refer primarily to so-called front-end life-cycle tools such as those supporting (structured) analysis and design. Each of those categories is discussed in the sections to follow.

In the rush to improve software productivity in the 1980s, grandiose claims were made for both of these classes of tools. Books with titles like *Programming Without Programmers* were published making the assumption that with tools of this calibre, programming would become trivial and anyone with a problem would be able to solve it regardless of whether or not they had programmer training.

With the passage of time, it has become obvious that these tools were not the breakthroughs that they were claimed to be. That is not to say that they do not have productivity advantages because, in fact, they do. What is demonstrably true, however, is that those productivity advantages, although important, are not as colossal as what had been claimed. In fact, in the 1990s most people are saying that the advantage of these tools lies more in quality than in productivity.

At the height of the exaggerated claims, it was also popular to engage in adversarial discussions as to which was the more important breakthrough, 4GL or CASE. The presumption seemed to be that only one breakthrough was allowed per computing installation, and that a choice had to be made! But in fact the two concepts are not necessarily incompatible. 4GLs eliminate certain portions of the life cycle and thus CASE tools to support those activities are not needed, but basically what is true is that no matter what language you program a solution in, you still need tools to help implement that solution. In that sense, the notions of 4GL and CASE are largely compatible. Furthermore, for those applications where 4GLs are inappropriate (we discuss that subject later), clearly lower-level languages amply supported by CASE tools are an essential approach.

The message here, then, is that 4GL and CASE approaches are:

- helpful to productivity but not breakthroughs
- beneficial to quality as well as productivity
- not necessarily incompatible

REFERENCES

ACR90—"Guide to Software Productivity Aids," *Applied Computing Research,* 1990. *A comprehensive guide (350 pages!) to software tools; published semiannually.*

DATAPRO90—"Datapro Directory of Software," Datapro Research Group, 1990. *An even more comprehensive guide (three large volumes) to software tools; updated quarterly.*

KNUTSON90—"Four Software Tools Catalogs: A Comparative Review," Software Maintenance News, Aug. 1990; Jef Knutson. *Evaluates four tools catalogs and finds various advantages to each. Catalogs evaluated were [ACR90], above; [Datapro90], above; "Software Maintenance Tools," published by Software Maintenance News, a catalog solely about maintenance tools; and "Testing Tools Reference Guide," published by Software Quality Engineering, a catalog solely about testing tools.*

2.11 4GL

4GLs are powerful tools for expressing a problem solution in a language very close to the problem. Their heritage lies in a concept called problem-oriented languages, which was a popular research topic about 20 years ago.

Because they are close to the problem (rather than close to the computer), these languages tend to be

- application focused (they are designed to be used with a particular narrow class of problems)
- user programmable (the person with the problem, rather than a professional programmer, may develop the solution in the language)

In addition, often the languages may be nonprocedural. That is, the problem may be stated in a manner independent of solution approach, especially solution order.

4GLs tend to be extremely powerful problem-solving tools for the class of problems they are designed for. The chief benefit of using them is productivity; problem solutions can be written extremely rapidly (up to 25 times faster than with conventional 3GLs, such as COBOL). They also offer some quality advantages:

- Solutions coded for 4GLs that run in a number of computer settings will be portable.
- Succinct 4GLs result in code that is highly modifiable and understandable.
- Assuming the 4GL language processor itself is reliable, then 4GL solutions should be extremely reliable, especially because the programmer has far fewer opportunities to make errors than in lower-level languages.

The quality benefits of 4GLs are not universal, however. Efficiency is reduced, often by significant factors. (Glass [91] reports a large variance in efficiency loss. Sometimes a 4GL solution will run faster than its COBOL equivalent, for example, but more often the 4GL solution will run up to 100 times slower, and on at least one occasion a 4GL solution ran for 24 hours without producing a solution and had to be aborted!) In addition, if the problem to be solved does not mesh well with the 4GL chosen, language workarounds must be employed that are considerably uglier than those in standard 3GLs (e.g., unstructured and unmodular). Thus, a 4GL must be chosen with great care with the applications to be solved firmly in mind.

Recall that in Chapter 2.4.4 we recommend the use of the highest level of language possible given the problem to be solved and its quality requirements. Certainly that advice is applicable to the use of 4GLs. If there is a 4GL that solves your problem, and if (in a benchmark test, for example) it does not degrade efficiency too badly, then it should be the programming language of choice.

REFERENCES

GLASS91—"CASE and 4GLs: What's the Payoff?" *The Software Practitioner,* January 1991; Robert L. Glass. *Summarizes empirical findings on the relative merits of 4GLs versus earlier approaches. Finds benefits but not breakthroughs. Warns that some 4GLs are incredibly inefficient (while others are sometimes better than COBOL!), and that programming some problem solutions in a 4GL can be quite clumsy.*

IEEE88—Special issue on "Shedding Light on 4GLs," *IEEE Software,* July 1988. *Contains two very useful papers comparing third- and fourth-generation language approaches to building software.*

MATOS89—"An Experimental Analysis of the Performance of Fourth Generation Tools on PCs," *Communications of the ACM,* November 1989; Victor M. Matos and Paul J. Jalics. *Explores costs/benefits of 4GLs; finds productivity benefits for 4GLs, but huge variations in performance effects.*

2.12 CASE

Fourth-generation languages probably number in the dozens. CASE tools, on the other hand, number in the hundreds. There has been an incredible explosion in the number and capability of tools available to the software developer.

Because of that, it is virtually impossible to talk about CASE tools without some qualification. First of all, the concept is divided into classifications. CASE [88] sees three classes of tools: front end (systems analysis, prototyping, and design), back end (coding, test, and maintenance), and project support (management/clerical). On the other hand, and at a finer level of detail, one tools catalog [ACR90] offers 25 classes (e.g., comparators, debugging aids, program analyzers/optimizers, screen generators). Certainly the plethora of tools is spawning a plethora of classes of tools.

In both discussion and use, however, front-end CASE predominates. In Figure 2.17 for example, we see from a survey that projected use of systems analysis CASE tools far exceeds that of any other category, making a spike on the figure. It is not at all uncommon to find that a discussion of CASE is really a discussion about systems analysis and design. Probably this reflects a natural progression in computing history. Management attention focuses on front-end problems/solutions early on historically because those are the ones they understand best and where, therefore, the payoffs are most visible. Gradually, over time, attention trickles back to focus on back-end coding, testing, and maintenance, where the grubwork of poking in code previously had warded off management attention. Recall from an earlier section of this book the long time it took for source-level debug to become universally available, and the fact that test coverage analyzers are still far from universally used tools.

There have been interesting trends in CASE perceptions, also reflected in survey findings. For example, the early euphoria of huge productivity payoffs has nearly vanished. Transfer of technology of CASE concepts proved painful, often because (at least front-end) CASE tools are designed to support a methodology, and programmers needed to understand and accept the methodology before the tools could prove useful. In this stage, two things happened:

- Many CASE tools became "shelfware," unused and symbolically placed on the shelf.

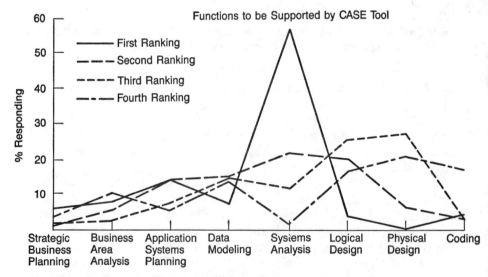

Figure 2.17 CASE usage. Systems analysis support is the main early focus of CASE tool usage (from [CASE 88]).

- For those who persisted past this problem, productivity actually diminished in the early stages of use, as the learning curve for the tools was absorbed, and the productivity payoff, if and when it did occur, was slower in coming than predicted.

Nevertheless, users surveyed have generally been "satisfied" with CASE usage (Figure 2.18), although the hoped-for productivity improvement (Figure 2.19) dissolved into the reality of "improved quality of design" (Figure 2.20). (Note that in the category of achieved benefits, productivity does not even show up!)

In addition to these survey findings, there are small amounts of quantitative experimental data about CASE benefits. Glass [91] reports a 9 percent benefit in productivity using a largely front-end tool, and a postulated higher benefit in quality that had not been achieved at the time of the study. Certainly more such studies are needed before any conclusions can be firmly drawn, but it is apparent that CASE is far from the productivity breakthrough that it was originally claimed to be.

Meanwhile, several trends are developing. While CASE users were struggling with the *benefits* of using these tools, the *cost* has become an important consideration as well. Two trends have developed:

1. Mainframe and minicomputer vendors, such as IBM and Digital Equipment, have jumped on the CASE bandwagon and offer integrated architectures for CASE. For example, IBM offers AD/Cycle, a still growing collection of tools centered on a repository (a data dictio-

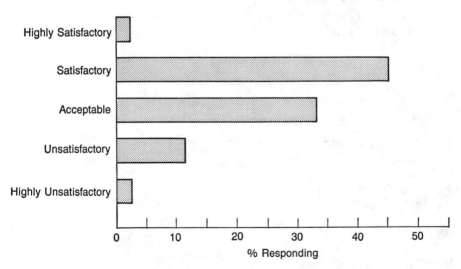

Figure 2.18. CASE usage. Most CASE users are pleased with their results (CASE88]).

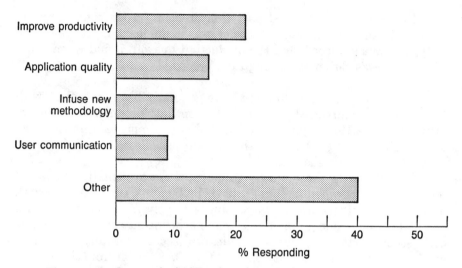

Figure 2.19. Reasons for CASE tool purchase. Productivity improvement has been a leading goal of CASE tool acquisition ([CASE88]).

nary specific to the needs of software development) and utilizing non-IBM software tools vendors to augment the offering. The cost to an installation of IBM's approach is estimated to be $40,000 to $60,000 *per programmer* [Yourdon89].

Digital's offering ("Cohesion"), estimated to cost 25 percent to 50 percent less than IBM's [Yourdon90], still costs an astounding amount of money.

2. Microcomputer software vendors have for some time offered many of the same kinds of CASE tools that are beginning to be available on

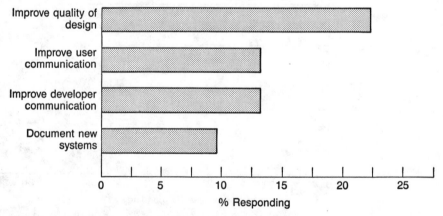

Figure 2.20. Benefits of using CASE tool. Quality improvement (not productivity!) has been the chief benefit of CASE ([CASE88]).

the larger computers. Because of the economies of scale of selling to the micro market, tools there often cost less than a tenth the price of a comparable tool on the bigger hardware. As a result, many software-developing institutions are switching a portion of their work to micros, perhaps doing analysis, design, code, unit test, and some documentation on a micro before switching to the target large computer for final test and production. (See Figure 2.21 for the prices for the same software product, in this case, a library of mathematics routines, on a variety of hardware platforms.)

These cost problems for CASE have not yet caused a groundswell of change to early life-cycle development on micros, but they may. The tradeoffs in this transition involve balancing the cost of the CASE tools (lower on the micros) with these facts:

- If multiple copies of the micro tool are needed, multiple copies must be paid for. (On a mainframe, one copy may be shared among multiple timesharing users.)
- If a necessary database exists only on a mainframe, micro development can become awkward.
- Porting the program during development from the micro to the mainframe can be painful unless careful planning is followed.
- Team coordination may be easier on a shared mainframe than a collection of (even networked) micros.

IBM's compromise solution to this problem is to offer access to AD/Cycle from a PS/2 micro connected to a host mainframe with a host-resident repository. Digital's solution is an open architecture (PCs or Macintoshes or other micros can access a VAX host, with a central repository that provides for distributed data).

Certainly profound changes may be in store for the software field as the implications of the IBM approach, the Digital approach, and the micro approach are understood and evolve.

(Example)	
MathAdvantage from QTC (object code prices, 1988)	
This same software product is sold for these computers:	at these prices:
Supercomputers (e.g., Cray)	$15K
Mainframes (e.g., IBM 30XX)	$10K
Big minis (e.g., DEC VAX 86XX)	$7.5K
Minis (e.g., DEC VAX 11/7XX)	$5K
Workstations (e.g., Sun)	$2K
Micros (e.g., IBM PC/PS2, Apple Mac)	$.5K

Figure 2.21. CASE pricing strategies.

CASE has raised another dilemma. For a long time, software products built by the large collection of software vendors have had at best awkward interfaces between them. Without the existence of a standard interface approach, and with little motivation among the many vendors to define one, and with the users of these products apparently uninterested in taking the reins, we have a state of the practice where a collection of CASE tools may not play at all well together. The repository, discussed previously in the context of the IBM and Digital CASE approaches, is an attempt to solve that problem. Some vendors have attempted to solve the problem in another way, building an integrated and "somewhat" complete set of CASE tools themselves. This "integrated CASE" (ICASE) approach, as of this writing, has not proved very effective, however. The result to date has been integrated collections of mediocre tools. The best CASE advice for purchasers, as of the beginning of the 1990s, is to buy a collection of "best in class" individual tools that have some hope of playing together, albeit awkwardly, rather than to buy an integrated but less capable collection.

How can one determine what is "best in class"? In-house comparative analysis, using competitive tools on a "real" problem is probably the best way. Another way is to talk to users of the tools of interest. Some conferences on CASE (there are an astounding number of them!) focus on user experience presentations; talking to the speakers, and to others in the conference hallways, can be an extremely illuminating experience. (Vendor presentations, on the other hand, are typically *not* illuminating as they focus on exaggerated claims and optimistic experiences.)

And there is one other way. There is now a thriving computer press. Magazines specialize in a variety of niche fields, especially the micro niche and the mainframe niche. Often, some of these magazines carry tool evaluations, much like *Consumer Reports* does for more general consumer products. These reports are another good source of information on product capability.

The federal government, faced with this "best in class" problem some years ago, decided through its Government Services Administration (GSA) to choose a collection of tools appropriate to the government agency user. Because a predominant part of this work was software maintenance in an IBM mainframe, COBOL setting, the collection of tools they chose supported that environment.

We now present a brief summary of the tools chosen by the GSA. For more complete information, contact them at

Government Services Administration,
Office of Software Development and Information Technology,
5203 Leesburg Pike, Suite 1100,
Falls Church, VA 22041,
hotline (703)756–4500

Tools chosen were:

- *Rand Development Center*—an interfacing system to tie the diverse tools together, from Rand Information Systems
- *Analyzer*—a test coverage monitor, from Aldon Computer Group
- *Transit*—a translator (COBOL to COBOL) system, from UCCEL Corp.
- *DCD II*—a cross referencer, from Marble Computer
- *Retrofit*—a restructurer, from Peat Marwick
- *CSA*—a data name standardizer, from Marble Computer
- *Hawkeye*—a reformatter, from Blackhawk Data Corp.
- *Data-Xpert*—a file/database manipulator from XA Systems Corp.
- *Pathvu*—a documentation and metrics analyzer, from Peat Marwick
- *Comparex*—a comparator from Sterling Software
- *Via/Insight*—a source code analyzer from Viasoft, Inc.

CASE is, then, a diverse collection of useful tools, whose value lies to some extent in enhancing developer (and maintainer) productivity, but probably to a larger extent in improving product quality. Because the state of the art and practice of CASE is alive and growing, it is vital for the concerned software person to stay abreast of this technology.

REFERENCES

CASE88—"The Annual CASE Survey," QED Information Sciences, Inc., 1988. *Findings of a survey of CASE users conducted by CASE Research Corp. Because of the complexity of conducting the survey, the report has turned out to be less than "annual."*

GLASS91—"CASE and 4GLs: What's the Payoff?" *The Software Practitioner,* January 1991; Robert L. Glass. *Summarizes experiments reported on in the literature. Finds that the productivity and quality benefits of 4GLs and CASE, though significant, are by no means "breakthroughs." Quantizes those benefits.*

YOURDON89—"AD/Cycle," *American Programmer,* December 1989; Ed Yourdon. *An insightful analysis of IBM's CASE offering, written soon after the original announcement.*

YOURDON90—"DECCASE," *American Programmer,* January 1990; Ed Yourdon. *An analysis comparing IBM and Digital Equipment CASE approaches, written shortly after both had made their first announcements.*

3

The Management of Quality

3.1 OVERVIEW

The acceptance test for project TOPNOTCH was under way. Trevor Clever, the manager for the project, listened to his technologists make the presentation and give the demonstration. Things were going well, the customers seemed pleased . . .

A less pleasant memory flitted through Trevor's mind. It was the preliminary design review several months back, and the TOPNOTCH designers were obviously struggling to find the right solution. The customer, attending the review to see that the design really would satisfy the requirements, spotted some high-level glitches. Technical peers shredded the rest of the design. It was obvious at that point that Trevor's people hadn't yet gotten a handle on the problem.

Trevor had felt uneasy about that, since he was a brand-new manager, in charge of his first software project. But there was more to it than that. He, himself, had only seen about 25 percent of the problems. How could he manage a project where his technical people knew more than he did about what they were doing? And what would happen if they got all the way to the end with continuing problems that neither he nor his technical developers could spot?

It was at that review that Trevor had come to realize that no matter how hard he worked the schedule, budget, and quality problems, he was going to have to rely on others to help him. With appropriate, unbiased technical watchdogs, plus his own management skills, he would be able to bring TOPNOTCH to completion. Without that assistance, success and failure would be difficult to distinguish in advance.

Making that decision and carrying it out had been two different things. Trevor wanted to pull out all the stops, use all the quality management techniques he had read about in books, but he had a schedule and a budget to contend with. After that preliminary design review, Trevor had thought a lot about the fine line between quality on the one side and schedule and budget on the other. Finally he chose a management method that trod that fine line, and made it work.

. . . "And that's the end of our demonstration." Trevor's troops were finishing the acceptance test. He looked around at the others at the review, and just as he did, spontaneous applause broke out among the customers in attendance. Trevor let the sound of the applause sink in slowly. It was explicitly meant for the developers of the software, of course. But it told Trevor that that fine line he had found had been the right one.

What was the fine line Trevor found? It would be nice to draw it right here, on this page, and label it with a cost-effective set of techniques that could maximize a manager's chance of his or her people building a quality product, on schedule and within budget. But it's not that simple. The choices, unfortunately, are going to be project dependent. Just as the software technologist chooses carefully from a menu of quality techniques the set that best works the problem at hand, so must the software manager. The good software manager is the one who is aware of the menu, aware of the trade-offs, and has the judgment necessary to make the right choices. That's a pretty tall order.

3.2 MANAGEMENT CONCERNS _____

What form does the manager's quality menu take? In this section, we talk about management's role in these areas:

- planning
- organization
- measurement and prediction
- documentation

But before we do, let's take a look at overriding concerns that should steer the software manager's thinking.

Goals. First of all, there are the goals the manager is trying to achieve. A quality product. On schedule. Under budget. We have already seen in the preceding scenario that achieving this mix of goals is not as easy as it sounds.

Once upon a time there was a very proud software manager.

The manager was in charge of a software project which was looked upon in his company as a model for how to build software.

The project was, to be brief, under budget and on schedule.

And in the halls of management, where accolades are passed out for performance on the project, there is no finer thing to be than Under Budget and On Schedule.

Once upon a time there was a very proud quality assurance manager.

The manager was in charge of quality assurance for the software on the Under Budget and On Schedule project.

The project was, to be brief, configuration managed and standards conforming to a fare-thee-well.

And in the halls of quality, when the subject of quality itself arises, it is generally agreed that configuration and standards are What It Is All About.

Once upon a time there was a customer. The customer was very sad. The software product the customer received was a pile of excrement.

The software was produced well under budget. And on schedule. It was impeccably configuration managed. And standards conforming.

But it did not do what the customer wanted. It did not fit in the customer's computer's memory. It did not operate as fast as the customer wanted it to. It was abysmally difficult to modify, so that the customer could not even change it to be what *was* wanted. And when it did operate, it failed more often than it worked.

Once upon a time there was a corporate president.

The corporate president was in charge of the manager who was Under Budget and On Schedule. The corporate president was in charge of the quality assurance manager who managed configurations and audited standards.

But the corporate president was not in charge of everyone. There was, for example, the customer.

When the customer spoke to the corporate president, he spoke of value received. He spoke of useability, efficiency, maintainability, and reliability. In brief, he spoke of Quality. And he was upset. The corporate president listened.

Then the corporate president spoke to the two managers. "What went wrong here?" he said.

"I was under budget and on schedule," said the software manager.

"I achieved configuration management and standards conformance," said the quality assurance manager.

"But who is looking out for product quality?" cried the exasperated corporate president.

No one answered.

From *Software Soliloquies*, Computing Trends, P.O. Box 213, State College PA 16804, 1981; Glass.

We can see that budget + schedule is not enough. But even considering quality in the expression of budget + schedule + quality is still not enough.

People. The manager must also optimize the use of his or her people. Keep them productive. Keep them motivated.

Keeping people productive means using effective control, giving effective support. Keeping people motivated means using effective communication, giving effective rewards.

All of these people principles have been boiled down over the years into basic management strategies. One expression of those strategies is the following [Boehm88, Frank88]:

Theory X emphasizes management control. It says that people inherently dislike work, they have to be coerced into doing it, and they like to be told what to do.

Theory Y emphasizes technologist control. It says people don't inherently dislike work, they can exercise self-direction, they can learn to work responsibly, and commitment to objectives depends upon appropriate rewards.

Theory Z emphasizes shared control. It says that people work best toward goals that they have helped establish, that once people buy into those goals you can trust them to perform, and if the people share a common set of values they can develop workable project goals.

Historically, software engineering has progressed from a Theory Y approach to a Theory X approach and is now moving toward Theory Z. The progression has occurred because

1. Theory Y (relying on the responsible technologist) was seen to be inadequate as software projects moved from the moderate to the huge.
2. Theory X (relying on the controlling manager) was seen to be inadequate because it stifled the creativity and responsibility essential to producing a quality software product.
3. Theory Z (relying on shared responsibility) is being seen as the only logical way to build huge projects requiring creative and skilled technologists.

Thus, we come to a new expression for software:

$$budget + schedule + quality + people$$

The expression is easy to write down, but it is a lot harder to achieve. Because it *is* hard to achieve, let's take a more in-depth look at the quality part of that expression.

Organization. Is there some organizational magic that the manager can sprinkle on a project to help guarantee quality? Well, the answer is yes and no.

The good news is that there are lots of organizational strategies that focus on quality, and we discuss them later.

The bad news is that organization by itself is not the solution to the quality problem. In fact, no matter how well the manager of a project organizes to achieve quality, there is one fundamental fact that cannot be overcome: The developers of the software make the primary determination of product quality.

No amount of organizational additives can overcome this fundamental fact. What this fact means is that, for the manager concerned about quality, the prime focus must be on selecting the developers and ensuring that *they* do a quality job.

Once that fact is understood, it is still important to consider organizational assists. Recall that Trevor Clever realized that he needed technical watchdogs to help him ensure product quality. We can call these watchdogs the quality supplement.

The quality supplement can take the form of a quality assurance organization, a change review board, a product test organization, independent verification and validation, or a mix and match of these and other approaches that we spend more time on later.

However, for certain kinds of projects, there may be no call for a quality supplement at all. If the project is of low criticality, low lifespan, low budget, or (more likely) a combination of these factors, the quality supplement may be minimal to nil.

When a quality supplement *is* used, there are certain functions it *must* perform or it will be valueless. It must

- enhance the expertise of the developers with new levels of knowledge or focus
- provide an objective view to complement the subjective view of the developers
- provide effective feedback to the manager in charge of both development and the quality supplement

There is one other vital concern here. Once a quality supplement is chosen, there is a great danger that responsibility for quality itself, now split between the developers and the quality supplement, will be diluted. That is what happened in the story of the On Schedule, Under Budget project. It must be the responsibility of someone, probably the manager above both the developers and the quality supplement, to make sure that this does not happen. A clear delegation of this shared responsibility is vital.

This distinction can be called the difference between quality design and quality control. Quality design is implementation oriented; it is the developer's task of *building* a quality product. Quality control is inspection oriented; it is the quality supplement's task of *assuring* a quality product. Quality control can perform planning, assess procedures, and assess the product.

How might the developers and the quality supplement fit together from an overall organizational point of view? Whatever method is chosen, it is vital to maintain organizational independence between the two so as to maintain the objectivity that we mentioned earlier.

The following organization chart depicts a carefully thought-out, independent quality supplement. There is a program manager to whom both development and the supplement report. The supplement in this case consists of both an in-house quality assurance organization, and an independent verification and validation (V&V) contractor who provides an out-company level of objectivity to the quality process. Below the level of these three organizations, there is some ambiguity that needs to be resolved. Who is responsible for objective testing of the product—a separate test group reporting to development, or the same kind of group reporting to quality assurance? Does development assume responsibility for configuration management, or does quality assurance? Are audits performed, when necessary, in house or by the out-company people? There are not necessarily any right or wrong answers to these questions, except that *there must be answers* or the organizational entities and the responsibility may fall through the crack.

What about the quality assurance (QA) organization itself? How can it be organized? Here are a couple of ways.

In the first, we see a project approach, much like the preceding chart, with a special quality assurance organization for each corporate project.

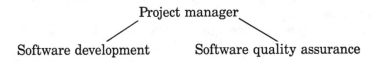

In the second, we see a central quality approach, one quality assurance organization which lends support to separate projects as they arise and need it. One advantage of this approach is that the quality assurance organization can support project-independent research and development. For example, a central QA organization might evaluate and procure testing tools for use on several or perhaps all corporate projects.

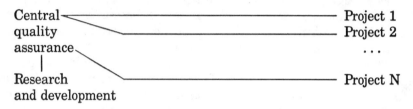

We are used to reading articles about what management wants from its employees. But here was an article about what employees want from their management!

It appeared in the "Software Manager" column of *IEEE Software,* one of many regular columns that *IEEE Software* now carries on fairly pragmatic subjects. This one (March 1990) was titled "Would the People You Manage Hire You?" and it was written by Elliot Chikofsky of Index Technology.

What did the article say? Software engineers want:
- direction (clear decisions, with explanations)
- support (barriers removed, facilitation of efforts)
- freedom to accomplish (leave room for creativity)
- communication (two-way)

In the mix of how-to information available for the harassed software manager, this simple set of ideas should perhaps rank near the top.

Constituencies. The world of software quality is also a political world. The manager concerned with quality must not only consider the organization under his or her control, but also the surrounding organizational world including the constituency groups with which interaction must occur.

There are, first and foremost, the *customer* and the *user*. The customer pays for the software; the user makes use of it. Sometimes they are in the same constituency group and sometimes they are in different ones. But they share one vital concern—they want to make sure that the product they receive will have the quality they want it to have. They care about schedule and cost too, of course, but they have the highest vested interest in ensuring a quality product.

This strong motivation can be used to the benefit of the software development organization. It is important that the customer and the user play a very strong role in the early life-cycle processes of requirements definition and preliminary design. Later in the life cycle, they should play a strong role again in test case generation and test result verification.

Note that even the customer and the user have differing goals, however. The customer would like to maximize quality while holding budget and schedule constant. The user, on the other hand, wants to maximize quality while holding schedule constant, with possibly less concern about budget. (It may not, after all, be his or her money they are spending!)

Another constituency of vital importance is the *developer*. The developer is, as we have already said, the producer of the software and the prime ingredient in product quality. The developer wants to achieve quality within budget and schedule constraints, but feels the brunt of the inherent conflicts in doing so.

The constituency group to which the developers report, *developer management,* has the same interests and goals as the developers themselves, but in the traditional corporate climate this level of management is sometimes evaluated on budget and schedule more than product quality. Thus, they become strong advocates for budget and schedule.

The *quality supplement* constituency was created to help balance the conflict between budget and schedule on the one hand and quality on the other. Like the developer, the quality supplement person wants to achieve all three, but he or she must play an advocacy role, arguing on behalf of quality against management advocates who may favor budget and schedule.

A very interested bystander in the constituency world is the eventual *maintainer* of the software product. The maintainer's vested interest, much like that of the quality supplement, is for quality above budget and schedule, especially maintainability quality. Barry Boehm, in a 1987 Distinguished Lecture at the Software Engineering Institute, suggested that the eventual maintainer be part of the quality supplement organization during development for that reason.

In the political world, everyone's most important constituency group is *upper management.* The upper management for the software developers plays more of a behind-the-scenes role than the customers and the users in determining software quality, but in the last analysis they play an even more important role. They set policy; they control budget and resource allocation; they resolve conflict. If there is trouble on the software development/quality/customer-user ranch, they are the court of resolution. And they have the power to make decisions stick. For budget/schedule/quality trade-offs, this is where the final decisions are likely to be made.

Problems. Experience tells us where software quality problems may arise. The most dangerous problem is *unstable requirements.* If the requirements evolve as the software evolves, there is no way the developers can build a successful product. They find themselves shooting at a moving target, sometimes throwing away design and code as fast as they can produce it.

It takes clout on someone's part to announce "the requirements are now frozen, and we will accept no further change," but it is a vital position to take. Often the conflicting forces here are: the customer/users, who now want features they failed to see originally; the software developers, who want to accommodate the customer but are losing control of the product they are building; and development upper management, which must step in and hold the line if the developers themselves are unable to.

Holding the line on requirements does not make it impossible for the customer to make changes, by the way. If the changes are truly vital, then the new requirements can be accommodated in the context of a revised project, with new budgetary and schedule estimates and new resources defined. It is everyone's tendency, unfortunately, to "slide one more change through under the current agreement," and eventually that one more change becomes the straw that breaks the camel's back.

Another complex problem area is *oversimplification of design*. It is always the software developer's goal, of course, to minimize the complexity of a software product, and everyone appreciates a clean and elegant solution. But some problems are inherently messy, and simple solutions to complicated problems are the cause of the most severe reliability problems in software.

What tends to happen here is not intentional oversimplification, but a lack of ability to stretch the mind to accommodate all the facets of a problem. Experiments into the nature of high-risk and high-cost software problems [Glass81] have revealed that the problems that hurt the most are the ones that arose when the design was too simple for the problem being solved. An example? An IF statement which tested two conditions but neglected to include a third important condition.

A more subtle problem area is *inadequacy of tools*. Neither tools nor techniques nor methodologies are the magic solution to the problem of software quality, and it is important that quality-concerned people realize that. But we are often at the opposite extreme in software development. Not only have we not poured a lot of resources into a methodological approach, we have often not put in any at all.

Look back at the tools and techniques listed in Chapter 2 of this book. There are over five dozen. Most software developers have access to a small percentage of them, at best. There is no standard minimal set of tools which all software developers have access to regardless of where they work, but there should be [Glass82]. The fact of the matter is that we wish software could be built scientifically, and we spend a lot of money on research into how to accomplish it; but we continue to build software pretty much as a craft and then fail to provide the craftspeople with the necessary tools to do the job well. It is in the quality world where this particularly hurts, since quality is so elusive and yet so much in need of tool support.

It will take a partnership of the software developers wanting the tools, the customers insisting on the importance of quality, and upper management providing the resources if this problem area is to be overcome.

One last but vital problem area is *poor estimation*. Because building software is a fairly new field, we really don't have a clear picture of how long it takes to build. Yet all the economic forces of our system demand that we do estimate cost in advance. Sometimes we overestimate, in order to protect ourselves later on; but much more often, we underestimate, either out of naiveté or the need to be competitive in cost.

Now consider the project that is approaching its estimated (and, as it turns out, unrealistic) deadline and is considerably behind schedule. There is enormous pressure on the developers to make a miracle and pull the project in on time. Look at the software life cycle—what is going on when that pressure mounts? It is testing, a quality-critical phase. All the economic and social pressure that exists on the project is pressing for a relaxation of testing—and, therefore, quality—as the deadline comes nearer. It takes a strong person indeed to say "damn the pressure, I'm going for quality," and most software developers cannot do it. Often, in fact, it would be politically unwise to do it. But until the chronic problem of underestimation is solved, quality will always be at risk on all such software projects.

Input from other disciplines. Analogy is one of the ways in which the mind is able to grasp new ideas. Concept X1 may be totally new, but if it is reasonably close to concept X then we can start from there and extrapolate new understandings.

Software is still a new field, and it is important to be aware of the workings of other similar disciplines in order to seek analogies and borrow solutions. At this point in time, the most promising disciplines from which to borrow appear to be the hardware engineering disciplines.

There is good news and bad news in taking this approach. The good news is that these concepts transition well from our more seasoned colleagues:

Prototyping: It is common for hardware developers to build a model, tweak it for awhile, and then pattern the final solution on it. As we saw in an earlier section, the software developer is learning to use the same approach, and payoffs have been achieved.

Review, (checking): It is also common for hardware developers to use people specifically for review and evaluation of a product. One task in some large companies, for example, is that of "checker." This person may or may not create new ideas, but his or her main function is to evaluate and critique the ideas and creations of others. The use of the many kinds of reviews discussed in Chapter 2 is evidence that software is borrowing this technology successfully.

Product Test: Just as checkers are people set aside to analyze creative work, testers are also people set aside in the hardware world to examine the product for faults. Software has borrowed this idea, also. Later on in this section we discuss the "product test" organization.

Assembly from Parts: The hardware engineer expects to have a parts catalog and a storehouse of parts from which to create a new product. Furthermore, he or she is expected to use them. In the history of software, this idea burst forth fairly early in the form of reusable library routines. Math libraries and sort/merge capabilities are the earliest examples, but since then the concept has bogged down. Some say it is because we haven't worked the problem of generic solutions hard enough; others say it is because, given the complexity of software and the diversity of its applications, generalization of solution is lamentably not possible. This is an area of enormous interest; probably the most activity in the area of borrowing analogies will happen here in the next decade.

And now for the bad news. There are certain areas in software that are so different from hardware engineering that there are whole classes of analogies which can never be borrowed. What are these differences?

Separation of Development and Manufacturing: Hardware development is a prelude to hardware manufacturing. The cost of manufacture is so high that development costs often pale in comparison. This can give the hardware engineer a little more latitude in taking on extra cost approaches in development to assure product quality. But in software, development is practically all there is. Manufacturing of software is a cookie-cutter problem; we simply produce another copy, about as easily as photocopying. That is one of the big benefits of software, of course, but it also means that the entire focus of cost concern in software is on development. Adding 10 percent to development costs to boost quality of hardware may only add 1 percent to total project cost, but with software it adds 10 percent. The result is an inherent conservatism in considering new development ideas. "Everyone says the cost is too high already, for heaven's sake. How can we afford to take on more?"

Quantity Costs: Hardware costs roughly N times as much to make N copies as it takes to build one. Software costs for N copies are essentially the same as for one. This is another facet of the manufacturing dilemma we discussed previously.

This ought to be good news for software people, and for the most part it is. But there is a tendency in a mixed hardware-software system which will be manufactured in quantity to transfer as much complexity to software as possible, since this can result in dramatically lowered costs for the manufacturing run of the system. This means that the software developers may have a higher percentage of total system cost than is at first apparent because of the costs of this complexity.

Aging: Hardware can grow older and eventually wear out. Software does not. David Fisher of the Department of Defense Ada world said it best: "Hardware deteriorates in the absence of maintenance, but software can only deteriorate because of the presence of maintenance." This means that hardware metrics, such as mean time between failure, must be examined in a whole new light for software. Most hardware metrics do not borrow well for just this reason. Even the word *maintenance* means something different for software.

The softness of software: The word *hardware* implies rigidity, and the word *software* implies its absence. Once again, the softness of software is to its benefit in that problems solved in software can more easily be modified later on, but it is also a problem. Just as the low quantity cost of software spawned a problem because complexity is allocated to it, so does its softness. Software will be used in many cases precisely because it is easily changed. But change of software, though easy in a relative sense, is still hard. It is harder, for example, than original development, since the maintainer's creativity is constrained by what already exists. Once again, this means that software workers are toiling in an area where the costs are higher than analogy says they ought to be.

Product Variance: It has been said that software is the most complex undertaking ever attempted by humanity, and that the complexity of hardware pales alongside it. One of the ways that this becomes important to quality and analogy is in the area of product variance. For any given hardware problem, especially those involving high reuse of component parts, there is only a limited number of ways that the problem can be solved successfully. But for software, even considering optimized solutions, there is a near-infinite number of possible correct solutions. A software checker, for example, would have considerable difficulty in pronouncing a particular design or coding solution as wrong. The costs of quality review are inevitably driven up by the fact that erroneous solutions are difficult indeed to detect.

The difficulties of making analogies which work for software is a problem. It is an increasingly critical problem as the focus of so many problem solutions evolves to software.

It is common to read such pronouncements as "software is that part of a complex system which is always behind schedule, over budget, and unreliable." *The software crisis* is a phrase that has been coined, and in articles such as Canan [86] we see ominous statements like:

- "Software costs have skyrocketed so high that they dominate the costs of military electronics and are headed for runaway proportions."
- "The national shortfall of some 80,000 civilian and military software personnel is expected to swell to 1,000,000 by 1990 [did it?], and only a few U.S. universities offer advanced degrees in software engineering."
- "Software quality is spotty."

Some of the dimensions of this software crisis are real, of course. But there is an implication in some of these cries of concern that if software people would only "do it right" (i.e., doing what people in other disciplines have been doing all along, such as assembly from parts), the crisis would subside. That kind of thinking is naive, as we have seen here. The problems of software must be considered both in the context of a broader world and in its own unique world. Attempts to simplify the problem run the risk of being mere hand wringing.

As we in software try to borrow ideas from older and more mature disciplines, we find ourselves coming to understand better both how we are like older disciplines and in what ways we differ from them.

This is a set of 14 principles for improving quality in manufacturing, as articulated by the legendary quality guru W. E. Deming. How many of them can be extrapolated into software?

1. Establish constancy of purpose for improvement.
2. Adopt the new philosophy.
3. Eliminate dependence on inspections.
4. End the practice of awarding business on price alone.
5. Constantly improve the process.
6. Institute training on the job.
7. Institute leadership.
8. Drive out fear.
9. Break down barriers between staff areas.
10. Eliminate slogans and posters imploring people to improve.
11. Eliminate numerical quotas and goals.
12. Remove barriers that rob people of pride of workmanship.
13. Institute a vigorous program of education and self-improvement.
14. Put everybody in the company to work to accomplish the transformation.
   It is easy to see when we try to apply these ideas to *our* field, why Deming ran into a stone wall getting his ideas accepted in the United States and found his

> success in a much more receptive Japan! Eliminate inspections? Slogans? Quotas and goals? Even in this new field of software, some of these ideas seem radical, indeed!

REFERENCES

BOEHM88—"Theory W," *System Development,* May 1988; Barry W. Boehm. *The reference is to an account of a Boehm lecture in which the Theory X, Y, and Z management philosophies are analyzed. Boehm proposes "Theory W" (win–win) as an alternative.*

BROOKS75—*The Mythical Man-Month,* Addison-Wesley, 1975; Frederick P. Brooks, Jr. *The most important book on software ever written!*

BROOKS87—"No Silver Bullet—Essence and Accidents of Software Engineering," *IEEE Computer,* April 1987; Frederick P. Brooks, Jr. *Takes the position that software development is hard and always will be. Warns that breakthroughs should not be expected.*

CANAN86—"The Software Crisis," *Air Force Magazine,* May 1986; Canan. *The article from which some of the quotes about the crisis used earlier in this section were taken. Describes the Air Force's "Project Bold Stroke," a software management action plan for coping with this "crisis."*

FOX82—*Software and Its Development,* Prentice-Hall, Inc., 1982; Joe Fox. *A tough and pithy book about software development by a man who managed major software efforts for the IBM Federal Systems Division.*

FRANK88—"Two Concepts of Quality," Washington D.C. American Society for Quality Control publication, December 1988; Norman C. Frank. *Analyzes quality from the Theory X, Y, and Z point of view.*

GILB87—*The Principles of Software Engineering Management,* Addison-Wesley (England), 1987; Tom Gilb. *Methods and case studies about software management, written by a European consultant.*

GLASS81—"Persistent Software Errors," *IEEE Transactions on Software Engineering,* March 1981; Robert L. Glass. *Identifies the most serious software errors as those stemming from product oversimplification.*

GLASS82—"Recommended: A Minimum Standard Software Toolset," *ACM Software Engineering Notes,* October 1982; Robert L. Glass. *Examines existing toolsets and finds little consistency; recommends that a minimum standard toolset to be used by all software developers be defined, and suggests one.*

HUMPHREY87—*Managing for Innovation: Leading Technical Teams,* Prentice Hall, 1987; Watts S. Humphrey. *Discusses management styles suited to leading and motivating creative people.*

METZGER87—*Managing Programming People—A Personal View,* Prentice Hall, 1987; Metzger. *A readable, light-hearted, but often right-on book about the complexities of managing the people who build software.*

PRESSMAN87—*Software Engineering—A Practitioner's Approach,* McGraw-Hill, 1987; Roger S. Pressman. *One of the best of an excellent lot of textbooks on software engineering.*

3.3 A DIFFERENT VIEW OF THE "SOFTWARE CRISIS"

In the previous section, we briefly mentioned the "software crisis." Let us spend a little more time talking about that.

There have been papers and articles proclaiming a "software crisis" in the computing literature now for over a decade. Words like those quoted in the previous section have been seen so frequently for so long that almost everyone believes them by now.

Pressed for a definition of this crisis, most people would say, "Software is always over budget, behind schedule, and unreliable." To support this definition, examples are given of projects where that was indeed true.

But there is a curious dilemma in this crisis. If there is truly a software crisis, then how can we be sending vehicles far into space? Running our banking system successfully with computers? Depending on reservation systems for most of our travel needs? Creating a multibillion dollar software industry? Waging war in whole new ways? The prevalence of these successful software solutions suggests that something about the software crisis doesn't add up.

There is a "lack of data" problem here. Certainly, there are software projects that have suffered over budget, behind schedule, unreliability problems. That makes it easy to create an anecdotal picture to support the crisis. But until recently, there were very few data available. What we needed was a credible statement of the form "X% of software projects suffer from this problem."

Then along came a government report that seemed to supply these needed data. The U.S. Government Accounting Office (GAO) prepared a report showing an astoundingly high percentage of software projects that failed in one way or another. (Sixty percent of projects were behind schedule, 50 percent were over cost, 45 percent of the delivered software was unusable.) Speakers and writers everywhere began using the GAO data to "prove" that there was a software crisis.

But there was a problem with these data. The projects studied by the GAO were selected for study *because they were in trouble.* In other words, the GAO study concluded that a fairly high percentage of troubled projects are never completed successfully. And that, of course, was more self-fulfilling prophecy than it was illuminating new information.

Let us step back and take a somewhat calmer look at this crisis. First of all, why have so many jumped on what we begin to suspect is a bandwagon?

Initially, it is important to admit that the anecdotal view of the crisis can be validated. What some call "runaway" software projects abound. Lederer [90] cites that the state of Oklahoma, initially estimating a half million dollars for a project, eventually spent four million; Allstate Insurance initially estimated eight million and, with the project still under way, increased that estimate to 100 million; and 35 percent of Peat Marwick's clients admit to "major cost overruns." If anecdotal evidence is all that is needed, there is plenty of it.

But given that the data to support a generalization of this claim has not yet been presented (note that when 35 percent of clients have runaways, it does not mean that 35 percent of their *projects* were runaways), why has the cry of crisis resounded so broadly?

The answers to that question would appear to be self-interest and a copycat syndrome. It is in the best interest of vendors of products and researchers into solutions that might affect this crisis to cite the crisis as a reason for money to be spent on their efforts. Once that pattern is launched, it is easy for others, perhaps not as self-interested, to cite the earlier references as fact.

An examination of the goals of those who use the crisis as a motivation for funding their work shows that the proposed solutions to the crisis, almost without exception, would involve new technology. Better languages, better tools, and more formal processes seem to be the answers that are offered. But there is another interesting dilemma here. Has anyone ever shown that the cause of the crisis is poor technology?

In fact, a deeper analysis of the GAO data shows an almost shocking fact, given these technology-focused solution efforts. Those troubled projects that failed, almost without exception, failed not because of poor technology, but because of organizational and goal problems [Blum91]. Putting that another way, the GAO projects failed due to areas within the control of management, not technology!

What were these failure causes?

- *Unstable requirements.* Customers were unable to pin down exactly what problem was to be solved, and developers kept shooting at a moving target.
- *Poor contracting.* The contract written did not properly define the terms, conditions, processes, and products involved.
- *Optimistic evaluation.* It probably never was possible, from the beginning, to complete the project in the estimated time.

Let us summarize where we are so far in this analysis of the software crisis:

1. The software crisis, although widely described, has neither been proven to exist, nor analyzed as to its causes.
2. Often the software crisis is cited as a justification for a research study into a technical aspect of the problem. But if there is a crisis at all, we begin to see here that its cause is more likely to be managerial than technical.

If we assume that the software crisis is indeed a management problem, what can we do about it? The first obvious answer is "Do a better job with requirements, with contracting, and with estimation." But like many obvious answers, it is easier to say than to do.

Nevertheless, there is value in marking these danger zones for software managers. Stable requirements, careful contracting, and accurate estimation are indeed vital areas of focus for the software manager. How does this book help with those obviously quality-critical subjects?

In an earlier section of this book, we dealt with the aspects of good requirements, but that was a technical view. The key to managing requirements is to

- Establish a firm baseline definition of requirements as soon as possible, whenever it is possible.
- If it is not possible, allow flexing of requirements to meet evolving customer needs, but tie budget and schedule considerations firmly to all such flexing.

With respect to contracting, there is material in a later section of this book ("acquisition management") that should help with that problem.

With respect to estimation, there is also material to come, in this case the "Prediction" material under "Metrics." But an extra word of warning is appropriate here.

Management of software projects can solve the requirements and contracting problems with a reasonable dose of good business practice leavened with a positive view of human relations and good old common sense. These problems require dedication and lots of attention, but they are solvable.

Estimation is another matter. Software has several endemic problems in the estimation area:

1. We provide estimates of project completion *before we define the requirements* for a project.
2. Estimates historically have been very bad, and they are not getting much better.
3. Estimation algorithms and automated tools have helped improve estimation capabilities, but not enough.
4. The climate in which estimates are given is heavily political. Marketing and upper management frequently override project management and technologist. (Lederer [90] . . . contrasts *rational estimation* and *political estimation.*)
5. Estimate revision based on actual project progress is frowned on, and reestimation, if it happens at all, comes far too late to be helpful.

Thus we see that estimation is a critical and troubled danger zone for software managers. To add to the concern, consider that to the extent there is any software crisis, all of it could be caused by poor estimation techniques.

Obviously software that is over budget and behind schedule could be in that state because the original estimate was far too optimistic. But note what happens to an over budget, behind schedule project. Panic attempts to make up time and cost begin at the point where it becomes obvious how serious the problem is. And what is usually happening at that time? We have already seen the answer: testing. As a result, testing is cut back to strive for budget/schedule compliance, and reliability suffers.

Thus, it is possible that there is one (management!) problem causing the concern about a software crisis. Poor estimation techniques, coupled with a heavily political estimation climate, can indeed produce software that is "over budget, behind schedule, and unreliable"!

That is a sobering thought, indeed, for the manager responsible for a software project. If there is one management danger zone to mark above all others, it is software estimation. As was previously mentioned, we return to that subject in a later section.

REFERENCES

BLUM91—"Some Very Famous Statistics," *The Software Practitioner,* March 1991; Bruce I. Blum. *Debunks the use of the Government Accounting Office data to prove the existence of a software crisis. Says "software's biggest problems can be traced back to uncertainty regarding what we want when we start a software project."*

CARD88—"The Role of Measurement in Software Engineering," *Proceedings: Second IEE/BCS Software Engineering Conference,* Liverpool UK, July 1988; David N. Card. *Points out that "cost estimation occurs at an earlier stage in software development than in most other engineering disciplines," and goes on to say that "most engineers can wait until after preliminary design to estimate product cost."*

LEDERER90—"Information System Cost Estimating: A Management Perspective," *MIS Quarterly,* June 1990; Albert L. Lederer, Rajesh Mirani, Boon Siong Neo, Carol Pollard, Jayesh Prasad, and K. Ramamurthy. *Uses a case study as a vehicle for presenting the notion that software cost estimating is based both on a (documented, approved) "rational model," and an (undocumented but ever-present) "political model."*

3.4 PLANNING

The fine line that Trevor Clever found on project TOPNOTCH involved working with his technical people, planning his relationship with them and their approach to the technology of software quality.

That is only one aspect of the complexity of the software manager's concern for quality. The world of management is a sandwich, with a heavy and vital steering force pressing down from above, and an equally heavy and vital achieving force pressing up from below. In the midst of that sandwich, it is rarely enough for the software manager to make shoot-from-the-hip decisions. Some kind of planning is needed to integrate all of the needs and forces the manager is balancing.

In the sections that follow, we elaborate on what kinds of planning the manager must do, and how the planning might best be carried out.

3.4.1 Planning for Power

The real world is a blend of technology and politics. A manager is expected to possess and wield certain amounts of power in the political world:

- Power on behalf of the company, to make sure that corporate interests are at the forefront of any decision-making process.
- Power in dealing with upper management, to make sure that enough resources are provided to get the job done.
- Power on behalf of the subordinates, to make sure that no barriers stand in the way of their getting the job done.
- Power on behalf of himself or herself, to make sure that the manager and workers are fairly represented in the give and take of corporate affairs.

Now, given that political power is one of the requirements of a software/quality manager, what are the problems and possible solutions here?

The first fundamental problem is that software is often "the new kid on the block," poorly understood and sometimes resented in the traditional corporate power structure. There is no effective power base for the software manager to draw on. It must be newly constructed, no small task in an organization where everyone else may have 20 or 40 years of historical positioning to start from.

What does this mean to the software manager? In the battle for resource allocation on a particular project, the software manager will have to fight extra hard just to carve out acceptable amounts. In the battle for project schedule definition, the software manager who sees his or her team on the critical path may have to be particularly vocal to be believed. In the assignment for blame if the project goes badly, the software manager may automatically carry a heavy load even before fairness and reason come into play. The attitude "I don't understand software, and if I had my way we wouldn't use it on this project" may very well be trickling down from above, and be constantly eroding the power base the software manager must have.

Now add the complication of "quality" to "software." Quality people independent of the software function may have some traditional organizational power, but at the same time quality may have been resented by some of the corporate "doers," who see quality not as a helping force but as an inhibiting one. Now we have the stigma of quality added to the resentment accompanying software. The combination, if not dealt with, can be lethal. To make matters worse, the quality people may be resented by the very software people they are trying to help, just as quality may have been resented by the other traditional disciplines.

The solutions to these political problems are themselves political. The first level of solution is "clout." Somehow, a power base must be constructed that enables the software/quality people to function effectively without running for help every time a small issue arises.

Clout can be obtained from:

- *Contractual requirements.* If the project is being built under contract, what the contract says to do is effectively law. It is vital that the software/quality people play a key up-front role in negotiating and defining contractual terms. In the military world, there is a whole host of government standards which, if included in the contract, will bring contractual clout to the software/quality people (e.g., DOD-STD-2167, which elaborately defines quality practices in the construction of software). There is a fine line to be trod here, of course. The corporate goals of the company doing the work are best served by minimizing contractual constraints, yet the software/quality people may welcome those constraints which give them a power base. Software/quality people must never be seen as sacrificing corporate goals to their organizational needs.

- *Corporate policies and procedures.* These mechanism form the basis for deciding what actions to take; but equally important, they form a baseline of defense for people who are acting in conformance with them. If they support what you want and need to do, don't hesitate to use them to "hit opponents over the head" in the case of conflict over an action. If they do not support what you want and need, then move forward to change them before a crisis arises.

- *Upper management belief.* Battles which are not resolved by paper power (contracts, policies, and procedures) will be resolved by human power. The upper managers who make key decisions must be educated into becoming supportive of the software/quality function. It is unfair, but the software/quality manager has an uphill battle here, in that there are already well-entrenched traditional disciplines highly visible to the upper managers. It may take a lot of imaginative presentations about the importance of software and quality to change that situation. Upper managers got where they are by power and brilliance; they will understand immediately what you are up to. Imaginative, therefore, means more than just clever. It means both technically strong and interpersonally skillful.

The battlefield for power is large and dangerous. The software/quality manager who approaches it must be prepared. A strategy for achieving power is a necessary prelude to stepping onto the battlefield.

In the overall complex planning efforts the software/quality manager must undertake, planning for power is a vital first step.

3.4.2 Planning for Resources

The establishment of a power base is an ongoing problem. While that problem goes on, the software manager must also plan the resources for each project which arises in his or her domain. Resources can mean people, equipment, and facilities. It is the manager's job to create the optimum mix of these resources to get the job done properly. That is no easy task.

We have already discussed the fact that schedule prediction is one of the serious problem areas in software development and software quality. Schedule prediction is, of course, one of the critical factors in planning for *people resources*. How many people are needed, and for how long? The two questions are intertwined. If the schedule must be short, the number of people must be increased (being careful to pay attention to the admonitions of Brooks [75] who said "adding people to a project which is already behind schedule will make it even later"). If the schedule is driven by the number of available people (software skills are nearly always in short supply), then people resource planning must work around that. The key factors here are:

- What critical skills are needed?
- How can we get those skills?
- How many people are needed, with what skill mix?
- How long are those people needed for, starting when?
- Where can we find those people?
- Are there any personnel or personality problems to work around?

These are not necessarily complex questions. But getting the answers to them, and mapping out how those answers mesh with the project, is a vital part of the manager's resource planning.

Before we pass on to the subject of planning other resources, there is one vital point about people that must be made here. *The best way to guarantee a quality software product is to use a high-quality software development staff and a high-quality software quality team.* No amount of technology or management can overcome the problem of inadequate people.

It is well known that people differ in their capabilities by orders of magnitude. No known technology or management increments can give orders-of-magnitude improvement in software development in the 1990s. The reason that we pay attention to technology and management issues is not because they overcome people problems, but because once the people issue has been settled and the people chosen to do the job, there are still improvements to be made within those constraints by appropriate technology and management choices.

The problem, of course, is that no matter no much we believe in the value of high-quality people, there are not enough of them to go around, and we have no scientific way of determining who those quality people are. Because of that, the prime focus of planning for quality is in the areas of technology and management because we understand a bit more about the costs and benefits in those areas than we do in the people areas.

What about *computing resources?* What kinds of hardware are needed to solve the problem at hand? There is size to think about, and speed. The issue of proper computer speed and capacity is a difficult *technical* issue; but it is the manager's job to ensure that appropriate lead time for those technical tasks is set aside so that the issue is settled before anyone needs the equipment.

Computing resources do not just come in tangible form. Someone must establish the software tools to be used on the project and obtain those which are not already in house, allowing the necessary lead time to obtain them. It takes good turnaround/response time to support software development, and someone must decide what development environment is going to provide that.

There are also *facilities* to be planned for. Is a special building or other architectural work necessary for this particular project? What sort of work environment should the software developers have: private offices, cubicles, an open bay of desks? Are there special storage needs, terminal or personal computer needs, communication needs?

It is not unusual to find that the manager does not have complete freedom in planning. There are preestablished constraints which must be met by the planning process. Were the budget or schedule established by a process such as market need or competitive bidding? Are the appropriate skills and people tied up elsewhere so that a less-than-optimum approach must be used? Is there sufficient lead time to get the proper facilities or tools?

And overriding all of these resource planning activities is the issue of *planning the budget.* What will it cost to meet all the previously discussed resource needs? Are we planning only for the cost of software development, or should we plan for a quality supplement?

In planning for quality activities, whether they are done by an organizational supplement or not, some say 35 percent to 50 percent of the software budget should be set aside for them. Some companies have even established methodologies and computer programs for estimating the quality portion of a software budget. Typically, these estimates are based on calculating what percentage of the development budget should go for quality.

The difficult thing about planning is usually not the doing of it (although optimizing a plan can be complex) so much as ensuring that time is set aside for it. Planning must be done so early in a project that the pressure and motivation may still be forming. And yet inadequate planning, particularly for long lead-time items, can scuttle a project even before it starts.

If compromises are made in the planning process, it is very likely that quality will suffer. Therefore, all software planning, whether it is purely for development activities or more specifically for quality issues, is important to achieving quality software.

3.4.3 Planning for Technology

Software is a field of deep and evolving technology. It is difficult if not impossible to manage software development and achieve a quality product without having a grasp of that technology.

And therein lies a problem. Because software is an evolving field, even the manager who starts out technically knowledgeable runs the risk of becoming obsolete after an all-too-brief passage of time. The manager who starts out without any software knowledge at all is going to have to develop a managerial style that delegates heavily to trusted technologists.

Fortunately, there are plenty of books, periodicals, short courses, conferences, and workshops for the manager who finds himself or herself slipping behind the field. Even here there is danger, however. Many short courses are run by people who have a point of view and perhaps even a methodology to sell. Presenters at conferences and authors of articles in periodicals may also be selling, but in this case a theory-based view of software reality. The software manager may find himself or herself the victim of a huckster who is selling something that simply won't play back home in the manager's shop.

It is important that the manager of software keep up to date with frequent learning experiences, but it is equally important that those learning experiences be balanced and filtered through a healthy mixture of skepticism and receptiveness. It would be wise to pick courses where the instructor is presenting information and not selling anything but that information. It would be wise to respond most positively to presentations that are objective with an understanding of alternate points of view.

The manager of a software product will be called upon to make choices about methodological approaches. At the very least this means making decisions as to which tools and techniques to procure and utilize. If a request comes in for $X,000 worth of tool XYZ, the manager needs to have some feel for whether XYZ has enough benefits to overcome the cost. Perhaps the manager, concerned about the challenges of a new software project, will in fact initiate the move toward new technical approaches. Since any kind of change of this sort involves risk and cost, it is vital that the manager have at least a qualitative feel for judging that risk and that cost, and the benefits that may overcome them.

One place to start gaining that kind of knowledge is in the earlier sections of this book. If you are a manager of software projects who has skipped over the technology sections of this material on the grounds that it was not of direct interest to you, think again—it is your job to decide that technique ABC is preferable to tool XYZ for the project for which you are responsible, and you need to understand both ABC and XYZ to make that decision.

Typically decisions of this kind are not only technically demanding, but they involve long lead times as well. If a project that is going to use the Ada language waits until the beginning of coding to explore the availability of Ada compilers, it is too late, and serious problems are inevitable. New tools and techniques require time for an analysis and a decision to be made, time for the procurement or development, and time for a training program for its users. The total of all this time can be termed *technology transfer time,* and it will run into at least weeks, and perhaps even months or years for a technology of any complexity. Obviously, this lead time becomes a compelling factor in management planning for technology.

One common pitfall in planning for new tools is that a tool that sounds good and available may in fact not be. The tool may be on the wrong computer, or run on the wrong operating system, or support the wrong programming language, or even be proprietary to another company. It is easy to find out whether any of these situations is the case, but if the time to do so is not planned for then trouble, again, will arise.

Up until now, this discussion has focused on the management of change in technology—decision about new tools and techniques. But the day-to-day management of software development involves decision making about the status quo as well as about change. If Thread RRR of Project Z is running behind schedule, should we add people or schedule overtime or postpone some activities or ask for a schedule extension? Once again, the manager of the technology of software must be on top of that technology in order to manage it effectively.

The summation of all of this planning is sometimes presented in a document called the *software development plan.* To find out more about what goes into a document of that kind, see Glass [88].

There is one recurring rule that is useful to the manager planning for technology. Many things in the technical world follow the "80/20 rule" (i.e.,

80 percent of the X lies in 20 percent of the Y). Investigations which make use of this rule are called *Pareto analysis.*

For example, it is commonly true that 80 percent of the errors in a piece of software are found in 20 percent of the code. It is also commonly true that 80 percent of the running time of software is consumed by 20 percent of the code. A manager who understands this can concentrate the efforts of his or her people on the 20 percent that matters. For example, the extra effort by Space Shuttle software people on peer reviews of code looking for data resetting errors, mentioned in an earlier section, was clearly the result of a Pareto-like analysis that found an uncommonly high percentage of such errors occurring. The rule of thumb for management here is that there are vulnerable areas in software, and the wise manager will put extra effort into identifying and working the problems of those critical areas.

REFERENCES

AMER90—Special issue of *American Programmer,* July/August 1990, on "Peopleware," with articles on "Managing the Real Leverage in Software Productivity and Quality," by Bill Curtis, "Performance Management: A New Approach to Software Engineering Management," by Susan Webber, and others.

DeMARCO87—*Peopleware,* Dorset House Publishing Co., 1987; Tom DeMarco and Timothy Lister. *Entertaining and important collection of essays on people in software development.*

GLASS88—*Software Communication Skills,* Prentice Hall, 1988; Robert L. Glass. *Describes choices for the form and content of most software documents, including the software development plan.*

HUMPHREY89—*Managing the Software Process,* Addison-Wesley, 1989; Watts S. Humphrey. *Sees process or the steps taken to build the product as the key to software development. Discusses planning, establishing, and controlling that process.*

3.4.4 Planning for Standards

Standards are both a technical issue and a management issue. Because of the evolving nature of the field, it is dangerous to impose standards by management directive without providing fairly frequent technical review to ensure that the standards are not enforcing outdated methodologies.

A technical discussion of standards appeared earlier in this book. Chapter 2.4.5 ("Standards and Enforcers") is particularly relevant to this management discussion of standards. The reader should go back and scan that section briefly before proceeding here. (The referenced section deals with the need to minimize standards and then enforce that minimum set vigorously. It also suggests candidate areas for standardization.)

For managers in most software-developing companies, the standards issue may look deceptively simple. There is probably already a corporate standard for software development, and the manager can edict and enforce that standard. This is not a bad position to take if the corporate standard is well chosen and up to date. But it is important that the manager who is planning for standards be aware that there are now national and international standards for software development. Those standards do not have the force of law, but they certainly have the force of communal wisdom, and all software managers should include a study of those global standards in any standards planning activity. In a way, the software manager who does not have a corporate standard to use as a starting place may be at an advantage here, since there is more freedom to use the global standards.

Even these global standards are evolving. The IEEE, for example, has several standards committees at work as this book is being written. We summarize some of their areas of standardization in Chapter 1.5.1. Software quality assurance plans, test documentation, configuration management plans, and software requirements specifications are already covered by standards. But because these standards are constantly evolving, the wise manager will pursue the latest information on these standards from the following contact points:

- To order the latest IEEE standards:
  IEEE Standards Sales (under $10 each)
  (201) 981-0060
  445 Hoes Lane
  Piscataway NJ 08854
- To attend a seminar on IEEE standards:
  S. Havranek, Seminar Marketing Manager
  (212) 705-7907
  IEEE Standards Board
  345 E. 47th St. P-7
  New York NY 10017

To give an example of the rapid evolution in this area, here is a list of standards currently in work by IEEE committees.

- Software Reliability Measurement
- Guide to Software Quality Assurance
- Quality System-Model for Quality Assurance of Software in Specification, Design/Development Test and Maintenance
- Guide for the Use of Ada as a Program Design Language
- Software Engineering Standards Taxonomy
- Software Unit Testing Standard

- Guide to Software Design Descriptions
- Software Reviews and Audits Standards
- Classification for Software Errors, Faults, and Failures

Furthermore, here is a list of areas in which the IEEE has proposed to work.

- Guide for Software Configuration Management
- Software Productivity Metrics Standard
- Software Quality Metrics Standard
- User Documentation Standard
- Guide for Third-Party Software Acquisition

For the manager planning for software standards, this list almost becomes a menu of best approaches which might be used.

The IEEE is not the only standards body, in fact. The International Standards Organization (ISO) operates at the international level, and there has even been a Corporation for Open Systems (populated by representatives of major companies) which attempted to focus on standards important to hardware/software vendors and users. Unfortunately, many such organizations tend to polarize into a vendor camp and a user camp, and politics then weakens the achievements.

It must be noted one more time that standards are an area requiring careful thought. The first question the planner must deal with is "Are standards really needed?" Only if that is answered in the affirmative should the next issue of selecting the best standard be pursued. Recall the message of the earlier section that standards are not worth having if they are not enforced. There is cost to enforcement, so the standards chosen should be vital requirements. One informal article [Johansen85,] summarized the issue very well:

> One company I worked for established a department whose sole responsibility was to develop standards and procedures for the programming staff to follow. Perhaps you can imagine the result: they continually issued a stream of new rules. If they ever stopped issuing new rules, they would no longer have a raison d'etre, and the company might decide to fire the lot of them.

REFERENCES

DOD2167—"Military Standard: Defense System Development," DOD-STD-2167a. *Contains requirements for the development of "Mission Critical" software for the U.S. Department of Defense. Defines standards for a uniform development process.*

DOD2168—"Military Standard: Defense System Software Quality Program," DOD-STD-2168. *Defines the requirements for ensuring that a U.S. Department of Defense software program is successfully carried out.*

JOHANSEN85—"The Trouble with Standards," *Datamation,* February 15, 1985; Johansen. *A very personal discussion of the problem areas in standards.*

3.4.5 Planning the Costs

Management is, for the most part, a subjective art rather than an objective science. That subjectivity becomes especially important when it comes time to talk about the costs of achieving a quality software product.

There are several positions commonly taken about the cost of the quality constituent of software:

- Quality activities should be allocated a percentage of the software development costs, perhaps 35 percent to 50 percent as suggested earlier in this book. Many companies base the dollar support for quality activities and organizations on this kind of method. Note that this method lumps all quality activities together regardless of where they are performed organizationally.

- Quality activities performed by a quality supplement organization should be separately provided for. One way of establishing how to do this is to look at typical staffing of development versus the quality supplement. The ratio of quality assurance people to development people is roughly 1:100, according to a recent survey. This would suggest an allocation of 1 percent of development funds to the special quality function.

- Quality activities are an essential part of the software development process and cannot be neglected. There is no need to break down separate dollar amounts for quality, it is all part of the same whole. As Crosby [79] puts it, "Quality is free." It is the cost of *not* having it that is the real concern here.

That is quite a mixed picture. The cost of quality can be either nothing, or 1 percent of development costs, or 35 percent to 50 percent of development costs, depending on what it is we are really talking about.

It is apparent from this discussion that the cost of quality is intricately intertwined with the attitudes and approaches toward quality. Just as the main character in Pirsig [74] lost his sanity for a while trying to define the elusive concept of quality, so too we find massive difficulty in discussing its cost.

Of course this is not a sufficient conclusion for a discussion of this matter. Regardless of the complexity, a method must be used to establish dollar allocations for ensuring that quality is achieved. Perhaps the best answer is the one we started with: The cost of achieving quality is going to be about 35 percent to 50 percent of development costs. Some of that amount should be split between separate organizations such as quality assurance or product test. But some of it should remain in the hands of the developers, who are as we previously discussed the prime constituency in any quality process. How much is split between separate organizations, and where we stand on the 35 percent to 50 percent spread, should be a function of the product requirements. If some attribute(s) of quality are critical, then there should be more quality supplement work and the numbers should be on the high side of the spread. If not, the converse should be true.

Whatever else is said about the cost of quality, the fundamental truth is that Crosby is right: If poor quality results in product malfunction or recall, customer resentment, or perhaps even litigation or death, then the cost of the lack of quality may very well be as high as or higher than the entire cost of the development process itself. The focus of concern regarding the cost of quality must be on achieving it, not costing it.

REFERENCES

CROSBY79—*Quality is Free: The Art of Making Quality Free,* McGraw, 1979; Philip Crosby. *Takes the position that it is the absence of quality that costs money.*

PIRSIG74—*Zen and the Art of Motorcycle Maintenance,* Morrow, 1974; Robert M. Pirsig. *A fictional story about quality, its pursuit, and the effect on the pursuer.*

3.5 ORGANIZATION

Remember Trevor Clever? He is the software manager whose team failed the software preliminary design review but came back strong to get applause at their acceptance test.

Remember that when things were at their lowest Trevor decided that he was going to have to rely on others to help him complete a quality product? A large number of those others were his own software developers. But in addition there was the idea of the quality supplement.

The quality supplement consists of one or many organizations which complement the developers and focus on specific aspects of quality. In the sections that follow, we first explore what those specific quality supplements are from a functional point of view. Then we talk about organizational packages which might be used to mold and enable those functions. The quality assurance organization, one of the most popular packaging techniques, is discussed there.

3.6 QUALITY FUNCTIONS AND TASKS _____

We already established that the developers of the software make the primary determination of product quality. The quality functions and tasks we are about to discuss can all be performed by these software developers. If they do that, of course, there is no quality supplement. But that does not mean that the tasks will not or should not be performed.

Because of the complexity of software quality, however, it is often desirable to have separate groups of people assist in the quality creation and quality analysis functions. These functions include:

- Reviews and audits performed by people who can help direct the development effort onto quality paths
- Product test performed by people who can objectively create tests and analyze test results
- Configuration management performed by people who defend the product baseline against loss
- Change and error control performed by people who make sure that all changes are recorded and tracked
- Contract management performed by people who ensure that purchased software is of sufficient quality
- Independent verification and validation performed by people who have an outside objective view of the product

3.6.1 Reviews and Audits

Reviews and audits are events where project outsiders are invited to analyze and critique either the evolving software product or its process of evolution, or both.

A *review* is usually a planned event, focusing on a specific subproduct or process (e.g., a preliminary design review examines the first cut at design and the artifacts which define and support the design). An *audit* is usually an invoked event, focusing on a particular problem or concern (e.g., project XYZ is deeply over budget and an objective view of why is needed).

The word *usually* occurs in both of the preceding definitions. There are no hard and fast rules for reviews and audits; for example, the U.S. Department of Defense requires two events called the functional and the physical configuration audits which are actually planned events focusing on a delivered software product. In that sense, even though the DoD calls them audits, they fit our definition of a review.

What is unique about reviews and audits from an organizational point of view is that they are transient; that is, a group of people are called together for a short time to perform a task, and then the group disbands.

The other organizations we talk about in this section are usually permanent; that is, they function for a major portion of the duration of the project. Thus, it is important to know when to call a review or an audit, and when to terminate them.

With reviews, the answer to that issue is simple. Management decides what kinds of reviews are needed during the planning process (e.g., requirements review, design review(s), code review, acceptance review), and puts onto the project schedule the points in time where the reviews need to be started ("select review team; invite reviewers to review and notify them as to what tasks they are to perform") and terminated ("obtain minutes of review and disband review team").

With audits, the answer is case specific. Through its normal project monitoring process, management may spot an anomaly which deserves further study. In that event, an audit team is established and presented with a definition of tasks and desired findings, and given resources to complete its assignment. When its findings are presented, the audit team is disbanded.

Generally for a review, it is vital to have:

- qualified and available team members
- resources to enable the team members to perform
- a predefined agenda
- a clear picture of the goals of the review

Generally for an audit, it is vital to have:

- qualified and available team members
- resources to enable the team members to perform
- a clear picture of the goals of the audit
- a commitment from the developers that they will not obstruct the audit team's search
- the clout to enable the use of the findings of the audit

3.6.2 Product Test

The basic motivation of a software developer during testing is to show that the software works. But the goal of testing is really to find places where the software does not work.

This basic conflict can be resolved by (1) having the developers overcome their basic motivation through a strong feeling of responsibility for the product, and (2) having a separate organization supplement the testing done by the developers. This separate organization is often called *product test*.

Both approaches are important. We have noted several times that quality emerges first of all from the developers, and the level of testing that must inevitably be done by them—unit testing—is a vital first step in the testing process. If developers believe that a separate organization is going to be responsible for testing, they may skimp on that first level of testing unless they see the product and its reliability as an example of their own professional prowess.

On the other hand, no matter how responsible the developers feel, there are built-in biases and blind spots which prevent them from doing a thoroughly objective job of error removal. The services of a separate organization complement those biases and blind spots.

The fundamental purpose of the product test organization, then, is to do *objective* testing of the software product. The product test organization must supplement and not replace the testing efforts of the developers. Often this happens via a phaseover approach, in which the developers do the early testing and the initial integration testing. The product test performs additional integration testing and begins to assume the dominant testing responsibility, such as system testing.

No matter what the timing of the relative responsibilities, the task of product testing is error detection and not error removal. Knowledgeable software developers must be utilized to analyze and remove the errors found by product testing.

Because the product test organization will be increasingly responsible during the later stages of testing, it is commonly true that they take over responsibility for the formal documents of testing such as test plans, procedures, and test reports.

It is important that quality supplement organizations, especially product test, be seen as helpers and not adversaries by the software developers. There will naturally be adversarial moments, as when product test finds yet another error that the developers must fix. But if product test is also seen as an organization which removes some of the documentation burden as well as some of the testing burden from the developers, the relationship is much more likely to be successful.

Bell Labs has developed a set of priorities for their product test organizations [Petschenik85]. In summary, they advocate the following:

1. As a practical matter, it is not possible to be 100 percent thorough in testing. A cost-effective solution is to use about 15 percent of the test cases which a test theoretician would consider thorough.
2. Testing the system's capabilities is more important than testing its components.
3. Testing old capabilities is more important than testing new capabilities.

4. Testing typical situations is more important than testing boundary-value cases.

Some of these guidelines seem controversial at first thought. Certainly a 15 percent solution would seem to be totally inadequate. But this simply repeats in a numeric way what we have already said, that fully rigorous testing of software is neither practical nor even possible.

Testing capabilities over components is simply a restatement of our earlier position that requirements-driven testing must take precedence over (but not replace) structure-driven testing.

Placing high priority on the testing of old capabilities is also a restatement of an earlier position that during maintenance, regression testing is a vital part of the overall testing process. And performing typical testing is closely related to statistics-driven testing for customer visibility. Thus, although these statements taken out of context may seem striking and perhaps even argumentative, in fact there is an important element of truth to all of them. Seen here in the context of the role of the product test organization, they form an important basis for the functioning of that organization.

REFERENCES

PETSCHENIK85—"Practical Strategies in System Testing," *IEEE Software,* September 1985; Petschenik. *A discussion of how system testing is done at Bell Labs.*

3.6.3 Configuration Management

The worst nightmare stories in computing are about the loss of a total system. Somehow, the only copy of the source code is deleted from disk or otherwise lost, and the system can only be replicated from the object code.

The defense against this ultimate loss is embodied in a function called configuration management. For simple software systems, configuration management is something that the developers do. In more complicated situations, often it becomes a quality supplement task.

The task of configuration management is simple in concept, as we said earlier in Chapter 2.6.2, to establish baseline inviolate versions of the software, totally protected from any possibility of loss. This generally involves having one copy of the software which can never be touched (written to) by anyone. (Changes can only be made by making a copy to be modified.) It also involves keeping backup copies of the baseline product, often at a remote location, so that even if fire or other disaster strikes the computer center there are copies of the important products available.

The execution of this simple concept rapidly gets complicated. As multiple versions of a product evolve, and as the baseline tracks source code, object code, documentation, and the modules which make up the product, the task of configuration management quickly escalates. It is largely clerical but it requires careful and responsible attention to a well-defined set of tasks; it need not be staffed by skilled software developers, but it is vital that it be staffed by especially responsible and intelligent clerical people.

The procedures for configuration management must include a definition of how product evolution will be handled and in fact facilitated without threatening the baseline. Sometimes configuration management organizations become too vested in protection and do not cooperate in supporting change; this position is almost as dangerous to the software product as no configuration management at all.

The central core of configuration management tasks is shown in Figure 3.1. The complexity of configuration management lies in the iterative repetition of this central core.

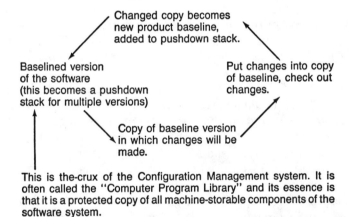

Figure 3.1.   The configuration management baseline and the process of change.

REFERENCES

BERSOFF80—*Software Configuration Management,* Prentice-Hall, 1980; E. H. Bersoff, V. D. Henderson, and S. G. Siegel. *A readable, thorough book on the methods of configuration management.*

TOMAYKO87—"Software Configuration Management," Software Engineering Institute Curriculum Module SEI-CM-4, April 1987; James E. Tomayko. *Presents a good description of, and bibliography for configuration management; for educators who want to teach the topic.*

3.6.4 Change and Error Control

Rarely does software go into production status in an absolute, final form. There are errors remaining to be corrected, and there are inevitably requirements changes which will also result in program revision. In this section, we refer to both requirements changes and the corrections resulting from error detection as *changes.*

As the change reports reach the software maintainers (or the software developers if the product is being configuration controlled but has not yet reached production status), it is important for management to decide whether the technical team will prioritize the tasks resulting from the change requests, or whether management wants to play a role in that prioritizing. Commonly, a change review process and board are defined to provide management control in this area. The change review process is usually prepared in the form of a procedure given to the maintainers. A change board is usually a fairly high-level team defined to meet periodically and make decisions about which changes should be made and when.

The level of the people chosen for the change board is application dependent, but it should involve key users and key maintainers and thus it should report fairly high up the management ladder, perhaps immediately under the project manager or at the very lowest directly to the software maintenance manager. For some NASA work, such as on the Space Shuttle, the change board is the place where key project decisions are made, and its population is the top Shuttle managers.

Not every error report or change request should be implemented. The first decision for a change board to make is "Do we accept or reject this proposal?" Following that decision, the board must then decide the relative importance of the change request, if accepted. This can be a complicated issue, especially if the number of such proposals is high. It is not just the nature of the change, but also the date needed which must determine the priority. For example, an unimportant change which, if it is to be done at all must be completed by a week from Tuesday, may be prioritized higher than an important change which is not needed for six months.

Once the change is prioritized, it is important to track the progress of the change. The change board needs to know what changes have been made, which ones are about to be made, and which ones are scheduled for a later date. The user of the software needs to know when a change of interest to them is going to be available in the production version of the software, and what changes are in which versions. The maintainers need to know what they are currently working on, what they will work on next, and how the changes will be packaged into versions. The management of the maintainers needs to know how the product is progressing. (Is it getting better or worse? Is it satisfying the customers?) Management also needs to know how the maintainers are progressing. (Is the backlog of changes increasing or decreasing?) All of this information must be supplied by a change reporting system.

Often a change reporting system is done manually, but simple report generation, database tools, or perhaps even project-specific tracking programs may be created. The reports resulting from the system, however it is done, will obviously be distributed widely, to all of the destinations mentioned in the preceding paragraph.

The question of how often should a change board meet arises. Obviously, the answer must be project specific, but there are two considerations here: (1) that decisions be made responsibly and without pressure, and (2) that critical decisions be made as rapidly as possible.

Clearly it is difficult to achieve both of these goals together. The usual solution is to convene a change board on a regular basis, perhaps once a week during key activity periods, and to provide a process for emergency decision making which can then be reviewed at the next regularly scheduled meeting.

The change board must work closely with and be appreciative of the efforts of the configuration management body. The configuration management people essentially place a protective shield around baseline versions of the software product; the change board decides when that protective shield will be penetrated.

The source of a change request is usually a formally defined piece of paper. With such information as:

1. an identifying number or name for future tracking
2. the nature of the change or the symptoms of the error
3. (later) a first analysis of the implementation of the change
4. (even later) a description of the eventual change
5. configuration information, such as the version in which the problem/analysis was identified or performed, and the version in which the change will reach production
6. findings, such as what workaround is available to users, if any, or estimates of when the work might be completed
7. names, such as the name of the change originator, the name of the first analysis maintainer, and the name of the eventual change maintainer
8. any information relevant to any management metrics being collected on changes.

Status report for software problems, system ARGH				9/23/90
SPR number	Originated	Correction	Version	Description
25	9/20/90	10/20/90	4.7?	Audible signal when system finishes lengthy procedure
26	9/20/90	10/17/90	4.7?	Archive directory link broken
27	9/21/90	9/22/90	4.8	No record of archive action
28	9/21/90	10/20/90	4.7?	Check part command invalid
29	9/23/90	9/23/90	4.6	Operator message not logged

Figure 3.2. Status report for software problems, system ARGH 9/23/90.

This information will not only be on the forms themselves, but also be presented in appropriate places on the reports produced to track the changes.

Examples of change reporting system outputs are shown here. The first chart is a good example of the information needed by maintainers and users. The second chart, the trend chart, might be of interest to maintenance managers and the change board. It shows that the software represented here is becoming stable (fewer new changes are being requested) but that the maintenance team is not keeping up (the total number of

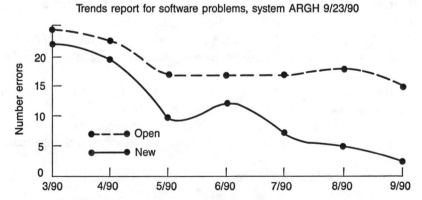

Figure 3.3. Trends report for software problems, system ARGH 9/23/90.

changes to be made remains relatively high even though the reporting of new changes is decreasing).

3.6.5 Acquisition Management

Software need not always be built in house. Whenever the requirements for the software can be satisfied by an existing package, that solution should be chosen. Prebuilt software is usually more reliable and certainly should be cheaper. When package software often does not meet the requirements at hand sufficiently well, then the software must be built. However, there is still a choice.

There are many software companies which specialize in certain kinds of software. Often the right solution will be to contract with a specialty company to build the needed software. Most computing installations, for example, do not have the skills to build efficient, optimized compilers. If the situation arose where you needed a new compiler built, you would be smart to contract with a company that had been building them for several years, knew what problems to avoid, and had the tools to do the job properly. (It is still true, of course, that the vast majority of application software will be built in house because either its requirements are too company specific or because the application skills are at least as strong in house as outside.)

When software is built by an outside company, it is essential that a contract be drawn to govern the work and the product to be built. The task of ensuring that the outside company satisfies the contract is known as *contract management* or *acquisition management.*

A contract will usually consist of a product definition, against which the evolving and eventually the delivered product can be measured, and a process definition, telling how the software will be built. The product definition, for example, might discuss the specific application requirements to be satisfied, and the performance the product must achieve, while the process definition might discuss the reviews to be held and any staffing considerations (such as defining what skills those participating in the development must possess).

The items a contract should cover and how it should cover them are best described in a book devoted to such topics. (See, for example, Glass [88].) The contract, it must be noted, is an essential part of producing a quality product, since those items stated in the contract must be done by the contracting company, and whatever is not stated in the contract will quite likely not get done.

It is the task of contract management, then, to assure that the conditions of the contract are carried out. Often this means that contract managers must be responsible for all of the tasks which determine product quality—everything else we have discussed in this book! For example, the contract manager will see to the following procedures (assuming that the contract calls for them):

- reviews and audits of the product and the process
- product decisions within the scope of the contract
- contract scope interpretation
- in-house test of the delivered product
- configuration management of the delivered product
- change and error control
- product acceptance
- product transition to in-house use

The contract manager's first goal is always to get a quality product delivered on time and within budget. If it is apparent that that is not going to happen, then the contract manager must decide what to do about it. For example, if the contractor is badly behind schedule, the contract manager can:

- demand contract compliance and pressure the contractor to do whatever is necessary to get the product completed on time
- relax the contract schedule in order to ensure getting a quality product
- eliminate or postpone certain contract requirements to make possible a partial delivery on schedule

These decisions clearly must be made with the visibility and often the direction of upper management. If the contractor is to be pressured, for example, upper management has more power to do so. If contract provisions are to be relaxed, upper management must decide the matter. Because of this, it is not uncommon to find contract managers reporting fairly high up the management chain. In essence, the contract manager is managing the people the contractor has assigned to the job. Seen in this light, the contract manager is a product manager as well.

There are two important skills which the contract manager must possess: thorough knowledge of the application domain for which the product is being built, and a working knowledge of the rudiments of contract law. The contract manager must also have ready access to upper management (as we have already seen), corporate buyers (for advice on handling contractors), and corporate lawyers (for in-depth advice on contract law).

What this usually means is that software contract managers must be fairly senior people. Note that this adds some expense to the bid price of contracting software to an outside company. That is, the price of obtaining the software is not only the price agreed upon when the contract was signed, but also the price of the contract manager's time. It is vital not to try to skimp on contract management; the result may be at least unnecessary animosity between the contractor and the company ordering the product, and at worst the failure to deliver an acceptable product.

Most computing installations do very little contract management, preferring to build their software in house. But some companies, as a matter of policy, buy most of their software outside. In the latter kind of company, much of the software staff would be contract managers.

REFERENCES

GLASS88—*Software Communication Skills,* Prentice Hall, 1988; Glass. *Describes the kinds of communication software people must perform. Includes a section on negotiating and writing contracts.*

3.6.6 Independent Verification and Validation

The quality of software need not always be monitored only in house. If the software is particularly critical, it may be desirable to hire an outside company to supplement the work of any in-house organizations.

Independent verification and validation (IV&V) is the name commonly given to this function and to the companies which perform it. IV&V is the ultimate in objectivity, in the sense that the contracting IV&V company is motivated only to seek problems in the software, not to demonstrate the lack of them. Typically, IV&V contractors may play any or all of the roles we have discussed in this book, sparing little expense in ensuring that a quality product is produced. For example, IV&V companies sometimes analyze and verify requirements by constructing a prototype or model of the system defined by the requirements to see if the result is what the customer really wants. IV&V companies may also use or produce special tools to augment the developer's own verification and validation efforts. IV&V is most commonly used on U.S. Department of Defense and Space systems, where there is a particularly severe need for product quality. Under those circumstances, the typical cost of the IV&V contract may range from 10 percent to 60 percent of the development cost.

REFERENCE

IEEE89—Special issue on "Verification and Validation—Its Place in the Life Cycle," *IEEE Software,* May 1989. *Contains six papers on software V&V, including an overview paper and one predicting what V&V will become over the next decade.*

REIFER79—"Airborne Systems Software Acquisitions Engineering Guidebook for Verification, Validation and Certification," Air Force Technical Report ASD-TR-79-5-28; Donald J. Reifer. *A government-funded report on the value and conduct of IV&V.*

V&V STANDARDS AND GUIDELINES

The concepts of V&V emerged in the late 1960s and 1970s as the use of software in military and nuclear-power systems increased. Initially, individual programs' standards addressed the need for V&V. Then government and industry began to develop V&V standards so they would have a specification of this methodology for contract procurements and for monitoring the technical performance of V&V efforts. Today's V&V standards and guidelines serve large, heterogeneous communities and are applicable to many types of software. They include:

- Federal Information-Processing Standards Publication 101, *Guideline for Life-Cycle Validation, Verification, and Testing of Computer Software.*
- FIPS Pub. 132, *Guideline for Software Verification and Validation Plans,* which adopts ANSI/IEEE Std 1012-1986, the *Standard for Software Verification and Validation Plans.*
- the US Air Force's AFSC/AFLC 800-5, *Software Independent Verification and Validation,*
- the American Nuclear Society's ANS 10.4, *Guidelines for the Verification and Validation of Scientific and Engineering Computer Programs for the Nuclear Industry,* and
- the NASA Jet Propulsion Laboratory's JPL D-576, *Independent Verification and Validation of Computer Software: Methodology.*

Table A shows you how to develop a V&V effort based on the strength of the guidance in these standards and guidelines.

TABLE A.   PLANNING V&V WITH GUIDANCE FROM V&V DOCUMENTS

Activity	Procedure	Guidance
Scope the V&V effort	Criticality assessment	AFSC 800-5
	Organization	AFSC 800-5, ANS 10.4
	Cost estimation	AFSC 800-5
Plan the V&V effort	Planning preparation	FIPS 132/IEEE 1012,
	Objectives	ANS 10.4, FIPS 101
		FIPS 132/IEEE 1012,
		FIPS 101, ANS 10.4,
		JPLD-576
	General V&V task selection	all
	Minimum, required	FIPS 132/IEEE 1012
	Optional	FIPS 132/IEEE 1012
	Criticality levels	FIPS 101, AFSC 800-5
	Test management	FIPS 132/IEEE 1012
	Test types	FIPS 132.IEEE 1012,
		FIPS 101, JPLD-576
	Objectives	FIPS 132/IEEE 1012
	Documentation	FIPS 132/IEEE 1012
	Coverage	FIPS 101, FIPS 132/

(continued)

TABLE A.   PLANNING V&V WITH GUIDANCE FROM V&V DOCUMENTS (continued)

Activity	Procedure	Guidance
	Planning	IEEE 1012, ANS 10.4 all
	Planning V&V for maintenance	ANS 10.4, FIPS 132/IEEE 1012
Manage the	V&V management tasks	FIPS 132/IEEE 1012
V&V effort	Reporting	FIPS 132/IEEE 1012, ANS 10.4

From "Software Verification and Validation: An Overview," *IEEE Software,* May 1989, Dolores R. Wallace and Roger U. Fijii © 1989 IEEE.

3.6.7   Process Group

A relative newcomer in the world of quality supplement organizations is the process group. The purpose of the process group is to develop and ensure the use of appropriate software processes; the belief of the advocates of the process group is that good process is the surest determiner of software product quality.

What do we mean by process? According to Humphrey [87], we mean "the sequence of tasks which, when properly performed, will produce the desired result." Becoming more specific, Humphrey [87] says that process, to be effective, "must consider the interrelationships of all the required tasks in building software, the tools and methods used, and the skill, training and motivation of the people involved." Examples of good process would include things like "using coding standards," "tracking software code and test errors," "using computer tools to measure test coverage." The expectation is that a process group will enable and ensure the use of good process.

The process group by this name may be a new concept, but some aspects of the idea have been previously employed in groups called *methods* or *technical staff*. The development center, to be discussed later, is also related.

It is the role of the process group to improve process through

- advocating improved process
- tracking and procuring new technology
- training software people in new process concepts
- monitoring the use of improved process

There is no doubt that paying more attention to software process can improve the quality of work being performed. In fact, some computer hardware companies are now using process evaluation to screen out "undesirable" software houses for building products for use on their computers, and the U.S. Department of Defense is actively pursuing process evaluation as a tool for improving its ability to select software contractors. However, some questions remain:

1. Can defined process lead to predictably high-quality products?
2. Is process really the best determiner of product quality?

We have already seen that in most respects people are the keys to quality. However, given that a project has obtained the best people it can commensurate with the task to be performed, then certainly good process is more likely to lead to quality products than the lack thereof.

REFERENCES

AP90—Special issue on "Software Process Models," *American Programmer,* September 1990. *Contains such papers as "Introducing Process Models into Software Organizations," by Watts Humphrey, and several papers linking CASE tools to process modeling.*

HUMPHREY87—"Characterizing the Software Process—A Maturity Framework," and its companion volume, "A Method for Assessing the Software Engineering Capability of Contractors," Software Engineering Institute Technical Report CMU/SEI-87-TR-11, June 1987, Watts S. Humphrey. *Describes software process levels and achievement of process maturity, and proposes a program for improving the performance of software development organizations. The companion volume lists the all-important detail-level criteria upon which the evaluation is based.*

HUMPHREY90—*Software Process Maturity,* Addison-Wesley, 1990; Watts S. Humphrey. *The book describing Humphrey's views on process groups and improving software process. Suggests that software quality assurance should have 5 percent to 10 percent of the people of the development organization, and that the process group should have 1 percent to 3 percent.*

OSTERWEIL87—"Software Processes are Software Too," *Proceedings of the Ninth International Conference on Software Engineering,* 1987; Leon Osterweil. *Controversial keynote presentation in which the author suggests that software process is programmable, and subject to the creation of process programming languages. Examples of such a language are presented.*

3.6.7.1 Process measurement and improvement

In the previous section, we mentioned that process evaluation has led to process rating and even scoring of software developers. What do those ratings and scorings look like?

Humphrey [87] defines five levels of software process maturity. Presumably, as a software organization progresses and improves, especially with the help of a process group to lead the way, it will gradually rise from a low level to higher ones. The levels are:

1. *Initial.* A site not yet under statistical control, in the sense that repetition of roughly the same work will produce roughly the same product.
2. *Repeatable.* A stable process under statistical control, achieved by initiating rigorous project management of commitments, cost, schedule, and change.
3. *Defined.* The process is stated and followed, resulting in consistent implementation.
4. *Managed.* A defined process where process measurement is employed.
5. *Optimized.* The defined and measured process allows the search for the best software processes.

By means of the evaluation criteria mentioned in the previous section, and these levels of process maturity achievement, many industrial and governmental software organizations have been evaluated. Evaluation teams from Humphrey's organization in the Software Engineering Institute, or teams trained by them, make on-the-spot evaluations.

The result of these evaluations is depressing. Most software sites evaluated to date have been at level 1, a few have been at level 2, and hardly any have been at level 3. By this rating scale, the state of the practice of software engineering is apparently quite bad.

A challenge to this viewpoint was presented at the 1989 International Conference on Software Engineering, when DeMarco [89] reported after examining the practices of software practitioners building real software under experimental conditions that most modern technical methods are employed. (They evaluated the experimental results on their uses of modularity, cohesiveness, information hiding, structured coding, and others).

If practitioners tend to use the best-defined technology, why then have the process evaluation results been so dismal?

That question actually was asked at the conference, and Watts Humphrey rose to respond to it. "The process evaluation findings," he said, "are about the *management of software,* whereas the DeMarco [89] findings were about the *technology.*" Once again, in this exchange, we see that the critical area in software in the 1990s appears to be management rather than technology.

Another curious finding resulted from DeMarco [89]. The experimenters examined several programs written by people from an institution that enforced use of a common methodology. The issue was if the products produced by the individuals using this methodology converge on a common design and implementation solution. Note that at stake here is the process evaluation concept of repeatable products resulting from repeatable process. In this study, at least, the answer to the question was a resounding "No." "There was no sign at all of convergence of design concept . . . Their programs had as few as 4 and as many as 23 modules with an even distribution between the extremes. They didn't even code in a very similar style . . . "

More research work is needed here showing the relationship between defined process and predictable product. These admittedly early informal findings suggest that any such relationship may be problematic. But there is enormous enthusiasm in the software world for process methods and process evaluation. The wise software manager and the technologist in the 1990s will pay close attention to what is happening here.

REFERENCES

DeMarco89—"Software Development: State of the Art vs. State of the Practice," *Proceedings of the 11th International Conference on Software Engineering,* May 15–18 1989, Pittsburgh; Tom DeMarco and Tim Lister. *A report on a study of software techniques used in practice, based on the results of so-called "Coding War Games" in which nearly 400 programmers solved the same problem. Found that the state of the practice was surprisingly close to the state of the art.*

3.6.7.2 Statistical process control

There is another benefit from the use of a predictable and controlled process, according to the advocates of this process technology. Once the process is defined, in place, and some data on normal process behavior have been collected, it is possible to measure a software project's progress against the norm for many previous projects.

By this technique, for example, it might be easy to spot those Pareto principle anomalies, the 20 percent that cause 80 percent of the problems. Thus, management attention can be focused on problem areas as deviations from the norms of past history rather than relying on intuition or subjective views of participants in the process.

This idea called *statistical process control* is borrowed from older technologies, especially manufacturing, where sampling techniques are used to examine products on an assembly line. If the norm for this line is 98 percent good products and this lot achieves only 65 percent, clearly management has a problem to be solved.

It is an extremely appealing idea, since it allows management to use quantitative judgment instead of subjective analysis to make decisions. The question is, "Can it be used for software?"

Early use of the method has been relatively successful. Most companies now track software errors, measuring number of errors per thousand lines of code. They have determined their own corporate norms, collected the corporate norms of others, and know when a project has an unreasonably high number of errors.

Beyond that, how well has it done? The honest answer, as this book is being written, still lies in the research and development domain. How many other processes in software can have quantitative norms meaningfully defined for them? How easy is it to gather the data to define those norms and how helpful is it to apply those norms to specific projects? There are many more questions than answers.

One serious concern lies with the attempt to apply schemes used for mechanistic processes to the more intellectual/creative process of software development. The early findings of DeMarco [89], for example, suggest that even with stringent process controls a wide variation in resulting product will occur.

Again, it is too early to come to conclusions on this matter, and it is important for the concerned software manager/technologist to track the progress of these concepts. There are many who predict that software management/development in the future will use predictable process to produce predictable products where deviations from the norm can be identified and dealt with. If that is indeed possible, software people should embrace these ideas with open arms.

3.6.8 Development Center

The development center is very similar in concept to the process group. It is an organization responsible for improving the way software is built in general, rather than improving the way software for a particular project is built.

What kinds of activities could a development center engage in on behalf of the software professionals it serves? It can *do* certain things:

- provide metrics
  - define goals
  - define data to be collected
  - provide for collecting the data
  - determine ways of using the data
  - use the data to improve recommendations
- provide coordination
  - facilitate cross-project communication
  - provide for project feedback, "lessons learned"
  - use the results to improve recommendations

- provide training
  - determine needs
  - decide to "make" or "buy" appropriate training
  - facilitate courses
- provide information
  - determine needs
  - analyze alternative sources
  - obtain the needed information
  - (note that this might include establishing a computing library)

The development center can also *recommend* certain things:

- methodologies
- processes
- representations (languages)
- tools
- standards
- guidelines

For example, suppose your software organization has decided to explore the ideas presented in this book in order to improve the way you build software. The development center could analyze the ideas, determine which ones are useful under what circumstances in your setting, define the standards and guidelines for enabling them, provide the training, perhaps establish a small library of key books and periodicals, and in general oversee this technology transfer.

3.6.9 Information Center

The information center is to the user as the development center is to the software professional. It provides users with whatever information is needed to help them use the computer power of the enterprise.

In the 1990s, there is some controversy in that. There are essentially two rather different roles that computing people see for users:

1. Making use of the corporate (usually, large) computers, software solutions, and centralized database provided by the computer center (sometimes known as the *closed-shop* approach).
2. Making use of the most convenient computer power to provide their own solutions, even to having their own computers, writing their own software, and keeping their own databases (sometimes known as the *open-shop* approach).

Although it is important for an enterprise to decide which of these approaches is to be the corporate culture, fortunately the information center can facilitate either the closed- or open-shop approach. In the closed shop, the emphasis is on optimizing use of the central computing facility and the corporate data to the benefit of the enterprise. In the open shop, the emphasis is on optimizing the problem-solving capabilities of the users, also to the benefit of the enterprise. (Note that we see later several variations on the open shop, ranging from total independence of the users with some facilitating help by the computer people, to carefully restricted user capabilities with monitoring provided by the computer people.)

There is no obvious "best" choice here. Both closed and open shops have been around since the beginning of computing. Although it is not unusual to see an article in a popular computing periodical extolling the virtues of one of these approaches or the other, it is probably true that the choice is solely dependent on the corporate culture and the management personalities of the enterprise making the choice.

What might the information center do in these various circumstances?

Closed shop:

- provide information on how to use the computer center
  - hardware
  - software
  - data

Completely open shop:

- provide the information mentioned earlier
- provide information on computer procurement
- provide information on software procurement
- provide information on software development
- provide information on data management

Largely open shop:

- define an "approved list" of computer hardware and software
- facilitate purchases from the approved list
- define approved ways of building software
  - methodologies
  - processes
  - representations
  - tools

- standards
- guidelines
- provide training in software construction
  - problem solving
  - requirements definition
  - design approaches
  - database unification and sharing
  - tools and their use
- define preferred ways of handling enterprise data

Somewhat open shop:

- provide centralized procurement for users
- police the exclusive use of the approved list
- monitor software development versus the approved approaches
- require and facilitate/control software construction training
- control enterprise data and their access

In addition to these tasks, the information center can help with coordination and communication between the several organizations of users, giving them a vehicle for talking among themselves and helping each other. Many of these kinds of ideas were presented in an earlier section on user satisfaction. And, like the development center, the information center could establish a small library of user-relevant books and periodicals. (Note that user participation in purchase decisions could be vital here.)

3.7 QUALITY ORGANIZATION PACKAGING ⸺⸺⸺⸺⸺⸺

The most important content in this book is the concepts and ideas available to enhance the quality of software. How those ideas are packaged organizationally is considerably less important.

This, by some standards, is a radical notion. Most books that deal with software quality do it from the point of view of the quality assurance organization. This is a very common quality supplement approach that packages most concern and responsibility for product quality into a separate organization. For example, most of the functions listed in the previous section would be done by, or controlled from, such an organization.

There are some dangers in this approach. First of all, it is hard to get qualified people to do software quality work. To be responsible for software quality and to work in tandem with presumably skilled developers, the software quality assurance person would need to be a senior software person, knowledgeable enough about product quality to negotiate with and occasionally override developer judgments.

Historically, this has simply not been the case. Early software quality assurance people were retreads from other quality disciplines, and could be little more than superficially helpful in achieving software product quality. Even now that software professionals for the most part have replaced these interim people, there are still problems. Most top software people would rather develop software, a creative assignment, than monitor the quality of someone else's creation. Again and again I have asked the experienced software professionals in my software quality classes how many of them would like to do software quality assurance work. Again and again the answer has been that few of them would care to.

This problem will not go away. In deciding how to distribute the software quality tasks defined in the previous section, management must take into account that it will be hard to get very many top-notch software skilled people to join a quality assurance organization.

The second danger in this approach is one that we have already discussed. It is vital that the developers never give up prime responsibility for product quality, because some aspects of software quality are purely under their control. Quality cannot, in many cases, be added on by outsiders—it must be in the product from the beginning.

This has been a rather negative discussion until now. It would be easy to conclude, based on what has been said here, that the job of software quality should always be done by the developers. That would be an erroneous conclusion.

The objectivity that a separate organization can bring is essential. The focus that a central organization can bring is vital. In many situations involving critical software, it could be a terrible mistake to let quality be entirely in the domain of the developers.

Let us talk a little more here about how such an organization might function.

There are essentially three levels of strength which might be used in a quality assurance organization, depending on the requirements of the application in question. Those levels of strength are (1) a weak QA function, (2) a process QA function, and (3) a product QA function.

In the weak QA function, the development group does most of its own quality supplement work. This might happen because the project has a small budget and/or low criticality. With this kind of QA approach, the developers would perform their own reviews, perhaps calling on others to assist on an as-needed basis. The developers would also do their own testing configuration management, change control, and manage their own contracts (if any). Audits, if needed, would be called by management using an independent team specially selected for the event. A separate product test organization might be called on for the final system testing, and a change board might be separated off as the product went into production status, but basically the developers would have almost complete responsibility for the quality of the product.

In the process QA function, a separate quality assurance organization is established to ensure that the software developers use appropriate quality processes. That is, the quality assurance organization does not look at the product as it evolves, but instead pays special attention to the steps the developers use in producing the product. This is probably the most common form of quality assurance organization and is advocated by many who write about the quality assurance function. It is useful on projects where quality is a serious concern, but budget limitations prevent a full-blown quality effort, such as applications whose quality is important but not life critical. With this approach, the developers still "own" most of the quality assurance tasks, but the quality assurance organization audits developer performance and alerts management of any deviations from quality planning. Typical tasks of such an approach to quality assurance would include:

1. ensuring that a development plan is created and followed
2. ensuring that standards are defined and enforced, and guidelines are available and advocated
3. ensuring that reviews are conducted when scheduled, and that audits are invoked when needed
4. ensuring that appropriate documentation is produced when planned
5. ensuring that configuration management and change control processes are in place when called for
6. ensuring that the test plan is sufficient, and that it is executed properly

The basic assumption of the process-level quality assurance function is that the developers have a vested interest in a quality product, and that QA simply has the task of helping them achieve that interest.

In the product QA function, the quality assurance organization looks not just at the process but at the product. That is, quality assurance participates in all the reviews, making technically competent inputs; quality assurance decides when audits are needed and invokes them; quality assurance owns product test and configuration management and other similar organizations; and, in short, quality assurance takes responsibility for the quality component of the delivered product. This level of quality assurance is used when projects involve enormous budgets or lives depend on the execution of the final product. Here, the technical competence of the quality assurance organization is vital; this level of quality assurance participation should not be attempted without having the personnel with superior software skills. Typically, with this level of quality assurance organization, QA has the power to "stop work." That is, QA may dictate that, because of a quality infraction on the part of the developers, no work can continue until the infraction is corrected. Thus, not only must the technical competence of the quality assurance personnel be beyond question, but the political clout to back up quality assurance positions must be firmly in place.

Tasks which must either be ensured or performed in these quality assurance approaches include:

1. *Planning.* Preparing a plan not just for software development but for the quality aspect of software development.
2. *Verification.* Ensuring that the product of each development phase (such as the life-cycle phases) conforms to the requirements for that phase.
3. *Validation.* Ensuring that the final software product conforms to the original requirements.
4. *Testing.* Paying special attention to the test plans, test procedures, and test results, and ensuring that test results match the expected test results.
5. *Tools and methods.* Ensuring that appropriate tools and methods are selected, planned for, and used.
6. *Configuration management.* Ensuring that appropriate techniques are planned and used, such that baselines are saved and products cannot be lost.
7. *Acceptance.* Ensuring that acceptance criteria are defined and approved in advance, and that at the acceptance process the criteria are achieved.

REFERENCES

BROWN86—"Assurance of Software Quality," Software Engineering Institute Curriculum Module SEI-CM-9, November 1986; Bradley J. Brown. *Describes the principles, practices, and philosophy of quality assurance, for use by an educator wanting to teach the topic.*

BRYAN88—*Software Product Assurance,* Elsevier, 1988; William L. Bryan and Stanley G. Siegel. *A practitioner-oriented fundamentals book written by Grumman product assurance people.*

CHRISTOFF89—"Five Steps to Quality MIS," *InformationWEEK,* August 14, 1989; Kurt Christoff. *Popular-press, tongue-in-cheek article on what not to do to achieve quality software.*

EVANS87—*Software Quality Assurance and Management,* John Wiley, 1987; M. W.

Evans and J. J. Marciniak. *A readable and comprehensive treatment of quality assurance from a Department of Defense point of view.*

IEEE87—Special issue on "SQA—In Pursuit of Perfection," *IEEE Software,* September 1987. *Contains such papers as "Quality Assurance Technology in Japan," "Quality Assurance in Future Development Methods," "Counting Down to Zero Software Failures."*

TICE84—"SQA Contributions to a Quality Software Product," *Proceedings of the Annual Reliability and Maintainability Symposium,* 1984; Tice. *Reports on SQA as practiced at Tektronix. Lists eight major activities and discusses their value.*

If you are going to establish a quality assurance organization, concise advice about how to go about it would be useful.

In the case studies section of this book later on (Chapter 4), we describe the specific steps certain companies have taken. But in the meantime, here is a short list of do's and don'ts, taken from the July 1990 special issue of *System Development;* the topic for that issue was a report on the 1990 International Conference on Information Systems Quality Assurance.

DO'S AND DON'TS FOR QA START-UP

DO:

1. *Set up a mechanism for measuring the cost of quality.* This will enable QA to show what its contribution is in terms of "added value" to the organization.

2. *Determine what the customer/user perspective of quality is,* and devise a way of monitoring it. Keeping a finger on the pulse of changing perspectives will enable appropriate action in a timely manner.

3. *Educate everybody,* management and staff, in quality concepts and practices.

4. *Develop a quality implementation plan and stick to it,* but also include checkpoints over time to allow mid-course corrections as environments, priorities, and management perspectives and requirements change.

5. *Aim to get library management, product verification, and process management structured, stabilized, and under control.* Then as QA matures, migrate library management to operations, and product verification to development. This rightfully leaves QA with process management.

6. *Develop a QA charter and publish it.* Then, because those who have received it will not find the time to read it, take every opportunity to disseminate the charter's contents to anyone who will listen.

7. *Develop a sense of business.* Success will favor your quality implementation effort if you can tie benefits directly to business indicators.

8. *Always focus on statistics that expose weaknesses in processes.* QA may certainly uncover defects in products, but that should only be regarded as symptomatic of a flawed process.

9. *Use recognized authorities to get started with charters, plans, standards, and procedures;* e.g., IEEE, ASQC, QAI. In nearly all cases, they will provide you with more information than you need at start-up. But adapting them to your organization will not only give you the required deliverable, it will teach you a lot.

10. Remember, whereas 30 percent and 70 percent of your effort at start-up may be expended on prevention and appraisal respectively, as QA matures, *the goal should be to reverse those figures—70 percent prevention and 30 percent appraisal.*

DON'T:

1. *Don't let QA get caught in the middle of functional groups* through any formal activity that connects them both; e.g., change control responsibility between applications development and operations.

2. *Don't allow QA to be equated solely with testing.* It forces QA into a decision-making role on a product rather that a process. Furthermore, testing is an after-the-fact rather than a preventative activity.

3. *Don't implement "QA signoffs" for deliverables.* Once again, it assigns decision-making responsibility on a product to QA. Rather, QA should identify risks and provide appropriate information for management to make a decision.

4. *Don't operate on an informal basis.* Undertake all assignments on a contract basis and get management to prioritize projects.

5. *Don't forget to develop a sense of curiosity.* Don't use statistical data except to look for trends and to determine problem causes.

6. *Don't ever do anything that can be interpreted as evaluating people.* Always let your focus be explicitly on process management.

7. *Don't make enemies.* If QA is successful, you will eventually need everyone as an ally. Rather, try and establish yourself as intermediary between hostile groups. QA must be a facilitator for improved communications.

(From "A Report on the 1990 International Conference on Information Systems Quality Assurance," System Development, 1990.)

3.8 METRICS

Trevor Clever, we have already seen, is the new software manager who learned that he needed to rely on others to help him achieve a quality product. We explored in the last section the functions others might perform on his behalf.

Trevor is content with getting feedback from quality supplement people to help give him confidence that his people are doing a good job. But still, he wishes that there were more help available.

For example, he wishes that he had a way of running his team's newly produced software through an automated quality checker which would give the software a quality score and point out areas where improvements are needed.

For another example, he wishes he had a way of automatically evaluating a piece of software to tell whether it would be able to withstand two or three more years of significant enhancement, or whether it should be scrapped soon and rewritten.

For yet another example, he wishes he had a baseline productivity figure available so that he could tell whether his people were really working as hard and intelligently as they are capable of.

As Trevor scratches his head and thinks about these things, he is beginning to see that they all have something in common. They all involve *measurement*. The study of what we can measure, and how we can measure it, is known as *metrics*. What Trevor is wishing for is a set of good, useful software metrics.

There is good reason for that wish. It is easy to see, from the examples in Trevor's mind, value in being able to quickly measure the goodness or badness of something. With this kind of objective input, managers could begin to quit relying so heavily on the more subjective sources of information they normally have to use. When it became time to make a decision about something like the competitive purchase of a new software tool, the candidate tools could simply be run through a metric process and out would pop a score for the quality of each product. When software built either inside or outside the company was delivered, it could be run through the same tool in order to make an acceptance decision. Quantitative judgment based on metric information is generally considered to be a higher-quality judgment process than qualitative judgment based on subjective information.

But there are a couple of problems here. The first is that metric information always looks good, no matter how good it really is. That is, metric values obtained from a back of the envelope calculation using an equation with an error in it look just as good to a decision maker as rigorously produced metric values run through a completely correct computer program. In other words, there are numbers and then there are numbers, and the ones that are completely accurate look no better than the ones that are contrived and fake.

The second problem is that the world is made up of things that are not easily measured. There are times when a good dose of intuitive decision making based on the input from an educated and experienced person is better than any amount of questionably generated numbers could ever be.

Now those problems are an important prelude to any further study of software metrics. Metrics, to the extent that we can get good ones, are a powerful tool for management decision making.

Let us explore the state of software metrics. First we look at the state of the theory. Theory, as you might imagine, sees great potential as the science of metrics evolves.

Then we look at the state of the practice. Here we see some disdain for theoretical metrics, and the substitution of entirely different ones.

In other words, in the material that follows we see that software metrics is a subject struggling for a valid identity, with enormous potential but great uncertainty as to how that potential might be achieved.

REFERENCES

CONTE86—*Software Engineering Metrics and Models,* Benjamin/Cummings, 1986; S. D., Conte, H. E., Dunsmore, and V. Y. Shen. *Thorough coverage of the breadth of software metrics.*

GRADY87—*Software Metrics: Establishing a Company-Wide Program,* Prentice-Hall, 1987; Robert B. Grady and Deborah L. Caswell. *Describes the introduction of a software metrics discipline into Hewlett-Packard. Lists the metrics used and shows how they are collected and used.*

MILLS87—"Software Metrics," Software Engineering Institute Curriculum Module SEI-CM-12, October 1987; Everald E. Mills. *Surveys the theoretical approaches to metrics, for use by an educator wanting to teach the topic.*

3.9 QUALITY METRICS

Analyzing Trevor Clever's metrics wish list, we begin to see that there are really two categories of software metrics: those that deal with the quality of a software product, and those that deal with predictions about the future of a software project. Because of that, we break this discussion of metrics into two subsections: quality metrics, and prediction metrics.

There are really two separate and quite different major thrusts in the topic of quality metrics: theoretic approaches, and practical approaches. We devote a section to each of those topics.

Regarding theoretic approaches, first, we look at the idea of measuring the aggregate quality by measuring its disaggregated individual attributes. The U.S. Air Force has sponsored considerable research work toward that goal. Those findings are presented and discussed. At the same time, we present an academic approach to quality metrics, which focuses primarily on measures of complexity, using a collection of methods sometimes called *software science.*

Then, in the section discussing the state of the practice, we see an almost entirely different set of activities. A framework for progress in the achievement of quality software is presented, in which the highest level of achievement is a phase of *quantitative measurement*. Various industry approaches to that quantitative measurement are discussed.

3.9.1 State of the Theory

The appeal of software metrics, as we saw in the last section, is undeniable. That appeal is best articulated by the theorists working in the metrics area.

The concept behind the theory is quite simple. If we want to measure the quality of a software product, we take the attributes that make up quality, find a way of evaluating each of them, and then by a simple formula calculate overall product quality:

Product Quality = *SUM* (score of attribute i * weight for attribute i)

where *SUM* is taken over all N quality attributes (we have chosen to use seven in this book). The score for each attribute is obtained by a means discussed later, and the weights are assigned based on the relative importance of each attribute for the product being built.

Assigning weights can be a simple process. The weights for the attributes could be arbitrarily assigned such that they sum to 100 percent, for example, so that for a given product we might have something like

Reliability	50%
Understandability	15%
Modifiability	15%
Testability	5%
Human Engineering	5%
Efficiency	5%
Portability	5%
Total	100%

This leaves the only difficult part of the formula as the obtaining of the scores for each of the attributes. As it turns out, that is a difficult problem indeed.

To best illustrate the nature of that problem, let us look for a little while at a field called software science, which sprang up several years ago to try to establish a scientific and quantitative way of looking at the field of software. The essence of software science was that the evaluation of quality could be performed by a white-box analysis of the program product under study. That is, if we dissected the program and counted such things as the number of

- operators and operands
- decision points

- statement types
- executable statements
- connections between data items
- connections between logic points
- assumptions shared
- errors
- testedness

we could then use those numbers in an algorithm to draw quantitative conclusions about the program's complexity, or its quality, or about another entity of interest.

Over the years, software science has been something of a philosophical battleground. Lots of work has been completed and published in the field. Measures of complexity, for example, have been developed, and touted, and modified and touted some more. Noted computer scientists like Halstead and McCabe and Thayer have explored the basic science and ways of making it better.

But in recent years, software science has lost a lot of ground. For one thing, the carefully developed measures didn't seem to correlate very well with anything meaningful happening in practice. For example, the various measures of software complexity seem to produce fairly consistent results no matter whose formula is used, but those results correlate fairly well also with the trivial metric "length of program in lines of code," which is so easy to obtain that the other metrics become pointless by comparison.

The doubters of software science began surfacing as early as the beginning of the 1980s. A paper called "A Critical Examination of Software Science" was published in the *Journal of Systems and Software* in June 1981. A presentation called "Is Software Science a House Built on Sand?" was the only applauded paper at a 1982 metrics workshop. An internal Boeing Company report, published in 1982, said software science appears to be "a group of ad hoc relationships derived from empirical data, but not . . . a science." And one of the trade periodicals published an item called "Software Science is more likely an art," making an analogy between TV dinners as the product of a science, and cooking as an example of an art. The battle lines, drawn fairly clearly then, have persisted to this day. The field has its advocates, but they are at least balanced by those who see no value in current software science practices.

In a somewhat parallel but separate effort, the U.S. Air Force has funded a comprehensive study of the measurement of quality through its attributes. The work began in 1976, and continues to this day. It involves the development of comprehensive worksheets, on which analysts evaluate each of the quality attributes (the Air Force uses 13) in order to quantize the quality of a software product.

The focus of the Air Force work is broad, on quality as a whole, as seen through its attributes (as opposed to the software science approach, which tends to build higher-level measures out of such low-level entities as number of operators and operands). The goal is noble, but to date the breadth of the investigation seems to have thwarted the achievement of useful results. Two studies of the value of the work, completed in 1987, found the approach "sound" and "reasonable," but expressed concern about the metrics being "arbitrary" and lacking in a "real-world basis for the contentions of the measurement methodology."

Specifically what has the Air Force achieved? In the early work, primarily done in the 1970s by General Electric, lengthy metrics worksheets were developed, on which the quality analyst could record findings about a piece of software like "the number of major functions," "the number of logic paths," "the number of overlays," and so on. In more recent work by Boeing Aerospace, the approach has been refined and the worksheet findings are summarized on *factor worksheets,* one per Air Force quality attribute, in order to get a quantitative finding for each quality attribute.

The Boeing work focused on use of the measures by Air Force acquisitions managers, the people who buy software from contractors for Air Force applications. The intent of the work is to allow the acquisitions manager to predict the eventual quality of the software product while development proceeds, and to evaluate the quality once work is completed. Raw data for filling out the worksheets can be obtained by interviewing the developers or having them record information, formal inspections of the software, resource utilization of the working software (e.g., to measure efficiency), and behavior of the working software (e.g., to measure errors per line of code).

The Air Force is serious about this effort. They have funded two studies of the effectiveness of the material [Pierce87; Warthman87], both of which were supportive while suggesting significant further study and change, and has even seen to the development of two supportive tools, the Assistant for Specifying the Quality of Software (ASQS) and the Automated Measurement System (AMS). The former tool is expected to be useful to the acquisitions manager *specifying* the quality of a procured software product, while the latter is to be useful in measuring the quality of the *completed* product. Some people connected with this effort have defined a "software quality life cycle," consisting of specifying the quality, predicting the quality (during development), estimating the quality (as development proceeds), and assessment (of the quality upon product completion). These tools fill two slots in that framework.

Those who have tried the method report lengthy information gathering time (from 4 to 25 hours per metric worksheet), but find that the final results from the factor worksheets (one per attribute) match the developers' intuition about the products in question.

Like most of the work in software metrics, this area deserves further tracking. The contractors involved in the effort themselves have suggested use of the methodology on "trial programs" involving "selected contracts." Certainly more work is needed in this area.

What is the problem here? Even when we break quality down into its measurable components, measurement is still difficult and elusive.

Some attributes are easy to measure because they are visible. Human engineering can be evaluated, for example, by looking at the user interface.

Some attributes are easy to measure because the way of measuring them is obvious. Efficiency can be evaluated by timing the execution of a benchmark test case.

Some attributes are not easy to measure but at least we know how to do it. Reliability can be measured by the percentage of correct executions over a large spectrum of test cases (see statistics-driven testing, section 2.5.2.2.3.1), or by discerning what percent of the logic paths of a program have been successfully executed (see test coverage analyzer—logic, 2.5.2.2.6)

Some attributes are simply not easy to measure no matter what we do. Understandability, modifiability, portability, and testability all require a thorough inspection of the code of the software product, and even then it is not obvious what the inspectors should be looking for, nor what algorithms to apply once the data have been found.

It is important to keep one thing clearly in mind. Although software metrics to date have not produced any software quality results which are useful in practice, the potential is always there for findings which *are* useful. When that happens, it is vital that software managers be ready to adjust their ways of doing business and incorporate metric methods.

Software quality metrics, then, remain a primitive art form. (Software predictive metrics, which we discuss in Section 3.10 are somewhat more advanced, but that is another topic.)

For many years before the advent of the Ada programming language, there was a language called JOVIAL which was used by the U.S. Air Force as its standard language.

Actually, there were several languages called JOVIAL. As happens for most programming languages, variants had formed over the years, and as this story opens there were two main versions of the JOVIAL language, each backed to the hilt by militant proponents. It was obviously in the best interests of the Air Force to eliminate one of the languages and settle on the other for all the benefits that standardizations of this kind bring, but no one was willing to buck the opposition in either camp in order to do it.

What made the decision difficult was that the languages were really pretty equivalent in power and capability, and there was no particular reason to choose either one over the other.

As the Air Force cast about for a way to confront the problem and make a decision, someone suggested that even if the languages were similar, perhaps the compiler for one of the languages was better enough to allow the decision to be made on *that* basis.

It was a good idea. Those of us familiar with the compilers for both languages knew at the gut level that one of the compilers *was* clearly better than the other. Now the problem became, "How can we evaluate compiler quality?"

The answer was as elusive as the whole issue of software quality metrics. The surface-measurable quality attributes, such as human engineering and reliability, yielded no important differences. Some of us knew that the merits of the better compiler lay in its modularity and thus its understandability and its modifiability, but there was no way to translate that knowledge into something measurable by the decision makers.

Finally, in the absence of any good compiler quality metric data, the decision came down—the compilers as well as the languages were equivalent in quality. It was the wrong decision, of course, but it was the state of the art of quality and not stubbornness or politics that forced the incorrect decision.

Then, as a dramatic anticlimax to the story, the Air Force solved the problem in a most unusual way. Since it was not possible to choose either language over the other on any meaningful basis, and since the militant proponents for each language were willing to fight to the death to defend their version . . . the Air Force contracted for and defined a whole new version of JOVIAL!

You could say that neither faction had lost the battle, if you wanted to.

But of course what really happened is that everyone lost! For want of a measure of software product quality, a ludicrously wrong political decision had been made.

REFERENCES

BOWEN85—"Specification of Software Quality Metrics," RADC-TR-85-37, February 1985; Thomas P. Bowen, Gary B. Wigle, and Jay T. Tsai. *Describes the results of an analysis of Air Force quality metric work. Volume I presents recommendations for use of the metrics in software acquisition; Volume II describes how quality requirements might be specified; and Volume III describes how quality can be measured.*

CARD87—"Resolving the Software Science Anomaly," and "Comments on Resolving the Software Science Anomaly," *Journal of Systems and Software,* March 1987; D. N. Card and W. W. Agresti. *Identifies serious problems with software science.*

HALSTEAD77—*Elements of Software Science,* Elsevier Science Publishing, 1977; M. H. Halstead. *The definitive book on software science.*

JSS90—Special issue on "The Oregon Workshop on Software Metrics," *Journal of Systems and Software,* July 1990. *Contains 14 papers on metrics, including a description of the European ESPRIT "METKIT" approach.*

PIERCE87—"Software Quality Measurement Demonstration Project II," RADC-TR-87-164, October 1987; Patricia Pierce, Richard Hartley, and Suellen Worrells. *One of two studies assessing the feasibility of using the findings of Bowen [85] in software acquisition.*

Ross90—"Using Metrics in Quality Management," Quality Time section, *IEEE Software,* July 1990; Niall Ross. *Describes experiences beginning a metrics program at STC Technology, and some lessons learned.*

VALETT89—"A Summary of Software Measurement Experiences in the Software Engineering Laboratory," *Journal of Systems and Software,* January 1989; Jon D. Valett and Frank E. McGarry. *Describes experiments conducted and lessons learned at NASA-Goddard and its Software Engineering Laboratory. Fascinating findings, not always matching conventional software wisdom.*

WARTHMAN87—"Software Quality Measurement Demonstration Project (I)," RADC-TR-87-247, December 1987; James L. Waerthman. *The second of the two studies assessing the feasibility of Bowen [85].*

3.9.2 State of the Practice

The promise of software metrics is no more fulfilled in the practice of the field than it is in the theory. But there are a few glimmerings of hope.

For example, Bill Perry, executive director of an organization called the Quality Assurance Institute, has defined what he calls the evolution of a quality assurance organization:

- *Phase 1.* The "judge and jury" phase. QA people try to tell the developers what to do. According to Perry, one third of all QA organizations get stuck here and fail.
- *Phase 2.* The "attribute" phase. QA people establish methods, processes, and standards, and then evaluate software against them.
- *Phase 3.* The "quantitative measurement" phase. Statistical evaluation of quality is performed, perhaps using tools to do so. QA organizations, according to Perry, should be striving to reach this phase.

Perry defines a process for reaching this quantitative measurement phase. In five steps, the quality assurance manager should:

1. Establish measurement objectives (define what is to be measured).
2. Develop acceptable measures (narrow the list to the things which *can* be measured).
3. Educate the measured (train and motivate the people who will participate in the measurement).
4. Implement the measures, gathering information from such sources as
   a. time reporting information
   b. budget reporting
   c. project status reports
   d. production run logs
   e. incident reports

    f. byproducts of operational software

    g. carefully designed surveys

    h. baselines of historical information

5. Use the results of the measures to change current practice where desirable.

Now this is a carefully thought-out set of ways and means and goals, all based on the assumption that we know enough about metrics to take these steps and achieve the phase 3 position.

Do we? The news from the world of theory was not terribly encouraging. Where do we stand in practice?

The most important clue to answering that question lies in examining the previous lists of ideas. Notice that "baselines of historic of information" is one of the sources of metric information. Obviously, in order to measure how good a new concept or methodology is, we need to compare it against a baseline of traditional data. Do we have those baselines?

The answer, for most companies building software, is "No." With a few exceptions, such as Hewlett-Packard and portions of IBM, most companies have neither defined the information they would like to gather, nor begun gathering it. Since preparing this baseline of data is a long-lead-time prelude to any other metric activity based on comparisons, most companies are nowhere near the place when they could even consider moving to phase 3 as defined by Perry.

There is identifiable progress, however. The following brief snapshots show ideas being explored by a variety of practitioners.

The U.S. Department of Defense has developed a military standard for evaluating quality ("Software Quality Evaluation," DoD-STD-2168, February 28, 1985). It contains a lot of direction on what the contractor should do but very little help on how to do it.

At one IBM location [Fenn85] the following kinds of metrics are gathered, and in fact IBM is attempting to manage software productivity against these metrics:

Metrics gathered	*Desired trend*
Errors per design page	1.1, trying to achieve .4
Errors detected by inspection versus total	63 percent, trying to increase to 83 percent
Inspection hours per error	4.9, trying to reduce to 2
Unit-test-detected errors versus total test-detected errors	54 percent, trying to achieve 81 percent
Defects per 1,000 lines of code	1.7, trying to reach .7
Problem reports	200/quarter, trying to reach 50/quarter

The information gathered *does* give the manager good visibility into the quality of the process, and some perspective on progress, but it is difficult to imagine that management could feel confident about achieving what appear to be arbitrarily chosen quantitative goals. Once again, the use of a metric runs the danger of being an end in itself (trying to achieve ever better numbers) rather than a means to an end (the production of quality software).

One other practitioner [Meas85] has proposed what he calls the "Ten Best Data Processing Measures." They are:

1. Defects per 1,000 lines of code
2. Mean time between failure
3. Return on investment
4. Spoilage (cost of rework/development cost)
5. Change from baseline data
6. Productivity increase
7. Degree of risk in application
8. Cost per unit of work (e.g., per copy of product shipped)
9. Over/under measures (actual versus projected)
10. User satisfaction

One Japanese company keeps another metric called the *bug leak rate* for a program, which measures the number of bugs which survive the debugging process:

Bug leak rate = (number of bugs caught during production usage)/(total number of bugs)

There are two interesting observations here. There is very little correlation between what the practitioners are proposing and what the theorists are investigating; and very few practitioners are doing even what the practitioners propose.

The bottom line, then, for software quality metrics is that they are very primitive, and (because baseline data for comparisons are still largely nonexistent) they are likely to stay that way.

This should not be taken as an excuse to quit trying to improve the state of the practice. For example, it is important to use quantitative rather than qualitative requirements whenever possible:

Not	*But*
Accuracy shall be suffi-cient.	Errors shall be < 1 degree.
Testing shall be adequate	At least 85 percent of logic segments shall be tested.

Not	*But*
The program shall be modular.	Modules shall implement only a single function and hide their methodology from the callers.

It is nearly impossible to devise a satisfactory test for a qualitative measure. On the other hand, the right-hand column of the preceding requirements is testable.

Thus, the use of metrics on a "wherever possible" basis is well within both the state of the theory and the state of the practice.

REFERENCES

FENN85—From a speech by Jack Fenn, quality assurance coordinator for the IBM Sterling Forest (NY) facility, speaking at the 1985 Quality Assurance Symposium. *Discusses metrics gathered during the development and maintenance of manufacturing control software at one particular IBM location.*

IEEE90—Special issue on "Metrics," *IEEE Software*, March 1990. *Contains seven papers, many quite practical, including "Implementing Management Metrics: An Army Program."*

JSS90—Special issue on "Using Software Metrics," *Journal of Systems and Software*, October 1990. *Contains seven papers, including three viewing metrics from the point of view of a software user/buyer.*

LI87—"An Empirical Study of Software Metrics," *IEEE Transactions on Software Engineering*, June 1987; Li and Cheung. *Reports on an evaluation of some software metrics via FORTRANAL, a source code analysis tool. Sees more such analysis needed.*

MEAS85—From the Third National Conference on Measuring Data Processing Quality and Productivity, 1985. *Nominates the "ten best data processing measures."*

PETSCHENIK85—"Practical Priorities in System Testing," *IEEE Software*, September 1985; Petschenik. *Discusses the applications of testing theory at Bell Research. Reports findings of the metric "defect per 1,000 lines of code" ranging from .8 to 3 in practice.*

3.10 PREDICTION METRICS

Trevor Clever not only wishes he knew how to measure what is; he would also like to be able to measure what will be. Even with the best theoretic and pragmatic software quality metrics in the world, there are still important things that Trevor would like to get a handle on that have to do with the future of a software product.

For example, he would like to know at the outset how long it is going to take to build the product. Trevor is painfully aware of the fact that software quality gets badly squeezed when software schedules are slipping. Realistic schedules, Trevor believes, could do an awful lot for software quality.

For another example, he would like to do in-process tracking of the original schedule prediction against as-built progress. Even with a good schedule estimate up front, projects can get in trouble if unexpected occurrences (or perhaps even expected ones) begin to twist and warp the original schedule plans.

As a main case in point, Trevor would like to know when he can really consider the checkout phase to be complete. Oh, he knows that checkout is over when the last bug is found, and he knows that the last bug is never really found, but still he would like to know when his team is close enough to that elusive last bug to turn the product over to its users. Checkout consumes more software development dollars and time than any other development life-cycle phase, Trevor knows, and getting a handle on it is essential to getting a handle on development schedules in general.

And for yet another example, Trevor would like some way of knowing how good the reliability of the software, once delivered, really is. If it is working now, what are the chances that it will still be working 10 minutes or X runs from now, an hour or Y runs from now? In hardware, Trevor knows, they measure mean time between failure. Can we do that for software? Trevor would sure like to.

What Trevor is discovering here is that the subject of metrics extends beyond quality metrics into another area we collectively call prediction metrics. The alert software manager would like to have metrics that help him or her look into the future. What we discuss in what follows is the status of that kind of metrics.

3.10.1 Cost and Schedule

Traditionally, cost and schedule prediction for software has been done by the seat of the pants. Some software person who has been there and done that before is called upon to come up with a best guess as to how long it will take to do it again. If it has never done before, things get a lot harder fast.

Traditionally, cost and schedule prediction for software has been very bad [Abdel-Hamid86]. In spite of the best efforts of grizzled veterans, the estimates are often not very reliable; usually they are far too optimistic. There is a strange streak of optimism in most software practitioners (and in theorists, for that matter!) that says "Of course I can do that in a jiffy." Usually it takes anywhere from two jiffies to ten, instead.

We have been aware of this failing in our field for more than 30 years now. The problem is not awareness, but knowing enough to fix the problem. Starting over 20 years ago, theorists and practitioners alike began exploring algorithmic prediction methods to see if a more scientific approach could produce more scientific predictions.

The best summary of that approach appears in Mohanty [81]. In that study, the author invented a hypothetical software project, established a consistent set of parameters defining it, and then applied 20 different algorithmic prediction models to it to see what they would predict.

The data required by the various algorithms were impressive, perhaps even oppressive. Between the 20 of them, the author had to provide an estimate of:

- productivity of the programmers to be used
- complexity of the project to be built
- number of inputs and outputs
- application type
- programming language to be used
- development environment
- size of the database to be used
- number of interconnections between product modules
- documentation requirements
- mileage to be traveled by the developers
- number of lines of code in the final product

Some data made a lot of sense (obviously product application type and complexity, for example, will have a major impact on schedule), but some were at best bizarre. For example, many of the algorithms required the estimator to provide the number of lines of code expected in the final product. But this is begging the question; if you do not know how long it will take to build a product, how can you possibly know how many lines of code will be in it?

The bottom line of the study was unfortunate but probably predictable: "It is unlikely that any two models will estimate the same cost for a given project." For the hypothetical project in question, cost predictions of the various models ranged from one third of a million dollars to nearly three million dollars, a spread of a factor of 10! Schedule predictions were tighter, but still varied from 14 person-months to 26 person-months, a factor of two. Clearly, algorithmic methods have as much variance built into them as the seat-of-the-pants methods we had been using before. (These findings, unfortunately, have been confirmed in more recent studies such as Kemerer [87], Rubin [87], and Martin [88].

Help is coming. New algorithmic techniques now count functional capabilities to be implemented in a product (the *function-point* method, Albrecht [83]) to produce an estimate of lines of code in order to use some of the earlier models discussed previously. Some models have become very popular (Boehm [81] and his COCOMO model, for example) so that there is consistency if not correctness among people who do predictive modeling. Commercially available products are now in the marketplace [Reifer 87] along with analyses of when they work best and how best to work with them. Because software schedule prediction is so vital, a great deal of work continues to be done here, and there is discernible but slow progress.

At this point in time, there is one generally accepted predictive technique which seems to represent the state of the art. Most people employ two approaches—the best seat-of-the-pants estimate they can get, and the results of their favorite automated algorithm. The two results are compared, and a realistic blending of the two is used.

The result is still not a solid, algorithmic, scientific projection, but it is the best the state of the art and practice has to offer.

REFERENCES

ABDEL-HAMID86—"Impact of Schedule Estimation on Software Project Behavior," *IEEE Software,* July 1986; Tarek K. Abdel-Hamid and Madnick. *Finds that "different estimates create different projects," since software developers gear their work to the estimate. Suggests that "more accurate estimates are not necessarily better estimates," since the estimate itself may become the cost driver.*

ABDEL-HAMID88—"Understanding the '90% Syndrome' in Software Project Management: A Simulation-Based Case Study," *Journal of Systems and Software,* September 1988; Tarek K. Abdel-Hamid. *Finds that poor estimation and poor visibility are the twin causes of the "90% complete syndrome," where software is considered 90% complete for an unreasonably long period of time.*

ALBRECHT83—"Software Function, Source Lines of Code, and Development Effort Prediction; A Software Science Validation," *IEEE Transactions on Software Engineering,* November 1983; Albrecht and Gaffney. *Describes the function-point method of algorithmic prediction. This method can be used to estimate source lines of code, which are needed by most other estimation algorithms.*

BOEHM81—*Software Engineering Economics,* Prentice-Hall, Inc., 1981; Barry W. Boehm. *Describes and rationalizes the COCOMO model for software cost and schedule prediction.*

KEMMERER87—"An Empirical Validation of Software Cost Estimation Models," *Communications of the ACM,* May 1987; Kemmerer. *Evaluates four algorithmic estimation models. Finds that (1) they must be calibrated for a particular usage environment; and (2) even then they "do not model the factors effecting productivity very well."*

MARTIN88—"Evaluation of Current Software Costing Tools," *ACM SIGSOFT Software Engineering Notes,* July 1988; Rick Martin. *Reports on an evaluation of four cost estimation tools; finds results with " . . . variations of at least one order of* magnitude," *especially resulting from the multiplicity of definitions for terms such as lines of code* used in the tools.

MOHANTY81—"Software Cost Estimation: Present and Future," *Software—Practice and Experience,* Volume 2, pages 103–121, 1981; Mohanty. *Compares 20 algorithmic schedule prediction models. Finds enormous variance in their predictions.*

MYERS89—"Allow Plenty of Time for Large-Scale Software," *IEEE Software,* July 1989; Ware Myers. *Examines estimation techniques for programming-in-the-large projects.*

REIFER87—"SOFTCOST-R; User Experiences and Lessons Learned at the Age of One," *Journal of Systems and Software,* December 1987; Donald J. Reifer. *Describes a commercially available software estimation product, and positive and negative experiences in using it.*

RUBIN87—"A Comparison of Software Cost Estimation Tools," *System Development,* May 1987; Rubin. *Presents a comparative study of cost estimation tools first presented at the 1985 International Conference on Software Engineering. Finds differences in estimates of as much as 8 to 1.*

SD89—Special issue on "Function Points," *System Development,* August 1989. *Defines, rationalizes, and evaluates the use of function points for measuring software developer/maintainer productivity, and estimating software product size and complexity.*

VERNER88—"Estimating Size and Effort in Fourth Generation Development," *IEEE Software,* July 1988; June Verner and Graham Tate. *Explores the applicability of contemporary estimation techniques to 4GL software development, and finds them largely wanting. Interesting findings from one case study.*

3.10.2 Reliability

When will the software be ready for productive use? That is an important question, and one that looms over the checkout process as errors are gradually removed. An answer to that question could help a great deal in management's ability to control the software process, and everyone's ability to keep the customer and user informed about when they might take delivery of their product.

One attempt at an answer is covered earlier in the discussion of statistics-driven testing. With that method, testers run randomly selected tests from a profile of typical usage, and can state things like "the software is now running 86 percent of typical input cases successfully." This answer does not predict when the software will become available, but it does give everyone a feeling of how ready it will be when it is.

But as checkout drags on, and errors continue to be found, that process begins to feel interminable. Wouldn't it be important to know, perhaps based on the rate of error removal to date, when the software might be sufficiently error free to turn over to its users? Then, when the developers once again take the traditional position that the software "is 90 percent ready" (that 90 percent readiness response often seems to happen through 50 percent of the project!), management would have a more objective figure to base their progress reporting on.

Software reliability prediction is the name given to statistical attempts to answer that question. Over the last decade or two, a number of (sometimes competing) methods have been defined to try to provide the needed answers.

All of these methods work roughly the same way. They mathematically model the past error history into a curve fit to the historic data (on dates X, Y, and Z, there were X1, Y1, and Z1 errors found, respectively), and then they extrapolate that curve to see when it crosses a "zero errors found" axis.

Over the years, these models have become extremely sophisticated, so that underlying intuition and actual mathematics are difficult to relate to each other. This is a "good news, bad news" situation. The good news is that the sophistication is a natural result of a process of refinement and improvement, but the bad news is that it is now difficult to stand back and take a "common sense" look at what has happened.

That "common sense" problem would not be a concern if the models behaved well in practice. However, in the worst case, attempts to evaluate various models against software projects where the actual data and results are known has shown that in general the models either (1) fail to predict actual known dates, or (2) worse yet, fail to predict any date at all (because the curve fails to converge on any prediction, or because it comes in tangent to the "error-free axis" and thus never crosses it).

Work continues enthusiastically in this area, however. Advocates for various approaches publish refinements to their past work. It is important for the concerned software engineer to be aware of this work, because if there is eventually a payoff, it will be important to build on that payoff.

(There is an interesting side-effect of this work. Factional contentions in the field of computing and software usually stay hidden below the surface of public meetings and professional journals. However, the software reliability people are an exception. At conferences where such work is presented, hostile and barbed questions erupt from the floor immediately after the speaker concludes. It is probably safe to say that, as long as researchers in this area are at odds with each other, they have not found a workable solution to the problem of reliability estimation!)

A related area of software reliability prediction is the desire to predict software's mean time between failures (MTBF). Traditionally, we like to judge the future reliability of a product by its past reliability. When *Consumer Reports* magazine says that surveys have shown 1987 model Straightarrow automobiles to be unreliable, we are reluctant to buy one for fear that our experiences will be (future tense) the same as that of others (past tense).

It makes sense to try to apply that same measuring stick to software. Would we fly on a 7X7 aircraft whose avionics software had failed on three of its last twelve flights? Quite likely we would not.

Studies of past failure frequencies result in what we call mean time between failure (MTBF) data. MTBF gives us the numbers on how frequently the product has failed in the past, so that we can estimate the frequency of failures into the future.

There is a fundamental problem here with respect to software, however. In the traditional disciplines, when we measure MTBF we are measuring product fatigue and breakage. But when we measure software MTBF, we cannot measure fatigue and breakage because software never breaks and never wears out. With software, we are measuring an entirely different animal with MTBF—the possibility that some lurking error which was built into the software during development is still there and will rise up and bite us this time.

Thus, MTBF studies are predicting future error rates on past error discoveries, but in software it is not necessarily true that past error rates have anything to do with future error rates. That is, if we found twelve errors in the software last week, we might feel very bad about the prospect of finding more this week, but on the other hand we might feel very good about it because those twelve errors were found using a superb set of test cases designed to flush out all remaining errors.

The problems with MTBF studies does not negate their value. In the absence of any other information, most software professionals will use MTBF as a way of predicting future reliability because even though we understand that the data may not have the same value they have in other disciplines, they are all we have.

In fact, in some high-reliability applications there is a demand for MTBF data for software. The Federal Aviation Administration (FAA) demands MTBF data on all components of commercial aircraft, for example. If software is considered to be a component, then not only must MTBF data be provided, but those data must show a sufficiently high value to give confidence that a software failure will not be the cause of an aircraft failure.

Fortunately, unlike the other metrics we have talked about earlier in this section, MTBF is easily calculated and does not require sophisticated mathematics. MTBF is measured in hours (or minutes or seconds) elapsed, on average, from one failure to the next. For most software products in production usage, MTBF should be a fairly large number and growing larger all the time. MTBF is especially easy to calculate for continuously running programs, like operating systems and certain real-time systems. For programs which run on demand instead of continuously, it may be more a matter of calculating the ratio of successful runs to unsuccessful ones over time (e.g., this month we have twelve successful runs for every failure; last month it was only eight).

Overview. Looking back at what we have seen here, we see software predictive metrics as an area of enormous potential and unsatisfactory achievement. The guideline for using these metrics at this point is to use them as an important supplement to more traditional approaches, not as a stand-alone technique. As with the other areas of metrics, progress in these metrics must be monitored. There are dedicated people actively at work here, and real progress could happen at any time.

REFERENCES

BROCKLEHURST90—"Recalibrating Software Reliability Models," *IEEE Transactions on Software Engineering,* April 1990; Sarah Brocklehurst, P. Y. Chan, Bev Littlewood, and John Snell. *Cites the problem that "there is no universally applicable software reliability growth model which can be trusted to give accurate predictions . . . in all circumstances. Worse, we [cannot] even . . . decide . . . which of many models is most suitable in a particular context." Suggests the solution that users apply all models, apply smoothing to their predictions, and recalibrate the models for the program in question.*

DACS86—"The DACS Measurement Annotated Bibliography," published by the Data and Analysis Center for Software (DACS), Rome Air Development Center, Griffiss AFB NY 13441. *Contains citations on a collection of over 600 software measurement documents, including reliability modeling. Much of the work in reliability modeling has been funded by RADC.*

EHRLICH87—"Modeling Software Failures and Reliability Growth During System Testing," *Proceedings of the Ninth International Conference on Software Engineering,* 1987; Willa K. Ehrlich and Thomas J. Emerson. *Analyzes the underlying mathematics of some reliability models and raises theoretical questions about the validity of some of the approaches used.*

FARR84—"An Interactive Program for Software Reliability Modeling," *Proceedings of the Ninth Annual Software Engineering Workshop,* NASA Goddard, 1984; William H. Farr and Oliver D. Smith. *Describes a software tool (called Statistical modeling of reliability functions for software, or SMERFS) which implements eight of the better-known reliability models, allowing automated analysis of error reliability data. Contains references for the eight models employed.*

IEEE86—"Special Issues(s) on Software Realiability," *IEEE Transactions on Software Engineering,* December 1985 and January 1986. *Two collections of papers on reliability estimation, modeling, management, and techniques.*

MUSA89—"Quantifying Software Validation: When to Stop Testing." *IEEE Software,* May 1989; John D. Musa and A. Frank Ackerman. *A summary of the state of the art. Reports successful applications at Hewlett-Packard and AT&T.*

3.11 DOCUMENTATION _____

Trevor Clever really savored the applause his development team got at the acceptance test. It came mostly, he knew, from their collective skills and the quality of the product they demonstrated.

But Trevor also knew that part of the credit for the quality of that product went to its underlying documentation. The user manual's clarity, for example, had been one of the factors in the applause. So had the test report, designed both to make an honest presentation of the testing that had been done, and to give confidence to the prospective users that thorough testing had been done.

The software product has always been an elusive one. Is it just object code? Plus source code? Plus documentation? Trevor was not one of those managers who managed the documentation, figuring that the software itself would follow along in good order. But at the same time he knew that quality documentation is an essential part of a quality software product.

There is a dilemma here, a trap for the unwary software manager. Documentation is readable by the manager, and it is easy to monitor software progress by what documentation has been produced. But imagine the worst-case scenario, that is, that the developers produce impeccable documentation but never even begin to build the software itself. Clearly, the software manager must pay attention to the software, not just its documentation.

The opposite scenario, of course, is the more traditional one. The developers produce impeccable code, but with no documentation to support it at all. Or if there is documentation, it consists of an unreadable user's manual, an obsolete maintenance manual, and a collection of in-process documentation artifacts which haven't had any value since the product was delivered. Clearly, the software manager must pay attention to the documentation, not just the software!

The trap for the unwary manager, then, is to pay too much attention to either the software or its documentation, to the neglect of the other. It is a dangerous trap, and a common one. What do we mean, specifically, by documentation? A thorough discussion may be found in Glass [88], but in brief what we mean here is any written reports which are important to the process of developing the software or supporting it after delivery.

For examples, the list that follows is fairly complete. As we have discussed before, quality on a particular software product may involve all of these documents or only some of them. The nature of the product should be the determining factor in that decision.

The early-phase documents supporting project start-up are:

- the concept paper, which contains the idea for a project and the request to proceed with it

- the plans of action, such as
  - the computer program development plan, which describes how the project will be attacked
  - the software quality management plan, which describes procedures specific to insuring product quality

The implementation-phase documents supporting product development are:

- the requirements specification, which defines the problem to be solved
- the design documentation, which describes how the problem will be solved
- the interface specification, which lays out the interactions within the product and between the product and its outside world
- the database specification, which defines the data to be used in the product, both in terms of form and content
- the test plan and procedure, which describe the steps to be taken to insure that the product is reliable

The project windup-phase documents supporting turnover to a user are:

- the user manual, which tells the user how to get the product to do what it is supposed to
- the operations manual, which tells operations support personnel (if any) what they must do to make the product useful
- the maintenance manual, which describes for the maintenance programmer what the product is all about
- the configuration management plan, which describes the procedures for keeping the product safe from loss
- the test reports, which describe how the testing process went, and how any problems were resolved

The ongoing documents needed because of product usage are:

- the software problem report, which describes the symptoms and the fixes for errors discovered in the product
- the software change notice, which describes changes requested in the product, the rationale for them, and the level of authorization for them

The task of assuring software product quality, of course, must encompass not just the software itself but this documentation. Someone must review these documents to see to it that they, too, have quality.

Quality supplement organizations must play a role in this regard. For example, a quality assurance organization will probably take on the responsibility for reviewing all of this documentation, and in addition they will probably write some of it. Examples of the latter might include the software quality management plan, the configuration management plan, the test plans, procedures, and reports, and the problem reports and change notices.

To the extent that most software developers dislike documentation tasks, quality supplement organizations may be at their most supportive when they take over as much of this documentation role as makes sense. It makes a great deal of sense for such an organization to do the quality planning documentation, for example; it may make less sense for them to do the maintenance documentation, since that requires an intimate knowledge of the internals of the software product.

If a strong quality assurance organization exists on a project, there is another role it must play. It must define and reach agreement on its own workings. The quality assurance policies, procedures, and directives become written documentation just like any other form of project documentation. Such documents are usually organized in a form like the following:

1.0   Purpose of policy (why does it exist)
2.0   Applicability (when and to whom should it be applied)
3.0   Policy (the statement of the policy itself)
4.0   Responsibilities (who does what to whom)
5.0   Procedures (how is the policy to be carried out)

These policies might include such subject areas as:

- definition of the roles of QA versus developers
- creation and function of an audit team
- establishment of a configuration control board
- definition of the change and correction process

At its essence, documentation is the glue helping to put the software project together and hold it in place. If the project is large or critical and therefore formal, the documentation requirements will also be formal. If not, the documentation can be less formal, even skipping certain documentation types. Formal documentation adds considerably to software project costs and schedules; when it is needed, that cost *must* be paid. When it is not, that cost should not be incurred. It is vital that the software manager have the judgment to know when the price for formality must be paid, and when it need not be.

REFERENCES _____

GLASS88—*Software Communication Skills,* Prentice Hall, 1988; Robert L. Glass. *Discusses all forms of communication that a software practitioner may use. Emphasizes project documentation form and content. Includes national documentation standards.*

PERRONE88—"Primary Product in the Development Life Cycle," *Software Magazine,* August 1988; Giovanni Perrone. *Popular-press summary of documentation support tools commercially available.*

PRICE84—*How to Write a Computer Manual: A Handbook of Software Documentation,* Benjamin/Cummings, 1984; Price. *A how-to book on creating, writing, and editing computer documentation.*

4

Case Studies

4.1 OVERVIEW

It is one thing to read a textbook on software quality; it is quite another to see quality pursued in practice. The purpose of this chapter is to lend reality to the words that have preceded it.

The goals of software quality are fairly well defined by the seven attributes of quality that most everyone would agree we are striving to achieve.

The means of achieving these goals are also fairly well defined by reviews and audits of various kinds, methodologies galore, plenty of well-known tools and techniques (and some that are less well known), and then of course there is always testing.

It is when we in the business of building software begin to put together the means to achieve these goals that complications may arise. One institution will do one collection of things, another institution will do another. One person within one institution will stress one set of procedures, another person will stress another. It is almost as if there are too many good ways of achieving quality for anyone to agree on what a "best" set of ways might be.

One of the reasons the quality supplement organization known as quality assurance has become popular is because it, on paper at least, brings order into this mini-chaos. You want quality? Get a QA organization to be responsible for it, and they'll know what to do—reviews and audits, product test, configuration management, change and error control; it's as simple as that.

But, of course, life is seldom that simple. We may see how simple it is by looking at the software quality efforts of several different institutions in the sections that follow.

To bring a bit of order into *this* discussion, we divide the material into sections: (1) institutions whose end product is computing, (2) institutions where it is not, (3) a survey of ten anonymous companies and government agencies, and (4) a report on Japanese efforts.

In each case, the raw material for these case studies is a report published in the open literature, usually written by people from that institution. A reference to that raw material is included with the discussion.

4.2 COMPUTING-FOCUSED COMPANIES _____

For some companies, the quality of the software produced and the productivity with which they produce it directly influence overall corporate success. In the sections that follow, we see the approaches taken at two such companies, Computer Sciences Corporation and IBM.

Computer Sciences Corporation (CSC) is a sprawling software giant with offices on both U.S. coasts as well as overseas. It does a lot of business with various U.S. government agencies, and a lot of business with the private sector as well. Its greatest success has been in large systems using large computers.

If CSC is to be financially successful, they must be successful at building software. Their products must be built productively and with quality. In the following material, we see some of the ways they have gone about doing that.

IBM is the quintessential computing company; the name personifies computing in most of the world. Best known as a builder/marketer of mainframe and microcomputer products, it also does considerable systems development and integration business with various branches of the federal government. It is from this latter business that we draw a description of IBM's approach to software product quality.

Although IBM primarily depends on computer hardware for its revenue, its software drives the solutions that cause its customers to buy the hardware; in other words, IBM must build quality software in order to sell hardware. Software solutions are especially vital in their government agency work.

For both CSC and IBM, then, the success of the enterprise is dependent on the success of their software.

4.2.1 Computer Sciences Corporation

A corporate program. CSC's approaches to quality are a particularly good place to start these software quality case studies, because we can begin at the beginning.

About a decade ago, CSC was concerned enough about software product quality to make the decision to start a corporate software quality assurance program. This is the story of how they went about doing that.

Like most major activities, this work began with a plan. The plan for CSC's software quality approach contained sections on:

- organizational approaches
- procedures to be followed
- activities to be utilized
- staffing approaches

Recall that quality people are in many ways the key to quality software products. CSC focused extra attention on the latter section. Early on a decision was made that people joining the QA organization would have to be:

- senior people
- up-to-date in their knowledge
- willing to do QA work
- particularly good communicators

Once the plan of approach was defined, initialization of the QA program itself was begun. Key people

- obtained management buyoff for the plan
- reviewed the quality assurance literature
- defined the basic software life cycle to be used at CSC
- defined the processes and deliverables for each life-cycle phase
- created new job titles for software people, using levels of competence

(i.e., systems architect, chief programmer) instead of levels of seniority (i.e., senior member of the technical staff)
* obtained management buyoff for these initial steps

With the foundation poured (planning), and the initial framing up (initialization), establishment of the program began in earnest.

Staffing came first. A strong core of senior software specialists meeting the criteria described previously was obtained. A management commitment was obtained along with them that, in times of corporate staffing pressure, these people would *not* be taken away from QA to work on more direct revenue-producing activities. (Other companies have found that problem rampant.) The senior people were supplemented by a set of key clerical people, chosen for their adeptness in software support roles.

Provision was made for the establishment of two review groups, one to review the *technology* of software quality, and one to review its *management*.

Having worked the people problem, CSC next turned to standards and procedures. Mechanisms for quality including enforcement mechanisms were put in place so that everyone would know what was expected of them, and so that QA would have the procedural underpinnings necessary to allow them to act on behalf of quality. Particular emphasis was put on software reuse. Mechanisms were defined to motivate and facilitate the construction of reusable software, and provision was made such that no new software could be built without evidence that an earnest search had been made for existing software to do the same job.

With the plan underway, people and procedures in place, CSC at that point was ready to support software projects needing advice and assistance on matters of QA. We will visit CSC again in the next section, six years later, to see how all of this worked on one particular project.

We leave this section with a word of warning. At the outset, the feeling was that there would be a heavy cost for this software quality assurance approach, perhaps up to doubling the cost of an ongoing software project. Coupled with that, however, was the hope and expectation that early life-cycle efforts would markedly *decrease* the costs of software maintenance.

REFERENCES

GUSTAFSON82—"Some Practical Experience with a Software Quality Assurance Program," *Communications of the ACM*, January 1982; G. G. Gustafson and Roberta J. Kerr. *The report on which the foregoing analysis has been based.*

A project report. Six years have passed. CSC's software QA program, initiated as described in the previous section, has been in place for some time. How is it working?

Fortunately, we have an answer to that question. On a particular CSC project, a real-time packet processing program for NASA-Goddard, not only is a project-focused quality assurance program in place, but the people involved get the time to describe how it worked in the literature.

First of all, how was QA defined on this project? It had

- organizational independence (the QA manager reported to the manager of the total project, not the software development manager, who had the power to override lower management decisions)
- dedicated people (the QA people were only QA people)
- a standards and procedures document specific to the project
- authority to inspect all intermediate and final products

With that definition, what did QA do?

- product inspections, as described previously
- collected error data and tracked problems
- collected productivity data and developed metrics
- performed product and process audits

And what came of all this?

- the QA program cost 4 percent of project resources (imagine the relief when it did not double them!)
- regarding product quality
  - no significant changes had to be undertaken during implementation
  - all functional and performance requirements were met or exceeded
  - the defect rate was 2.2 defects per 1,000 lines of source code prior to delivery, dropping to .2 afterwards (CSC norms had been 30 and 5)
  - testing efficiency (the percent of errors removed before or at system test) was 93 percent (CSC norm had been 80 percent)
- regarding productivity
  - project-basing estimates exceeded actuals by 25 percent
  - COCOMO estimates exceeded actuals by 67 percent
  - compared to past (premethodology) CSC norms, productivity was up 300 percent
  - all schedule commitments were met

According to the CSC report, then, the corporate QA plan translated into an effective and workable QA project activity. One word of warning is probably appropriate here, however. When a report is as glowing as this one, it is wise to leave a little niggling question at the back of the brain. When did *anything* ever go this well? Given that here we have dramatic success, with quality and productivity dancing hand in hand with a successfully completed project, one cannot help wondering if there weren't at least some negative lessons learned here along with the positive ones!

REFERENCES

KIM88—"A Comprehensive and Aggressive Quality Assurance Program as a Foundation for Improving Software Productivity," *Proceedings of COMPSAC 88,* Chicago IL 1988; Marcia M. Kim and Walter R. Hall. *The report on which this discussion is based.*

4.2.2 IBM

A project upgrade. Via CSC's reports, we have seen the beginnings of a corporate QA approach, and a follow-up on the use of that approach on a particular new project.

For completeness, it would be nice to report on software quality approaches on some already developed software. Fortunately, IBM's reports give us a chance to do precisely that.

The first IBM report, in fact, is almost prototypical of the software industry in the 1990s. We see here a 15- to 20-year-old software application, written in a combination of assembly language and obsolescent high-order language, huge in scope, with totally inadequate maintenance documentation. IBM's assignment, which it chose to accept, was to renew the software.

The application in this case was the Federal Aviation Authority air traffic control system, one that we all care about since our lives depend upon it every time we fly aboard a commercial airliner. The obsolete language was JOVIAL, an Algol-derivative language, in this case a very early version of a language that evolved many times over the years before finally being replaced for the most part by Ada. The huge system was 1.5 million lines of source code, complex not only because the application itself is complex, but because the software system included a specialized operating system (not unusual for real-time systems), language processors, utilities, and data reduction packages, as well as the application software itself.

How did IBM tackle this monster? First of all, it isolated the changes to be made. Out of that 1.5 million lines of code, it discovered that about 100,000 had to be modified, and another 50,000 rewritten entirely.

Given that there was a significant amount of change (even though there was an even more significant amount that was not changed), IBM next defined standards for the changes to be made. Most of the standards focused on design activities and methods. Once the standards and practices were defined, formal training in the standards was given to the software people responsible for the changes. Meanwhile, a steering group was established to enforce the standards.

Recall that Harlan Mills, one of the pioneers in software methodologies such as cleanroom, was prior to retirement a long-term IBM employee. For this project, management elected to use many of Mills's ideas, calling the approach "mathematically-based":

- An understanding of the existing software had to be gained through manual reengineering from the source code (this was a necessary addition to the Mills approach).
- Redesign was to be top-down, by stepwise abstraction.
- The design representation was to be "semi-formal," using a state machine (not uncommon for real-time applications, which typically are executing in one of several states) and program design language (PDL) for detail-level representation.
- The design, once constructed as previously stated, was then mapped into new code, and modifications of existing code.

And how did this gigantic effort come out?

- The revision was on schedule.
- Defect rate (through system acceptance) was 7 per 1,000 lines of source code (recall that CSC, in a development project, reported 2.2 and a norm of 30).

Here again, we have a happy ending with no negative lessons to be learned. Once again, some niggling doubt is probably appropriate.

Note also the enormous variance in defect rates. Certainly 2.2 and 7 are considerably better than 30, and thus something to be proud of. Yet 2.2 and 7 vary by a factor of over 3. And, in reports yet to come in this book, we will see even more variance in these numbers. The state of the practice in defect rates appears to be that we have some bad historical strawmen to view with alarm, but we still do not have a very stable picture of what should allow us to point with pride.

REFERENCES _____

BRITCHER86—"Using Modern Design Practices to Upgrade Aging Software Systems," *IEEE Software,* May 1986; Robert N. Britcher and James J. Craig. *The report on which this analysis has been based.*

An ongoing project. Not only is most software activity in the 1990s maintenance, but in fact the typical maintenance task is not so much to massively upgrade the software, as we saw in the previous IBM report, but to continually upgrade it. In this sense the Space Shuttle software is even more prototypical than the air traffic control software. It is changed so often that it doesn't have a chance to get massively out of date!

Just as with the FAA software, the Space Shuttle software cannot afford to fail. Here, quality is at its highest priority. Spending an extra $100,000 here and there to improve the quality of the software that controls the system is peanuts compared to the cost if the software somehow fails in flight. In a sense, it is the software quality person's greatest dream—resources cannot be an impediment to quality! But it is the greatest nightmare as well, for if the software fails, the whole world will know about it immediately.

It is the nature of the Space Shuttle that existing software is reused for each new flight, but with significant mission-dependent change. How does IBM, the contractor responsible for accomplishing this activity, handle these dramatic software quality requirements?

First of all, say the Shuttle managers, "no breakthroughs in technology" are used. (An old saying, "the pioneers take the arrows," explains why). Even though this is IBM at work, for example, Shuttle management considers the software "too complex" to use such formal approaches as cleanroom, developed at IBM.

Instead, we see rigorous use of straightforward approaches:

- quality circles at the first line supervisor level (in order to focus as much attention as possible at that level on quality)
- process definitions understood by all
- rigorous inspections of all work products
- independent software verification
- defect-cause analysis (to insure that lessons learned are not lost)
- error tracking

And what is the bottom line here?

- on-board (most critical) software has .11 errors per 1,000 lines of code
- on-ground software has .4 errors per 1,000 lines of code

In this quick snapshot, we see high use of people-intensive quality approaches (quality circles, inspections, tracking, and monitoring), with the highest payoffs we have yet seen in software reliability as measured by defects.

REFERENCES

MYERS88—"Shuttle Code Achieves Very Low Error Rate," *IEEE Software,* September 1988; Ware Myers. *The report on which this analysis is based.*

More on Space Shuttle. Fortunately, we have more than the preceding brief report on which to base our understandings of Space Shuttle software. In what was to have been one in a series of interviews with key software project people (for the most part, the idea died not too long afterward), the editors of *Communications of the ACM* talked to key software players on the Space Shuttle about four years before the glowing defect rate findings described earlier.

From those interview results, we can augment our picture of quality approaches on the Space Shuttle. For example, at least at the time of the interviews, Space Shuttle had 100 people developing software and 80 doing verification and validation. Certainly this is a higher rate of quality activity by far than anything we have discussed previously in this book.

Keys to the quality approaches are

- Configuration management (in effect, every new mission is accompanied by a major enhancement to the existing software, and the management of those changes becomes synonymous with management of the mission).
- IV&V (responsibility for quality, especially reliability, is organizationally separate, including out-company verification and validation)
- Testing is primarily requirements driven, supported by heavy use of simulation (of flight performance in real flight situations), 100 percent requirements conformity is required, and over 1,000 test cases are used to achieve it.
- A key attribute of quality is modifiability. Heavy use is made of table- and file-driven logic, with specialized tools for maintaining such data.
- Requirements are completely traced to test specifications, test procedures, test cases, and test reports.

The process of making changes gets lots of special attention. For each module to be changed

- a verification analyst is assigned
- changes are clearly identified by use of a comparator
- all changes are tracked to their authorization for change
- all changes are tested

Testing consists of

- unit test (structure driven, to see if the code conforms to the design)
- IV&V test (requirements driven *plus* additional structure-driven testing and code inspection)

The testing is extremely rigorous (simulation runs are made on a three shift per day basis, for example!) and yet over half of the software errors are found by code inspection, and there are rigorous design inspections as well. (More recent reports [Kolkhorst89] claim that over 90 percent of Shuttle errors are found by inspection.)

REFERENCES

KOLKHORST89—Presentation at Oregon Center for Advanced Technology Education seminar on Real-Time Software Testing, June 1989; Barbara Kolkhorst. *Shows Space Shuttle "early detection" of software errors improved from 50 percent in 1982 to 90 percent in 1989.*

SPECTOR84—"The Space Shuttle Primary Computer System," *Communications of the ACM,* September 1984; Alfred Spector and David Gifford. *The report on which this analysis has been based.*

4.3 NONCOMPUTING-FOCUSED COMPANIES

Not all institutions view software as being at the heart of the enterprise. Yet even in these institutions, software almost always reaches toward that heart.

Imagine a high-technology company like GTE or TRW without computing and software. Of course, the business of the business would be severely handicapped. How could all the accounting functions for a vast enterprise be performed without computer power?

But even more to the point, imagine the products of these companies without computing and software. Could GTE and TRW control communications networks without computer power? The world has moved a long way past that possibility.

Whether it is in the back rooms of business, or the front rooms of product, the commercial world of today is built on a computing base. For the companies we discuss in this section especially, quality of the software they use is critical in indirect, if not direct, ways to the success of the business. GTE, TRW, and Boeing have electronic-related end products. Monsanto uses computer power in at least its manufacturing processes. And Hallmark, perhaps the least computer-dependent company presented here, still bases its marketing and decision-making strategies on capable computer power.

It is fair to say that even for noncomputing-specific companies, quality software is critical to today's corporate success. We explore how these kinds of companies pursue software quality in the case studies of this section.

4.3.1 GTE

Earlier we saw how Computer Sciences Corp. began a corporate-wide software quality organization. Here we see something similar. GTE, realizing software's importance to its future success as a broad-based telecommunications company, took a corporate approach to the broader subject of software engineering.

GTE is a farflung, decentralized company with a lot of relatively independent business units. Each business unit tends to have its own way of operating because each has its own customer set. But that causes a problem. In software, for example, there was no unifying theme for corporate-wide systems, such as management information and networking/switching.

A steering committee was established, around a decade ago, to set corporate directions for software. The importance of the steering committee was reflected in the fact that it reported to an already established engineering council (which consisted of engineering vice presidents).

The committee meets four times per year, and it also holds an annual corporate software engineering conference. (Several other companies, such as CSC and GE, also hold such internal software conferences.)

From the outset, the committee sought to define a corporate software development methodology and the establishment of a mechanism for software special-interest groups, with early meetings of groups interested in

- high-level languages
- tools
- methodologies
- metrics
- networking
- quality assurance

When the committee was first established, the prime concern was with real-time software, and that was the sole application of interest to the committee. Over the years, however, concern for software management information systems has been added.

What did GTE mean by a corporate software development methodology?

- taking a hierarchic approach to overall systems architecture
- establishing a life-cycle model
- defining an integrated tools environment
- the rigorous use of configuration management
- defining the documents to be produced
- constructing a standard GTE glossary of software engineering terms
- standardized symbols for commonly used terms and expressions
- provision for review of the methodology itself

Technology transfer has been a slow process in most American corporations. At GTE, to help encourage the movement of new ideas out of the laboratory and into general use, a *business advocate* system is used. The job of the business advocate is to coordinate the new technology offerings coming out of GTE's research and development laboratories with the business needs of particular corporate units. The committee saw the business advocate system to be important for software technology transfer, especially in performing experiments with new software ideas before they are put into business unit work, if necessary.

One of the functions of such a steering committee is looking ahead. What does GTE's group see in the software future? Some things are not surprising, some are. In the surprising category, " . . . the major influence on software development will *not* be new software technology. Rather, it will be high-performance, robust personal computers used as software engineering workstations."

In the less surprising category, these directions are either set or anticipated:

- use of 4GLs when they are appropriate
- use of Ada and Ada Programming Support Environments (APSE) when appropriate
- use of relational database tools "when performance constraints are overcome"
- use of the Unix operating system as a basis for developing real-time executives
- building a tool for requirements processing

- building a tool for generating test plans
- building a tool for building compilers on a common underlying framework

While the committee takes a pragmatic, product-oriented view of the future, other branches of GTE take a more research-oriented view. Here, computer scientists see " . . . the dominant software engineering research themes at GTE Laboratories will be specification, integrated environments, reusable software components, and the application of knowledge-based systems to the software development process."

The conflict in the committee view and the research view was not highlighted in the paper. But it interestingly and probably accurately reflects the struggle with the future of software in many institutions. Different arms of GTE appear to be pursuing different and perhaps conflicting goals, and that is probably appropriate to the state of the software art and practice in the 1990s!

REFERENCES

GRIFFIN84—"Software Engineering in GTE," *IEEE Computer,* November 1984; William G. Griffin. *The report on which this analysis was based.*

4.3.2 TRW

In preceding sections we have seen CSC focus on software quality and GTE on software engineering at the top levels of the company.

Here, we see the focus of TRW on software productivity. But although the focus is on an apparently different topic, in each of these case studies we see much similarity in the topics that arise. To achieve good software engineering productively and with quality, there is a common set of themes that must be explored. We see many of those same themes, some with new twists, in this section.

TRW is another broad-based company. Perhaps its strongest and best-known presence is in the defense business, but you also run into TRW in such other areas as auto parts and credit approval.

The decade of the 1980s could be characterized as the productivity decade. Almost everyone in the software business was touched in some way by a worldwide concern for productivity improvement. The software productivity project at TRW was a natural outgrowth of that world climate. It was also an outgrowth of a productivity survey that had been conducted within the company at the beginning of the decade.

Early in the project, topics for possible productivity improvements were identified. The software productivity system, resulting from the software productivity project, was to include strategies for the improvement of

- the work environment
- processes for evaluating and procuring hardware equipment
- communication via a local area network capability
- project support via master project databases, to include project metric data
- techniques through construction of an integrated software toolset
- technology transfer by the establishment of a responsible organization

In an unusually frank report for corporate America, the paper on which this case study is based [Boehm84] reported both positive and negative results from the work defined previously.

The area in which they felt they achieved the most success was in work environments. Here, they defined a *productivity environment* as private offices with soundproofing, carpeting, plenty of storage, and a terminal or workstation. This work, TRW believes, resulted in 10 percent to 25 percent productivity improvement. (Note that this finding tracks interestingly with GTE's expectations, as reported in the previous section.)

Underlying this productivity environment was a well-defined set of computer power—host VAX computers running the Unix operating systems, with target workstations (the choice of what workstation had not been made at the time the article was written), and good support for electronic mail and electronic file transfer.

TRW also made good progress in software technology transfer. Courses were developed. Documentation was prepared. Consulting was established. The software developers who would be the users of this technology were informed and involved from early on.

It was in two other areas where TRW did not progress as far as they hoped to. With respect to the project database, the expectation was that it would contain plans, specifications, standards, code, data manuals, and metrics for at least all resource expenditures, but much remained to be done at the time of writing the article. (Note here that this effort appears to parallel the project repository notion that emerged half a decade later in the CASE community.)

The integrated software toolset was also an area of less progress than expected. Goals were well established:

- reusable tools, portable across projects
- Unix based, with a mix of buy/build/port from other projects

But specifying these goals and achieving them are two different matters. It is relatively easy to identify what tools are to be bought or built. What is difficult is integrating the collection of tools so identified. TRW is not the first company to run into that problem.

At the time the article was written, enough steps had been taken to provide measured results. The new technology had been used in "several" production software projects and on several other software research and development efforts. Via survey and measurement, certain findings were made.

Opinion Findings: The "productivity office" was felt to improve productivity by 39 percent to 47 percent. Of the percentage, the contributions of individual components of the office were felt to be

software tools	16%
personal terminal/workstation	14%
private office/furnishings	8%

Metric Findings: Using all of the productivity system components together, the total productivity improvement was measured to be 142 percent. Of this total, the biggest benefit was reuse, which contributed a little over 100 percent.

What conclusions did the TRW study come to?

- Productivity gains require an integrated program, with a sustained effort over a long term.
- The payoff expectation by 1990 was a factor of 4 improvement.
- Reuse has the biggest long-term payoff.
- Integrated toolset approaches are still too immature to make predictions about their contribution.
- Immediate access to whatever tools are available is a must.
- Office automation and clerical support are important background factors.
- Focused workstations, private offices, and networked computers are important.
- Acceptance of new ideas by the target audience will be gradual and must be nurtured.

REFERENCES

BOEHM84—"A Software Development Environment for Improving Productivity," *IEEE Computer,* June 1984; Barry W. Boehm, Maria H. Penedo, E. Don Stuckle, Robert D. Williams, and Arthur B. Pyster. *The paper on which this analysis was based.*

4.3.3 Monsanto

Maintenance is increasingly the common focal point for corporate software improvement campaigns, as more and more of the software dollar is spent in enhancing old software.

Certainly that was true at Monsanto, a scientific product conglomerate, six or so years ago. Maintenance of management information systems (MIS) software was the concern, both from a quality and productivity point of view.

Corporate management is not always in touch with just what software maintenance is. As a result, Monsanto's first step was to define *what software maintainers do*. This is what they came up with:

- enhancement and new development
- emergency repairs
- consulting with users
- evaluations of other products and approaches
- planning future work
- training users and other maintainers

Following that, they prepared a list of *why they do it:*

- required by law or policy (e.g., enhancements, repairs)
- tangible business benefits (e.g., enhancements, new development)
- intangible business benefits (e.g., preventive maintenance, consulting, evaluations, planning, training)

And then they generated a *mission statement* for the software maintenance organization:

To provide cost-effective systems to support Monsanto business requirements in a timely manner.

They also gave it a departmental charter:

We must continue to provide "required" services.
We will anticipate and facilitate business change.
We will demonstrate contributions to productivity and cost reduction for our users.
We will demonstrate internal improvement in productivity and quality.
We will provide leadership and direction in managing the MIS function.
We will be recognized as being competent, responsive, and valuable.

Now, with the platform for action in place, Monsanto began taking those actions. Intent on improving software maintenance quality and productivity, they started an attitudinal/motivational campaign, and a management/technical campaign, designed to get everyone oriented to the common goal in both emotional and rational ways.

For motivation, they

- used motivational displays and posters
- emphasized humor and fun
- linked productivity and quality to client service

With a management focus, they

- emphasized goals
- provided for bottom-up participation in goal setting
- gave responsibility and authority to the maintainers
- increased top-down communication
- initiated a metrics program, counting
  - number of people per task
  - software inventory in programs, modules, lines
  - activities per maintainer and over time (e.g., abends, transactions, repairs, enhancements, consultations, batch runs, compiles)
- wrote a Business Practices Handbook

With a technical focus, they

- emphasized training and education
- hired capable employees
- obtained maintenance CASE tools or began new technologies
  - PATHVU, for complexity and architectural metric measurement
  - XPEDITER, for on-line debugging
  - RAMIS, for report creation
  - JAD (Joint Applications Design), for user-supported requirements definition
- internally built tools for
  - data capture
  - information dissemination
  - on-line logging of emergencies
  - on-line logging of consultation
  - on-line logging of requests
- provided dial-up terminals for maintainer emergency use *at home*
- procured optimizers for TSO/CMS response time, dropping the average from 1.8 to .7 seconds

It was an interesting mix of activities, this Monsanto program. Starting with the need to add clarity to the maintenance activity at the highest management levels (this need is probably present in all, or nearly all, companies), it extended all the way down through motivational programs to very specific tools and improvements at the lowest technical level.

REFERENCES

LANDSBAUM89—*Measuring and Motivating Maintenance Programming,* draft manuscript submitted to Prentice-Hall, reviewed by the author of this book in 1989; Landsbaum, Jerome. *The material on which this analysis was based.*

4.3.4 Hallmark

By all respects, Hallmark might be the ultimate nontechnical computer and software using company. Their products are not high tech, and their corporate use of computers lies in the data processing strategic systems area—finance, marketing, order processing, distribution, personnel, and manufacturing. Motherhood and apple pie from mid-America (the corporate headquarters is in Kansas City), you might think.

But with respect to software quality, you would be wrong. In an era where most companies are moving toward separate organizational responsibility in quality assurance, independent testing, and separate maintenance, Hallmark is doing just the opposite.

They call their software development activities (mainframe/COBOL) a *software factory.* They call their software technique *just in time,* based on Japanese manufacturing concepts. But for Hallmark's software, JIT principles are interpreted into their software factory in interesting ways:

JIT PRINCIPLE	HALLMARK SOFTWARE INTERPRETATION
1 Line management control	No separate QA
2 Correct one's own errors	Developers responsible for own testing, error correction, maintenance
3 Continuous error detection throughout the process	Emphasis on test planning, inspections, postimplementation audit
4 Easy-to-see quality	Metrics collected and reviewed Postimplementation audit

Note the strength of the commitment to developer responsibility. Developers inspect their products, test their products, and maintain their products.

So specifically how is this responsibility translated into quality in this kind of setting? At Hallmark, it means three main things: heavy emphasis on testing, careful tracking of unusual condition reports (UCRs), and use of a postimplementation audit. Let's look at them one at a time.

Testing. The four levels of testing, unit, integration, system, and acceptance, are pretty much as we have described them earlier in this book. At the unit-test levels, "all logic paths" must be tested. With respect to the other three levels, they must be planned in advance and documented in a formal test plan. Hallmark cares enough about these test plans that they circulate their best ones to serve as guides for future ones.

Unusual condition report. Operational quality is the prime concern at Hallmark; the software must be dependable once it's put in production status. To track operational quality, they count UCRs, and that count becomes the base metric for an algorithm that tells them how they're doing. They divide lines of code for a product by its UCR count, and they expect that over time a software product's ratio will exceed 8,000. (Note that LOC/UCR is the inverse of the more usual errors/lines of code ratio. Note also that when this count exceeds 8,000, we are talking about an errors per 1,000 LOC of .125, pretty good by all the standards we've discussed in earlier sections.)

Postimplementation audit. To ensure that product quality remains a visible focal point, postimplementation audits are held with the customer to determine how well the developers/maintainers have done. Questions like the following are asked at the audit:

- How well has the product performed?
- Is it easy to use?
- Are the users satisfied?
- How many enhancements have been requested?
- Has maintenance been relatively easy?
- Is operations satisfied and able to meet schedules?
- How many UCRs have been written in the first three months?

Hallmark knows that what they are doing is unusual. "This approach may not apply to every organization, but it does work for Hallmark," they say. In any case, it illustrates very well what we said at the outset of this book. No one has yet identified a best approach to software quality. That makes the search for it all the more fascinating.

REFERENCES ───────────────────────────────────

JOHNSON90—"Hallmark's Formula for Quality," *Datamation,* February 15, 1990;
James B. Johnson. *The material on which this analysis was based.*

4.3.5 Boeing

Like many massive companies, the huge aerospace conglomerate Boeing is
divided into many smaller companies, each with its own way of doing
business.

Boeing Commercial Airplane Company, for example, is strongly influenced by its commercial airline customers and by the Federal Aviation
Authority. If the FAA requires software, as a component in newer-genera-
tion commercial aircraft, to have a mean time between failure just like all
the other components in the airplane, then a way of calculating MTBF for
software will be devised.

Boeing Aerospace Company, as another example, builds products for
the U.S. Department of Defense. Their way of building software is heavily
influenced by DoD directives, such as DOD-STD-2167 and -2168, which
say a lot about what software quality should mean in the DoD software
process and product.

As a third example, Boeing Computer Services provides computer-
related support to other branches of the Boeing company and to some
outside companies. Their approach to quality is driven by what the customer wants. For example, when they support Boeing Aerospace, they use
the DoD software quality requirements.

However, there are centralized approaches across these organizational and customer-oriented lines. There are corporate standards for producing software. There is corporate research and development into what
software quality means and how it can be achieved. There are thorough
and elaborate documents describing what activities make up software
quality assurance:

- planning
- standards
- documentation
- design control
- test control
- tools and techniques
- verification

And documents describing software product assurance:

- configuration management
- problem reporting
- change control
- audits

There is even a quality assurance algorithm for estimating what portion of a project's cost should be allocated to QA, and a computer program for calculating the algorithm.

But a strange thing happens in the midst of these many documents describing what software QA is or should be. On any particular project, the software QA-assigned persons tend to apply that portion of the total definition that they are most comfortable with or interested in. For example, if the QA-assigned person on project Wings Aloft sees quality as primarily a standards conformance activity, then there may be elaborate reviews at which the code is checked to make sure that no standards are violated.

As a result, for all the centralized planning and definitions, QA becomes a very personalized thing.

REFERENCES

Recollections of the author as a Boeing employee, 1965–1970 and 1972–1982.

4.4 SURVEY FINDINGS

The preceding sections of these case studies have been based primarily on papers in the open computing literature, written by computing and software people from the institution in question. That is a good-news and a bad-news situation. It is good news because the source of the information is as close as possible to the information itself, and thus accuracy should be optimal; but it is bad news because it is corporate policy in most institutions to put only a positive face on all corporate news.

Chances are that each paper that served as the basis for these case studies was routed for approval to a corporate public relations (PR) organization. The job of these organizations is to create and protect an institutional "look-good." Therefore, even if at the outset there were negative lessons learned in any of these papers, put there by the technically-aware authors, PR probably would not approve the work for publication until it was deleted. Recall that sometimes, at the end of the discussion of a paper, there were niggling doubts about why no negative findings had been presented in the paper? Now we have a reason why that may have been so.

How can we overcome this problem? In this section, we try one answer to that question. Here we report on a *survey* of corporate software quality approaches. The survey was conducted by a disinterested organization on behalf of a truth-seeking funding source. Institutional responses were treated anonymously. Thus, none of the parties involved had any reason to paint an optimistic picture over the survey findings. What we lose in "inside" reporting, we gain in objective findings.

However, this survey is over a decade old. Its findings must, therefore, be met with another kind of niggling doubt. It is fair to say that at the time of this survey, its findings were accurate as well as objective. Now, it would be better to consider this as a snapshot in time. No doubt advances in our ability to build quality software have advanced the state of the practice in the surveyed companies. But here we have a picture of how things once were.

Who were the players in this survey? Boeing Computer Services conducted the survey on behalf of what was then called the National Bureau of Standards, looking at five companies and five government agencies. What it surveyed was the "Verification and Validation Standards and Practices" of those organizations; what it found was a picture of quality practices and concerns rather different from the rosy views of the case studies we have just read. Here, in our "snapshot in time," we find a depressing and backward view of software quality practice.

Where does the truth lie? With the rosy-hued PR-approved descriptions of corporate insiders? Or with the backward and obsolete survey findings? Probably the answer is "somewhere in between." And, judging by the findings of Tom DeMarco in his "Coding Wars" studies reported in an earlier section of this book (on software process), in this case the rosey hue is probably closer to being correct.

4.4.1 Five Government Agencies

The survey divided the target institutions into U.S. government agencies and corporations. In both cases, the application domain of interest was commercial data processing. This is a report on what the government agencies did.

First of all, these government agencies were very decentralized and therefore project oriented in their approach to quality. Different projects used different rules and methods. On a particular project, however, standards and constraints were common.

Perhaps the most striking characteristic of these government agencies was that they were not very receptive to new technology. How it was done before strongly influenced how it would be done in the future. It is interesting that this reinforces a stereotype about government agencies and progress.

There was a wide variance between the agencies in the use of formal approaches to software. None of the agencies, however, used a formal quality assurance program. (This is one of the areas where time has undoubtedly changed practice; a more recent survey would likely show different results.)

What *techniques* (as opposed to tools) did these government agencies use?

Reviews and inspections were used by four of the five. So was testing with large "live" files of data.

Standards may have differed across agencies and projects, but three of the five used some kind of standards for coding and documentation.

An independent test organization was used by two of the agencies.

And one agency each used a Programmer's Handbook, a commercial design methodology (here is another area where things no doubt have changed), and structured programming.

What about *tools* for these government agencies?

Three of the five used a test data generator, most commonly extracting live data from real files.

File comparators and configuration management systems were each used by two.

And one each used a debugger (this is an almost frightening finding), a cross-reference lister, and a performance analyzer.

4.4.2 Five Commercial Companies

What did the commercial companies do, and how did they differ from the government agencies?

At the philosophical/organizational end of the scale, there were significant differences. Where the government agencies had been decentralized and project focused, in the commercial companies operations were centralized, with data processing reporting high up the management ladder.

Where the government used lots of standards and constraints, there were few in the commercial companies. Interestingly, the commercial companies were much more open to new technology.

But there were some threads in common. Again, there was wide variance in the use of formal techniques. A separate quality assurance organization was used, for example, by only one of the companies (recall that for the government agencies none used it).

Regarding *techniques:*

All of the companies used reviews and inspections (four of the five government agencies did, too).

Four of the companies used coding and documentation standards (it was three of five for the agencies).

Two used a commercial design methodology (one more than the agencies).

And one each used an independent test organization, internal audits, and a user steering committee.

Not a very advanced picture of quality approaches, but a picture nevertheless better than the comparable one for government agencies!

Tools?

Three used debuggers. (Recall that only one government agency did. This makes *that* finding all the more depressing, because it means that at that time debuggers were commonly available!)

Two used test data generators (here is the only place where the government agencies, with three, were more advanced than their commercial counterparts).

Two used configuration management tools (the same as the agencies). Two used data dictionaries.

And one each used cross-reference listings, performance analyzers, file comparators, and test tracing tools.

Remember, now, this is a fairly old picture. A more recent survey, we would all hope and expect, would show a higher percentage of technique and tool usage in both the government and commercial companies.

REFERENCES

SMITH81—"A Report on a Survey of Validation and Verification Standards and Practices at Selected Sites," Boeing Computer Services document number BCS-40345, June 1981; Mark K. Smith and Donna R. Hudson. *One volume of the multivolume report on which this analysis was based.*

4.5 AN INTERNATIONAL PERSPECTIVE

The early dramatic progress in software as both a discipline and as an enterprise was first an American phenomenon. Before too long, however, that success spawned software companies and software solutions all across the globe.

While the explosion of the software industry was happening worldwide, another explosion at work was the rapid rise and success of the Japanese industrial machine, and in particular the quality capabilities of that machine. Have the Japanese been able to blend into their newly emerging software industry some of the quality magic of their industrial colleagues?

In the material that follows, based on a paper written by Japanese software experts, the answer is "no." Although there are cultural differences at work, the bottom line in software quality appears to be that the Japanese, like their American and other international counterparts, are still struggling to define a preferred way of building quality software.

REFERENCES

MATLEY87—*National Computer Policies,* IEEE Computer Society Press, 1987; Ben G. Matley and Thomas A. McDannold. *An excellent analysis of the national government computer policies of several nations: Japan, France, Britain, South Korea, Taiwan, Singapore, Brazil, Australia, Israel, and the European Economic Community; and the lack of such a policy by the United States.*

4.5.1 Japan

The Japanese computing effort splashed prominently onto the computing scene a decade ago with several governmental initiatives, the most prominent of which was the Fifth-Generation Computer project. But, like many projects with splashy beginnings, results of that effort have been evolutionary instead of revolutionary. There is no evidence that the Japanese attempt to leapfrog the technology of the 1980s has had any dramatic payoff in the 1990s.

In particular, Japanese software development seems remarkably like that of the United States. Different companies use different life cycles and processes to achieve quality. The amount of tool usage is similar to that in the United States, with choices being dependent on what the chosen hardware vendor supplies, and with what makes sense for the application domain in question. And, just as in the United States, in the 1980s productivity improvement was emphasized more than quality improvement.

Error identification and removal techniques, too, sound like an echo of U.S. practices. Reviews are heavily used. Audits are common practice. Testing, including "severe" testing by independent testers, is the backbone of error detection.

There are a few differences, however. Total quality control (TQC) is commonly used, and includes quality circles and quality improvement campaigns. Special emphasis is put on documentation, with intermediate document review by the software developers. Intermediate software products (e.g., detail design) are evaluated against metric goals (e.g., errors per page of detail design).

And maintenance is different from many U.S. firms. The developers maintain the software, rather than using a separate maintenance organization. (Japanese employees expect a long-term affiliation with their companies, and developers are typically around long enough to maintain a product, unlike U.S. employment patterns!)

In some larger companies, the *software factory* approach is used. There is a separation of labor for various kinds of tasks; systems analysts do just systems analysis, for example, and not the follow-on design and coding. These companies tend to standardize on the form of the requirements specification, and use formal reviews to analyze the specification for errors and omissions.

What is the bottom line of software quality in Japan? Kishida [87] says "Quality control in Japan, especially TQC, has seen successes in the manufacture of computer hardware and automobiles. But software quality control is new to Japan, and so awaits its evaluation."

REFERENCES

KISHIDA87—"Quality-Assurance Technology in Japan," *IEEE Software*, September 1987; Kouichi Kishida, Masanori Teramoto, Koji Torii, and Yoshiyori Urano. *The paper on which this analysis was based.*

4.6 CONCLUSIONS

These case studies reinforce some of the thoughts mentioned earlier in this book. The achievement of quality is complex, with no one institution having found that "best" way that we would all like to find. Approaches to quality are application dependent, organization dependent, institution dependent, people dependent, and even to some extent nation dependent.

Certainly we see a lot of high-level corporate interest in software. Companies call their focus "quality" or "productivity" or even "software engineering," but at heart they are all looking at the same thing, that is, how to build this strange phenomenon called software more effectively and more productively.

There are a few common threads in the case studies. A couple of companies seem to feel that enhancing the work environment of the software producers, especially with software engineering workstations, could be particularly helpful. Reviews, inspections, and testing form a strong backbone for error removal. Tentative efforts at metrics are beginning, but without much similarity in what is being measured except errors per line of code. Similarly, tentative steps are being taken into formal approaches, although as often as not a closer inspection would find what is being done is partly lip service and only partly truly formal.

And there is one final common thread. Most institutions spend a lot of time talking about what makes them look good. Few talk about mistakes they make along the way. That is, of course, both human and institutional nature, but still, many learning experiences are lost because we are not open enough to share them, and the learning experiences that *are* shared must be taken with a grain of salt.

But differences seems to dominate likenesses. Even the cost of quality seems subject to enormous differences of opinion. Computer Sciences Corporation spoke of doubling the cost of an ongoing project, then found much to their relief that it did not, and that the actual cost for a particular project was four percent. (But notice what that says about how little we understand this business.)

And the result of quality efforts seems equally variable. Different companies brag about different error rates. Certainly anything over 30 errors per 1,000 lines of code appears, in the 1990s, to be a "bad" rate. But how can companies be pleased with error rates (7, 2.2, .4, .1) that still differ by nearly two orders of magnitude?

Here we are, still well inside the first half-century of using software as a practical problem-solving tool, still trying to figure out how to do a good job of it. The struggle is probably quite predictable. Perhaps we should rejoice in the common threads we *have* found, rather than despair about the ones we still seek. After all, this is a *very* young field.

5

Issues in
Software Quality

All through this book we have seen a plethora of techniques for building quality software and multiple choices from that menu of techniques used by different projects at different institutions. This suggests that in the midst of this plenty, there are plenty of differences of opinion. In this section we try to focus on some of those differences.

Why focus on differences of opinion? For the same reason that some scholars would rather talk with someone who disagrees with them than with someone who agrees—we learn from disagreement, not from agreement.

And for another reason: a difference of opinion probably indicates an underlying issue worth exploring. People tend to spend their energy differing with each other only over something that is worth that energy.

So in this chapter are topics that may be worth spending a bit of extra time on. Why do people disagree on these issues? What should you, the reader, do about these disagreements? Perhaps here, in these areas of difference, are key decisions you can make on behalf of your institution.

5.1 ERROR DETECTION AND REMOVAL TECHNIQUES

The choices here are fairly straightforward. To detect and remove errors, we have reviews, inspections, testing, and proofs of correctness. There are several issues here. First, how much emphasis should we put on each technique? Reviews are fairly formal and high level. Inspections may or may not be formal and detail level. Testing comes in a lot of flavors, as we have already seen. And proof of correctness holds a great deal of promise but is little used in practice, for some very good reasons.

Attempts to focus on issues in this topic area have sometimes had spectacular repercussions. When one company considered using fault-tolerant software techniques to eliminate unit testing, for example, a debate erupted in print and on electronic bulletin boards and spread across the Atlantic to a personal confrontation in Bremerhaven, Germany.

Analogously, some academics have suggested that all of testing can be replaced by rigorous proof-of-correctness techniques. And that has led to several eruptions. On at least two separate occasions, some scholars have cast doubts on the value of proofs, other scholars have leapt into the fray, and the resulting personal name-calling in the professional journals was truly a sight to behold!

Clearly, these issues have generated a lot of heat, and perhaps some light, already! What, precisely, are the issues?

1. What mix of techniques is the most effective?
2. Should the traditional approach [review/inspect/test (requirements + structure)] prevail over the cleanroom approach (proof/independent test/statistical test)?
3. Is there a place at all for proof of correctness?
4. Are reviews and inspections really more efficient and cost effective than testing, and if so how thorough (100 percent of all code? 100 percent of critical code?, and how formal (informal walkthroughs? Fagan formal inspections?) should we be in doing them?

The point of this chapter is not to answer the questions raised in these issues (we have had our opportunity to do that in the earlier sections of this book!), but to focus the reader's attention on them. Here are probably some of the most important questions you will be called upon to answer in your software career.

5.2 DEVELOPER QUALITY APPROACHES VERSUS SEPARATE QUALITY ASSURANCE

Who does quality assurance is probably at least as important as what it accomplishes. We have already seen in several sections of this book and one of the case studies disagreement on where responsibility for quality should reside. It has been popular for a couple of decades to equate quality with quality assurance, and opt for a separate organization responsible for it. I have had the personal experience, in having the manuscript for this book reviewed, that reviewers have assumed that since the manuscript had *quality* in the title that it must be about *quality assurance*. (Those reviewers have been consistently disappointed, sometimes even angered, by what the book does contain!)

But under what circumstances should your organization opt to do quality with and without a quality assurance organization? And if you do establish a separate QA organization, how should it and the developers divide the tasks of quality? (Remember that there are the options of a weak QA, a process-oriented QA, and a product-oriented QA.)

Once again, this chapter is not the place where easy answers to difficult questions are being attempted. The fact that different companies have different approaches suggests that the issue here is legitimate, and one that you can expect to focus some energy on.

5.3 STANDARDS

The issue of standards is peculiar because although everyone agrees that standards are a good thing, almost no one has attempted to standardize on what the standards are!

Well, that's actually not quite right. There are lots of candidate standards, defined by many national and international standards bodies. The problem here is that those standards are ignored by most institutions in favor of home-grown (dare we call them nonstandard?!) standards.

There is a further problem with standards. As we discussed earlier, those who provide standards usually favor thorough standards documents. And the standards that result from that process are frequently ignored in practice.

So the issues in standards, then, are these:

1. Do we use international standards, or our own?
2. Do we have complete and elaborate standards, or lean and mean ones?
3. Do we spend the money needed to enforce the standards we are using?
4. Is quality the same as standards conformance, and if not what more does it mean?

5.4 SILVER BULLETS

Since the beginning of software history, new ideas have floated out on the research and development breeze that were to revolutionize the construction of the product. In the 1950s it was high-order languages, in the 1960s it

was computer science education, in the 1970s it was structured meth-
odolgies, in the 1980s it was CASE tools and 4GLs, and in the 1990s it is
object-oriented approaches and cleanroom.

The question that becomes an issue is how much attention should be
paid to each of these breakthroughs?

We have already done a retrospective on most of these ideas in the
earlier chapters of this book, and we will not repeat those thoughts here.
The important issue here is how high should we jump for each new idea
that comes along?

The answer to that question is not obvious. For each of these ideas,
there is/was obvious promise behind the idea when it first emerged. But in
each case, no one had measured how much that promise could be expected
to translate into payoff. For many, it was easier to jump on each new
bandwagon as it started up than it was to run the risk of being accused of
falling behind. But the cost-benefit trade-offs of these new ideas have never
been properly worked.

So what happens when the next breakthrough idea comes along?
There can be no question but that there will be more. Ed Yourdon has even
postulated twelve new breakthroughs ahead:

1. Better management of human software resources
2. Software metrics
3. Better programming languages
4. Reverse engineering
5. Software reuse
6. Software engineering
7. Object-oriented design
8. Software maintenance
9. Prototyping
10. CASE
11. End-user development
12. Software quality assurance (!)

This list is a curiously mixed bag, since some of the ideas are not and
cannot be breakthroughs. But still, the point here is that with this kind of
volume of new and exciting ideas to contend with, the alert software person
must answer these questions over and over again:

1. How do I evaluate this new idea?
2. Are its benefits to me and my organization higher than its costs?
3. If I am going to adopt this new idea, how do I proceed?

The wise software person will think about these issues in advance, rather than waiting for the emotional appeal of each new "breakthrough" idea to wash over him or her.

REFERENCES _____

YOURDON—"12 Silver Bullets," *American Programmer,* April 1990; Ed Yourdon. *Lists Yourdon's twelve candidates for future software breakthroughs.*

5.5 OUTSOURCING _____

This topic is an exception to the others in this chapter. It has not been previously covered in this book. *Outsourcing* is the act of contracting some or all of the computing tasks of an institution to another, outside company.

For the most part, outsourcing applies to computer facilities management, and therefore has little relevance to software. The software job should be the same no matter who is tending the hardware store.

But there are exceptions to that rule. Some companies have farmed out some or all of their application software development. Some have farmed out reverse and reengineering activities of software under maintenance. Certainly, when the hardware is outsourced, the care of the system software for that hardware equipment is also outsourced.

On occasion, the outsourcing decision is software based. For example, one small university whose administrative computing application specialists could not keep up with the request load of new work and changes chose to bring in an outside company that offered reusable, standardized administrative computing software. (It happened that the software ran only on IBM hardware, and thus the hardware accompanied the software in being outsourced.)

The issue in outsourcing is in-house control versus the presumption of out-house efficiency. With hardware outsourcing, there is the important fringe benefit that the company doing the outsourcing need no longer own computer power; there may be immediate cost savings. (Note that the same is not true for software outsourcing.)

The outsourcing trend is fairly recent, as this book is being written. There are no experiential data one can study to draw any conclusions. What does seem to be true is that the strength and competence of the in-house organization should determine the decision to outsource. If your people are good, stay with them. If they are not, here is a good way to solve the problem.

Lingering in the background, however, is the concern that once control has been given up, it may be hard to retrieve. For example, if an institution comes up with a computing-related idea that promises an important competitive advantage, will an outsource company attack the solution with the same energy and secretiveness that an in-house group would apply? Therefore, the important consideration here is how to gather the appropriate information needed to make an effective outsourcing decision which fits the best interests of your institution, should this need ever arise.

6

Summary

Where have our travels led us, between the covers of this book, wending our way through software quality land?

Not, I hope, searching for the holy grail of software, the one magic bullet that will bring quality to all our software efforts.

Not, I hope, oohing and aahing over the latest in software break-throughs, the structured buzzword approach to software quality.

Not, I hope, viewing quality through a narrow knothole that says "if I can get all of the errors out of my software, it will have high quality." Or a very broad knothole that says "if I meet all my requirements, I have built quality software." Or a very personable knothole that says "if I can satisfy my customers, I have built quality software."

But, I hope, slogging earnestly through a very large collection of ideas that, taken in concert, can lead to very high-quality software products. Where quality is a lot broader than absence of errors, in some important ways narrower than meeting requirements, and just plain different from user satisfaction.

At the beginning of this book I defined its basic premises:

1. Software is very complex. Building quality software adds complexity to an already complex topic.

2. There are no "best" approaches to quality, no silver bullets.
3. Several factors must be considered in achieving quality:
   a. The nature of the application.
   b. The practices of the organization.
   c. The quality of the people.
4. Layered over the application, the organization, and the high-quality people, building quality software still demands good tools, techniques, and organizational strategies.
5. The purpose of this book has been to present a menu of those tools, techniques, and organizational strategies, and information to help you form the wisdom to make judgments about them. The emphasis has been on breadth in the menu rather than depth. References are given to help you find depth when you want it; recommendations and author biases have been presented to help you narrow the breadth to a manageable menu. In addition to breadth instead of depth, we have tried to focus on ideas instead of rules, and concepts instead of skills, using the belief that there is no point in developing in-depth skills and understanding the rules for a technology that has little relevance to what you are trying to do.

I believe that I have achieved what I set out to do here. I hope you agree with me.

It is time to tidy up this book. Perhaps the best way to begin tidying up would be to get a high-level perspective on software. In this book, we have covered material on tools, methods, metrics, and management. Is there any perspective on where we in software engineering are making the most and the least progress?

Several times in this book we have made reference to various papers presented at the Software Engineering Workshop, sponsored each year in November/December by the NASA-Goddard Software Engineering Laboratory. Some of the most pragmatic research findings in computing are reported here each year. About six years ago, the sponsors of the workshop polled those who attended, asking them where software engineering had improved most over the past ten years, and where the greatest disappointments were. Here are the results of that poll:

- Greatest improvements: tools, methods
- Greatest disappointments: metrics, management

So, for what it's worth, there's the opinions of some pretty savvy, pragmatic people. Has the situation changed in the intervening years? Probably not. Perhaps in software metrics, where there are lots of new ideas and tools. But basically, once again we see that the technology of software seems to be pretty solid; it is the management aspects where we are still troubled.

Scattered throughout the prior chapters of the book have been references to further reading about specific ideas. Here, we draw the book to a close with broader references, books that tackle in breadth the same subject area that we have just traversed.

Recall that in this young field we are still sifting through ideas, and it is difficult at times to tell good ones from bad ones. It is important that your reading about software not be limited to just one book, whether it be this one or any other one. Here are particularly important books about building software in general:

The Mythical Man-Month, Addison-Wesley, 1975; Frederick P. Brooks, Jr. *The most classic of all the classic software books. Tells the lessons learned on a huge software project, with insight and accuracy.*

The Art of Software Testing, Wiley-Interscience, 1979; Glenford Myers. *The classic book about software testing. There are newer testing titles with newer thoughts, but this one is still hard to beat for completeness and insight.*

Software and Its Development, Prentice-Hall, Inc., 1982; Joseph Fox. *A pithy book by an IBM insider with very definite ideas on how software should be built.*

Software Metrics: Establishing a Company-Wide Project, Prentice Hall, 1987; Grady and Caswell. The *book to read on pragmatic approaches to metrics, as experienced at Hewlett-Packard.*

Here are important books about *managing* the construction of software:

Characteristics of Software Quality, North-Holland, 1978; Barry W. Boehm et al. *Contains the attribute definition of quality that forms the foundation of this book.*

Software Engineering Economics, Prentice-Hall, Inc., 1981; Barry W. Boehm. *The book to read about the dollar side of software construction. Particularly interesting ideas on estimation.*

Peopleware, Dorset House, 1987; Tom DeMarco and Tim Lister. *Wonderful, anecdotal book containing a lot of ideas that fly in the face of computing conventional wisdom.*

Managing for Innovation, Prentice Hall, 1987; Watts S. Humphrey. *One of the few management books that understands the innovative nature of software, and presents management approaches for fostering innovation.*

Software Quality Engineering, Prentice Hall, 1988; Michael S. Deutsch and Ronald R. Willis. *Broad coverage of software quality from an engineering management point of view.*

Managing the Software Process, Addison-Wesley, 1989; Watts S. Humphrey. *The book to read on the importance of good process in the construction of software.*

Here are important books that bring us insight from other fields:

Systemantics, Association for Systems Management / Pocket Books, 1978; John Gall. *A tongue firmly in cheek book containing a surprising amount of truth about systems analysis and design. Contains 32 axioms, including "People in systems do not do what the system says they are doing," and "The system takes credit for what would probably have happened anyway."*

To Engineer is Human, St. Martin's Press, 1985; Henry Petroski. *An anecdotal book that makes the point that failure is an important component of success.*

And finally here are important books about quality in general, independent of software:

Quality Is Free: The Art of Making Quality Free, McGraw, 1979; Philip Crosby. *Argues that it is the* absence *of quality that is costly.*

Quality Without Tears: The Art of Hassle-Free Management, McGraw, 1984; Philip Crosby. *A book about enabling the infusion of quality.*

Quality, Productivity and Competitive Position, Center for Advanced Engineering Studies, 1982; William Deming. *Advocates Theory Z management, where management's role is the facilitation of a team of responsible, caring workers.*

Quality Control Handbook, McGraw, 1974; Joseph M. Juran. *The classic by a classic author on quality.*

Quality Planning and Analysis: From Product Development Through Use, McGraw, 1980; Joseph M. Juran. *Juran and Deming are the fathers of the quality movement in post-World War II Japan.*

7

Recommendations

The purpose of this book has been twofold: to provide a menu of software quality techniques, and to increase your ability to make judgments about choices from that menu. To that end, as techniques and tools are presented in the earlier chapters, some biases are presented as to the value of using them.

None of these biases are without controversy. In this young field of software engineering, there are few demonstrable right answers to the question of what is the best way to produce high-quality software.

Nevertheless, the development of computer science theory and practitioner experience has led to strong opinions about that "best" way, and few computer scientists and software engineers exist who do not have at least some strong opinions on the matter. The problem is that those opinions frequently differ.

It is with this background that I present my own strong opinions on how to achieve quality software. These opinions are based on my own personal background and set of experiences:

- nearly 30 years of industry experience in software engineering, largely in the aerospace business. My application mix has been 50 percent systems software, 35 percent scientific software, 10 percent commercial software, and 5 percent real-time software

- five years of academic experience teaching in a graduate software engineering program
- a year spent ruminating on these experiences at the Software Engineering Institute

My biases, then, are strongly flavored by my practitioner background and my systems/scientific applications background, tempered somewhat by the unusual breadth of this background. The opinions that I present in what follows reflect these biases and may be evaluated in that light.

7.1 ORGANIZATION OF RECOMMENDATIONS

Not only is there no one best route to software quality yet, but there may never be. This is because there are many, many differences between software projects, and these differences often determine what techniques should be used on the various projects.

Because of this, I present here tabular information containing my recommendations about how to build quality software. These tabular recommendations are actually four tables—for a "normal" project, a large one, a critical one, and a particularly small or throwaway one. These tables are my attempt to incorporate the following important differences in software projects.

Application-type differences. Computer scientists and software engineers are just beginning to appreciate that the type of application plays a heavy role in the techniques used for that application. For example, data structure design may make a great deal of sense for a file or database-oriented commercial application, but it makes very little sense for an algorithmically-based scientific application. Although I have mentioned a few application-specific choices in the text of the description of the techniques presented earlier, I make no further recommendations here based solely on application type. Much work remains to be done in the research community before we can fully appreciate which techniques are best for each application domain; in fact, at this point, there is not even a generally accepted classification of what those application domains are.

Project size. It has been over a decade since the phrase *programming in the large* was coined to represent applications needing huge amounts of resources with large numbers of software developers, certainly more than 30, to produce massive amounts of code, certainly more than 50,000 lines.

We are beginning to learn facts about programming in the large that we didn't know a decade ago, but progress is slow and painful. Research into problems with programming in the large and their solutions is prohibitively expensive, and research which targets the problem area all too often degenerates into research in the small.

In spite of that, because of the experience we do have with programming in the large, I have chosen to produce a set of recommendations specific to that problem area. Table 7.2 is a set of recommendations for putting quality into programming-in-the-large projects. (Note that the first table, Table 7.1, is a set of recommendations for a "normal" software project. To make use of Table 7.2, it must be treated as including Table 7.1.)

Project criticality. Critical software is that upon which lives or huge amounts of money depend. The avionics software running on board an Airbus or a 767 may very well determine the destiny of the several hundred passengers on board. The decision-support software for top-level executives in a megamillion dollar corporation may very well assist in the determination of the future success or failure of that corporation. The utility software produced by a successful microcomputer software company for doing spreadsheets in millions of offices and homes certainly bears the future of its producing company on its back, and perhaps even some portion of the future of its millions of users. Criticality, in other words, comes in a lot of disguises, but all of those disguises have one thing in common—the software *must not* fail.

To address these unique problems, I present another set of recommendations in Table 7.3. Table 7.3 can only be used as a superset of Tables 7.2 and 7.1; in other words, the recommendations in the three tables should be used cumulatively.

Project weight. *Weight* is a strange term to find used in software. After all, software is not only invisible, it is weightless! Nevertheless, there is a special meaning I am assigning to the term here. All software developers, at one time or another in their careers, are asked to produce a software product that is of low importance. Perhaps it is to be used once and discarded. Perhaps it is to produce rough answers to support studies of a complicated question. Perhaps it is to serve as a prototype of a more complete software solution later on. Whatever it is for, the care to be put into this project is of necessity less than that usually used in building software. In that sense, the software has little weight; it is not very important in the overall scheme of things.

For that class of software, it is absurd to require software developers to use all the quality techniques normally used for "heavier" projects. Because of that, I present in Table 7.4 a set of *standalone* recommendations for what I call a small or prototype/throwaway project.

Unusual quality attribute needs. Some software will always need special care just because of the project, not necessarily the application, needs. For

TABLE 7.1 NORMAL PROJECT

Recommendations for software quality technique and tool usage

Technique	Ref. in book
Requirements	
Prototyping if appropriate	2.2.1.2.2
Informal specification	2.2.1.2.3
Review	2.2.1.3.5
Design	
Functional or data structure design	2.2.2.1
Design review, at least preliminary	2.2.2.4
Implementation	
Top-down or bottom-up, depending on experience	2.2.3.1
Modular programming	2.2.3.2
Structured coding	2.2.3.3
High-order language	2.2.3.4
Standards and enforcers	2.2.3.5
Standardized elements if available	2.2.3.6
Checkout	
Desk checking	2.2.4.1.1
Source language debug	2.2.4.2.1.1
Performance analysis, if needed	2.2.4.2.1.4
100% requirements-driven testing	2.2.4.2.2.1
80% structure-driven testing	2.2.4.2.2.2
Unit, integration, system testing	2.2.4.2.2.4
Environment simulator, if appropriate	2.2.4.2.2.7.3
Independent testing	2.2.4.2.2.12.1
Acceptance testing	2.2.4.2.2.12.3
Beta testing, if appropriate	2.2.4.2.2.12.2
Interactive debug, if available	2.2.4.2.2.13.1
Test documentation, minimal set	2.2.4.2.2.12.5
Test review, at design review	2.2.4.2.2.12.6
Maintenance	
Preventive maintenance	2.2.5.1
Configuration management, rigorous but informal	2.2.5.2.2.2.3
Change review, informal	2.2.5.2.3.1
Regression testing	2.2.5.2.2.5
Error reporting	2.2.5.2.3.2
Cross-referencing	2.2.5.2.2.2.1
Comparator	2.2.5.2.2.2.3
Conditional compilation	2.2.5.2.2.2.4
Management	
Reviews and audits	3.4.1.1
Product test organization	3.4.1.2
Acquisition management, if needed	3.4.1.5

For large projects, add this table to Table 7.2. For critical projects, add this and Table 7.2 to Table 7.3. For small projects, see Table 7.4.

TABLE 7.2   PROGRAMMING-IN-THE-LARGE PROJECT

Recommendations for software quality technique and tool usage	
Technique	Ref. in book
Requirements	
Modeling and simulation	2.2.1.1.1
Formal specification if appropriate	2.2.1.2.3
Traceability	2.2.1.2.4
Design	
Automated design checking	2.2.2.3
Design reviews	2.2.2.4
Implementation	
Standards and enforcers, full set	2.2.3.5
Checkout	
Peer code review, key parts	2.2.4.1.2
Structural analysis, as available	2.2.4.1.3
Statistics-driven testing, if customer wants	2.2.4.2.2.3.1
Test manager	2.2.4.2.2.2
Test coverage analyzer, logic	2.2.4.2.2.1
Test coverage analyzer, data, if available, applicable	2.2.4.2.2.2
Test data generator, if available	2.2.4.2.2.8
Standardized testing, if available	2.2.4.2.2.9
Postdelivery review	2.2.4.2.2.12.4
Test documentation, full set	2.2.4.2.2.12.5
Maintenance	
Code analyzers	2.2.5.2.2.2.1
Data analyzers	2.2.5.2.2.2.2
Change analyzers	2.2.5.2.2.2.3
Constructors	2.2.5.2.2.2.4
Testers	2.2.5.2.2.2.5
Configuration management, formal	2.2.5.2.2.2.3
Change review, formal	2.2.5.2.2.3.1
Management	
Configuration management	2.4.1.3
Change and error control	2.4.1.4
Process group or development center	3.4.1.7 or .9
Quality assurance	3.4.2
Quality metrics	3.5.1
Prediction metrics	3.5.2

Use all techniques listed in Table 7.1 plus the ones listed here.

example, software built to execute on most microcomputers will need to be highly portable. Software built with the expectation that it will be changed will need to be highly understandable and modifiable. Software built to execute using the least resources will need to be very efficient. Those special quality requirements cause the need for special techniques. The achievement of those special needs, we have already seen, is covered in

TABLE 7.3 CRITICAL PROJECT

Recommendations for software quality technique and tool usage	
Technique	Ref. in book
Design	
Fault-tolerant design	2.2.2.2
Checkout	
Peer code review, all parts	2.2.4.1.2
Proof of correctness, critical parts if applicable	2.2.4.1.4
Assertion checking	2.2.4.2.1.2
Structure-driven testing, at least 95%	2.2.4.2.2.2
Risk-driven testing	2.2.4.2.2.3.2
Mathematical checker, if appropriate	2.2.4.2.2.10
Management	
Independent verification and validation	3.4.1.6

Use all techniques listed in Table 7.2 plus the ones listed here.

Chapter 2.8 of this book. Because of that, there are no tables presented here for those special needs.

It is interesting to note the hierarchic relationship of the tables discussed in the previous sections. Essentially, the relationship is

small < normal < programming in the large < critical

where "<" is used in the sense of "being a subset of."

According to these tables, as we move up the quality scale from small to critical, what we need to do is simply add more techniques to the bag of tricks we use in building the software. It is not quite that simple, of course, because each technique added to the set used must be integrated into the total picture. Yet, at least at the conceptual level, it is nice to know or at least to believe that critical projects need not be approached in fundamentally different ways from, say, normal ones.

The use of that hierarchic relationship as presented here, however, is somewhat unique. Many authors talk about software engineering techniques as if all of them should be applied to any project, regardless of its size, weight, or criticality. My bias is that this is an erroneous view. Using formal verification techniques on a throwaway program, for example, would be a gross waste of software development resources. Recall in the first paragraph of this chapter that I said the purpose of this book has been not only to present a menu of techniques, but to provide the judgment for choosing from that menu. Here, in matching technique to project type, is where that judgment must be used.

It is also true that few other authors have presented this hierarchic relationship between weight, size, and criticality. Because this is a relatively new idea, the reader is especially cautioned in its use. If you use

TABLE 7.4   SMALL OR PROTOTYPE/THROWAWAY PROJECT

Recommendations for software quality technique and tool usage	
Technique	Ref. in book
Requirements	
Prototyping if appropriate	2.2.1.2.2
Very informal specification	2.2.1.2.3
Informal review	2.2.1.3.5
Design	
Functional or data structure design	2.2.2.1
Implementation	
Top-down or bottom-up, depending on experience	2.2.3.1
Modular programming	2.2.3.2
Structured coding	2.2.3.3
High-order language	2.2.3.4
Standardized elements if available	2.2.3.6
Checkout	
Desk checking	2.2.4.1.1
Source language debug	2.2.4.2.1.1
Performance analysis, if needed	2.2.4.2.1.4
100% requirements-driven testing	2.2.4.2.2.1
60% structure-driven testing	2.2.4.2.2.2
Unit, integration, system testing	2.2.4.2.2.4
Interactive debug, if available	2.2.4.2.2.13.1
Maintenance	
Configuration management, very informal	2.2.5.2.2.2.3

these tables at all, either to guide project quality approach choices or to use them as a basis for forming your own set of recommendations, be careful of any oversimplifications that this hierarchy contributes. For example, for a programming in the large project I recommend "formal specification if appropriate," where "if appropriate" means "if your people are comfortable and/or experienced with the concept." Using the hierarchic relationship of the tables, that same choice is then valid for critical software. But for deeply critical software, the importance of having accurate requirements may transcend the problem of having comfort and experience; for some projects, it may be important to use formal specifications even if a large training program is needed to introduce them.

Index